D1612279

CRITIQUES: Critical Studies in Architectural Humanities

A project of the Architectural Humanities Research Association

Series Editor: Jonathan Hale (University of Nottingham)

Editorial Board:
Sarah Chaplin (Kingston University)
Mark Dorrian (University of Edinburgh)
Murray Fraser (University of Westminster)
Hilde Heynen (Catholic University of Leuven)
Andrew Leach (University of Queensland)
Thomas Mical (Carleton University)
Jane Rendell (University College London)
Adam Sharr (Cardiff University)
Igea Troiani (Oxford Brookes University)

This original series of edited books contains selected papers from the AHRA Annual International Conferences. Each year the event has its own thematic focus while sharing an interest in new and emerging critical research in the areas of architectural history, theory, culture, design and urbanism.

Volume 1: Critical Architecture
Edited by: Jane Rendell, Jonathan Hill, Murray Fraser and Mark Dorrian

Volume 2: From *Models* to Drawings: Imagination and Representation in Architecture
Edited by: Marco Frascari, Jonathan Hale and Bradley Starkey

Volume 3: The Politics of Making
Edited by: Mark Swenarton, Igea Troiani and Helena Webster

AHRA provides an inclusive and comprehensive support network for humanities researchers in architecture across the UK and beyond. It promotes, supports, develops and disseminates high-quality research in all areas of architectural humanities.

www.ahra-architecture.org.uk

From *Models* to Drawings

Imagination and representation in architecture

Edited by Marco Frascari, Jonathan Hale and Bradley Starkey

Routledge
Taylor & Francis Group

LONDON AND NEW YORK

First published 2007
by Routledge
2 Park Square, Milton Park, Abingdon, Oxon OX14 4RN

Simultaneously published in the USA and Canada
by Routledge
270 Madison Ave, New York, NY 10016

1005614537

Routledge is an imprint of the Taylor & Francis Group, an informa business

Typeset in Univers by Wearset Ltd, Boldon, Tyne and Wear
Printed and bound in Great Britain by TJ International Ltd, Padstow, Cornwall

British Library Cataloguing in Publication Data
A catalogue record for this book is available from the British Library

Library of Congress Cataloging in Publication Data
Frascari, Marco.
From models to drawings : imagination and representation in architecture / Marco Frascari, Jonathan Hale, and Bradley Starkey.
p. cm. – (Critiques, critical studies in architectural humanities)
Includes bibliographical references and index.
ISBN 978-0-415-43113-2 (hardback : alk. paper) 1. Architectural drawing. 2. Architectural design. I. Hale, Jonathan. II. Starkey, Bradley. III. Title.
NA2700.F727 2007
720.22–dc22
2007012601

ISBN13: 978–0–415–48798–6 (pbk)
ISBN13: 978–0–415–43113–2 (hbk)

Contents

Contents

Illustration credits

Contributors

Soumyen Bandyopadhyay is Senior Lecturer in Architecture at Liverpool University where he is Director of Studies for the MArch programme and director of India in the World Research Centre. Since 1983 he has been in architectural and urban design practice in Oman and India. He heads an AHRC-funded study of the Rock Garden in Chandigarh, on which he has recently published a book (Liverpool University Press 2007).

Richard Coyne is based in Architecture and is Head of the Graduate School in the School of Arts, Culture and Environment at the University of Edinburgh. He researches in the areas of computer-aided design, digital media and design theory. He is the author of three books on the implications of information technology and design with MIT Press, and is co-author of a recent book with Adrian Snodgrass, *Interpretation in Architecture: Design as a Way of Thinking* (Routledge, 2006). He currently heads a research project on the relationship between voice and public space and a research cluster on Non-Space, both funded by the Arts and Humanities Research Council.

Nader El-Bizri is a Research Associate at The Institute of Ismaili Studies (London), a Chercheur Associé at the Centre National de la Recherche Scientifique (Paris). He lectures at the Department of History and Philosophy of Science, University of Cambridge, and he previously held a lectureship in architecture at the University of Nottingham, and taught at Harvard University and the American University of Beirut. His research focuses on architectural humanities, phenomenology and history of science. He is the author of *The Phenomenological Quest between Avicenna and Heidegger* (Binghamton, 2000), and has published numerous philosophy articles.

Paul Emmons is an Associate Professor at the Washington-Alexandria Architecture Center of Virginia Tech, where he coordinates the PhD programme in architecture. Dr Emmons received a PhD in Architecture from the University of Pennsylvania in 2003 and a Master of Architecture from the University of Minnesota in 1986. His research in representation and design focuses on the imaginative role of diagrams and technical drawing. Conferences where this work has been presented include: Academia Eolia Revisited (Costozza, Italy); Intimate Metropolis (AA, London); Other Voices, Other Drafting Rooms (Society of Architectural Historians). Some of this work has also appeared in recent publications including: *Journal of the Society of Architectural Historians*; *Architectural Research Quarterly*; *AA Files*; and *Body and Building* (MIT Press). Dr Emmons is a registered architect and maintains a small architectural practice.

Marco Frascari was born under the shadow of the dome of Alberti's Sant'Andrea in Mantua. He achieved a Dottore in Architettura at the 'verum IpsUm fActVm' (Istituto Universitario di Architettura di Venezia) in 1969. He began his professional career as an architect in Verona and at the same time taught at IUAV. Later he moved to the United States and earned an MSc in Architecture at the University of Cincinnati and a PhD at the University of Pennsylvania. He has taught at several institutions in North America and is presently Director of the School of Architecture at Carleton University in Ottawa. He has written extensively on topics in architectural theory, representation and tectonics. Since he graduated from Venice, he has always run a small architectural practice. He believes strongly that architectural theory and the resulting buildings should make life happy (*vita beata*).

David Gissen is a theorist, historian and designer working at the intersection of achitecture and contemporary geographical concepts. He is the editor of *Big and Green* (2003) – an exporation of architecture, urban environmentalism and globalization – and author of the forthcoming *Techno-Nature Handbook* (2008) – an exploration of new methods for producing nature with buildings – both published by Princeton Architectural Press. David's writing, research and design have appeared in *Cabinet Magazine*, *Interiors*, *Metropolis*, *Thresholds*, *Blueprints*, *The Journal of Architectural Education*, *Architectural Record*, *Architecture*, the *New York Times*, the *Village Voice*, and in the edited collections *Design Ecologies* (Princeton Architectural Press, 2008), *Saved!* (Monacelli Press, 2008), *Urban Writing* (Routledge, 2007), *Dirt and Architecture* (Taylor and Francis, 2007), *Disability and History* (Duke University Press, 2006), *Amphibious Living* (01 Publishers, 2000) and *The City of the Next Millennium* (Marsilio, 2000). David is also an active curator with exhibitions staged at The National Building Museum (*Big and Green, Federal Design Now!*), Museum of the City of New York (*Big and Green*), the Chicago Architecture Foundation (*Big and Green*), Yale University Architecture Gallery (*Big and Green*), and The Lower East Side Tenement Museum (*New York's Floating Bathhouses*). For the exhibition and book *Big and Green* he was awarded a Graham Foundation Grant, the Richard Carroll lectureship at the Johns Hopkins University, and in 2006 *Metropolis Magazine* named the exhibition one of twelve of the most significant architecture and design exhibitions of the last twenty-five years. He is currently an assistant professor of architecture and visual studies at the California College of the Arts, San Francisco.

Federica Goffi is an Assistant Professor at the School of Architecture, Carleton University, in Canada where she teaches studio, a workshop on aural architecture and advanced building systems. She also taught studio, architectural representation and a graduate seminar focusing on 'time' as a design material at the Interior Architecture Department of the Rhode Island School of Design. She holds a Dottore in Architettura, University of Genoa, and is a registered architect in Italy. She is currently a PhD candidate in Architectural Representation and Education at the Washington–Alexandria Architectural Center, Virginia Polytechnic Institute and State University, Alexandria, Virginia, where she is working under the guidance of Director Marco Frascari (Carleton University, Ottawa, Canada) and Professor Paul Emmons (Virginia Tech). Her dissertation focuses on a 'redefinition' of the concept of 'conservation' through a phenomenological approach. Following a conjectual hypothesis and micro-historical procedures, the dissertation focuses on a specific drawing of Saint Peter's in Rome to deal with the concept of sempiternity in architecture and how that reflects in the process of conservation.

Katja Grillner (PhD, Docent) is an architect and critic based in Stockholm, Sweden. She is a Senior Lecturer at the KTH School of Architecture, the director of AKAD, and a member of the board of the Swedish Architecture Museum. Among her recent publications is *01.AKAD – Experimental Research in Architecture and Design* (AxlBooks, 2005), for which she was the main editor.

Jonathan Hale is an architect and Associate Professor in Architecture at the School of the Built Environment, University of Nottingham. He is Course Director for the Master of Architecture (Design) and the interdisciplinary MA in Architecture and Critical Theory. His research interests include: architectural theory and criticism; the philosophy of technology; the relationship between architecture and the body; and architectural exhibitions. His publications include: *Rethinking Technology: a Reader in Architectural Theory* (with William W. Braham, Routledge, 2006); *Ends Middles Beginnings: Edward Cullinan Architects* (Black Dog, 2005); *Building Ideas: an Introduction to Architectural Theory* (John Wiley, 2000), and *Moving City: the Electronic Guidebook*, a guided-walk and exhibition, part of an ongoing collaboration with the School of Computer Sciences, University of Nottingham. He is Coordinator and a founder member of the Architectural Humanities Research Association (www.ahra-architecture.org.uk).

Catherine Hamel is an Assistant Professor in Architecture at the Faculty of Environmental Design at the University of Calgary, Canada. Her research focus is the experience of forced displacement. Recent projects include the essay 'Beirut, Exile and the Scars of Reconstruction', in *Memory and Architecture* and a solo exhibit of drawings entitled 'displace/graft/retrace'.

Jonathan Hill, an architect and architectural historian, is also Professor of Architecture and Visual Theory and Director of the MPhil/PhD by Architectural Design programme at the Bartlett School of Architecture, University College London. He is the author of *The Illegal Architect* (1998), *Actions of Architecture* (2003) and *Immaterial Architecture* (2006). Jonathan is the editor of *Occupying Architecture* (1998), *Architecture – the Subject is Matter* (2001) and the 'Research by Design' issue of *The Journal of Architecture* (2003). He is co-editor of *Critical Architecture* (2007). Galleries where he has had solo exhibitions including the Haus der Architektur, Graz, and Architektur-Galerie am Weissenhof, Stuttgart.

Donald Kunze has taught Architecture Theory and Art Criticism at Penn State University since 1984. He received his professional degree in architecture from NC State University and his PhD in cultural geography in 1983. His research has engaged a range of topics dealing with the poetic dimensions of experience. He was the 1997 recipient of a Shogren Foundation grant to develop a graphical approach to problems of the boundary in art, architecture and geography; during his 2003 Reyner Banham Fellowship at the University at Buffalo, he extended this project to include film study.

Katie Lloyd Thomas has worked in architectural education for ten years and is currently completing a PhD at Middlesex University. She edited *Material Matters: Architecture and Material Practice* (Routledge, 2006) and researches and publishes in the areas of architectural representation, materials and feminism. She collaborates with artist Brigid McLeer on an ongoing project *In Place of the Page* which has been exhibited in Ireland and the UK, and is a founder member of the feminist group *Taking Place*.

Christina Malathouni is currently a PhD candidate in Architectural History at the Bartlett School of Graduate Studies, University College London. Her doctoral research focuses on architects Claude Bragdon (1866–1946) and Theo van Doesburg (1883–1931). Broader research interests include the significance of 'space' in such diverse disciplines as philosophy, mathematics, physics and psychology, and how this relates to architecture. She has lectured on her work on the 'fourth dimension' and presented related papers in several international conferences. As a qualified architect in Greece, she has also practised architecture.

Judith Mottram is Professor of Visual Arts at Nottingham Trent University. She is Associate Dean for Research and Graduate Studies for the College of Art & Design and the Built Environment. Her research interests cover two main areas: understanding constructed and environmental visual phenomena, particularly relating to drawing, pattern and colour; and the inter-relationships between subject knowledge, creativity, research and practice. She is a team member of the Review of Practice-led Research in Art, Architecture and Design.

Antony Moulis is Head of Architecture in the School of Geography, Planning and Architecture at the University of Queensland, Australia. His current research on the history of the plan in twentieth-century architecture incorporates work undertaken at the Foundation Le Corbusier and the Alvar Aalto Academy in 2006. He received his PhD from the University of Queensland in 2002 with the dissertation, *Drawing Experience: Le Corbusier's Spiral Museum Projects.*

Betty Nigianni trained as an architect at the Technical University of Athens and studied history and theory of architecture at the University of East London. She has practised as an architect and is currently Lecturer at the University of East London. She also works towards the completion of her doctoral thesis, which examines literary representations of modern Athens to discuss the role of subjective narratives within spatial experience. Publications include articles in: *Gramma: Journal of Theory and Criticism* and *Urban Mindscapes of Europe* by Rodopi (forthcoming).

Alberto Pérez-Gómez is Bronfman Professor of Architectural History at McGill University, Montreal, where he chairs the History and Theory division, and is Director of Post-Professional Programs. He studied architecture in Mexico City, at Cornell University and the University of Essex. He has taught at universities in Mexico, Houston, Syracuse, Toronto and the Architectural Association. His book *Architecture and the Crisis of Modern Science* (MIT Press, 1983) won the Hitchcock Award in 1984. Later books include the erotic narrative theory *Polyphilo or The Dark Forest Revisited* (1992), and more recently (with Louise Pelletier) *Architectural Representation and the Perspective Hinge* (1997), which traces the history and theory of modern European architectural representation. He is also co-editor of a series of books entitled *Chora: Intervals in the Philosophy of Architecture.*

Raymond Quek is Director of Architectural Studies at University of Nottingham.

Mathanraj Ratinam is the Director of Lmno Studio and a research candidate in the School of Architecture and Design at RMIT, Australia. He resides in New York, practising and publishing in the area of digital representation and visual effects for film and television, and teaches in the Architecture programmes at Columbia University, Parsons School of Design, and maintains an ongoing Visiting Professorship with the TU Innsbruck, Austria. (The animation described in the present paper can be viewed at: www.lmnostudio.com/research.)

Peg Rawes is Co-ordinator of Diploma History and Theory at the Bartlett School of Architecture, UCL. Publications include: *Spatial Imagination*, Peg Rawes and Jane Rendell (eds) (AHRC/EPSRC and Bartlett School of Architecture UCL, 2005); 'Plenums: Rethinking Matter, Geometry and Subjectivity', Katie Lloyd Thomas (ed.), *Material Matters* (Routledge, 2007); 'Reflective Subjects in Kant and Architectural Design Education', *Journal of Aesthetic Education*, Spring

2007, volume 41, no. 1 (University of Illinois Press, 2007); *Irigaray for Architects* (Routledge, 2007).

Jane Rendell, BA (Hons), Dip. Arch, MSc, PhD, is Professor in Architecture and Art and Director of Architectural Research at the Bartlett School of Architecture, UCL. An architectural designer and historian, art critic and writer, she is author of *Art and Architecture* (2006), *The Pursuit of Pleasure* (2002) and co-editor of *Critical Architecture* (2007), *Spatial Imagination* (2005), *The Unknown City* (2001), *Intersections* (2000), *Gender Space Architecture* (1999), *Strangely Familiar* (1995).

Sam Ridgway is an architect and Lecturer in Construction and Design in the School of Architecture, Landscape Architecture and Urban Design at the University of Adelaide, South Australia. His research examines the current conceptual and structural split between construction and design (body and mind) in architectural pedagogy and the profession. The aim of this research is to reconceive construction knowledge in a less instrumental fashion as the embodiment of the intangible in material form and as indistinguishable from design.

Bradley Starkey is a Lecturer at the Institute of Architecture, University of Nottingham and is a member of the school's Architectural History & Theory Group. He was on the organising committee of the second AHRA International Conference, *Models and Drawings: the Invisible Nature of Architecture* and is presently completing a PhD by Architectural Design at the Bartlett School of Architecture, UCL on the subject of Architecture and the Post Secular. He is a registered architect and has practised in South East Asia, USA and the UK.

Teresa Stoppani is an architect. She taught Design and Theory at the IUAV, Venice (1995–1999) and at the Architectural Association, London (2000–2002). She is currently Senior Lecturer in Architecture at the University of Greenwich, London, where she directs the MA/MSc Architecture programme and coordinates Histories and Theories. Recent publications include: 'The Reversible City', *Urban Space and Cityscapes*, C. Lindner (ed.) (Routledge 2006), 'Voyaging in Piranesi's Space', *Haecceity Papers*, 1:2, (2006), and the edited journal 'Antipodes/Measuring the World', *Haecceity Papers*, 2:2 (2006).

Nicholas Temple is Professor of Architectural Design and head of the School of Architecture at the University of Lincoln. A Rome Scholar, he has previously taught at the University of Liverpool, Nottingham University, University of Pennsylvania and Leeds Metropolitan University. He has a PhD on early-sixteenth-century urbanism in Rome and has published widely on architectural history and theory, most recently *Disclosing Horizons: Architecture, Perspective and Redemptive Space* (Routledge, 2006).

Qi Zhu is a Researcher in the stream of Architectural Representation and Education at the Washington-Alexandria Architecture Center of the Virginia Polytechnic

Institute and State University. Her interest covers traditional Chinese architecture and building construction through comparative reflection with the western tradition. She holds a Bachelor of Architecture Degree from Tongji University in Shanghai, China, and a Master of Architecture Degree from Virginia Tech where she is currently a PhD candidate. Her dissertation investigates the cultural concept of Shi, derived from Sun Tzu's *The Art of War*, as potentials born from dispositions and its implication in traditional building practice in early-nineteenth-century China.

Acknowledgements

The editors would like to thank everyone who took part in the conference *Models and Drawings: the Invisible Nature of Architecture* held at the University of Nottingham in November 2005. Despite the cold(!) it was a fascinating event, drawing delegates from around the world. Apologies must go to all those whose work we were not able to include within the limited scope of this book, but appreciation is due to everyone who contributed to making it such a successful and enjoyable event. The theme of the conference was set by Marco Frascari, who at the time was serving as a Leverhulme Visiting Professor at the University of Nottingham. Thanks must go to the Leverhulme Trust for supporting the conference in this way. The Humanities Research Centre at Nottingham (via the interdisciplinary *Images Project*) also sponsored another of the keynote speakers, Professor Don Ihde of the State University of New York, whose paper we were not able to reprint in this collection due to copyright restrictions. The event would not have succeeded without the 'backstage' assistance of the indefatigable Lyn Shaw, plus the more visible input of a number of energetic Nottingham students, most especially Fidel Meraz Avila, Yan Zhu, Eirini-Maria Gerogianni and Amy Tang.

The editors would like to express their gratitude to Hannah Dolan at Wearset for guiding the book efficiently through the production process and to Martyn Hale for helping with proofreading. Special thanks must also go to Caroline Mallinder and her team at Routledge Architecture, not just for their work on this book, but also for their long-term support of the AHRA.

Introduction

Models and drawings – the invisible nature of architecture

Marco Frascari

In an age in which unconsidered consumerist interests have exploited architecture, when a hasty abuse of public and private edifices has reached institutional intensity, and when buildings are the target of technologies of absurd variations, it is imperative to re-evaluate the graphical procedures involved in the conceiving of buildings. It is vital to recognize the processes of conversion and transformation taking place within the highly undisciplined discipline of architectural imagination, in order to provide architecture with a measure of resilience and resistance.

Nowadays we are fully aware of the kinds of drawings and models that architects or architectural practices produce. The profession generally follows a misguided interpretation of what tradition and contract jurisprudence has codified, for the purposes of billing clients and guaranteeing products and services – without any doubt, a properly principled set of criteria. Nevertheless, most of these codifications have been the outcome of some not-so-proper market-driven and technologically biased events that have disguised themselves beyond the manifold masks of professional appropriateness. The depressing consequence of all this is that current architectural graphic productions have reached an unchangeable and highly sterile phase of inert classifications and taxonomies, based on a pseudo-transparency of scope and a pseudo-scientific justification of the functions and roles carried out by the different kinds of architectural representations.

Even though the majority of the existing handbooks, manuals and pseudo-theoretical texts on the subject of architectural representation claim that they are presenting innovative directions for elaborating professional and/or poetic two-dimensional or three-dimensional modeling, when subjected to deeper scrutiny they always confirm and support the immobile categorizations and nomenclatures of the conveniently dominating conventional practices. These handbooks and manuals describing how to read and produce elaborate renderings, design and technical drawings provide the dullest compilation of platitudes that a profession that has lost any critical reference could possibly put together. They offer, as a panacea for the deficiency in architectural imagination, the most insidious graphic banalities that can be applied in a set of architectural drawings as allegedly effective means of design and communication.

These publications spread easy formulas and ready-made clichés, or smooth, ever-so-accommodating confirmations of graphic conventions that prevent any critical dispute of the most pedestrian and prosaic design protocols. Their instructions reduce both the discipline and the profession of architecture to a trade without a tradition. Even the present digital production of architectural drawings is pseudo-efficient and often unnecessarily precise, fulfilling the sole purpose of mechanically describing visual appearances that are utterly insignificant from a properly imaginative way of architectural thinking. Mimicking only the visual make-up of traditional architectural drawings, most digital representations are limited only to the communication of conscious intent, since within the realm of conventional computer-graphics there are two imperative aspirations: on the one hand, the aim is to produce 'photo-realistic' images that do not aim to emulate the human phenomenology of perception, but rather that of the photographic camera. On the other hand, the conceit is to describe future-built artifacts with a precision and accuracy that no-one within the existing building trades could possibly achieve during construction.

Architectural drawings have become highly deceptive and frustrating didactic and professional tools that magnify the false traits and values of graphic architectural articulation. They do this by concealing, in a contrived likeness and an artificial exactness, the actual suggestive and evocative power of real architectural drawings. Accordingly, the innovation and improvement of effective architectural representations becomes extraordinarily difficult and problematic. However, in the light of the new possibilities generated by the use of electronic media, a different and passionate challenge of these immobile and sterile circumstances is needed to alter the present perception of the nature, skills and means that govern the conceiving and making of architectural models and drawings.

The undigested understanding of the role of new electronic media brings into architecture the same predicaments as those fostered by the pseudo-innovative or backward-looking graphic handbooks and manuals. Unfortunately, those predicaments are exponentially augmented in their ennui by the continually increasing and extraordinary speed and power of computer workstation processors. The digital production of models and drawings is faster and more precise, but they can often result in relatively meaningless documents if they are considered from the point of view of analogical 'thinking within architecture'. The new electronic imaging prevents imagining, and the resulting representations promote acts of merely logical 'thinking about architecture' rather than bringing architects, contractors, clients and critics to think *within* architecture.

The use of drawings and models in advance of production makes the search for the resolution of uncertainty in the prediction of future buildings a fundamental and primary problem in architecture today. A way out has been proposed via a kind of 'information drafting', where the prediction of a future building can take place simultaneously with the computerized creation of details, schedules and levels of structure. This can therefore also provide product-specific installation requirements and 4-D construction scheduling that can automatically be tied to building elements for construction sequencing on site. In this digital 'Building Information Modeling' (BIM) system, when the architect 'draws' what is actually taking place within the shadows of the digital machine (hidden from architects' physical and mental senses), is that objects are being created in a database with an extensive array of standardized properties. This information is used to generate 'drawings', but it is used in many other ways as well, fulfilling the pseudo-proficient dream of a professional efficiency.

Efficiency is the disposition to be motivated towards the satisfaction of one's final desires. The problem of course is that in their search for the architectural 'final desire', the computer programmers who have predetermined the digital encoding cannot pinpoint the final cause of an imaginative architectural event. As this is always an essential aspect of the specific conditions of an architectural mandate, and thereby undeterminable in advance, so they substitute it with the most common pseudo-final cause – the ultimate desire of entrepreneurs for financially profitable results. Successfully substituting ongoing cosmopoietic tactics with cosmopolitan strategies, BIM is seen as a novel technology that is still under development, therefore justifying all of its various shortcomings. As David R. Scheer, a professional and a professor at the College of Architecture + Planning, University of Utah, points out:

> For millennia the design tools used by architects were a pencil, a straight edge, a triangle and a scale. 2-D CAD merely uses a computer to mimic these traditional tools. BIM is a genuinely new tool that is still in its infancy.[1]

The traditional design tools were analogical tools: the square used on paper to guide the tracing of lines corresponded to the square used on site to guide the erection of walls. Without any doubt the digital mimicking has been detrimental, but such programs as BIM are further removing from the process of conceiving of buildings the possibility of emotionally and bodily conjuring up of experimentations in architectural theory.

Whoever conceived the process of BIM has forgotten the two essential polar properties of architectural drawings and models: as forms of communication they are perceived as both categorical and inferential. Thus architectural modeling might be taken into account as a form of understanding in which part of the input happens to come in through the senses and part through cultural factors such as needs, expectations and beliefs. The output is the category of the construction being perceived. There is no distinction between a drawing of construction and a thought of construction. This correlation turns drawings into the most sophisticated expressions of architectural theory.

Analogy requires projection from a source to a target. A set of elements in the source matches a set of elements in the target. Another set of elements in the source is then transferred to the target to create new inferences. Analogy has been considered a binary relation between the source and target. However, we should also consider analogy as a ternary relation between the source, target and their category.

By the analogical nature of drawings, architects free themselves from a fixed modus operandi, which becomes habitual through the constant repetition of accepted building procedures. Before drawings, buildings were compulsory duplications and continuous replications of causal forms. However, in drawing, designers take part in a multi-modal dialogue played out on a surface with visible tracings. Viewing and responding to their own drawn lines, even as they trace them down, a compelling reflexivity emerges, born out of the relation occurring between the designers and their drawings. In their analogic procedures they follow the Vitruvian precept that indicates construction (*fabrica*) as 'a continuous and meditative process completed by the hands' (*fabrica est continuata ac trita usus meditatio, qua manibus perficitur*). Their thoughts engage a separate temporality from the flux of the cosmos by which effects occur indiscernibly before or after their causes.

Drawings make use of a particular sensory conjunction – that between feeling and seeing. By both looking at and feeling a surface of a drawing, designers are in contact respectively with both the outward appearance and finish of an edifice, and also the interior inauguration and solidity of construction. The chiasm among the senses makes the designer aware of the complex interplay between the inside and the outside. It thereby provides a new locus of architectural invention, since to draw is to enter into participation with both the inscriptions and the scribing that mark the surface of the drawing.

Architects are bound to treat as real that which exists only in an imagined future, and to specify the ways in which the foreseen things can be made to exist. In doing so they must predict the future nature of an artifact and that it will work as expected. In other words, the drawing process is a cosmopoiesis that can help to invent better futures and make potential worlds. A set of architectural drawings always corresponds to an infinite set of built possibilities. As Luigi Nono, an avant-garde music composer, a friend of Carlo Scarpa, has cleverly pointed out in the title of a piece composed to honor the Venetian architect: *A Carlo Scarpa architetto, ai suoi infiniti possibili per orchestra a microintervalli* (1984).[2]

Cosmospoiesis, or world-making, 'always starts from a world already at hand; the making is remaking'.[3] Architects carry out their communal or diverse styles of making in drawing by way of a sequence of operations based on composition and decomposition, weighting, ordering, deletion and supplementation, and deformation.[4] By tracing drawings, architects perform an act of world-making: a cosmographic expression that is also the root to future cosmospoiesis.

Buildings designed in the absence of real physical constraints might not work, and since conditions might well change by the time the artifact is actually made, design unavoidably entails a large amount of uncertainty and risk. Consequently, architects have developed drafting techniques that allow them to perform their thought-experiments (*Gedankenexperiment*) in sets of graphic analogies. Working from a 'great un-digital database' of instinctive information picked up from experience, by dividing, combining, emphasizing, ordering, deleting, filling and distorting, architects have worked out their thought-experiments on paper, discovering something new about the built world even though they have no new data. Out of this process they are able to re-conceptualize the world in a more effective way by relating the surface of paper with the surfaces of buildings.

The main stumbling block in this challenge to the present negative condition of the use and production of architectural representations is that the study of drawings is generally seen as subsidiary to the analysis of buildings. Where they are considered, these documents are figured out by means of rules of reproduction, recognition and similarity, rather than the rules of cosmospoiesis, i.e. of analogy, opposition and sympathy. Consequently, in elaborating theories of architecture, drawings are always considered – and presented – as ancillary components rather than being treated as the most important architectural agents, since they carry embodied in them the non-verbal essence of architectural theory. The chapters in this book aim to show that the origins and the critical nature of architectural theory must be derived from the phenomenology of the lines traced on site and on paper. This understanding is the proper way to breed the critical evolution that those lines will have in their future development as the 'input and output' of the new electronic media.

The motivation for the conference call to which the following chapters have brought fruitful responses was elicited from a profound and sincere dissatisfaction with much of contemporary architectural graphic education and production – exaggerated by its patently non-specific evaluations of the media used during the act of design. These chapters provide a reaction to the present conditions of the act of architectural modeling and drawing that have gradually created an exasperating set of circumstances. It is not difficult to discern that the majority of critical writings elaborated by historians and theoreticians of architecture generally lack an awareness of the cogency of the multifaceted semiosis and multiple intelligences operating within the realm of architectural representation.

Architectural drawings nowadays are more often appraised as pieces to be hung in art collections rather than as demonstrations of architectural thinking. Design drawings and renderings have become art pieces with an aesthetic value wholly separated from their architectural value. They should instead be seen as the essential part of architectural production, rather than works of art in their own right. During the Renaissance, architects began to collect drawings out of professional interest, and for the simple reason that they could understand the knowledge embodied in these 'theoretical artifacts'. They could read them not only as descriptions of future, present or past edifices, but also as a-temporal theoretical 'signatures' that could be read between the lines. Eventually the collecting enthusiasm spread to non-architects and the art market exploited these drawings as works of art for sale and display, bringing to an end the interpretative richness of their analogical essence. They have been gradually transformed into allegories – rather than analogies – by the reduced importance of the *Vis Imaginativa* embodied in the *Vis Disegnativa*, leading to pure autographic representations and empty and powerless images.

The recognition that in our age of digital imaging architects do not build buildings but merely draw them does not imply that what an architect traces is either worldly or unworldly, existing or non-existing, physical or mental, subjective or objective. Architectural drawing must avoid such labels. The only thing that the act of drawing assumes is that that which appears comes into view. Architectural drawing is, in other words, wholly based on an awareness of givenness and on a materialization of fluid invisible thoughts. Givenness is not understood as an objective fact but as a coming into appearance. Through the process of architectural drawing architects study how different visions move into the realm of visuality: the giving-act in which the given is given. Drawing is thus a 'shower of gifts', and this complex showering is the reality of architecture, understood graphically. Architectural drawings are psychophysical expressions of architecture.

By reading and drawing 'architectural imaging' line-by-line, architects read and draw 'between the lines' to foster architectural imagination. For architects, that which is between the lines is in reality earlier – more archaic and genuine – than the lines themselves; for that which is shown invisibly is that which appears most powerfully and most directly in architecture. Architecture is not represented directly; rather, it is that which lies between the lines that appears most directly as it is able to manifest itself, reveal itself, give itself, exhibit itself, arise and materialize. That which occurs in this invisible realm is not 'somewhere else', it is 'in' the drawing itself: the architecture that is able to be discerned in-between is not elsewhere. If two people in love sit in a park talking about ducks and the weather, what they are really talking about, using the invisible language of love, is not something that is elsewhere but something that is right there in the park: in looks, movements, lips, hands, postures, thoughts, hesitations, words, in other words in the synaesthetic articulations of the conversation. Others who pass by see this reality only incompletely; they see 'two lovers on a bench in a park', but they do not see the manifestation of love as such. In their drawings, architects seek to see Architecture 'as such'. Architects are not passers-by, since they linger, have patience and are in no hurry. They abide in the drawing where manifestation abides – just as lovers abide in their lake-front setting.

To read and understand 'between the lines' is not to read and understand elsewhere; it is not to look behind some sort of shutter, to lift a veil, or to remove a screen. For what is really there is standing right before us – not in some other place, not behind the lines, and not hidden out of view. Architectural drawing is thus the tracing of a 'metaphysics of presence'. This means that architectural cosmography is committed to the idea that truth is not elsewhere, not in some place other than presence, not 'beyond' the manifestation, but something that reveals itself in its own presenting of itself. Looking around, architects everywhere see a chaos of confused thinking, much of which is slack, easy-going, careless, unprofessional and unsystematic. Drawing research is often carried out in the natural attitude as woolly and undisciplined – unfortunately architectural culture and education does not tend to reduce this woolliness but only makes it more entangled. The history and understanding of the transformations of reading and drawing are the only histories genuinely worthy of study because they summarize what all the other histories tell us is of interest. The 'graphic' investigators of architectural representations are to most architectural critics and historians as archeologists are to stamp collectors.

At a deep level of elucidation, the processes of architectural representation are universal; the elaboration of a few simple structural values and principles result in a huge variation of architectural imagination which can cut all the way through temporal, spatial and cultural divides. If we have to understand architecture – to think within architecture rather than about architecture – then we have to understand something of the mechanism that drives representational thoughts, otherwise we are condemned to watch in despair as the architectural worlds created in the past continue to slip further and further away from our awareness and beyond our intellectual capacities.

To recall the definition of architectural vision offered in the original call for papers for the *Models and Drawings* conference: the real architectural drawing does not result from a vision of the absent, but instead it provokes one. Rather than resulting from the·gaze aimed at it, the drawing summons insight by allowing the invisible to saturate the visible, but without any attempt or claim of reducing the invisible to the visible lines of the drawing. The drawing attempts to render visible the invisible as such, and thus, strictly speaking, shows nothing. It teaches the gaze to proceed beyond the visible image into an infinity whereby something new of the invisible is encountered. Thus the true 'drawing-gaze' never rests or settles on the drawing itself, but instead rebounds upon the visible into a gaze of the infinite.

Notes

1   David R. Scheer, 'AIA Building Information Modeling: What About Architecture?' Online, available at: faculty.arch.utah.edu/bim/Website%20Info/Articles/BIM%20What %20About%20Architecture.doc.

2   John Warnaby, 'Only Travelling Itself: Reflections on Luigi Nono (1924–1990)', *Tempo*, New Ser., 176 (March 1991), pp. 2–5.

3   Nelson Goodman, *Ways of Worldmaking*, Indianapolis: Hacket Publishing Company, 1978, p. 6.

4   Ibid., pp. 7–17.

Historical perspectives

Introduction

In the opening chapter of this book, Alberto Pérez-Gómez sets out both a historical and a theoretical framework into which many of the subsequent chapters could be placed. Tracing a broad intellectual arc from Vitruvius to the present-day, he pinpoints a series of shifts in the scope, style and status of the architectural drawing, focusing on developments in the use of perspective. His skepticism as to the benefits of digital design technology (or, as he pointedly prefers to call it, 'computer graphics') is tempered by his contextualizing of these recent innovations in relation to previous historical ruptures in the habitual patterns of architectural vision. In Marco Frascaris' chapter, he questions the perception of paper as merely the passive support of the finished architectural drawing. Through a detailed historical analysis of the various media in which design has traditionally taken place, he highlights the subtle influence that the materiality of paper has had on the development of architectural thinking. Given that the process of drawing does not simply involve an automatic transcription onto a surface of ideas that are already clear in the architect's mind, he shows why the very materiality of drawings should be seen as part of the dynamic character of what he calls architectural *factures*, that is, the things (distinct from buildings) that architects can be properly said to 'make'. In the following chapter, through an examination of the role of the imagination in the perception, conception and construction of architectural representations, Nader El-Bizri interrogates the claim made in the conference call for papers, that 'the model-gaze reduces the possibilities of innovation' and 'stifles the pursuit of the absent referent beyond the present model'. This chapter suggests that the imagination is an integral phenomenon of direct vision and part of our perceptual experience and not simply illusory or fictional, and that it therefore plays a role within the model-gaze itself.

Raymond Quek revisits historical definitions of the problematic term *disegno*. By examining its use in the work of a number of philosophical commentators, he also draws out its continued relevance to contemporary debates on the notion of visual knowledge. The metaphor of Adam's navel is also used to highlight the problem of origins in the mystery of artistic creation. His chapter also illustrates the continuing tensions and reciprocities between conception, imagination and the process of visualisation. Picking up the threads of Marco Frascari's discussion of paper, Paul Emmons focuses on questions of scale in his historical account of architectural representation. In explaining how the use of scale makes the very process of design and comprehension possible, he also illustrates how the potential of CAD to produce one-to-one representations can actually lead to a loss of architectural understanding. Qi Zhu looks at two contrasting examples of twelfth-century Chinese architectural images. By comparing the graphical conventions common in technical drawings with those found in fine art, she illustrates the impact of both the cultural context of the production of images and the embodied actions of their producers. In their occasional misreadings of unfamiliar stylistic codes, the Chinese artisans involved in 'copying' technical drawings from the West often produced highly imaginative images of buildings that evoked the temporally ordered activities of their construction.

With reference to the thirteenth-century narrative of the 'King's Two Bodies', Federica Goffi discusses tangible/temporal and intangible/sempiternal aspects of the twinned bodies of kings and of architecture. To expand the analogy, she examines the role of drawing in relation to Tiberio Alfarano's ichnography of the Basilica of Saint Peter's in the Vatican during its Renaissance renovation. Conceived within an understanding of the twin persona of architecture, the chapter argues that drawing plays a significant role in allowing the imagination to grow and develop. Teresa Stoppani discusses the spatiality of Piranesi's *Campo Marzio dell'antica Roma* in contrast to that of Nolli's *Topografia di Roma*. With reference to Deleuze and Guattari's notion of the smooth and the striated, she argues that, by understanding space in terms of 'movement' rather than by the static objects within it, Piranesi constructed spaces that anticipated the spatial and temporal complexities of the contemporary city.

With reference to the study of the ruin in early sixteenth-century Rome and the 'fabricated' ruin in Le Corbusier's projects in India, this chapter discusses the theme of the 'unfinished' in the architectural imagination. Counter to the contemporary preoccupation with 'finished' states, where the messy processes of design are erased by the priority given to the uniformity of digital production, Nicholas Temple and Soumyen Bandyopadhyay discuss the redemptive potency of the unfinished in generating new horizons of creative intervention. In the final chapter in this section of the book, Antony Moulis explores the generative power of the architectural diagram by examining Le Corbusier's forty-year preoccupation with the graphical figure of the spiral. Whether vertically or horizontally employed, implied or explicit, Moulis highlights the significance of the spiral figure as a choreographer of movement. Beyond any symbolic or aesthetic value, the spiral is seen as an organisational device – in both the completed building and, more intriguingly, in the emerging design drawing.

Questions of representation

The poetic origin of architecture

Alberto Pérez-Gómez

Despite all the excitement about digital media, it is still impossible to argue that the integration of these concerns in the production of architecture has had an automatic positive effect on our built environment. The digital 'avant-garde' has degenerated into a banal mannerism, producing homogeneous results with little regard for cultural contexts all over the world. Clearly such means of representation are here to stay, and this poses enormous questions. Addressing primarily our vision (and not other senses of embodiment), experimental video, computer-graphics and virtual images have transformed our conceptual understanding of reality. Monopolising the discourse surrounding visual representation, discussions around the so-called 'digital revolution' often exclude more primary issues of meaning and ethics.

Paradoxically, the fragmentation and temporalisation of space initiated by film montage and modernist collage that opened up a truly infinite realm of poetic places for the human imagination still await their translation into architecture. During the last two decades, the seductive potential of virtual space has expanded beyond all expectations, through both technological breakthroughs and artistic endeavours, yet the architectural profession is still reluctant to question certain fundamental premises concerning the transparency and homogeneity of its means of representation.

Architectural conception and realisation usually assume a one-to-one correspondence between the represented idea and the final building. The fact that digital media *also* make this literal transcription more feasible through automation and robotics has resulted in an unwillingness to question this premise. Absolute control is essential in our technological world. Although drawings, prints, models, photographs and computer graphics play diverse roles in the design process, they are regarded most often as necessary surrogates or automatic transcriptions of the built work. To disclose appropriate alternatives to the ideological stagnation plaguing most architectural creation at the end of the second millennium, the first crucial step is to acknowledge that value-laden tools of representation underlie the conception and realisation of architecture.

The process of creation prevalent in architecture today assumes that a conventional set of projections, at various scales from site to detail, adds up to a complete, objective *idea* of a building. It is this assumption of the *ideal* as *real*, a conceptual inversion with roots in early Western modernity, that constitutes the first stumbling block. Whether the architect is effectively or legally responsible for the production of construction documents (working drawings), the assumption remains. These projective representations rely on reductive syntactic connections, with each projection constituting part of a dissected whole. They are expected to be absolutely unambiguous to avoid possible (mis)interpretations, and to function as efficient neutral instruments devoid of inherent value other than their capacity for accurate transcription. The architectural profession generally has identified architectural drawing with such projective tools.

The descriptive sets of projections that we take for granted operate in a geometrised, homogeneous space that was construed as the 'real' space of human action during the nineteenth century. Our implicit trust in the application of a scientific methodology to architecture derives from techniques prescribed by Jean-Nicolas-Louis Durand in his *Précis des Leçons d'Architecture* (1802 and 1813). Durand's *Mécanisme de la composition* was the first design method to be thoroughly dependent on the predictive capacity of these projections. For him, descriptive geometry was the modus operandi of the architect. Although descriptive geometry promoted simplistic objectification, this projective tool is a product of a philosophical tradition and technological world-view that defines the European nineteenth century and leads to our own 'world order'. It is, therefore, not something we can simply reject or pretend to leave behind. As Hubert Damisch has pointed out recently in his tour de force on the origins of perspective, the destructuring of perspectival depth by the avant-garde in twentieth-century art has not prompted our culture of television and cinema to make the projective distance 'a thing of the past'. In architecture, the issue is rather to define the nature of a 'depth' that the work must engage in order to resist the collapse of the world into cyberspace, a depth that concerns both the spatial or formal character of the work, and its programmatic, temporal or experiential dimension.

The technological world has generally embraced the pragmatic capacity of architectural drawing over its potential to construe a symbolic order. For architects it is important to remember that a symbol is neither a contrivance nor an invention, nor is it necessarily a representation of absolute truths or transcendental theological values. Symbols embody specific historical and cultural values, and buildings often possess experiential dimensions that cannot be reproduced in a conventional representation. Expecting architectural representations to embody a symbolic order – indeed, like any other work of art – will seem controversial unless we revise the common assumptions about art and its relationship to human life that have been with us since the eighteenth century. For architecture the difficulty of manifesting a symbolic order is necessarily double, since it concerns both the project and its 'translation' – an unfolding that is seldom present in other arts.

Projective drawing need not be a reductive device, a tool of prosaic substitution. Projection evokes temporality and boundaries. Defining the space between light and darkness, between the Beginning and the Beyond, it illuminates the space of culture, of our individual and collective existence. Closer to the origins of our philosophical history, projection was identified with the space of representation, the site of ontological continuity between universal ideas and specific things. The labyrinth, that primordial ground plan and image of architectural endeavour, is a projection linking time and place. Representing architectural space as the time of an *event*, the disclosure of order between birth and death, in the unpredictable temporality of human life itself, the labyrinth was literally the hyphen between idea and experience, the figuration of a place for human culture, the Platonic *chora*. Like music, realised in time from a more or less 'open' notation, inscribed as an act of divination for a potential order, architecture is itself a projection of architectural ideas, horizontal footprints and vertical effigies, disclosing a symbolic order *in time*, through rituals and programs. The architect's task, beyond the transformation of the world into a comfortable or pragmatic shelter, is the making of a physical, formal order that reflects the depth of our human condition, analogous in vision to the interiority communicated by speech and poetry, and to the immeasurable harmony conveyed by music.

Since the inception of Western architecture in classical Greece, the architect has not 'made' buildings; rather, he or she has made the mediating artefacts that make *significant* buildings possible. These artefacts – from words, to many kinds of inscriptions and drawings, to full-scale mock-ups – have changed throughout history. Changing has also been their relation to buildings. As late as the Renaissance, for example, the only drawings truly 'indispensable' for building (from a technological standpoint) were *modani* or template drawings, considered nevertheless important enough by their authors to be carefully protected from unscrupulous copying.

For architects concerned with ethics and not merely with aesthetic novelty, who seek the realisation of places where a fuller, more compassionate human life might take place, the appropriateness of mediating artefacts and tools is paramount. Architectural traditions are rich in potential lessons and alternatives. History offers ample evidence for an architecture resulting from a poetic translation of its representations, rather than as a prosaic transcription of an objectified image.

There seems to be an intimate complicity between architectural meaning and the modus operandi of the architect, his or her *praxis* at all levels, from abstract and ethical concerns to practical and technical issues. There is also a relationship between the richness of our cities as places propitious for imagery and reverie, as structures of embodied knowledge for collective orientation, and the nature of architectural *techne*, that is, differing modes of architectural conception and implementation. These relationships can never be grasped as merely causal, obeying some clear principle of mathematical logic. It is clear that the meaning of an architectural work is never simply the result of an author's will. In addition to the complex factors that contribute to bring to life an absent building, once the work occupies its place in the public realm, a multitude of additional considerations related to context, use, cultural associations, etc., have an impact on how it is perceived. Nevertheless, the architect responsible for initiating the dream cannot abdicate responsibility. The changing relationships between the intentions of architectural drawings and the built objects they describe hold important lessons for architects in order to exercise ethically the personal imagination and construe a better, richer place for human dwelling.

Prior to the Renaissance, architectural drawings were rare, certainly in the sense that is familiar to us. In the Middle Ages, architects did not conceive of a *whole building* and the very notion of *scale* was unknown. Gothic architecture, the most 'theoretical' of all medieval building practices, was fundamentally a *constructive* practice, operating through well-established traditions and geometric rules that could be applied directly on site. From the footprint of a building, construction proceeded by rhetoric and geometry, raising the elevation as discussions about the building's physiognomy continued, almost until the end. The master mason was responsible for constructing a model of the city of God on Earth; only the Architect of the Universe, however, possessed a comprehensive fore-knowledge of the project and was deemed capable of concluding the work at the end of Time. The various expressions of Gothic cathedrals were the result of different generations and diverse methods applied by itinerant bands of stone masons who migrated around Europe to work on various building projects. Multiple styles, as in the Cathedral of Chartres, or compromised geometric systems, as in Milan Cathedral, were regarded not as an inconsistency but as a layering of different responses to structural or symbolic problems during the course of construction.

Starting with the Renaissance, the relationship between architectural drawings and the buildings they describe should be considered with greater care than has been customary. From the most important architectural treatises and their respective contexts, it is evident that the maturation from architectural idea to built work was less systematised than we now take for granted. During the early Renaissance, the traditional understanding of architecture as a ritual act of construction had not been lost. The concept of a sympathetic universe, thoroughly alive, was prevalent throughout the fifteenth and sixteenth centuries. Different orders of reality – from a stone to God, from a point to a three-dimensional solid – were connected by a chain, by erotic links or *vincoli*. While this concept was based on the old Aristotelian cosmology, it was increasingly open to manipulation by magician-architects interested in propitiating a happy life, emulating the order of the heavens. This cultural context obviously demands a qualification of the 'instrumentality' of the tools or drawings of the architect. Projecting the geometric physiognomy of a building or city was a prophetic act, a form of conjuring and divining as we are told by Marco Frascari, and involved much more than the personal will of the author. Architectural drawings crystallised the miraculous power of the imagination and were therefore value-laden, never understood as neutral artefacts that might be transcribed unambiguously into buildings.

During the early Renaissance, Filarete discussed in his treatise the four steps to be followed in architectural creation. He was careful to emphasise the autonomy among proportions, lines, models and buildings, describing the connection between 'universes of ideation' in terms analogous to an alchemical transmutation, not to a mathematical transformation. Unquestionably, however, it is during the fifteenth century that architecture came to be understood as a liberal art, and architectural ideas were thereby increasingly conceived as geometrical *lineamenti*, as bi-dimensional, orthogonal projections. A gradual and complex transition from the classical (Greco-Arabic) theory of vision to a new mathematical and geometrical rationalisation of the image was taking place. The medieval writings on perspective (such as Ibn Alhazen, Alkindi, Bacon, Peckham, Vitello and Grosseteste) had treated, principally, the physical and physiological phenomenon of vision. In the cultural context of the Middle Ages, its application was specifically related to mathematics, the privileged vehicle for the clear understanding of theological truth. *Perspectiva naturalis*, seeking clear vision for mankind, was not concerned with artistic representation, but with an understanding of the modes of God's presence; it was part of the *quadrivium* of liberal arts, associated by Thomas Aquinas to music as visual harmony, and never to drawing or any other graphic method. Humanity literally lived *in* the light of God, under God's benevolent gaze, the light of the golden heaven of the Byzantine frescoes and mosaics, or the sublime and vibrant coloured space of the Gothic cathedrals.

The new understanding of a perspectival image in the Renaissance remained directly related to the notion of classical optics as a science of the transmission of light rays and to its underlying metaphysics. The pyramid of vision, the notion on which the Renaissance idea of the image as a window on the world was based, was inherited from the Euclidean notion of the visual cone. The eye was believed to project its visual rays onto the object, with perception occurring as a dynamic action of the beholder upon the world. Vitruvius (first century BCE) had discussed the question of optical correction in architecture as a direct corollary of the Euclidean cone of vision, demonstrating an awareness (also present in some medieval building practice) of the dimensional distortions brought about by the position of an observer. The issue, however, as is well known from the great examples of classical architecture, was to *avoid distorted perception*. Architects were expected to correct certain visual aspects (by increasing the size of lettering placed on a high architrave, for example), in order to convey an experience of perfect adjustment or regularity to synaesthetic perception, always primarily tactile. Renaissance architectural theory and practice never questioned this aim, which remained unshakeable until Claude Perrault's theoretical revolution at the end of the seventeenth century.

Neither did certain fundamental assumptions about perception change during the Renaissance. When queried about the truth of parallel lines, anyone would have answered that obviously, in the world of action, those straight lines *never* meet. The hypothesis of a vanishing point at infinity was both unnecessary for the construction of perspective, and ultimately inconceivable as the reality of perception in everyday life. Alberti's central point (*punto centrico*) of the perspective construction, for example, is often wrongly associated with such a 'vanishing' point. In fact the point of convergence in the *construzione legittima* is determined and fixed by the point of sight as a 'counter-eye' on the 'window' or, in contemporary terms, the central point on the picture plane. Even though fifteenth-century painters were experimenting with methods of linear perspective, the geometrisation of pictorial depth was not yet systematised and did not immediately transform the quotidian experience of the world, nor the process of architectural creation. It was impossible for the Renaissance architect to conceive that the truth of the world could be reduced to its visual representation, a two-dimensional diaphanous section of the pyramid of vision.

During the sixteenth century, treatises on perspective tried to translate the primarily empirical understanding of perspective into a system, and became increasingly distanced from treatises on optics. These new works, however, remained theoretical or mathematical elucidations and had almost no practical use in prescriptive representation. In Vignola's *Due Regole della Prospettiva Prattica*, a 'second observer' was introduced and became the distance point that allowed for a mathematical regulation of the foreshortening. The distance point was projected on the picture plane, on the horizon line at a distance from the central point equal to the distance between the eye of the observer and the plane of the image. In other words, Vignola's method introduced a second observer at the same distance from the central point, looking perpendicularly at the beholder, thereby adding an element essential for the representation of stereoscopic vision. Prior to this, with the apex of the cone of vision as a simplified eye, *perspettiva artificialis* had been, strictly speaking, a (very imperfect) monocular construction.

Before Dürer, a plan was generally conceived as a composite 'footprint' of a building, and an elevation as a face. Vertical or horizontal sections were not commonly used before the sixteenth century. It should not come as a surprise that perspective's emphasis on the truth of perception being a section through the cone of vision would be translated as a new emphasis on the importance of sections in architectural representation. Sections became the legitimate embodiment of architectural ideas, precise as composite drawings could not be, and therefore more adequate to embody a Platonic conception of truth. Yet, early use of sections betrays a fascination with the role of buildings as gnomons or shadow tracers. Vincenzo Scamozzi's design for the Villa Bardelini, in his *Idea dell'Architettura Universale*, is a fascinating instance. The co-ordination of the vertical and horizontal sections of the building reveal light and shadow as constitutive of the architecture's symbolic order, very much in the spirit of Vitruvius who had introduced gnomons as one of the three artefacts within the province of architecture, together with *machinae* and buildings. The possibility of taking measure of time (and space), in the sense of poetic *mimesis*, was the original task of the architect, and this hadn't been forgotten in the Renaissance. There was an overlapping of the notion of section as shadow or imprint, revealing the order of the deity, the presence of *light*, with that of section as a cut. The obsession to reveal clearly the insides of bodies, to magnify and dissect as a road to knowledge, is one that takes hold of European epistemology only after the mechanisation of physiology in the seventeenth century. Only then, light as divine emanation, as 'lighting' making the world of experience possible, indeed, as *projection*, becomes a passive medium, to the exclusion of shadows. Today, many architects remain fascinated by the revelatory power of cutting, but it is clear that in science this operation has reached its limits. Further cutting in biology, or particle smashing in physics, does not reveal a greater interiority.

More light without shadows is of no use. We are always left on the outside by objectified vision, and the architect at the end of modernity must clearly understand this if the 'enframed' vision is to be transcended. Understanding the nature of projections as ephemeral, dynamic and endowed with shadows may generate an architecture once more experienced as a flowing musical composition, in time, while the spectator glances compassionately at its material surfaces.

During the sixteenth century in Northern Italy, Daniele Barbaro, Palladio's friend and patron, emphasised that perspective was *not* an architectural *idea* in the Vitruvian sense. We may recall that in Vitruvius's *Ten Books*, the Greek word 'idea' refers to the three aspects of a mental image (perhaps akin to the Aristotelian *phantasm*) understood as the germ of a project. These *ideas* allowed the architect to imagine the disposition of a project's parts: *ichnographia* and *orthographia* would eventually be translated as plan and elevation, but do not originally involve the systematic correspondence of descriptive geometry. In his treatise on perspective, Barbaro offers a fascinating commentary on the Vitruvian passage. He believed that the translation of *sciographia* (the third Vitruvian idea) as perspective, resulted from a misreading of *sciographia* as *scenographia* in the original text, whose application was important only in the building of stage-sets. Thus he concludes that perspective, however important, was mainly recommended for painters and stage-set designers.

It is worthwhile to follow Barbaro's commentary in some detail in order to understand its implications. Sciagraphy or sciography derives etymologically from the Greek *skia* (shadow) and *graphou* (to describe). Scamozzi's villa comes immediately to mind. The etymology also speaks to the eventual relationship between the projection of shadows and linear perspective, an obligatory chapter in most seventeenth- and eighteenth-century treatises on the subject. In the architectural tradition, however, sciagraphy kept its meaning as a 'draught of a building, cut in its length and breadth, to display the interior', in other words, the profile, or section. This use of the term was still present in the nineteenth century (*Encyclopedia of Architecture*, London: The Caxton Press, 1852). Modern Latin dictionaries translate *scaenographia* (the actual term as it appears in the first existing Vitruvian manuscript) as the drawing of buildings in perspective, and generally assume that this word is synonymous to *sciagraphia*. The fact is that perspective was unknown in ancient Rome and even when Vitruvius speaks about the three types of stage-sets appropriate to tragedy, comedy and satire (Book V, ch. 6), there is no mention of perspective in connection with classical theatre. Vitruvius describes the fixed *scaena* as a royal palace facade with *periaktoi*, 'triangular pieces of machinery which revolve', placed beyond the doors, and whose three faces were decorated to correspond to each dramatic genre.

Barbaro argues that *scenographia*, which is 'related to the use of perspective', is the design of stages for the three dramatic genres. Appropriate types of buildings must be shown diminishing in size and receding to the horizon. He does not agree with 'those that wish to understand perspective (*perspettiva*) as one of the ideas that generate architectural design (*dispositione*)', ascribing to it the definition Vitruvius had given to *sciographia*. In his opinion it is plain that 'just as animals belong by nature to a certain species', the *idea* that belongs with plan (*ichnographia*) and elevation (*orthographia*), is the section (*profilo*), similar to the other two 'ideas' that constitute architectural order (*dispositione*). In Vitruvius's conception, the section 'allows for a greater knowledge of the quality and measurement of building, helps with the control of costs and the determination of the thickness of walls', etc. Barbaro, in fact, assumes that in antiquity 'perspective' was only applied to the painted representations on the sides of the *periaktoi*.

It was only during the seventeenth century that perspective became a generative *idea* in architecture, in the Vitruvian sense of the category. Both theology and science contributed to this shift. Within the Jesuit tradition, Juan Bautista Villalpando homologised perspective with plan and elevation in his exegetical work on Ezekiel's vision for the Temple of Jerusalem. Emphasising the notion that the human architect must share the divine architect's capacity for *visualising* a future building, he insists that plans and elevations are similar to perspectives, as they are merely 'pictures' of a building-to-come. The inception of the Cartesian modern world and the epistemological revolution brought about by modern science, introduced during the Baroque period a conflict between symbolic and mechanistic views of the world. A world of fixed essences and mathematical laws deployed in a homogeneous, geometrised space, much like the Platonic model of the heavens, was assumed by Galileo to be the truth of our experience of the physical world. As an example, Galileo believed, after postulating his law of inertia, that the essence of an object was not altered by motion. This notion, now an obvious 'truth' (as long as we keep making abstractions from contexts), was at odds with the traditional Aristotelian experience of the world in which perception, with its double horizon of mortal embodied consciousness and a finite world of qualitative places, was accepted as the primary and legitimate access to reality. The new scientific conception eventually led to a scepticism regarding the physical presence of the external world. In the terms of Descartes, man became a subject (a thinking, rather than an embodied *self*), confronting the world as *res extensa*, as an extension of his thinking ego. This dualistic conception of reality made it possible for perspective to become a model of human knowledge, a legitimate and scientific representation of the infinite world.

Baroque perspective in art and architecture, however, was a symbolic configuration, one that allowed reality to keep the qualities that it had always possessed in an Aristotelian world. During the seventeenth century, the primacy of perception as the foundation of truth was hardly affected by the implications of this new science and philosophy. Perspective, now a legitimate architectural *idea*, became a privileged form of symbolisation. The architecture of the Jesuit churches by Andrea Pozzo, for example, can hardly be reduced to their section or elevation. Pozzo's frescoes are inextricably tied to the three-dimensionality of the architectural space, revealing transcendental truth in the human world. Rather than remaining in the two-dimensional field of representation, the perspective is projected from a precise point situated in lived space and fixed permanently on the pavement of the nave. The possibility of 'real order' for mortal existence appears only at the precise moment that a human presence occupies the station point of the 'illusionistic' *quadrattura* fresco.

Even though the theory of perspective, as an offspring of the new science, allowed human beings to control and dominate the physical reality of existence, the arts, gardening and architecture during the seventeenth century were still concerned with the revelation of a transcendentally ordered cosmos. Thus it can be argued that by geometrising the world, humanity first gained access to a new transcendental truth. Even though perspective became increasingly integrated with architecture, perspectival systematisation remained restricted to the creation of an *illusion*, qualitatively distinct from the constructed reality of the world. Perspective marked the moment of an epiphany, the revelation of meaning and the God-given geometric order of the world. For a brief time, illusion was the locus of ritual. The revelation of order occurred at the precarious moment of coincidence between the vanishing point and the position of the observer.

While most seventeenth-century philosophers were still striving to formulate the appropriate articulation of the relation between the world of appearances and the 'absolute' truth of modern science, the work of Gérard Desargues appeared as an anomaly. Desargues disregarded the transcendental dimension of geometry and the symbolic power of geometrical operations. He ignored the symbolic implications of infinity and thus transformed it into a 'material' reality. He sought to establish a general geometric science, one that might effectively become the basis for such diverse technical operations as perspective drawing, stone and wood-cutting for construction, and the design of solar clocks. Until then, theories of perspective always associated the point of convergence of parallel lines with the apex of the cone of vision projected on the horizon line. Desargues was apparently the first writer in the history of perspective to postulate *a point at infinity*. He maintained that all lines in our ever-changing, mortal and limited world actually converged toward a real point, at an infinite distance, yet present at hand for human control and manipulation. Thus any system of parallel lines, or any specific geometrical figure, could be conceived as a variation of a single universal system of concurrent lines. Orthogonal projection as we understand it today was already for Desargues a simple case of perspective projection where the projective point was located at an infinite distance from the plane of projection. Desargues's method allowed for the representation of complex volumes *before* construction, implementing an operation of deductive logic where vision, perception and experience were supposed to be practically irrelevant. Perspective became the basic (and paradigmatic) prescriptive science, a new kind of theory prophetic of the epistemological shift that would take place during the nineteenth century, whose sole *raison d'être* was to control human action, the *practice* of applied sciences and our enframed technological world. The scientific revolution had witnessed in Desargues's system the first attempt to endow representation with an objective autonomy. Nevertheless, the prevailing philosophical connotations of infinity, always associated with theological questions, as well as the resistance of traditionally minded painters, craftsmen and architects, made his system unacceptable to his contemporaries. Desargues's basic aims would eventually be fulfilled by Gaspard Monge's descriptive geometry near the end of the eighteenth century.

Despite European culture's reticence to demystify infinity, perspective soon ceased to be regarded as a preferred vehicle for transforming the world into a meaningful human order. Instead, it became a simple re-presentation of reality, a sort of empirical verification of the external world for human vision. Pozzo's treatise, *Rules and Examples of Perspective Proper for Painters and Architects* (Rome: 1693, English trans. London: 1700), occupies an interesting, perhaps paradoxical, position as a work of transition. From a plan and an elevation, his method of projection is a step-by-step set of instructions for perspective drawing that establishes the homology of projections and an absolutely fixed proportional relationship of orthogonal elements seen in perspective. Pozzo avoids the geometrical theory of perspective, and his theoretical discourse amounts to a collection of extremely simple rules and detailed examples of perspective constructions, perhaps the first truly applicable manual on perspective in the sense familiar to us. The consequential homology of 'lived' space and the geometric space of perspectival representation encouraged the architect to assume that the projection was capable of truly depicting a proposed architectural creation and, therefore, to 'design in perspective'. The qualitative spatiality of our existence was now identical to the objectified space of perspective, and architecture could be rendered as a picture.

In the eighteenth century, artists, scientists and philosophers lost interest in the theory of perspective. Building practice, in fact, changed very little despite the potential of the new conceptual tools to transform architectural processes. The geometrisation of knowledge initiated with the inception of modern science in the seventeenth century was arrested by the focus on empirical theories spurred by Newton's work and by the identification of the inherent limitations of Euclidean geometry.

In this context, architects seemed nevertheless ready to accept the notion that there was no conceptual distinction between a stage-set constructed following the method *per angolo* of Galli-Bibiena, one where there was no longer a privileged point of view, and the permanent tectonic reality of their craft. Each and every individual spectator occupied an equivalent place in a world transformed into a two-point perspective. Reality was transformed into a universe of representation. The Baroque illusion became a potential delusion in the Rococo church. Even the vanishing point of the frescoes became inaccessible to the spectator, the new aesthetic chasm now to be bridged by an act of faith, while the building appeared as a highly rhetorical, self-referential theatre, one where the traditional religious rituals were no longer unquestionable vehicles for existential orientation. Humanity's *participation* in the symbolic (and divine) order of the world was starting to become a matter of self-conscious faith, rather than self-evident embodied knowledge, despite the pervasive (and unquestionably influential) Masonic affirmation of the coincidence between revealed and scientific truths.

Only after the nineteenth century and a systematisation of drawing methods could the process of translation between drawing and building become fully transparent and reduced to an equation. The key transformation in the history of architectural drawing was the inception of descriptive geometry as the paradigmatic discipline for the builder, whether architect or engineer. The École Polytechnique in Paris, founded after the French Revolution, trained the new professional class of eminent scientists and engineers of the nineteenth century. Descriptive geometry, the fundamental core subject, allowed for the first time a systematic reduction of three-dimensional objects to two dimensions, making the control and precision demanded by the Industrial Revolution possible. Perspective became an 'invisible hinge' among projections. It is no exaggeration to state that without this conceptual tool our technological world could not have come into existence. With Durand's *Mécanisme de la composition* and its step-by-step instructions, the codification of architectural history into types and styles, the use of the grid and axes, transparent paper, and precise decimal measurements allowed for planning and cost estimates. Descriptive geometry became the 'assumption' behind all modern architectural endeavours, ranging from the often superficially artistic drawings of the École de Beaux Arts to the functional projects of the Bauhaus. The rendering of drawings in the Beaux Arts tradition does not change the essence of the architecture it represents, nor does it succeed in formulating an alternative to the architecture of the École Polytechnique. The Beaux Arts does not retrieve myth through drawings, but rather only formalises appearances with a status of contingent 'ornament', in a similar way to 'post-modern classical' styles. This is indeed at odds with the possibility of retrieving meaning through a phenomenological understanding of symbolisation.

In this context, it is easy to understand that true *axonometry* could only emerge as a preferred architectural tool after Durand, who was already suspicious of perspective and what he believes are deceiving painterly techniques. Conversely, 'new' theories of perspective became concerned with depicting 'retinal' images, such as curved or three-point perspectives. Despite similarities, it is in the early nineteenth century and not in the work of Pozzo, that the tools taken for granted by twentieth-century architects see their inception.

Today the growing obsession with productivity and rationalisation has transformed the process of maturation from the idea to the built work into a systematic representation that leaves little place for the invisible to emerge from the process of translation. Computer graphics, with its seductive manipulation of viewpoints and delusions of three-dimensionality, are mostly a more sophisticated 'mechanism of composition'. The question concerning the application of computers to architecture is, of course, hotly debated and as yet unresolved. The instrument is not, simply, the equivalent of a pencil or a chisel that could easily allow one to transcend reduction. It is the culmination of the objectifying mentality of modernity and it is, therefore, inherently perspectival, in precisely the sense that we have described in this chapter. Computer graphics tend to be just a much quicker and more facile tool that relies on mathematical projection, a basic tool of industrial production. The tyranny of computer graphics is even more systematic than any other tool of representation in its rigorous establishment of a homogeneous space and its inability to combine different structures of reference. It is, of course, conceivable that the machine would transcend its binary logic and become a tool for a poetic disclosure in the realm of architecture. The issue, perhaps the hope, in our post-historical, post-literate culture, is to avoid delusion through electronic media and simulation, the pitfalls of further reductive, non-participatory representation. Conceivably, as a tool of representation, the computer may have the potential to head towards absolute fluidity or towards further fixation and reduction. The latter is the unfortunate result of the implementation of the techno-logical will to power, i.e. control and domination. The fact is that the results of computer applications in architecture, whether merely graphic, or more recently motivated by a desire to extrapolate 'complex natural orders' to practice, remain generally disappointing.

While descriptive geometry attempted a precise coincidence between the representation and the object, modern art remained fascinated by the enigmatic distance between the reality of the world and its projection. This fascination, with immediate roots in nineteenth-century photography and in optical apparatuses such as the stereoscope, responded to the failure of a modern scientific mentality to acknowledge the unnameable dimension of representation, a poetic wholeness that can be recognised and yet is impossible to reduce to the discursive *logos* of science, while it no longer refers to an intersubjective cosmological picture. Artists since Piranesi and Ingres have explored that distance, the 'delay', or 'fourth dimension' in Marcel Duchamp's terms, between reality and the appearance of the world. Defying reductionist assumptions without rejecting the modern power of abstraction, certain twentieth-century architects, including Le Corbusier, Alvar Aalto, Antoni Gaudi or John Hejduk, have used projections not as technical manipulations, but to discover something at once original and recognisable. These well-known architects have engaged the dark space 'between' dimensions in a work that privileges the *process* and is confident of the ability of the architect to 'discover', through embodied work, significant tactics for the production of a compassionate architecture. This emerging 'architecture of resistance', a verb more often than a noun, celebrates dreams and the imagination without forgetting that it is made for the Other, and aims at revealing depth not as homologous to breadth and height (3-D), but as a significant *first dimension* that remains mysterious and reminds us of our luminous opacity as mortals in a wondrous more-than-human world.

A reflection on paper and its virtues within the material and invisible *factures* of architecture

Marco Frascari

Since paper has become an essential ingredient of architectural conceiving, it has had – and always will have – an essential purpose in the development of an architect's thinking. In its continual material progression and its interfacing with other drafting paraphernalia and instruments, paper has regularly transformed the procedures of architectural conceiving. It has allowed architects to alter the temporality of the process of invention and to move away from the site during the making of their architectural *factures*. To speak of an 'architectural facture' is to consider both a piece of architecture and its drawing in terms of their making – as both can be seen as interfacing records of their own having-been-made (*facture* is the past participle of the Latin verb *facio, facere*: to make or to do).[1]

The constant fascination with an active rather than with a passive technology has always misled the human perception of reality since active technology prevents the knowledge of material objects in an immaterial way. As a passive instrument, paper is more important than an active instrument such as the printing press: if paper had not existed, Gutenberg could not have conceived of using movable characters. Regrettably, many architects and design critics perceive paper as merely a passive support of the finished drawing, since they do not realize that during the drafting procedure, subtle manipulations and changes in the paper play an influential continuo-counterpoint, essential for the play of an architect's imagination. The assortment of drafting papers cannot be deemed as mere supports for architectural representations, but rather their very materiality should be considered as part of the dynamic characteristic of the architectural *facture*. In Italian, a factura (*fattura*) is also a magical procedure, a ritual making that is done with the scope of increasing or reducing the vital and spiritual energy of individuals. By analogy, an architectural factura is a mounting or falling of the energies played out during the process of architectural conceiving.

Although the trash cans of architectural offices are gobbling up more paper at present than ever before, the widespread sycophantic claim is that we are in the age of 'paperless' architecture. The consequence of this symbolic 'trashing' is that the anagogic stipulation of any true architectural project – a vision above and beyond the drafting surface – is trashed together with the paper.

Drawing on paper does not involve an automatic transcription onto a surface of ideas that are already clear in the architect's mind, i.e. a merely figural delineation. But, rather, it provides a way to mediate and sublimate architectural factures of future edifications.

'And nothing else will suit the age ...'

Paper is a humble material that dominates our life. However, we do not reflect on its unthinkable presence until a paper-associated event strikes us for its omnipresent use. The pervasive use of paper was celebrated in London by a popular song entitled *The Age of Paper*, performed by Mr. Howard Paul – attired in a suit of paper – in the British music halls during the 1860s.[2] The refrain affirmed: 'For paper now is all the rage, And nothing else will suit the age'.[3]

Since then, paper has kept its position as one of the most significant technological presences in the building and design industry. Nevertheless, architectural critics and intellectuals do not often acknowledge its crucial and critical role. In January 1999, the *Daily Telegraph* carried out a cross-cultural survey on the Internet among leading scientists and mathematicians, asking: 'what were the most significant developments of the last two millennia?' In his answer, Clifford Pickover, a research staff member at the IBM T.J. Watson Research Center of During, assigned to the development of paper a crucial role in the advancement of humanity:[4]

> In AD 105 Ts'ai Lun reported the discovery of paper to the Chinese Emperor. Ts'ai Lun was an official to the Chinese Imperial Court and I consider his early form of paper to be humanity's most important invention and progenitor of the Internet. Both paper and the Internet break the barriers of time and distance and permit unprecedented growth and opportunity.

Because of the interaction of their material qualities with the conceiving of future buildings, the various kinds of drafting paper (as evolved during the centuries from the *carta bambagina* to *bristol boards*), should be taken into account as inspiring the more meditative aspects of architectural factures. An architectural meditation on paper is a consideration of an artefact in terms of its making – considered as a record of its own having-been-made – in that it becomes a way of casting it into the future.

On the one hand, a recent account of a house construction in Bosnia does reveal how paper was historically totally unnecessary, since the making of an edifice is, and always was, a facture. On the other hand, it also shows how immediate and spontaneous designations are the origins of architectural conceiving:[5]

> One day the owner of the neighboring garden brought a carpenter to the site and told him to build up a house. They stopped on a spot where the

ground sloped gently downwards. The carpenter had a look at the trees of the garden, the grounds, the environment and the town in the valley. Then he proceeded to extract from his cummerbund some pegs, paced off the distances and marked them with pegs. Then he came to his main task. He asked the owner which tree might be sacrificed, moved his pegs for a few feet, nodded and seemed satisfied.[6]

Although the facture of architecture originated in paperless procedures of immediate designation, architecture was never completely without mediated drawings. Early architects produced a few scale drawings on papyrus, vellum or parchment, but the major drawing activity took place on-site. Full-size details were drawn onto a skimming of plaster of Paris on the floor of the 'tracing house', or carved into the stone paving in the secondary parts of the building. Similar techniques had already been used in Roman and Greek architecture. Examples of these kinds of tracings can been found at the Temple of Apollo at Didyma or in Rome near the Pantheon.[7] Tracing floors still exist in many places such as the cathedrals of Strasbourg, Vienna, Prague, York and Wells, in many edifices in France and in other several locations around the world. It took a long time before drawing on paper could replace these very effective tracings. As late as the end of the seventeenth century, there were still instances of this tradition. The plans for Francesco Borromini's bell towers that once embellished the Pantheon in Rome (likened to 'donkey's ears', they were removed in the late nineteenth century) are detailed on top of the cornice stone slabs encircling the Pantheon's dome.

Architecture came into the age of paper during the fourteenth century. By the mid-eighth century, Chinese paper-making following the Silk Route reached Samarkand and from there the trade was introduced to the Arab world, where paper quickly became popular as a support for calligraphic works.[8] Through the Arab conquest of North Africa and Southern Spain, the craft of paper-making first reached the Moorish parts of Spain in the eleventh century. From the eleventh century on, Arabic papers were exported throughout the Byzantine Empire and Christian Europe. The first European paper mill was established in the mid-thirteenth century and the use of paper spread all over Europe, even though the earliest paper was very expensive, fragile and suffered from a strong cultural distrust: the Western Church initially declared that only parchment could carry the Sacred Word.[9] Of course, there were architectural drawings on papyrus and parchment before the emergence of paper, although they were merely replicas of the paperless drawings taking place on construction sites. Their materiality and portability allowed a new kind of considered cross-transcription, although not a conceiving transformation.

From parchment to 'bum-wad'

On architects' tables, slowly, paper began to reach the condition of enhancing the factures of architectural conceiving. Nevertheless, the majority of contemporary architects do not think too much of paper, ironically especially nowadays when paperless offices and studios are consuming much more paper than ever before. A remarkable sign of this predicament can be seen in the language of the drafting room, in the practice of using a play of assonance to identify the lightweight yellow tracing paper as 'trash' or – perhaps worse – the identification of it (without any metonymical flair) as 'bum-wad'. Professionals and students of architecture alike trace a few lines on a piece of 'bum-wad' and, if the result is not to their satisfaction, it is immediately trashed. Of course there are exceptions to this insensitive act, as witnessed by Louis I. Kahn's, Bob Venturi's and Michael Graves' famous drawings on 'yellow trace' – as notable exceptions they confirm the negative view.

The effect of this denial of the crucial active role played by these paper 'supports' is that two seemingly unrelated problematic events have combined to misrepresent the task performed by paper during the elaboration of the architectural project. On the one hand, there is the Cartesian metaphysical phenomenon of the separation between the image and its support and, on the other hand, the physical phenomenon of the way in which the profession has organized the billing of clients in relation to the production of drawings.

Architectural drawings have been always considered as sources and material for the historical investigation of architecture, to help reconstruct or analyse the history of buildings, cities or the work of individual architects. Drawings are seen as images of the idea, images of different phases of design, images of construction procedures, images of realized constructions, as finished or transformed by time. These drawings are seen as simulacra, conceptual or 'mythological' models that have no correlation or foundation in the physicality of drawing on paper, but only on a 'platonic' relationship with architecture. This deceiving notion can be traced back to Rene Descartes who, on the one hand, explains images as partial similitudes to their objects and, on the other, explains that images are just as ink lines laid down on paper: 'un peu d'encre posee ca et la sur du papier ...'[10]

In his compelling refusal of sensual perceptions, Descartes had not detected that the material reactions between papers and inks plays a key part in the making of drawings. These material reactions are necessary ingredients of the facture of any architectural image, since drawings are not the simulacra of works of architecture to be built, restored or modified, but they are works of architecture in themselves. However, giving to Caesar what belongs to Caesar, I must recognize that Descartes had remarkably set the conceptual basis for inkjet printers which produce images by laying ink here and there on any kind of support properly sized for fast-drying ink.

The digital and the *anagogical* imperative

During this new era of paperless offices and studios, it is crucial to reflect more broadly on the uses and functions of paper in the facture of architecture itself. As already noted, the act of drawing on paper does not simply involve an automatic transcription onto surfaces of ideas that are already clear in the architect's mind. Working on paper has been a way for many architects to handle the mediation and sublimation of architectural making. Following an often-misunderstood Vitruvian precept stating that making architecture is 'a continuous mental process completed by the hands,'[11] by working on paper, architects have added manifold interpretative dimensions to their manually performed intellectual work.

In 1994, on an Internet site, two architecture professors from Columbia University publicized their studio as an answer to the 'digital imperative':

> The 'digital imperative' to switch from analog to digital mode will manifest itself this year at the architecture school in the form of the Paperless Studio. Projecting ahead, we envision the inevitable and ubiquitous presence of advanced digital design and communication technologies. Architecture students will routinely use the best of new technologies within an information-rich and fully networked, multimedia environment.[12]

Of course they had not appreciated that architecture had begun as a paperless practice and that the use of paper had accomplished the move from an interpretation of architectural projects based on *analogical* expressions to the virtues of *anagogical* manifestations. To bring digital outputs from being simply 'analogical and replicas of paper representation' to become powerfully anagogical in their own right, a valid concern is to understand how the materiality of paper has interfaced with the intellectual activity of architectural facture in generating anagogical demonstrations. The term originated in textual biblical exegesis: anagogy became well known during medieval times with a memorable couplet attributed to Augustine of Dacia (previously considered by Nicholas de Lyra) describing the four senses of a text: 'Littera gesta docet, quid credas allegoria Moralis quid agas quo tendas anagogia'.[13] The word *anagogia* is a transliteration derived from the Greek '*anagoghe*', a composite word from *ana* (above, high) and from the verb *agein* (to lead). The proper Latin translation for the Greek '*anagoghe*' is '*sursumductio*', which can be found in the writings of Isidore of Seville, Venerable Bede or Rabanus Maurus. Anagogy belongs to the layer of deeper sense that summarizes and encapsulates in a final event the other three senses. In the list and description of the four senses of a piece of writing (literal, allegoric, moral and anagogic), anagogy always occupies the final place. Structural and qualitative reasons determine such a location, since anagogy not only constitutes the last of the four senses of writings but it is also their ultimate goal or *telos*.

Similarly, the four senses can be detected in architectural representations. On paper, concealed within the architectural delineation, the literal and the allegorical senses of a drawing strictly represent different analogical constructs that articulate the tectonic and formal imagination. The literal and the allegorical senses have an obviously didactic and parallel purpose since they both describe the building envelope, its materiality, and the various aspects necessary to represent the poly-functional nature of every building. The tropological or moral sense of the drawing addresses intellectual constructions and provides the reasons by which technological, religious and social codes are defined and transformed.

Resulting from the interlacing of the logical constraints of the other three interpretative senses, the anagogical sense illustrates the *telos* embodied in the architectural project by demonstrating an immaterial reality beyond its material condition. In the text of his *De Administratione*, Abbot Suger reveals that anagogy occurs when the connection between materiality and immateriality results in a suspension of time:

> Thus, when – out of my delight in the beauty of the house of God – the loveliness of the many coloured gems has called me away from external cares, and worthy meditation has induced me to reflect, transferring that which is material to that which is immaterial, on the diversity of the sacred virtues: then it seems to me that I see myself dwelling, as it were, in some strange region of the Universe which neither exists entirely in the slime of the earth nor entirely in the purity of Heaven; and that, by the grace of God, I can be transported from this inferior to that higher world in an anagogical manner.[14]

Closely related to anagogy is the idea of *transitus*, which refers to the viewer's mental journey across an image in the act of interpretation. In the mode of entrance there is a three-dimensional world depicted and the viewer is drawn directly into the heart of the universe of the image, and perhaps even to the world beyond the depiction itself.

The first condition for the use of paper as a conceiving tool was generated by the transfer of analogical and allegorical senses from the drawing performances taking place at the construction site to the surface of the paper on the drafting table. In his commentary on Vitruvius, published in Como in 1521, Cesare Cesariano offers us some extraordinary similes to help to understand the analogical and allegorical use of paper in architecture. In commenting on Vitruvius' definitions of architectural drawings, Cesariano reveals the role of paper in conceiving architecture by stating that a piece of paper is similar to a layer of dust, plaster or snow on a field, on which architects could trace the plan of a building with their footsteps by pacing around:

> *Icnographia* ... : *cioe una impreffione facta sopra il terreno aut pulvere uel pasta o neve: nel como i disegno fopra il papero: & uulgarmente fi dice etiam holme feu pedane.*[15]

The paper used by Cesariano was most likely the *carta bambagina*, soft as cotton wool (Greek, *bambax*, Italian, *bambagia*). With its multimodal qualities it could easily evoke a snow-covered field. On a sheet of *carta bambagina*, the legs of the compass could literally and allegorically pace out the dimensions of a plan. For Cesariano, ichnography – a scaled and dimensioned drawing of a plan – embodies an anagogical sense if it is accurately traced by a compass: an analogue for an architectural diviner. A compass and a ruler are analogical divinatory tools that operate in a similar fashion to the unburnable *lituus* employed by Romulus to trace the foundation plan of Rome – an implement used to achieve the *transitus*:

> Therefore Ichnography is nothing else than a modular designation on a surface, as it is said of the border (Circigatura) made with the ruler and the compass to indicate the object to be made. Similarly done with the unburnable wand – *lituus* used by the Master Romulus to indicate the foundations of edifices.[16]

The ordinary manner of taking the auspices, that is to define by divination the anagogical sense of the place, was as follows: Roman augurs first marked out with a wand, the *lituus*, designated a division in the heavens called *templum* or *tescum*, within which they intended to make their observations. The station where they were taking the auspices was also separated by a solemn formula from the rest of the land, and was also named *templum* or *tescum*. For Cesariano, the paper was the *templum* where architects as *auspices* could divine the *telos* of future buildings by a mental journey across an image. The compass and ruler tracings on paper, as *Lituus* tracings on the ground, consent to enter into a multi-dimensional representation and the viewer is drawn directly into the heart of the universe of the image, and to the world beyond it.

From recto to verso

If all the changes and interfaces that the different aspects of architectural drawings have undergone during the long 'age of paper' are examined step-by-step, it would take us well beyond the scope of this chapter. Therefore, I propose to jump over a few centuries and turn quickly to Vincenzo Scamozzi's didascalic recommendations on the use of instruments and papers given in his treatise *L'idea dell'architectura universale*, published in Venice in 1600. In the chapter entitled 'Of the instruments needed by the architect, of drafting materials, of models: instructions on how to make them well', Scamozzi discusses the virtues and qualities of paper in the facture of architectural drawings. The first step is to smooth, burnish and press the paper in an attempt to make the surface ready to accept the three kinds of marks necessary to an architectural drawing. The first kind of line is made with a dull metal point or bone and ivory scriber. These lines are grooved into the paper; they are those signs that, in his architectural writing, Sebastiano Serlio, a friend of the Scamozzi family, had called 'occult lines' (*linee occulte*). The second kind of line is the trace left by pencils or charcoal on the surface of the paper. The third kind is the ink line, together with the washes that are laid by the pen or run by brushes. However, although he does not mention them as a specific set of signs, Scamozzi discusses and uses in his own drawings a fourth kind of mark. These are indirectly revealed in a set of instructions for the quasi-alchemical making of a good type of ink – an ink that is metaphorically and physically full of 'spirit':[17]

Ink can be manufactured properly with excellent Rumanian wine, or white wine, and it must be quite clear (because it absorbs the substance better) and with the crinkled Gall growing in the peninsula of Istria, somewhat crushed and left infusing in the wine in a glass vase for ten days exposed to the Sun, in the summer heat, stirring it every day.... The excellence of the ink, something we have always pursued, is recognizable from the purple hue of its washes, which gives such elegance to the drawings, and from the fact that the slight markings appearing on the back of the paper are of the same color, which is a sign of the ink's quality, instead of an ugly yellowish color, or reddish or even rusty.

The markings on the back that infiltrated through the paper are important for Scamozzi's architectural factures, as revealed in his drawings of the section and elevation of the Salzburg cathedral. On the recto, the elevation and the section are carefully drafted, and on the verso, using the trace of the ink that had permeated through the fibre of the paper, Scamozzi had also drawn the section and the elevation of the dome.[18]

Furthermore, for Scamozzi, paper is not only a passive anagogical instrument but it also becomes an active tool of the facture. He advises the use of a piece of paper as *lituus*: a piece folded to resemble a triangle that may be marked to transfer dimensions and proportions – a piece of paper that becomes an effective drafting and implementing instrument. In applying this drawing procedure, Scamozzi states that the first step is the accurate tracing of two orthogonal crossing lines onto the drawing surface, exactly as the Roman augurs did in the delineation of the temple on the ground.

The development of the recto–verso relationship is closely related to the history of paper, which was only widely used in Europe from the sixteenth century. At first, the scarcity of the new resource pushed artists to use a sheet to its fullest capacity: in many cases they crammed both recto and verso with sketches, architectural plans and notes. Sometimes they drew on the backs of letters or receipts, which can help to identify the date of the drawings a few centuries later. In Italy the matter of the permeation between recto and verso in architectural factures on paper became a fundamental issue with the use of a special type of heavy tracing paper – especially in connection with the development and use of blueprints and the Italian architectural tradition in preparing drawings. Even when paper was becoming more accessible, out of convenience many artists continued to use both sides.[19]

Tracing the *transitus*

The physical phenomenon of *transitus,* a literal and 'spiritual' crossing of the fibres of a sheet of paper, is present in many architectural factures, as in a drawing of Saint Peter's by Bramante and Sangallo, and in many other examples of drawings from the Renaissance and Baroque periods.

To conclude this discussion let us focus on one special type of paper, a heavy tracing paper we should refer to by its traditional Italian name, *carta da lucido*. Italian architectural tradition in preparing drawings for reproduction – whether for presentation to clients or to be submitted to approving and controlling institutions – is quite dissimilar in nature from the market-dominated situation prevalent in North America.

In their discussion of American drawings, Gebhard and Nevins point out that new drafting technologies and codified processes of education had

> decidedly affected the uses to which architectural drawings were put. It was in the 1870s and 1880s that the threefold division of architectural drawings became fully solidified.... The first two aspects of drawing – preliminary sketches and especially presentation drawings – continued to have a loose tie with High Art [sic] drawing and painting.[20]

These changes configured the relations between architects and draftspersons in the production of architecture and architectural drawings.

In the larger offices, the principals would supposedly produce the underlying concept of the building primarily through sketches. After this had been worked out, the formalized presentation drawings would then be made by a skilled draftsperson or by an itinerant delineator. Once this had been approved by the client, working drawings would be produced: 'It became increasingly advantageous to employ professional renderers who could produce impressive formal drawings used to sell the product to the customer and/or to advertise the firm through publications'.[21]

Within the Italian tradition, architects prepare 'under-drawings': a blend of drafting and drawing combined with written and sketched marginalia generally carried out on paperboards and labelled *sotto-lucidi*. Then, interpreting this medley of graphic expressions and descriptions, the draftspersons or architectural interns trace the drawing in ink on heavy tracing paper tagged *carta da lucido* and that drafting is called *lucidare*. This anagogic *camera lucida*, i.e. *carta da lucido*, came into architecture from the practice of using oiled paper for preparatory drawings in painting.

In the attempt to envisage a future building, the roles played by presentation drawings and renderings and the *sotto-lucidi* are different, but both dominate during architectural gestations. The presentation drawings present themselves to a person's view and purport to be representations of a building-to-come and thus propose to offer knowledge pertaining to its otherwise invisible referents. This view does not progress once the presentation drawing is experienced and any further pursuit of the invisible beyond the drawing is effectively annulled. Any discussion of whether the invisible remains invisible or instead becomes visible belongs to the domain of the presentation drawing. The function of this drawing is to divide the invisible into that part which is reduced to the visible and another part which is invisible due to the viewer's inevitable fixation on the 'photo-realistic' precision of the presented image; this share of the invisible is thus invisible. These are the results of a metaphorical *camera obscura*.

As another category of drawings, the *sotto-lucidi*, however, do not result from a vision of the invisible, but instead they provoke one. Rather than resulting from the gaze aimed at it, the *sotto-lucido* summons sight by allowing the invisible to saturate the visible, but without any attempt or claim of reducing the invisible to the visible drawing. The *sotto-lucido* teaches the gaze to proceed beyond the visible into an infinity whereby something new of the invisible is encountered; this gaze never rests or settles on the drawing itself, but instead rebounds upon the visible into a gaze towards infinite possible worlds. The *sotto-lucido* becomes the 'flatland' where the *transitus* takes place.

What has this tracing on paper got to do with buildings? What makes these sheets relate to what we finally will call 'constructed' architecture? Nothing: different matter, different dimensions, another substance. Should we take the 'real' architecture to reside in the stones, the bricks or the paper? Conceivably, none of these are architecture. Rather it is something that escapes us when we describe it factually. It possesses, exactly, only the substance of a facture plus an extracorporeal essence – a 'subtle body' – foreshadowed by the badly inadequate character of the signs with which we attempt the impossible venture of ineffably representing that which cannot be desired, i.e. the beautifully vague traces of architectural factures that we can only grasp through *a speculum in aenigmate*, i.e. through a (Claude)-glass darkly – realizing a true architectural *recto–verso transitus*. So, let's praise the hybrid nature of paper and sing again:

For paper now is all the rage,
And nothing else will suit the age.

Notes

1   I am expanding the meaning of 'facture' as elaborated by David Summers (*Real Spaces: World Art History and the Rise of Western Modernism*, London: Phaidon, 2003, p. 74) to include a further influential dimension of the meaning: the use in Italian of the word *fattura* as related to conjuring and supernatural events performed through the making and assembling of organic and inorganic objects.

2   Howard Paul, a journalist whose comic magazine *Diogenes*, a would-be rival to *Punch*, failed shortly after its creation. His wife was a famous singer.

3   Howard Paul, *The Age of Paper* (c.1860).

4   With a zestier flavour, Pickover repeats the same remark in a book properly entitled *Calculus and Pizza: a Math Cookbook for the Hungry Mind*, Hoboken, NJ: John Wiley & Sons, 2003.

5   The Italian *disegnare* derives from *designare*.

6   D. Grabrijan and J. Neidhardt, *Architecture of Bosnia*, Ljubljana, 1957.

7   'The Construction Plans for the Temple of Apollo at Didyma,' in *Scientific American* (December 1985), pp. 126–32.

8   Quoted by Karen Garlick, 'A Brief Review of the History of Sizing and Resizing Practices,' in *The Book and Paper Group Annual*, Vol. 5, 1986. Available online, at: aic.stanford.edu/sg/bpg/annual/v05/bp05–11.html.

9   Dard Hunter, *Papermaking: the History and Technique of an Ancient Craft*, New York: Dover Publications (Margaret Starbird, 1943), 1970, p. 61.

10 'a touch of ink laying here and there on paper ...', Rene Descartes, *La Dioptrique*,
1 *De la lumiere*; A.T. VI, p. 81.

11 Vitruvius I,i.iii.

12 www.arch.columbia.edu/DDL/paperless/NEWSLINE.html.

13 The literal sense teaches what happened,
The allegorical what you believe.
The moral what you should do,
The anagogical where you are going.
(The distich is generally attributed to Augustine of Dacia, and was previously con-
sidered by Nicholas de Lyra.)

14 Abbot Suger, *De Administratione*, XXXIII.

15 Ichnography: an imprint made on the ground or in dust or plaster or snow: as in a
drawing done on the paper: and in the vulgar called steps or foot-marks.

16   *Aduncha Icnographia non uol dire altro che una modulata defignatione fuperfi-
ciale como e a' dire Circigatura facta con il circino & regula per indicare la cofa
fienda. fi como etiam con lo septro lituuo inconbuftibile che ufo Romulo prae-
cipue in indicare fundatione deli aedificii.*

(*Liber Primus*)

17 By the way, if you change the Istrian Gall for green walnut fruits you have a well-
known Northern Italian digestive liqueur, the ink-black Nocino.This is the recipe for
what my grandmother called *Nocino di Seconda*: Nocino is a sticky, dark-brown
liqueur from the central Po Valley and is made from unripe green walnuts steeped in
spirit. It has an aromatic but bittersweet flavour. The walnuts used for making it are
then recycled in a dry white wine to make a lighter digestive drink.

18 The terms 'recto' and 'verso' originally came from the world of manuscripts. Folio
recto was the 'right leaf' of an open book, from the Latin for 'right' or 'straight.' Folio
verso was the 'turned leaf,' the one on the left. As the opposite of 'right,' verso took
on a negative connotation as the less-desirable side. The development of the
recto–verso relationship is closely related to the history of paper, which was only
widely used in Europe from the sixteenth century.

19 The artist did not usually designate one side as recto; that decision was often left to
dealers, collectors or curators. Sometimes the designation for a particular drawing
changed over the years, depending on the owners' preferences, and the changes
help art historians to trace the development of taste.

20 Gebhard and Nevins, *200 Years of American Architectural Drawing*, p. 40

21 Ibid.

Imagination and architectural representations

Nader El-Bizri

Introduction

This chapter examines the role of imagination in architectural conventional representations in view of critically rethinking the experiential and intellective conditions of envisioning architecture *in absentia*. The physical manifestation of architectural entities (built structures, installations, representational models and drawings), along with their mathematical determinations, highlight the multiple performances of imagination in the conception, perception and construction of architecture, which entangle the sensible (visible) with the intelligible (invisible). Guided by selected analytic constructs from philosophy and the history of science, this inquiry interrogates the generalising claim that 'the model-gaze reduces the possibilities of innovation' and 'stifles the pursuit of the absent referent beyond the present model'.[1] Consequently, I explore the potentials of originality and discovery that architectural representations inspire beyond the expedient descriptive and constructive functions they perform in presenting expressions of constructible realities. In this sense, architectural models and drawings do not simply 'render the invisible visible as such', but furthermore offer pointers and directives to *events* that carry manifold possibilities of realisation, and are thus not reducible in their bearings to solely being geometrical and perceptual instruments that formally represent prospective physical habitable structures. The visible points to the invisible as that which conditions the very perception of what is physically present, while being experientially engulfed by an active imagining that hints to what remains 'other' and absent. Models and drawings become past approximations of present architectural built-forms, or may be grasped as being suggestive modalities of visualising what has not-yet-been materially accomplished or what might never be applied. The destining of such representational objects to be eventually lifted from the spheres of utility transforms them in their visionary properties into archival items. And yet, they may well be construed as being articles that get valued for their self-referential artistic and intellectual merits, or even carry a paradigmatic significance. Present representational models and drawings offer perceptual signs of future architectural domains that ontologically belong to the imaginary. Despite the confident technical knowledge that these represented spaces could be constructed and sustained as concretised experiential realms of dwelling and of multifarious inter-subjective appropriations, they nonetheless point to deferred places, in so far that they are in essence potentialities rather than actualities.

I

This inquiry focuses on basic phenomena associated with visual perception in view of examining some of the multiple functions of imagination in architectural conventional representation in the effort to also critically rethink the experiential and intellective conditions of 'envisioning architecture *in absentia*'.

The physical properties of architectural entities, along with their complex mathematical determinants, all highlight the variegated performances of imagination in the conception, perception and construction of architecture, which co-entangle the sensible-cum-visible with the intelligible-cum-invisible. Aided in this investigation by some analytic constructs from philosophy and by selected notions from the history of science, with an emphasis on phenomenology and classical optics (*Perspectivae* traditions), I shall interrogate the generalising propositions that 'the model-gaze reduces the possibilities of innovation' and 'stifles the pursuit of the absent referent beyond the present model'. After all, one would argue that the workings of imagination, which are at play in visual perception and in the contemplative as well as discerning intellection, are not readily constrained by what is visually given through modes of architectural representation.

Even in their conventional forms, architectural drawings or models ('*les maquettes*', in distinction from the paradigmatic sense of 'models' as 'exemplars') do in some instances inspire originality and discovery, beyond the expedient descriptive functions or generative operations that they perform in presenting concrete or hypothetical expressions of current or future constructible architectural realities. Moreover, the creative reception and adaptive assimilation of what architectural representations stimulate all reflect the imaginative capabilities of the designer, the critic as well as the contemplating observer. Imaginative associations and variations determine the potential unfolding of inventiveness in reference to the inspirational possibilities locked in time-honoured architectural representations. In this sense, notable architectural drawings and models ('*maquettes*') do not merely 'render the invisible visible as such', but they furthermore offer pointers and directives to *events* that carry manifold possibilities of realisation, and are thus not reducible in their bearings to solely being geometrical or physical instruments that formally represent prospective or actual habitable structures.

It is by way of imagination and its entanglement with discernment, comparative measure and contemplation that the visible points to the invisible, and that the unveiled refers to the veiled. Hence, invisibility conditions the possibilities of perceptual experiencing in terms of engulfing what is physically present by an active imagining. It thus points through what *presences* to what is '*other*', absent and deferred. Models and drawings become past approximations of present architectural built-forms, if they have informed the generation of such architectural works. They may also be grasped as being suggestive modalities of visualising what is 'not-yet' materially accomplished or what, in deferrals, might never be realised. Such 'representations' are determined against the horizon of temporality, in the sense that they are at times anterior to what they 'represent' (or *pre*-present'); hence, they are 'proto-presentations' in being prior to the realisation of what they point at. They could also be posterior to what they re-present, in being descriptive of what came to be eventually realised in actuality as an entity of 'generation and corruption' (namely as what is subject in its materiality to decay and ruin). They moreover accompany what they hint at of architectural entities in the very processional acts of producing them, descriptively or constructively, as instrumental and technical determinants of architecture. In retrospect, certain built architectural domains re-turn our contemplative perceptions to the drawings and models that pre-conditioned their realisation. In this sense, such architectural works *re-present* the pictorial and model-based 'representations' that facilitated their generation, or, in visionary and imaginative terms, pre-projected the possibilities of their reality.

The destining of representational objects to be eventually removed from the diverse operational spheres of utility transforms them in reference to their potentially innovative properties into 'archival' entities (namely as items to be displayed in museums or in 'conceptual' art/architecture exhibitions). Such representational objects may well be construed as being 'representative' articles that get valued for their self-referential artistic and/or intellectual merits; they may even carry a paradigmatic significance in being exemplary of 'influential' trends ('styles') under particular surrounding circumstances of their historical architectural-cum-ideological reception.

Some *present* representational models and drawings (namely those given to us in direct vision) offer perceptual design-signs of future architectural domains that belong in ontological terms to the imaginary (*l'imaginaire*). Yet, despite the confident technical knowledge that these represented architectural spaces could be constructed and materially sustained, as concretised experiential-cum-utilitarian realms of dwelling and of multifarious inter-subjective appropriations, they nonetheless signal deferred places, in so far that they remain in essence as potentialities rather than actualities.

II

In reflecting on the 'invisible' nature of architecture, we wonder about the conditions of visual experiencing that 'invisibility' furnishes. We are furthermore compelled to ask: 'what led to this theoretical interrogation about architecture?' And, are we moreover aiming 'to let what appears show itself as it appears itself'? Hence, of approaching our questioning about imagery by way of 'phenomenological methods' in investigating vision?[2] But, what should we most fittingly state about 'representation' in an era seen by many of our contemporaries as being marked by dislocating fragmentations, discordant semantics and relativist disseminations?

Architectural conceptions and constructions consist of multi-layered fragmentary processes of realisation. This matter is not restricted to the advent of technology, nor is it readily the result of specialised manufacturing, as much as it is also a reflection of the co-entanglement of geometry, physics, intellectual and artistic acumen in generating architecture, and in situating its rigorous manifestations with a carefully posited sense of historicity.[3]

Unlike the philosophers (that is, the metaphysicians in particular; namely those who supposedly inquire about the 'ultimate principles of reality' and do not hesitate on some occasions to attempt to resolve the riddles of philosophical sceptics), architectural theorists tend to trust what is offered by the outer senses, and customarily leave the ontological and epistemic premises that surround reflections on the visible and invisible almost unquestioned.[4] Without becoming too constrained by the metaphysical imports of thinking about the refraction of *what points to the invisible in visibility*, and in tune with the confidence by which sensory phenomena are received architecturally,[5] I shall assume herein (with suspended qua 'bracketed' judgement; namely, what phenomenology designates as: 'reduction' or 'epochê') that: what is offered to the senses of architectural entities is sufficiently grounded, in 'epistemic and ontological' terms, and that it can be posited as a pre-reflexive given of intuition. Nonetheless, I must add that architectural representations are not merely saturated with allegorical signifiers, which temptingly appeal to those who mediate the workings of architectural theory by way of eclectic and, at times, unreflective deferential borrowings from literary and critical theory. Consequently, we need to reflect on the modalities by virtue of which we are able to present soundly judged utterances and coherent propositions regarding the 'invisible nature of architecture', away from dogmatism.

Conventional modern architectural representations are essentially signs of scientific, mathematical and technological accomplishment, which render architecture a discipline that is not simply confined to a 'play of words' or the articulation of 'ecstatic' images, but more significantly as being a multivalent domain of cognitive excellence and integrity in *praxis*. It is in this sense that the field of 'Architectural Humanities' would not develop into a rigorous discipline unless it seriously interrogates the coherence of its research methodologies and their pre-conditioning theoretical grounds. This calls for more informed accounts of the intellectual evolution of 'concepts' and 'categories' of thinking based on scrupulous approaches to the history of science, the history of mathematics and philosophy, rather than merely continuing to err, with damaging speculative distractions, due to facile and at times groundless 'textual collages'.

III

Like the myriad sensible objects that we encounter in our quotidian dealings, architectural structures are not immediately visible in their plenitude. Their seen 'adumbrations' and perceivable aspects are rather unveiled in an experiential continuum of manifold appearances in space–time. It is through spatial–temporal bodily displace-ment (be it of the observer/experiencing subject, and/or of the kinaesthetic rotations of the object of perception) that the formal totality of what is seen can potentially be brought from concealment to un-concealment.

Architecture is invisible as a whole in its perceptual reality; since it is offered to vision in the partial yet sequential continuum of the manifold appearances of its visible aspects by way of journeying in space–time around and within the architec-tural objects of sense perception. This experiential invisibility of the plenitude of an architectural entity is also attested in another modality of perception with architectural representations like models and drawings. While a model is not solely a representa-tional entity, but is rather primarily a sensible object of visual as well as tactile percep-tion, it is itself experienced in fragments and in a continuum of the appearing of its manifold visible aspects. With drawings, we move from the realm of the objective and sensory presence of a physical sensible thing to the domain of graphical geometrical constructs that acquire the semblance of 'spatial depth' in pictorial projections. In the case of axonometric and perspective drawings, the level of representation is restricted to certain visible aspects of the represented entity; while with orthographical and ichnographical sections, elevations, and plans, 'normal views' of the multiple sides of a given architectural work are represented in a metric scale that facilitates the recollec-tion of the formal totality of what is represented. In this sense, mathematic representa-tions establish a geometric ground (fond géométral) for the manifestation of the formal plenitude of what is given to sight, and thus facilitate the verification and ascertain-ment of its eidos.

An architectural entity is visible in its totality from nowhere but offers itself in direct vision through the appearing in a continuum of its manifold visible aspects. It is, rather, seen through a multitude of perspectives in space–time, while its geometric constitution gathers its visible parts in a structural whole that remains itself invisible in its totality. The perceptual field opens out in its stream of manifold appearances by way of bodily movement. The visual is weaved with the manual in spatial–temporal experiencing. It is in spatial depth (profondeur), as the cleared and perceivable leeway for corporeal movement, that architecture becomes experientially visible. From the standpoint of classical optics, be it physiological or geometric, it is the very invisibility of the transparent medium that grounds the visibility of what is brought to light and is seen. It is the lit transparent medium, as the cleared leeway between the eyes of the observer and the object of vision, that offers the visible to sight. Depth as the distance between the observer and the object of sight was itself questioned in terms of its visi-bility within the radical immaterialism of George Berkeley.[6] In reference to historical precedence, the Arab polymath Alhazen (al-Hasan Ibn al-Haytham; died after CE 1040) affirmed the visibility of depth in his monumental Kitâb al-Manâzir (Optics; De aspectibus; Perspectivae).[7] Therein he demonstrated through experimental installa-tions that space as the depth (al-bu'd; al-'umq) between the eyes (al-basar) of the observer and the object of vision (al-mubsar) is itself visually perceivable; moreover, he classed it as being one of the 'visible properties' (ma'ânî mubsara; intentiones *visibiles*). His thesis reflected a classical meditation on the 'mystery of depth' that radically contrasted with the controversial and fragile doctrine that emerged centuries later in Berkeley's writings (without implying herein that a documented transmission of knowledge did historically connect the authors with each other). The affirmation of the visibility of depth gained further importance in the foundational modern studies of Maurice Merleau-Ponty as they were grouped in the section on space (*espace*) in his voluminous treatise, *Phénoménologie de la perception*.[8] The visible reality of depth was also confirmed in Edmund Husserl's *Ding und Raum*, in reference to the kinaesthetic constitution of space by the transcendental subject, and in Martin Heidegger's affirmation of the spatiality of *Dasein* within a temporal framework (at least as encountered in *Sein und Zeit*).[9] In all of this, the visibility of depth remained a mystery of appearing, wherein un-concealment is entangled with concealment.

IV

Imagination secures a ground for the discernment and comparative measure of the *eidetic quiddity* of a given object of visual perception (namely what classical scholars designated also as being a '*forma universalis*'; *sûra kullîyya*). Perceiving a thing in parts, and by way of the unfolding of a continuum of its manifold visible aspects, engages the imagination in revealing the structural fullness of the form of that thing, even if the thing is invisible in its wholeness. The formal plenitude of an object of vision supplements the immediately visible facets of this object with 'potentially perceivable' *imagined* aspects that may become unconcealed in actuality.

Seeing three surfaces of an opaque cube in immediate vision is sufficient to judge that what is seen is a 'cube', even though its other three sides are not visible. The wholeness of the cube as a geometric solid formed of six planar un-curved surfaces cannot be offered to vision in its entirety unless the cube is fully transparent. However, each of these surfaces can be visually inspected and verified by rotating the cube in space or moving around it. The cube is revealed in its visible aspects in the successive unfolding of its manifold appearances through movement in space–time. Seeing three surfaces of the cube as skewed and sharp-edged planes extended in depth, and identifying them as such as being three square-surfaces associable with a *cubic* geometric solid, is sufficient to judge with prior knowledge that this configuration of planes is 'a cube'. This phenomenon is founded on an experiential trust in the structure of what is seen, along with the perceptual confidence that what appears in parts is the whole that remains invisible in its plenitude. The fullness of the cube is thus revealed through 'authentic' visible aspects that are perceived in immediate direct vision and in presence, along with imagined supplements that are taken in trust to be the concealed 'potentially visible' aspects of that cube, which structurally complete its formal fullness. This phenomenon points to the perception of a unified objective structural identity within a stream of manifold appearances. Each visible aspect of an object is dependent on the structural whole of which it is a part. A stream of consecutive facets becomes a volume through kinaesthetic (ocular–corporeal) 'constitutions', which let the wholeness of the object gradually appear via the spatial–temporal gathering of its sequentially visible aspects; and yet, as time lapses, there are no warrants that it will be '*what it was*' in permanence. Hence, its *being as becoming* calls continually for verification. This process of direct vision happens in a very minimal lapse of time, which passes almost unnoticed by the beholder, though it is at work in the functions of imagining in visual perception.

V

Even though imagination assures the preservation of the invariance of geometrical entities, and secures their 'existence', its workings in mathematics are not the same as those in physics; given that in corporeal–sensory conditions we have mere approximations of mathematical '*idealities*'. And yet, imagination plays a fundamental role in abstracting the formal characteristics of a given object from its material appendages. Hence, it lets things appear in their *eidetic* essences as geometric *extensions* (what seventeenth-century philosophers called 'a primary quality').

Imagination was conceived in classical traditions in science and philosophy as being a mental capacity or faculty that is engaged in experiencing, constructing or manipulating mental imageries, and as being the source of fantasy, inventiveness and insightful thought. *Phantasia* referred to a process by virtue of which a 'mental' image is presented to the self (*ego*; *anima*), as well as being connected with 'common sense' and its capacity to apprehend sensible phenomena. Moreover, the tradition of the early-modern transcendental philosophy posited 'imagination' (*Einbildungskraft*) as a faculty that furnishes the *a priori* grounds of the possibility of subjective experiencing by synthesising the manifold of sensory impressions into the form of a unified image; hence, rendering our knowledge of the phenomenal world possible, as well as recollecting appearances into representations that underlie the concepts of 'understanding'.[10] Nevertheless, *imagery* is at times auxiliary to abstract forms of mental representation, and it is not readily the case that *the unimaginable is absolutely impossible* (or that whatever is *imaginable* is possible). After all, we are incapable of imagining 'curved space–time', or 'multidimensional space', yet we are 'informed' by contemporary physics, with all its mathematical intricacies, that these phenomena are not only possible, but are rather 'real'.

VI

Although imagination can be grasped as being a mental faculty or activity that forms projected images of potentially 'external' objects that are not present to the senses, the *imaginary* is not simply illusory (or fictional) in the sense of not corresponding with some formal counterparts or sensory material data. In mathematics, imagination sustains the hypothetical existence of geometrical–arithmetical entities to serve particular purposes in demonstration, construction, illustration or definition. It is, moreover, an integral phenomenon of direct vision and perceptual experiencing.

In visualising 'the invisible of the visible', imagination presupposes perceptual stabilities, patterns of congruence and objective structural plenitudes. It thus refers to an '*eidetic* vision' of the *quiddity* of what appears, which, in its existential status, has the semblance of constancy in presence, but is fundamentally determined against the horizon of time. It is in this sense that the transitory nature of visual experiences is contrastable with the distinctness, clarity and invariance of mathematical '*idealities*'. The transition from the sensible to the intelligible is thus undertaken by way of imagining, which also brings the visible to visibility by 'materialising the visual',[11] and by saturating the architectural *pictorial* order (and/or '*maquette*'), with animating imaginings of the 'inhabiting' of its spectacles.

Notes

1   As described by Marco Frascari in the Call for Papers for the conference *Models and Drawings: the Invisible Nature of Architecture*, 2005.

2   I am hinting in this context at Heidegger's explicative reflections on the meaning of 'phenomenology' as being what the Greeks named '*apophainesthai ta phainomena*'; namely, the condition of 'letting what shows itself be seen from itself, just as it shows itself from itself'. See Heidegger, 1977, section 7.

3   I place an emphasis on the phenomenological significance of 'historicity' rather than on objectified history, on historicism or historiography.

4   By 'ontological', I refer to metaphysical speculations concerning the question of *being* (*Seinsfrage*), whilst by the term 'epistemic' I evoke the phenomenal pre-conditions of knowledge, along with their subjective/inter-subjective determinations in reference to 'meaning' and 'truth'.

5   I am referring in this context to the prominence of the visual in the writings and design endeavours of a large number of eminent architectural theorists, historians, critics, pedagogues and practitioners.

6   This polemical doctrine was elaborated in Berkeley's *Theory of Vision* and *Three Dialogues between Hylas and Philonus*.

7   Ibn al-Haytham (Alhazen), 1989. This monumental work influenced mediaeval European scholars like Roger Bacon, John Peckham and Vitello, as well as impacting on the meditations of Renaissance theorists like Leon Battista Alberti (*De Pictura*) and Lorenzo Ghiberti (*Commentario Terzo*). I have addressed this question elsewhere, in Nader El-Bizri, 2004a, pp. 171–84; Nader El-Bizri, 2005, pp. 189–218.

8   Merleau-Ponty, 1945. I have also studied this issue in Nader El-Bizri, 2002, pp. 345–64; 2004b, pp. 73–98.

9   Heidegger attempted to derive spatiality (*Räumlichkeit*) from temporality (*Zeitlichkeit*) without success, as he later confessed in his 1962 seminar: *Zeit und Sein* (preserved in Heidegger, 1969).

10 Kant, 1965, A120–1, A141–B181.

11 Bachelard, 1962, pp. 14–15.

Bibliography

Gaston Bachelard, *Air et songes*, Paris: Corti, 1962.

Nader El-Bizri, 'A Phenomenological Account of the Ontological Problem of Space', *Existentia Meletai-Sophias*, 12, 3–4 (2002).

Nader El-Bizri, 'La perception de la profondeur: Alhazen, Berkeley et Merleau-Ponty', *Oriens-Occidens: Cahiers du Centre d'Histoire des Sciences et des Philosophies Arabes et Médiévales, CNRS*, 5 (2004).

Nader El-Bizri, '*ON KAI KHÔRA*: Situating Heidegger Between the *Sophist* and the *Timaeus*,' *Studia Phaenomenologica*, 4, 1–2 (2004).

Nader El-Bizri, 'A Philosophical Perspective on Alhazen's *Optics*', *Arabic Sciences and Philosophy*, 15, 2 (2005).

Ibn al-Haytham (Alhazen), *The Optics, Books I–III on Direct Vision*, trans. A.I. Sabra, London: Warburg Institute, 1989.

Martin Heidegger, *Zur Sache des Denkens*, Tübingen: Nieymeyer, 1969.

Martin Heidegger, *Sein und Zeit*, Frankfurt am Main: Vittorio Klostermann, 1977.

Immanuel Kant, *Critique of Pure Reason*, trans. Norman Kemp Smith, New York: St. Martin's Press, 1965.

Maurice Merleau-Ponty, *Phénoménologie de la perception*, Paris: Gallimard, 1945.

Drawing Adam's navel

The problem of *disegno* as creative tension between the visible and knowledgeable

Raymond Quek

Introduction

Ernest Gellner, in his discussions on nationalism, remarked that the existence or not of Adam's navel might end the riddle between creationism and Darwinian evolution. A similar riddle existed in the Renaissance: does visual creation follow nature or is it created in the mind?

Joseph Meder commented: 'the concept of *disegno* was a great theme for the hair splitting intellectuals of the late Renaissance.'[1] This hair-splitting is largely lost in the translation of *disegno* into the separate ideas of practical drawing and intentional design in the Anglophone world. Lucy Gent has identified this as occurring as early as 1598, with the English translation of Lomazzo's *Trattato* by Richard Haydocke.[2] Baxandall's study of the Anglophone anxiety with the polysemic nature of *disegno* records some interference with the French notion of *dessein*; further, he concludes that its closest translation should have been 'draught'.[3] The French notion of *dessein* is also similarly semantically disjunctive, as it also is in the German,[4] although the two Italianate semantic senses meet simultaneously in *disegno* and they are distinguished in contextual usage.

Though we inherit the weakness in translation in the modern day, the etymological hair-splitting in the days of Vasari, Zuccaro and Lomazzo has much to inform us about the creative tension that exists between visual and intellectual knowledge, between the imagination and its manifestation, most particularly in relation to architecture as a problem of creative knowledge. The metaphor of drawing Adam's navel then is the mystery in the problem of artistic creation – the reciprocities that continue in the struggles between conception, the imagination and the various possibilities of visualisation. The problem of intelligibility itself has very ancient roots.[5] This chapter will focus on aspects of *disegno* as a problem of knowledge, particularly in the *Cinquecento*, its formative role as the foundation of the arts, and note its transformation in the early twentieth century.

The problem of knowledge and the arts

Knowledge in the Middle Ages was classified into the Trivium and the Quadrivium. Beyond the liberal arts, further professional education in Law, Medicine and Theology derived from the base knowledge and skills of the Trivium and Quadrivium. The liberal arts comprise seven disciplines, which were believed to be connected to each other as an amalgam of universal knowledge. The Trivium was the basis of elementary education: Grammar taught the craft of reading and writing; Logic, of careful reasoning; and Rhetoric, of effective communication. The Quadrivium, on the other hand, was the basis of advanced education: Arithmetic taught the art of number; Geometry, number in space; Music, of number in time; and Cosmology, of number and time in space in relation to an overriding order.

Drawing, painting, sculpture or, for that matter, architecture fell into a lower category of the mechanical arts and did not belong to the formulation of universal knowledge. There is some mystery as to how builders and master masons communicated; and several arguments have been put forward on the oral tradition or the mysteries of medieval exempla or model books.[6]

We are, of course, concerned here with the mode of communication of architectural knowledge. The ability to communicate beyond the oral via ichnography has been an ability since ancient times as we have many historical maps and even what seem to be measured floor arrangements resembling floor plans of the modern day.[7] A communicative visual marking is at the root of this, and it is no surprise that the Latin root of the Italian vernacular of *disegno* is the verb *designare*. The modern notion still exists and serves to ascribe meaning in English, to 'designate', a marking that makes meaning. The medieval idea of the word had a connection with the medieval signature, a mark of the hand of a person, a designation of claim or an indication of ownership.

In the Trecento and early Quattrocento *bottega*, the vernacular expression of the idea as *disegno* was already in currency. Cennini's craftsmen's handbook notes: 'El fondamento dell'arte, di tutti questi I lavorii di mano il principio é il disegno e'l cholorire.'[8] Cennini's handbook was handed down from *bottega* to *bottega* and not really published until the nineteenth century, and it may be argued that the handbook did little to formalise the vernacular usage of *disegno* as 'fundamental'. Lorenzo Ghiberti also supported the idea of foundation, 'el disegno é il fondamento et teorica di queste due arti', though in '*due arti*' he was making reference to painting and sculpture.[9]

Brunelleschi formulated new confidence in *perspectiva artificialis* through his experiments on the image of the baptistery. The coincidence of natural and artificial perspective made possible the representation of phenomena as if 'alike to appearance'. The optical conversion of the baptistery into a subject of perspective in his primitive camera obscura achieved in one stroke two consequences. One, perspective is formalised and understood mathematically – *perspectiva naturalis*, can now be 'recreated' through the geometry of *perspectiva artificialis*. The entry of artificial perspective gives rise to the second consequence – that visual reality is there to be 'enframed, observed and investigated' through observation. Prior to Brunelleschi, *perspectiva naturalis*, the natural vision of the eye, was experiential rather than observant. The role of *disegno*, in the semantic sense of artificially created manifestation in perspective, is no less implicated in the coincidental meeting of vision and visual description.

Argan observed that Brunelleschi's usage of perspective differs markedly from his Trecento predecessors: he used perspective as an instrument of knowledge, simultaneously articulating and organising space as it was being represented. Unlike Massacio's spatial settings for the depiction of subjects, Brunelleschi's use of perspective was not imitating reality but ordering reality in itself.[10] This sense of a visual ordering of reality is similar in Alberti's *De re aedificatoria* where he variously describes *lineamenta* and *disegno* as '*imago quaedam ab omni materia separata*' ('A separation of image from all matter').

The term 'lineamenta' and its translation had itself a controversial history.[11] Semantically, its usage in Alberti's text varies, but we can infer from its usage a simultaneous sense of measured control, of contoured separation of matter, and of ordering. These senses are simultaneously visual and conceptual. Alberti in Book I of his treatise confers four aspects of the duty of *lineamenta*: the prescription of appropriate place, exact numbers, a proper scale and a graceful order.

Alberti further recognised the difference between the use of drawings in painting and architecture:

> The difference between the drawings of the painter and those of the architect is this: the former takes pains to emphasize the relief of objects in paintings with shading and diminishing lines and angles; the architect rejects shading but takes his projections from the ground plan and without altering the lines and by maintaining true angles, reveals the extent and shape of each elevation and side – he is one who desires his work to be judged not by deceptive appearances but according to certain calculated standards.[12]

Elsewhere he discusses the model, where he describes the futility of making elaborate details, preferring the model to be an essential schema.

The elevation of the mechanical arts

It may be useful at this point to observe that Alberti attempted to raise these actions from the lower classes of the mechanical arts by relating them to the forms of knowledge in the Quadrivium. *Della pittura* was written in three sections, and in the prologue of his Italian version, Alberti described the structure to Brunelleschi:

You will see three books: The first, all mathematics (*tutto matematico*) concerning the roots in nature which are the source of this delightful and noble art. The second book puts the art in the hand of the artist, distinguishing its parts and demonstrating all. The third, introduces the artist to the means and end, the ability and the desire of acquiring perfect skill and knowledge in painting.[13]

In Book II, Alberti follows the model of the rhetorical arts, relating this time to the Trivium. Painting is divided again into three: circumscription, composition and the reception of light.[14] Alberti wrote separately about painting, sculpture and architecture, opting to translate into Italian *Della Pittura* but not *De Re Aedificatoria*. Despite modelling his ten books on Vitruvius, the Vitruvian architectural text is a chronicle of past practice whereas Alberti proposes a theory of practice. Ludovico Dolce in his *Dialogo della pittura* also separated the labours of the painter into *inventione, disegno* and *colorito*.[15] This tripartite schema is similar to the art of rhetoric: *inventio, dispositio* and *elocutio*. Although separated, the notions of *inventione* and *disegno*, as in *inventio* and *dispositio* before them, share the senses of creation, ordering and cognate form. The elevation of the mechanical arts reached its acme in the Cinquecento when Anton Francesco Doni related it to 'divine speculation' – the first act of *disegno* is the invention of the entire universe, imagined perfectly in the mind of the prime mover.[16] The notion of the common source or foundation of the arts that was embodied in *disegno* is best described in de Hollanda's *Four Dialogues on Painting* who noted that technique separated the arts, but that *disegno* was the unity of the arts: 'the draughtsman will have the skill at once to build palaces and temples and to carve statues and to paint pictures . . .'[17]

With reference to the Trivium and the Quadrivium, the newly elevated *disegno*, as visual knowledge, could be seen to be a complete consequence of the liberal arts, which encompassed and united the arts as its common foundation. *Disegno*, simultaneously creative intent and expression, is a rhetorical cosmic revelation of a thousand words of ordered number in time and space. Painting, sculpture and architecture, of course, follow *disegno*. The boldness of this notion is formalised in the *Accademia del Disegno* in Florence, the first proper school of design, with Giorgio Vasari as the leading principal.[18] In the second edition of his *Lives of the Artists*, he inserted a long introduction.[19] The famous passage in which Vasari wrote of *disegno*:

Perché il disegno, padre delle tre arti nostre architettura, scultura e pittura, procedendo dall'intelletto cava di molte cose un giudizio universale simile a una forma overo idea di tutte le cose della natura, la quale è singolarissima nelle sue misure, di qui è che non solo ne corpi umani.e. degl'animali, ma nelle piante ancora e nelle fabriche e sculture e pitture, cognosce la proporzione che ha il tutto con le partie. che hanno le parti fra loro e col tutto insieme; e perché da questa cognizione nasce un certo concetto e giudizio, che si forma nella mente quella tal cosa che poi espressa con le mani si chiama disegno, si può conchiudere che esso disegno altro non sia che una apparente espressione e dichiarazione del concetto che si ha nell'animo, e di quello che altri si è nella mente imaginato e fabricato nell'idea. E da questo per avventura nacque il proverbio de' Greci Del-l'ugna un leone, quando quel valente uomo, vedendo sculpita in un masso l'ugna sola d'un leone, comprese con l'intelletto da quella misura e forma le parti di tutto l'animale e dopo il tutto insieme, come se l'avesse avuto presente e dinanzi agl'occhi.[20]

(*Disegno*, father of our three arts of architecture, sculpture, and painting, that proceed from the intellect, derives from many things a universal judgement of form or idea of all things in nature, and is unique in its measurements. This happens not only in human bodies and those of animals, but in plants as well and buildings and sculptures and paintings, recognising that the whole has a proportionate relationship to the parts and the parts to other parts and to the whole. From this we recognise a certain notion and judgement such that something is formed in the mind which, when expressed, is nothing other than a visible expression and declaration of that notion of the mind, and this we refer to as *disegno*. We may conclude that *disegno* is not other than a visible expression and a revelation of our inner conception, or that which others have imagined and given form to in their idea. And from this, perhaps, arose that proved among the ancient Greeks, '*ex ungue leonem*', when some worthy person, seeing carved in stone the claw only of lion, understood with the intellect from its measure and form, the parts of the whole animal and then the whole animal together as if he had it before his eyes.)[21]

The foundational role of *disegno* is both instituted and constituted at the same time; namely, its formalisation is recognition of a collected understanding, its embodiment in the knowledge of the time despite some variance. This is significant as its symbolic extensions depend on the maintenance of its institutional and constitutional coincidence. From this declaration, we have a whole multitude of ensuing problems and issues.[22] First, we have the issue of the relationship of the trinity of painting, sculpture and architecture to the transcendent or supra notion of *disegno*. This is reflected in the *paragone* problem, or the problem of comparison of the arts, which Leonardo Da Vinci, Benedetto Varchi and others mooted. Leonardo in particular seemed to favour painting.

Then we have the issue of '*giudizio*' or judgement – which Vasari presupposed prior to creation, but in his manner of declaration, introduced the notion of critical judgement of work. His *Vite*, the lives of the artists, it has been argued, is more than a biography of who's who, but can be seen in the later editions to be a narrative elaboration not dissimilar to ekphrasis.[23] Vasari's *giudizio del populo*, a notion he introduced in an anecdote describing how the public will make judgement on the sculpture of his champion, the Divine Michelangelo, was transformed by Varchi into *giudizio universale*. Vasari raised the visual to a dominant role, though elsewhere in his introduction he also spoke of the tactile. He raised the issue of ideality. He also raised the issue of the imagination and its relationship to nature, and also its relation to perception.

Panofsky derided Vasari's declaration as not fully understanding the Platonic notions before him.[24] The declaration itself is actually syncretic of Aristotelian and Platonic traditions, and this has been supported by more recent scholarship.[25] Of the contributors to the discussions on *disegno,* very clearly of the Platonic tradition, is the figure of Federico Zuccaro, brother of Taddeo the painter. In the creation of architecture and art, the problem of *disegno* was brought into sharp focus by Zuccaro as *disegno interno* and *disegno esterno* in his *L'idea de Pittori, Scultori et Architetti*.[26]

Although Zuccaro may have published his ideas of *disegno interno* and *disegno esterno* in his *Scritti*, they were neither startlingly novel nor entirely original as there had always been some recognition of the semantic differences and their distinction in context. In Alberti, we have seen the tendency to distinguish. It is not difficult to see a speculation on separation of the semantic senses as a plausibly obvious conclusion, though he made no show of this at his lectures. Zuccaro repeatedly assigned lectures on *disegno* to others, and when the assigned person was unable to cope, Zuccaro would waltz in and pontificate on the manifestation of the hand and the intellection of the idea.[27] He also made the conceited pun out of *disegno* of *segno dei* – the sign of God.

An earlier statement on the separation of imaginative intention from visual manifestation is noted here: 'Il disegno é di due sorte, il primo e quello che si fa nell' Imaginativa, et il secondo tratto da quello si dimostra con linee'.[28] This comment was uttered by no less than Benvenuto Cellini, commenting on the seal of the Academia in Florence. Here is a clear recognition of the two semantic senses of *disegno* outside of contextual understanding prior to Zuccaro, the abstract imaginative idea and practice of linear description. Wolfgang Kemp has made the plausible argument of Zuccaro's dependence on Cellini, though despite the separation of *disegno interno* and *disegno esterno*, Zuccaro maintained the foundational role of *disegno,* celebrated most dramatically in the ceiling fresco in the *Sala del Disegno* at the Palazzo Zuccaro.

The three sister arts surround the personification of father *disegno,* resembling God the Father, who holds a sceptre in his right hand. On his left, he wields the compass and square of architecture and the tools of sculpting and painting – hammer, ink pot and quill; and in the same hand, he also holds a painting. The iconography is comparable to the iconologies of *disegno* and *giudizio* in Cesare Ripa's *Iconologia* of 1603. The sceptre is thought to be representative of the moral intellect, whilst the relationship of *disegno* and *giudizio,* raised earlier in Vasari, can be seen to have a mutually dependent co-existence. Ripa's *disegno* is depicted as a well-dressed nobleman, carrying in one hand the compasses of measurement, and in the other the mirror of imaginative reflection. *Giudizio,* who is depicted naked and therefore honest, sits on the rainbow of a wealthy experience carrying a square, rule and compasses. The notion of *giudizio,* exemplified by the visual judgement of *giudizio dell'occhio,* is closely tied to the secret of *disegno.* In the story of Donatello's abacus, Marco Barbo sought the secret of Donatello's abacus, believing it to be the tool by which he measured his art.

Fresco at Sala Del Disegno, *Father Disegno and his three daughters*.

Donatello eventually revealed that he was himself his abacus – he had the ability of *giudizio dell'occhio* – the judgement of the eye.[29]

In a comparative study of a preparatory cartoon of the fresco, Hermann-Fiore argued that the sketch of a sphere corresponding to the indiscernible detail of the painting in the left hand of father *disegno* represents the sphere of the cosmos. In the cartoon, the pedestal is inscribed faintly with the word '*disegno*'. A more elaborate script is seen in the corresponding pedestal of the fresco: 'LUX INTELLECTUS ET VITA OPERATIONUM' ('The Light of the Intellect and the Operation'). We may see the cartoon as the fresco in shorthand, the inscription 'disegno' in the cartoon corresponding to the fuller inscription in the fresco with its expanded explication of the intellect.

G I U D I Z I O.

Di Cefare Ripa .

Giudizio

Giudizio from Cesare Ripa's *Iconologia.*

Fig. 139. Giuditio: **JUDGMENT**.

A naked Man, attempting to fit down upon the Rainbow; holding the Square, the Rule, Compaſſes, and Pendulum, in his Hand.

The Inſtruments denote *Difcourſe*, and *Choice*, Ingenuity ſhould make of Methods to underſtand, and judge of any thing; for he judges not aright, who would meaſure every thing in one and the ſame Manner. The Rainbow, that much Experience teaches Judgment; as the Rainbow refults from the Appearance of diverſe Colours, brought near one another by Virtue of the Sun-beams.

Description of *Giudizio* in Cesare Ripa's *Iconologia.*

The notion of 'SCINTILLA DIVINITAS' ('Divine Spark') written into the frame below the fresco adds further commentary.

We can see in both the fresco at the Sala del Disegno and its preparatory cartoon Zuccaro's position on the *paragone*. 'Architecture' is remotely connected to *disegno*, and her sister 'Painting' is closest to father *disegno*. It has been recorded that the short definitions of each daughter's inscription in relation to father *disegno* was agreed with principal Zuccaro. Further, discussions on the *paragone* were forbidden in the statutes of the academia. An even more curious observation of the statutes records that the *paragone* conflict pertained only to painting and sculpture, and that architecture was omitted. In the fresco, 'Architecture' is supported by the inscription

'PARENS COMMODITATIS', that which gives comfort. 'Sculpture' carries the inscription 'CUSTOS EFFIGEI', the appearance of form. The inscription 'AEMULA NATURAE' supports 'Painting' – she is the imitator of nature. The relationship to nature is reflected in the relationship to father *disegno*, the daughter 'Painting' is closest as she is the most universal of the arts.

Zuccaro elaborated on his metaphysical notion of *disegno interno* in his *Scritti*, he wrote that as God created nature after an idea in the mind, God might be said to possess *disegno interno*.[30] Zuccaro compared the *disegno interno* of God and angels to the *disegno interno* of man. Unlike animals, man has a soul, and unlike angels, man has a body. But for the body, man would be like a divine being. God created the world by bringing things into existence – man only apprehended them. Thus man is inferior to God; humanity is properly suited to the realm of acquiring

Di Cesare Ripa.

Disegno from Cesare Ripa's *Iconologia*.

Description of ***Disegno*** **in Cesare Ripa's** ***Iconologia***.

FIG. 93. Diſſegno : *DESIGNING.*
A Stripling, of a noble Aſpect, with a Garment of rich Cloth, Compaſſes in one Hand, and a Miroir in the other.
The Aſpect ſhews that all things made by Art, are more or leſs *handſom*, according to the more or leſs *deſigning*: The Compaſſes, that Deſigning conſiſts in *Meaſuring*; the Glaſs, a good *Imagination* requiſite.

knowledge through sense. Therefore, the human intellective soul has by nature a possibility of knowing through sense the 'spiritual forms representing all the things in the world'.[31]

This virtue, which comes from God, makes man 'almost a second God'. In this sense he is able to form a 'new world', a world of human creation. Man 'almost imitating God, and emulating nature may produce infinite artificial things similar to the natural, and by means of painting and sculpture, make us see new paradises on earth'.[32] *Disegno interno* is described as a 'light' that guides the lower sensing faculties. The *disegno interno* is at once transcendental, passive and active. It is passive in that it is susceptible to all things. It is also active as it has the nature of intellection. It has the capacity to 'form one image from many'. The transcendence

Preparatory cartoon, fresco at Sala del Disegno, *Father Disegno and his three daughters*, Federico Zuccaro.

Inscriptions: *'LUX INTELLECTUS ET VITA OPERATIONUM'* ('The Light of the Intellect and the Operation') and *'SCINTILLA DIVINITAS'* ('Divine Spark'). Detail from Fresco at Sala Del Disegno, *Father Disegno and his three daughters.*

of the *disegno interno*, its status as 'light' and 'divine spark', is dependent on God. The pun of *segno dei* is probably cleverer if seen in these terms than has been dismissed by various commentators.

Curiously, we can see some prior consideration of the divine spark in an earlier preparatory sketch for the central scene in the vault in the chapel of the Villa Farnese at Caprarola, outside Rome – *The Creation of the Sun and Moon* – two luminous bodies.[33] The work reveals a more conventional tendency within Zuccaro's representation of the Creation and his support of God's miraculous *creatio ex-nihilo*. On this evidence, we may comment that his ideas in his *Scritti* must have developed much later, particularly on the consideration of the body and soul in the question of *disegno*, which may have been a result of a forced attempt to elevate the visual arts through the academy. Quiviger has observed Zuccaro passionately believed in academies.[34] He had earlier tried to interest the literary academies with the idea of a Roman Academia del Disegno with no success. Mundy has argued that the rulings of the Council of Trent affected the spiritual quality of Federico's work.[35] This may have contributed a more spiritual turn against his earlier Michelangelo-influenced expression of the creation.

On the strength of his theories, Zuccaro gained admission into the Accademia degli Innominati of Parma and the Accademia Insensata at Perugia. His concern, it would seem, would be the ambition of parity that painting might have with poetry in the literary academies, via doctrine and respectable activity in the academy.[36] Indeed, as late as 1605, four years before his death, he published a lamentation on painting.[37] The Accademia di San Luca[38] was finally established in Rome. The annals recorded by Romano Alberti show that Giacomo Della Porta, who was to represent the voice of 'Architecture', was absent on several occasions and eventually replaced by others. Payne observed Zuccaro's exploitation of the situation to declare that *disegno* the root of all the arts, despite giving painting the edge.[39] Whilst this may be true on the evidence of the proceedings, it is also true that apathy on the part of other contributors led to the demise of Zuccaro's academy. Quiviger also noted that Zuccaro's parallel of visual thinking could be seen as similar to a philosopher's syllogisms:

Preparatory cartoon, fresco at Villa Caprarola, *The Creation of the Sun and Moon*.

You should know that there are two kinds of *disegno*, that is one called *intellettivo*, and one called *prattico*. This is because there are in us two intellects. One is called the speculative intellect, and its aim is to understand things universally, The other is the practical intellect, and its specific and ultimate aim is action [*operare*], or rather, it is the principle of our actions. It is therefore related to our [two] intellects. One is the subject of the speculative intellect, and represents to this intellect things universally understood [*le cose universalmente intese*]. The other is the object of the practical intellect and it represents individual things to the intellect.[40]

Zuccaro actually travelled to England to offer his services to the Queen. A letter of introduction from Belgium exists in the British Museum.[41] His *Scritti* have not really been translated to English, though various commentaries in English exist. We can only speculate what the possibilities might have been had he travelled and pontificated on *disegno interno* and *esterno*. A contemporaneous text, by Lomazzo, however, made it in 'translation' to the Anglophone world and had considerable influence on Inigo Jones, Roger de Piles and others. Haydocke translated Lomazzo's central subjects in the *Trattato dell' arte della pittura, scultura et architetettura*, as 'painting, carving and building'.[42] What *disegno* sought to unite in the different techniques of the arts is in fact unravelled and returned to its separate constituent techniques. Lucy Gent was scathing of the Haydocke translation: 'When Lomazzo writes about "arte disegnatrice", Haydocke is floored'.[43] Ironically, in the year of publication of Haydocke's translation, the Anglo-Italian Giovanni Florio's dictionary of Italian and English was also published; it accurately records a sense of purpose in the term *disegno,* and also the verb and plural forms.[44]

We have seen the modulation of the notion of *disegno* from Cennini to Zuccaro and its formulation in the academy. With Zuccaro, the modern split between drawing as manifestation and design as intent can be said to commence. Despite this variance in *disegno*, the word itself carries no special mystery. Its role as the foundation of the arts, or as the notion that gives the arts unity, is a curious one as we come to modern times. The pursuit of a possible unity of the arts after the Baroque, the last authentic *gesamtkunstwerk*, can be seen in the attempts of Richard Wagner, who privileged drama but saw architecture as its frame:

> Architecture can set before itself no higher task than to frame for fellowship of artist who in their own persons portray the life of man, the special surroundings necessary for the display of the human artwork. Only that

Frontispiece, Lomazzo's *Treatise on Painting*.

TO THE RIGHT

VVORSHIPFVLL THO-

MAS BODLEY

ESQVIRE.

SIR, it hath fo falne out (with what fucceffe I know not) that many my fpare howers of fecreation, haue bin occupied in the fweete Contemplation, and delightfull Practife of the more curious kindes of *Painting*, *Caruing*, and *Building*; as may in fome forte appeere, by my paines taken in tranflating this worke; the worth whereof I forbeare otherwife to commend vnto any other, then by recommending mine indeuours therein vnto your felfe; whofe foundneffe in variety of Learning, whofe skill in this and the better Languages, and whofe harty affection to all good Artes, though it were euery way fufficiently knowne to the moft, yet hath it more abundantly difcouered it felfe in that memorable Monument of your exceeding loue towardes this our Vniuerfity, begun already with no fmall charge, and happily heereafter to bee finifhed to your great Honour.

In regard-full acknowledgement whereof, I could wifh I were as worthy, as I am willing, to bee the firft, who fhoulde fteppe forth, to yeelde you Publique thankes, in the name of the

¶ ij Whole

Page from Lomazzo's *Treatise on Painting*.

edifice is built according to necessity, which answers most befittingly an aim of man; the highest aim of man is the artistic aim of man; the highest artistic aim – the drama.[45]

Wagner was not alone in recognising the possibility of unity: Bruno Taut proclaimed the *Zukunftskathedrale* – the Cathedral of the future:

Together let us build a stupendous structure! A building that is not only architecture, but in which everything – painting and sculpture – all together will form great architecture and wherein architecture once again merges with the other arts. Here architecture must be frame and content all at once.[46]

It was in the pursuit of similar ideals of unity that inspired a young Walter Gropius, who took these aims and developed the Bauhaus along the lines of a unity of the arts. Ironically, in the modern *gesamtkunstwerk* of Gropius, the merger of industry and the arts meant that the notion of design was to be seen quite differently. The elevation of vernacular craft into one where production was a consideration meant that the everyday product had to be conceived and visualised – in other words, products could be *designed* for industrial production.[47] In the literature of the time, design is often included as a sister craft, and is no longer father to the arts as in Zuccaro or Vasari. From his first manifesto of the Bauhaus, Gropius radiates the statement of his programme, which is quoted here at length to fully appreciate its evangelistic zeal bordering on vitriol:

> The ultimate aim of all visual arts is the complete building! To embellish building once the noblest function of the fine arts; they were the indispensable components of great architecture. Today the arts exist in isolation from which they can be rescued only through the conscious, cooperative effort of all craftsmen. Architects, painters and sculptors must recognize anew and learn to grasp the composite character of a building both as an entity and its separate parts. Only then will their work be imbued with the architectonic spirit which it has lost as 'salon art'.
>
> The old schools of art were unable to produce this unity, since art cannot be taught. They must merge once more with the workshop. The mere drawing and painting world of pattern designer and the applied artist must become a world that builds again. When young people who take a joy in artistic creation once more begin their life's work by learning trade, then the unproductive 'artist' will no longer be condemned to deficient artistry, for their skill will now be preserved for the crafts, in which they will be able to achieve excellence.
>
> Architects, sculptors, painters, we all must return to the crafts! For art is not a 'profession'. There is no essential difference between the artist and the craftsman. The artist is an exalted craftsman. In rare moments of inspiration, transcending the consciousness of his will, the grace of heaven may cause his work to blossom into art. But proficiency in a craft is essential to every artist. It is there that the primary source of creativity lies. Let us then create a new guild of craftsmen without the class distinctions that raise an arrogant barrier between craftsman and artist! Together let us desire, conceive and create the new structure of the future, which will embrace architecture and sculpture and painting in one unity and which will one day rise towards heaven from the hands of a million workers like the crystal symbol of a new faith.[48]

Curiously, the Bauhaus development of the split between creative intellection and manifestation and drawing, normally differentiated in Italian through contextual usage of *disegno*, enters Italian discourse in the early twentieth century with the industrial design of products as *disegno industrialle*. So we have come full circle. The split between creative visualisation and creative intellection is everywhere and is a thoroughly modern phenomenon. The institution of 'design' in the industrial sense has lost its coincidence with its constituted identity. The unity that existed in *disegno* has largely been lost; and lost with it is the integral relationship with *giudizio* – the capacity to make integral judgements. Without this integral relationship, *disegno* as separated manifestation and intellection suffers from an exposure to relativism. As if discussing architecture, Ernst Cassirer provided an uncanny description of the responsibility of the historian in analogy to a draughtsman:

> Even the historian, like the draughtsman, produces only caricatures if he sketches detailed circumstances and events merely as they seem to present themselves and as they follow upon each other. The apprehension of events must be guided continually by ideas; yet on the other hand these ideas must not be merely added on the history as an unrelated appendage – an error into which philosophical history so-called easily fell. The 'idea' can appear only in the natural connection of things and can never be separated from them as something independent and existing for itself alone.[49]

Goya, *Sleep of Reason*.

The relationship between knowledge and critical observation developed in the nineteenth century in the form of the modern novel, and in particular the modern novel set in the modern city.[50] Visual knowledge, in particular developed in nineteenth-century culture in the manifestation of the spectacle.[51] When we understand, we say 'I see'. In the legal accounting of truth, the eyewitness is all-important. Under the modern rule of law we have enshrined this hegemony of vision – vision is knowledge.[52] The unity of *disegno* married both the intellection and manifestation, and allowed for *giudizio* to be consequentially and integrally possible in a meaningful way. Goya, in the *Sleep of Reason*, used an integrated *disegno* to tell us this: that otherwise the sleep of reason produces hallucinatory monsters, or in the true sense of the word *monstra* – imagined constructions without the ability to construe.[53]

Acknowledgements

The author wishes to thank Marco Frascari, James McQuillan and Thomas Kong for many conversations in the preparation of this chapter. An earlier version of this chapter was published in *Architectural Research Quarterly*, and the author also wishes to thank the editors of *ARQ*. The author also wishes to thank Kim Veltman for generously casting his critical eye on the paper.

Notes

1   Joseph Meder and Winslow Ames, *The Mastery of Drawing*, 2 vols (New York: Abaris Books, 1978), I, pp. 22–23.

2   Lucy Gent, *Picture and Poetry 1560–1620: Relations Between Literature and the Visual Arts in the English Renaissance* (Leamington Spa, England: J. Hall, 1981), pp. 8–10.

3   Michael Baxandall, 'English Disegno', in *Words for Pictures: Seven Papers on Renaissance Art and Criticism* (New Haven; London: Yale University Press, 2003), pp. 83–97.
      Baxandall took a more prosaic perspective of the English reception of *disegno*. He described four senses of the word: (1) intention, (2) graphic expression, (3) ideation, design, (4) activity. We have no disagreement with this exposition of the semantic senses. Baxandall also noted the first appearance of the word 'design' in English is spelt 'dessein', which is closer to the French '*desseing*'.

4   Jacqueline Lichtenstein's entry for *disegno* in the *Dictionnaire de la langue française "le Grand Robert"* traces its etymology and its entrance into French, German and English thought.

5   Leen Spruit, *Species Intelligibilis: From Perception to Knowledge* (Brill: Leiden; New York, 1994).

6   See, for example, Joseph Rykwert, 'On The Oral Transmission Of Architectural Theory', *AA Files 6* (1984), pp. 14–27, and Robert Scheller, *Exemplum: Model-Book Drawings and the Practice of Artistic Transmission in the Middle Ages (c.900–c.1470)* (Amsterdam: Amsterdam University Press, 1995); the most famous of these is the exemplum of Villard de Honnecourt.

7   Vitruvius records *ichnographia, orthographia* and *scaenographia*. The Vitruvian text of course had famously lost its illustrations. *Orthographia* is not thought to have developed fully until the sixteenth century. See James Ackerman, 'Architectural Practice in the Italian Renaissance', *The Journal of the Society of Architectural Historians*, 13, (no. 3, October 1954), pp. 3–11.

8   Cennino Cennini and Fernando Tempesti, *Il libro dell'arte: o, Trattato della pittura* (Milan: Longanesi, 1975). Translated as Cennino Cennini, *The Craftsman's Handbook: the Italian 'Il libro dell'arte'* (New York: Dover, 1960). A nineteenth-century translation is Cennino Cennini, Giuseppe Tambroni and Mary Philadelphia Merrifield, *A Treatise on Painting* (London: Lumley, 1844).

9   Lorenzo Ghiberti, *I commentari* (Napoli: Ricciardi, 1947). Ghiberti's work was known since the Quattrocento but was not published until the twentieth century. A further tendency to recognise the value of the separated semantic senses can be seen in Angelo Poliziano's lecture on *Panepistemon*, which has been described to be 'a whole intellectual system in outline, based on the Aristotelian premise of the unity of knowledge … ' See David Summers, *Michelangelo and the Language of Art* (Princeton: Princeton University Press, 1980), pp. 242–261. In Poliziano's outline, the arts of design fell under the lower category of the practical arts, and these would include *architectura* and *graphike*. The latter idea of *graphike* is similar to *disegno*, both shared the semantic sense of the intelligible differentiated from the visible.

10   G.C. Argan, 'The Architecture of Brunelleschi and the Origins of Perspective Theory in the Fifteenth Century', *Journal of the Warburg and Courtauld Institutes*, 9 (1946), pp. 96–121.

11   S. Lang, 'De Lineamentis: L.B. Alberti's Use of a Technical Term (in Notes)', *Journal of the Warburg and Courtauld Institutes*, 28 (1965), pp. 331–335.
        Lang's conclusion that '*lineamenta*' is the ground plan is unsatisfactory. Also see the glossary in Leon Battista Alberti, *On the Art of Building in Ten Books* (Cambridge, MA: MIT Press, 1988).

12   Leon Battista Alberti, *On the Art of Building in Ten Books*, op. cit., p. 34.

13   Leon Battista Alberti, *On Painting*, trans. J Spencer (New Haven; London: Yale University Press, 1966), p. 40.

14   Ibid., p. 66.
        In *Della pittura* the words are *circonscrizione, composizione* and *ricevere di lumi*. The observation of the rhetorical model is well known, as has been discussed variously by many scholars. For a recent study, see David Rosand, *Drawing Acts: Studies in Graphic Expression and Representation* (Cambridge; New York: Cambridge University Press, 2002), pp. 54–55.

15   Mark W. Roskill, *Dolce's Aretino and Venetian Art Theory of the Cinquecento* (New York: for the College Art Association of America by New York University Press, 1968).
        Dolce was influenced by Pietro Aretino, and Paolo Pino before him. *Disegno*, as a Florentine or Roman notion, and *colore* as a Venetian notion were thought to be in conflict. The conflict is not in the ambit of this chapter, though elsewhere I develop a wider study that includes colour as a problem in the issue discussed here. An excellent resource on the problem is Maurice Poirier, 'The *Disegno–Colore* Controversy Revisited', *Explorations in Renaissance Culture*, 13 (1987), pp. 80–86. This was written as a rejoinder to Poirier's unpublished PhD Thesis on the controversy: *Studies on the Concepts of Disegno, Invenzione and Colore in the Sixteenth Century and Seventeenth Century Italian Art and Theory*, PhD dissertation, New York, University of New York, 1976.

16   James Haar and Paul E. Corneilson, *The Science and Art of Renaissance Music* (Princeton: Princeton University Press, 1998).

17   Francisco de Hollanda, *Four Dialogues on Painting*, trans. by Aubrey F. G. Bell (London: Oxford University Press, 1928), pp. 28–46 (p. 36).

18   See, for example, Mary Ann Jack, 'The *Accademia del Disegno* in Late Renaissance Florence', *Sixteenth Century Journal*, 7 (no. 2, Oct 1976), pp. 3–20. A more recent study is Karen-Edis Barzman, *The Florentine Academy and the Early Modern State: the Discipline of Disegno* (Cambridge; New York: Cambridge University Press, 2000).

19   Indeed it has been extracted and published on its own. See Giorgio Vasari and G. Baldwin Brown, *Vasari on Technique: Being the Introduction to the Three Arts of Design, Architecture, Sculpture and Painting, Prefixed to the Lives of the Most Excellent Painters, Sculptors and Architects* (New York: Dover, 1960). Various arguments have been made that the second edition was a reaction to both the ill reception his work, and of *disegno*, in response to Dolce and others.

20   Giorgio Vasari, Carlo Ludovico Ragghianti and Giorgio Vasari, *Le vite dei piu eccellenti pittori, scultori e architetti* (Milan: Rizzoli, 1945).

21   In my translation of the passage, I have left the word *disegno* as it was used. Other published English translations have either substituted 'design' or 'drawing' in place of *disegno*. A recent exegesis of Vasari's declaration can be found in Robert Williams, *Art, Theory, and Culture in Sixteenth-Century Italy: From Techne to Metatechne* (Cambridge; New York: Cambridge University Press, 1997).

22   A classic study is Maurice Poirier, 'The Role of the Concept of Disegno in Mid-Sixteenth Century Florence', in *The Age of Vasari: a Loan Exhibition Under the High Patronage of His Excellency, Egidio Ortona, the Ambassador of Italy to the United States at Art Gallery* (Notre Dame: University of Notre Dame, 1970), pp. 53–68. We have also seen recently in the work of Karen-Edis Barzman, Robert Williams and others a renewed interest in the exegesis of Vasari.

23   Svetlana Alpers has dealt with the moment of *ekphrasis* in Vasari, and David Summers has chronicled the issues on Judgement of Sense following the rise of naturalism.

24   Erwin Panofsky, *Idea: a Concept in Art Theory* (Columbia: University of South Carolina Press, 1968), p. 62.

25   Barzman, op. cit., pp. 149–151.

26   Federico Zuccaro, *Scritti d'arte di Federico Zuccaro*, curated by Detlef Heikamp (Florence: Olschki, 1961); containing facsimiles of Romano Alberti and Federico Zuccaro, *Origine, et progresso dell'Accademia del Dissegno, de' pittori, scultori, et architetti di Roma* (Pavia, 1604); Federico Zuccaro, *Lettera a prencipi, et signori amatori del dissegno, pittura, scultura, et architettura; con un lamento della pittura* (Mantova, 1605); Federico Zuccaro, *L'idea de' pittori, scultori, et architetti, divisa in due libri* (Torino, 1607). Federico Zuccaro was a somewhat difficult character, as has been famously noted in the incident involving his commission of a painting for Pope Gregory, which resulted in his banishment from Rome until 1583. Ten years after his return, he was elected as the principal of the Accademia di San Luca in Rome. He had tried earlier to organise the Roman Accademia del Disegno unsuccessfully on the model of the literary academy. See François Quiviger, 'The Presence of Artists in Literary Academies', in *Italian Academies of the Sixteenth Century (Colloquium) (1991 Jun: London)*, (London: Warburg Institute, 1995), pp. 105–112.

27   Meder and Ames, op. cit., I, p. 22. Many episodes resulting in the dominant soliloquy of Zuccaro can be seen in Romano Alberti, *Origine, et progresso* (Pavia, 1604); in Zuccaro, *Scritti*.

28   Cited in Wolfgang Kemp, '*Disegno*: Beiträge zur Geschichte des Begriffes Zwischen 1547 und 1607', *Marburger Jahrbuch für Kunstwissenschaft,* 19 (1974), pp. 219–240.

29   Summers, *Michelangelo and the Language of Art,* op. cit., p. 364.

30   Federico Zuccaro, *L'idea de' pittori, scultori, et architetti* (Torino, 1607); in Zuccaro,

Scritti. I have also consulted the following commentaries on Zuccaro: David Summers, *The Judgment of Sense* (Cambridge: Cambridge University Press, 1990), pp. 283–310; Anthony Blunt, *Artistic Theory in Italy, 1450–1600* (London: Oxford University Press, 1962), pp. 137–159; Panofsky, op. cit., pp. 71–153; Robert Williams, op. cit., pp. 123–186.

31 Summers, *The Judgement of Sense*, op. cit., p. 291.

32 Ibid., p. 292.

33 Federico Zuccaro worked on the decoration of the Villa Farnese in Caprarola after the death of Taddeo in 1566. Zuccaro's fresco is the central scene in the dome.

34 Quiviger, op. cit., p. 111.

35 Federico Zuccari, E. James Mundy, Elizabeth Ourusoff De Fernandez-Gimenez, Milwaukee Art Museum, National Academy of Design (US) and Taddeo Zuccari, *Renaissance into Baroque: Italian Master Drawings by the Zuccari, 1550–1600* (Milwaukee: Milwaukee Art Museum; Cambridge: Cambridge University Press, 1989), p. 19. For a background on the Council of Trent and Art, see Blunt, op. cit., pp. 101–136.

36 Quiviger, op. cit., p. 110. Blunt notes that Zuccaro and Lomazzo joined academies that had 'nothing in particular to do with their professions' (Blunt, op. cit., p. 147).

37 Federico Zuccaro, *Un Lamento della pittura* (Mantova, 1605); in Zuccaro, *Scritti*, op. cit., pp. 119–129.

38 St. Luke is the patron saint of artists.

39 Alina Alexandra Payne, *The Architectural Treatise in the Italian Renaissance: Architectural Invention, Ornament, and Literary Culture* (Cambridge; New York: Cambridge University Press, 1999), p. 228.

40 Quiviger, op. cit., p. 111; translation by Quiviger, taken from Romano Alberti, *Origine e progresso*, p. 19; in Zuccaro, *Scritti*, op. cit., p. 31.

41 Roy C. Strong, 'Federigo (sic) Zuccaro's Visit to England in 1575', *Journal of the Warburg and Courtauld Institutes*, 22 (no. 3/4, July–December 1959), pp. 359–360. Mundy notes greater activity in England: Mundy *et al.*, op. cit., p. 20. I argue though on the dispute over his portraits of the Queen, that given his known work the resemblance of his *maniera* in *disegno* pertaining to the English Queen is not strong at all.

42 Giovanni Paolo Lomazzo and Richard Haydocke, *A Tracte containing the Artes of Curious Paintinge Caruinge Buildinge written first in Italian by Paul Lomatius Painter of Milan and Englished by R.H. Student in Physik* (Oxford: Ioseph Barnes for Richard Haydocke, 1598).

43 Gent, op. cit., p. 9.

44 John Florio, *A Worlde of Wordes of Most Copious, and Exact Dictionarie in Italian and English, collected by John Florio* (London, 1598), p. 106.
    Disegno – a purpose, an intent, a desseigne, a draught, a modle, a plot, a picture, or pourtrait. See Frances Yates, *John Florio: the Life of an Italian in Shakespeare's England* (Cambridge: Cambridge University Press, 1934).

45 Richard Wagner, cited in Dieter Borchmeyer, *Drama and the World of Richard Wagner*, trans. by Daphne Ellis (Princeton; Oxford: Princeton University Press, 2003).

46 Bruno Taut, 'Eine Notwendigkeit', *Der Sturm*, 4 (nos 196–197, February 1914), pp. 174–175; translated as Bruno Taut, 'A Necessity', in *German Expressionism: Documents from the End of the Wilhelmine Empire to the Rise of National Socialism*, ed. by Rose-Carol Washton Long (Berkeley: University of California Press, 1995), pp. 122–139 (p. 126).

47 I use the word 'design' here thoroughly in the dominant modern sense of motivated intent, with minimal sense of visual manifestation. The other sense of 'design' as visual manifestation is still recognisable in the English language, as it is in French and German, but this usage is only possible after production. The paradigm of industrial

production is the real wedge that sustains 'design' as separated motivated intent from its visual manifestation.

48   Walter Gropius, 'Programme of the Staatliche Bauhaus in Weimar' (April 1919), in Hans Maria Wingler, *The Bauhaus: Weimar, Dessau, Berlin, Chicago*, ed. by Joseph Stein (Cambridge, MA: MIT Press, 1969), p. 31.

49   Ernst Cassirer, *The Problem of Knowledge: Philosophy, Science, and History Since Hegel* (New Haven: Yale University Press, 1950), p. 239.

50   There are numerous publications on the relationship of expanding vision and its parallels in literature, particularly in novels of the nineteenth century set in the bursting Urban environs. See, for example, Burton Pike, *The Image of the City in Modern Literature* (Princeton: Princeton University Press, 1981).

51   Jonathan Crary, *Suspensions of Perception* (London; Cambridge, MA: MIT Press, 2000).

52   David Levin, *Modernity and the Hegemony of Vision* (Berkeley: University of California Press, 1993).

53   Marco Frascari, 'The Tell-the-Tale Detail', in *Theorizing a New Agenda for Architecture: an Anthology of Architectural Theory 1965–1995*, ed. by Kate Nesbitt (New York: Princeton Architectural Press, 1996), pp. 500–514.

Drawn to scale

The imaginative inhabitation of architectural drawings

Paul Emmons

This small reflection on scale begins with remembering Jorge Luis Borges' wonderful tale of a certain seventeenth-century Spanish treatise describing a place where 'the Art of Cartography attained such Perfection' that a map of the Empire was made:

> whose size was that of the Empire, and which coincided point for point with it. The following Generations, who were not so fond of the Study of Cartography as their Forebears had been, saw that that vast Map was Useless, and not without some Pitilessness was it, that they delivered it up to the Inclemencies of Sun and Winters. In the Deserts of the West, still today, there are Tattered Ruins of that Map, inhabited by Animals and Beggars . . .[1]

Borges' full-sized map helps us to understand the delirious condition of scale drawing gone awry that occurs in CAD where buildings are claimed to be represented at 'full scale'. Rather than aspiring to the false exactitude of a map enveloping its territory, scale drawing invites imaginative projection between a plan and its future building. After thousands of years of developing architectural drawing in scale, it behooves our thoughtful study, as scale is not merely a technical issue, but a question of the nature of architectural conception.

A scale drawing is more than a miniature; it has a consistent specific ratio to its object.[2] The scale of an architectural drawing consists of equal parts measure and proportion where a unit of measurement is chosen and a ratio established between actual and apparent size.[3] Eighteenth-century surveyor Samuel Wyld captured this in his definition of scale as 'the true and exact Figure of the Plott, tho' of another Bigness'.[4] Scale is a stair providing the means for ascending and descending between the great and the small or in music between the high and the low.[5] 'Scale' is simultaneously an instrument for the hand to make drawings and for the mind to imagine buildings.[6] Scale drawings have been used for at least several thousand years.[7] From the middle of the second millennium BCE, for example, a statue of Gudea, leader of the City State of Lagash in present-day Iraq, is seated with a floor plan resting on his lap. Also carved on the tablet are a stylus and a scale rule, showing fine divisions of the finger measure.[8] Scale's presence in architecture is so enormous that it is almost imperceptible.

Representing scale

Modern architectural scale drawing began early in the Renaissance with the widespread use of paper and the separation of the architect from the construction site, so that early illustrated architectural treatises did not yet conventionalize representations of scale.[9] Measures were still directly related to the human body such as the finger, palm and foot, and exhibited similar amounts of variation. Sebastiano Serlio and Andrea Palladio give the full-size dimension of the basic measures, because as Palladio explains, 'units of measurement differ just as cities and regions do'.[10] Vincenzo Scamozzi's treatise provides a table of comparative foot measures, ancient and modern, for various locales.[11] Christy Anderson reports that Inigo Jones, in his personal copy of Scamozzi, added the English foot at the bottom of this table and tiny pricks reveal that he used dividers to scale drawings from the page.[12] Not only did the same measures differ geographically, they even differed within the same locale by material to be measured. The foot for velvet was shorter than the foot for cotton, reflecting the materials' different valuations.[13]

Early illustrated architectural treatises inconsistently provide scales with their drawings. Rather than a scale, Palladio records primary dimensions directly on plans, but their precise relationship to the drawing is unclear.[14] Serlio sometimes includes scales with plans and, where they occur, he often explains how to use them, suggesting graphic scales were not yet widely understood:

> This plan was measured with the ancient palm. ... I have scaled it down with the utmost care to this small, proportioned form so that the diligent architect can work out the measurements of the elements fairly accurately, using the small palms ... on the line divided up into ten parts. ... Thus, taking a pair of compasses in hand some of the measurements of this building can be deduced.[15]

Occasionally, Serlio explains that he does not provide a scale because the plan is well-proportioned:[16] 'I shall not put down all the measurements of the St. Peters because, being well proportioned, from one part of the measurements the whole can be derived.'[17] Serlio also interchanged measure with scalar proportion when writing: 'Anyone who wanted this gateway to be larger or smaller should increase or diminish the feet.'[18] Rather than changing the scale, the architect could simply use differently sized feet.

When a graphic scale is included in one of the early treatises, it is shown as a horizontal line with small vertical subdivisions and its midpoint is almost always located on the primary axial centerline of the plan. Since early architectural drawings were made to represent procedures on the construction site, the scale representations derived from the knotted lines of ropes or chains that were stretched on site to lay out the building in full size. The procedure was to begin by stretching a rope along the major axis and then subsidiary measurements were pulled from the centerline. The graphic scale line is drawn out on paper just as the rope lines are stretched on site. In present drafting convention, a line of dimensions is still called a 'string' and the short perpendicular marks subdividing the line are shown as 'arrows'. The corresponding Renaissance marks, however, have the arrowhead pointing into the scale line. This representation probably derived from site surveying techniques where, at the end of each length of chain, a pointed post was driven into the ground that had this shape and so was called an 'arrow'.[19] An eighteenth-century treatise directs that the arrows are to be 'prick'd down' into the ground, using the same terminology as for drawings.[20]

Scale drawing spread northwards from Italy during the sixteenth century. English maps first exhibited consistent scale around 1540.[21] Because units of measure were so variable, it was important to affix the physical scale to the drawing. By the end of the sixteenth century, architectural scales were engraved on the sides of drawing tools, such as the proportional compass or the square.[22] Bar-shaped scales on flat plates were developed with multiple scales on each side, including those from various locales.[23] These tools provide the image of the graphic bars still in common use for representing the scale on drawings. The renaissance graphic scales became elaborated through representing the drawing tools used in scaling.[24] Stretched over the ends of the subdivided dimension bar was usually an open compass or divider. Not merely decorative, it visually demonstrated how to use the scale because distances were always taken off the scale with dividers and then transferred to the drawing. Edward

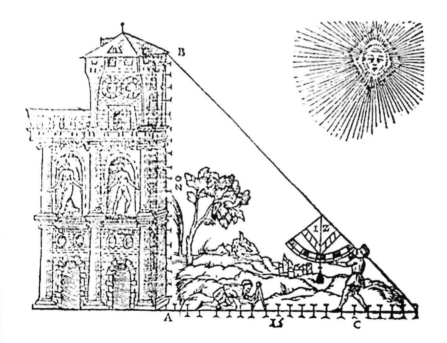

Surveyors measuring on-site.

committed in Landmeating.

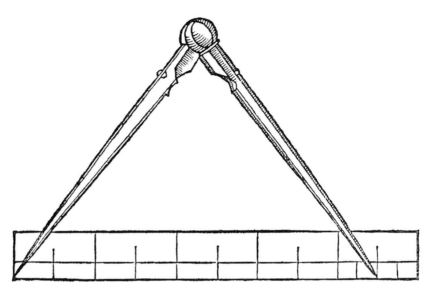

The use of
compasses on a
drawing scale.

Worsop, in 1582, explained: 'The knowledge, howe to apply the compasses to the scale, is commodious, for thereby … the Lord sitting in his Chayre at home, may justly knowe, how many miles his Manor is in circuite.'[25]

That the graphic scales were representations of tools to be used on the drawings is clearly evident in a sixteenth-century Italian map of England where the legs of the divider are drawn casting 'shadows' across the scale bar.[26] The surprisingly prominent size of the scale on plans such as those drawn by sixteenth-century English surveyor and architect Robert Smythson (1536?–1614), best known for Wollaton Hall outside of Nottingham and familiar with Dutch and Italian architectural treatises, is probably because the dividers are drawn as if in their full size resting on the paper.[27] The practice of using dividers to transfer scale onto drawings continued for hundreds of years.[28]

The sort of architectural scales in use throughout the twentieth century with a single scale at each edge of a straight edge were introduced toward the end of the nineteenth century.[29] In 1889, it was necessary to distinguish an 'ordinary' scale from a 'plotting scale, with the divisions on a fiducial edge, by which any length may be marked off on the paper without using dividers'.[30] The technique of using the scale directly on the paper replaced dividers only at the end of the nineteenth-century. In 1898, a drafting manual cautioned: 'A distance should rarely be transferred from the scale to the drawing by the dividers, as such procedure damages the scale if not the paper.' And by 1918, when Thomas French declared: '*Never* take dimensions by setting the dividers on the scale', the practice of scaling had forever changed.[31] Scaling moved toward becoming a solely mental act of measurement, and started to lose its related physical action.

Scaled literature

During the seventeenth and eighteenth centuries, questions of scale grew to prominence with the development and use of the telescope and microscope. These devices, in extending the ability of the senses, made new worlds visible. This scalar fascination was explored in *Gulliver's Travels* (1726) by Jonathan Swift and *Micromégas* (1738–1752) by Voltaire, both of which refer to telescopes and microscopes.[32] When Voltaire was exiled to England for three years, he was a student of English empirical science and developed a friendship with Jonathan Swift. Like an architect making drawings, these authors describe a person venturing into an imaginary world of another size.[33]

Both stories begin with bodily scale relationships. In Lilliput, Gulliver encounters 'a human Creature not six Inches high' giving him the scale of one inch to Gulliver's foot.[34] In his next voyage, Gulliver's scale proportionally becomes that of the Lilliputians as he meets a seventy-two-foot-tall farmer, making both lands the same ratio of 1:12, translating neatly between imperial feet and inches.[35] Swift's original illustrations are exclusively maps of the territories Gulliver accidentally discovered that show no scale and allows them to alternate between gargantuan and tiny.[36]

Voltaire gives Micromégas, a traveler from a Sirian planet, the Vitruvian Doric proportions of a well-formed man, but at enormous size, standing 120,000 Parisian feet tall, which is 24,000 times the size of a human. This proportion probably derives from Voltaire's *The Elements of Sir Isaac Newton's Philosophy* (1737), wherein he calculated the height of each planet's possible inhabitants in proportion to the planet's circumference based upon gravity.[37] Micromégas sees proportion everywhere, since the residents are small, their world is small. During Voltaire's lifetime, there was a spirited debate between Newtonians and Cartesians about the shape of the Earth. A French survey team was dispatched to the Arctic Circle to measure the length of a meridian to resolve the conflict. Voltaire was well aware of this voyage and used the survey team to populate his story when Micromégas discovers a ship returning from measuring the meridian of the Arctic Circle.[38] It seems likely that Voltaire was treating the relationship between Micromégas and the tiny humans as the proportion between planet and person; since the Earth's circumference was considered to be about 24,000 miles, Voltaire gives Micromégas' circumference (an otherwise unusual proportion) and in his scientific writings refers to the planets with the male pronoun 'he'. In the story, the relatively minuscule humans ascended and surveyed the reclining Micromégas to determine his height with exactly the same procedures as they did in reality at the North Pole. Voltaire's seven chapters of Micromégas match his proportional height as well as the number of known planets. Both of these stories project other possible worlds through proportional bodily presence.

Micrographia

A key source for both Swift and Voltaire was *Micrographia* (1665), prepared by Robert Hooke for the Royal Society to carefully document microscopic and telescopic observations, 'producing new Worlds and *Terra-Incognita's* to our view'.[39] Hooke was also Surveyor for the City of London and designed numerous buildings, including the Royal College of Physicians, Bedlam Hospital and many city churches with his friend Sir Christopher Wren after the great fire.[40] Hooke transferred his familiarity with scale from architectural drawing to the microscope.

Hooke organized his written and drawn observations in *Micrographia* progressively from simple to complex and minute to gargantuan by ending the book with telescopic planetary observations. Hooke began with the point, like a geometer, and then line, plane to volume, and ascended the chain of being from mineral to vegetable and finally animal. Observing first the point of a pin, which to the naked eye appeared like a geometric point but, under the microscope, as Voltaire wrote, it 'abounds with Eminences and rugged parts'.[41] Hooke next analyzed a dot made by a pen, and in a scalar reverie imagined this dot as the Earth in space. Emphasizing the importance of total engagement for observations through the microscope with 'Sincere Hand and Faithful Eye', Hooke advises: 'begin with the *Hands and Eyes*, and proceed on through the *Memory*, to be continued by the *Reason*; nor is it to stop there, but to come about to the *Hands and Eyes* again.'[42] Hooke's science required joining visual understanding with the dextrous knowledge of the hand.

Hooke explained his unique method of determining the microscope's scale of magnification by looking with one eye through the microscope as the other naked eye examines a ruler, simultaneously engaging both scales.

Magnified pin point, ink spot and razor edge.

> At the same time that I look upon the Object through the Glass with one eye, I look upon other Objects at the same distance with my other bare eye; by which means I am able, by the help of a ruler divided into inches and small parts, and laid on the pedestal of the microscope, to cast, as it were, the magnified appearance of the Object upon the Ruler, and thereby exactly to measure the Diameter it appears of through the Glass, which being compared with the Diameter it appears of to the naked eye, will easily afford the quantity of its magnifying.[43]

Since nature only exists in full scale, imagination is required to project a change of scale and it occurs through relation to a stable entity, our own body. As Lilliput appears quite ordinary without Gulliver's looming presence, Hooke keenly emphasised that the hand, as much as the eye, was necessary to understand scale.[44]

Malebranche's Cartesian dream

Nicolas Malebranche (1638–1715), an extremely devout Cartesian, was also stimulated by these new discoveries, but in a different direction. His first enthusiastic reading of Descartes 'caused him such violent palpitations of the heart that he was forced to interrupt his reading in order to breathe'. Sadly, he did not realize that this dramatic demonstration of the interconnection between mind and body already denied his new-found Cartesianism.[45] Malebranche argued for the relativity of perception by performing a thought experiment of an infinitely small creature on an infinitely small ball compared with an infinitely large creature on an infinitely large ball, which, without a constant bodily presence, appeared identical.[46] Contra Hooke, Malebranche severs the body to create a disembodied scientific eye:

> Since it is not certain that there are two men who view the same object as having the same size, and since sometimes even the same man sees things larger with his left eye than with the right …, it is clear that we must not rely on the testimony of our eyes to make judgments about size. It would be better to listen to reason …[47]

Like Voltaire and Swift, Malebranche concludes there is no such thing as true extent, only relative size proportional to ourselves. However, Malebranche's solution is to distrust the senses and rely on the mind's presumed direct access to ideas. The material world, 'the main cause of all our errors and miseries', he contrasts with the mind, which 'through God receives its life, its light, and its entire felicity'.

Cartesian computing

CAD applies this Cartesian approach to scale in architectural drawings by forgoing the senses to assume scale is solely in the mind. Data is recorded at 1:1 or full scale, but only as an abstraction. The size of the screen image indefinitely varies as the operator zooms in or out to consider various aspects, creating the inability to put the image into a perceivable relation to the operator's body. CAD only requires scale when printing in paper space. As Descartes transformed geometrical constructions into mathematical formulas, the CAD scale factor is a multiplier that converts the full-size measurement into a scale for the plot.[48] This relationship is merely numerical and must be known to the mind since it is not intuitive. This odd relation to scale is revealed by the necessity to put text into scale rather than the drawing so that the lettering is printed in an appropriate size. Only in paper space does the CAD representation take on a synoptic scale in relation to the observer. It is at this moment that computer-generated drawings may reveal their scalar limitations and fail to allow the imagination to focus on particular sets of issues.

CAD's myth of the exactness of full-scale drawing is in fact the absence of scale. This absence makes it more likely that the designer looks at the image as an object rather than projecting oneself into the image through an imaginative inhabitation. Scaled sight is not an abstraction; it is achieved through judging the size of things in relation to ourselves. With CAD, we do not operate at any particular scale because the image is severed from our (bodily) frame of reference. In moving from scaled drawings to CAD, 'man the measure' is replaced with 'man the measurer'.

The scalar imagination

Since the making of architectural drawings is a source for the imagination rather than a recording of prior ideas, scale assists in this effort. As drafting handbooks recommend, one must learn to think within a scale rather than translate from actual measure.[49] This valuable approach misleads some to believe that full scale is most desirable. Yet, the fiction of scale aids the architect in composing a story by providing a synoptic view that consistently asks for particular sorts of information. While Cartesian approaches assume that scale is merely numerical dimensions known to the mind, early explanations of scale show that empathetic bodily projection is critical to imagining a future edifice.

The virtuous Renaissance architect and author Filarete explains how the architect imaginatively begins to inhabit a scale drawing by subdividing a square into tiny squares that each represent ten braccia, a traditional measure from the elbow to the fingertip that is close to two feet in length. Filarete's early graphic scale was a proportional field like a tile floor rather than a line. He goes on to explain:

> If you want to understand this diminution clearly, take these compasses and divide one of these parts into ten. Then with the compasses, erect a perpendicular line that is three times as long as one of these parts. ... [M]ake a human figure of the same size. Then consider it to be as large as this. Then you would understand the diminution of the braccia and of every other measure.[50]

Filarete's human is drawn neither as a scale figure nor a measuring stick, instead as a vehicle to imagine measure through projecting oneself into the drawing. As this imagined miniature self inhabits a drawing, traditional representations of the human soul picture a tiny self that often stands on the person's shoulder or in the hand.[51] With measures deriving from the human body, the tiny body of the architect *is* the measure and the conscience of the project. Filarete continues:

> by pretending that man is small, all the measures drawn from him are small. … Even though this drawing seems small in appearance to us who are large, if men were as small as it is, it would seem as large to them as it will to us when it is all walled up and completed.

Filarete drew his explanation from Alberti's more philosophical discussion in *On Painting*:

> [I]f the sky, the stars, the seas, the mountains and all living creatures, together with all other objects, were, the gods willing, reduced to half their size, everything that we see would in no respect appear to be diminished from what it is now. … all these are such as to be known only by comparison. Comparison is made with things most immediately known. As man is best known of all things to man, perhaps Protagoras, in saying that man is the scale and the measure of all things, meant that accidents in all things are duly compared to and known by the accidents in man.[52]

Voltaire chides Malebranche in *Micromégas*, and explicitly in his book on *Newton's Philosophy*, where he writes: 'Father Mallebranche, whose Genius was more subtle than true, and who always consulted his Meditations, but not always Nature, adopted the Elements of Descarts (sic) without Proof'. Voltaire, against Malebranche, argues that our senses do not deceive us, but they must assist each other mutually, as Hooke's methodology of hand and eye demonstrated. For example, the idea of distance is known only through combining touch with vision.[53] The making of architectural drawings must engage the entire body into the physical act of imagination to understand scale.

Imaginative inhabitation of drawing

The synoptic scalar view invites imaginative inhabitation of the drawing. When no clear relation exists between body and drawing, this inhabitation is at best partial and shifting. Perhaps this relation of the designer in the drawing, like Hooke's two eyes focusing simultaneously at full and scaled relations, explains why dividers were used for centuries to scale plans. The compass *becomes* the architect walking across the drawing.[54] As the draftsman's language shows: the 'foot' of the compass grips the paper, and the two 'legs step off paces' to measure a distance.[55] John Soane, who kept a tiny set of drawing instruments including a compass and an ivory scale hidden inside the top of his walking stick, made a direct connection between the architect's

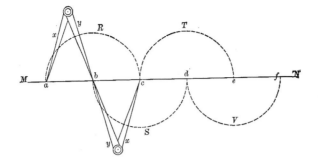

Procedure for walking the compass legs in scale across a drawing.

bodily measures and drawing measures.[56] The shaft of the cane holds two rules that can be joined to measure sixty inches, which is a fathom or two paces. Walking the compass to measure a drawing was analogous for Soane to perambulating London with his cane. Similarly, when Gulliver was in a land of giants, like the architect's scalar imagination, he walked across a map, explaining that: 'I [measured the city] myself on the Royal Map, which was laid on the Ground for me, and extended an hundred Feet; I paced the circumference Bare-foot, and computing by the Scale, measured it pretty exactly.'[57] This ability to project a tiny self into drawings allows architects to imagine inhabiting the building that the drawings represent.[58] American architect Claude Bragdon invented the character Sinbad for his 1924 treatise, who climbs out of Bragdon's ink bottle to represent his own imagination (or soul?) and is then seen per-ambulating throughout Bragdon's architectural drawings.[59] Borges' criticism of full scale as the myth of exactness reveals its ultimate uselessness.[60] Rather than scaled drawing limiting accuracy as the Cartesian approach assumes, scale makes the com-prehension of drawn worlds possible. A drawing is scaled for its destination toward a *fitting* understanding.[61] Architectural drawing assumes a plurality of worlds to describe an environment inferior to our size so that we may comprehend a possible future place which is superior.

Notes

1   Jorge Luis Borges, *On Exactitude in Science* (*Del rigor en la ciencia*), in *Collected Fictions*, trans. by Andrew Hurley, New York, 1998, p. 325.

2   This is made clear by the French phrase for scale: *Echelle de proportion*.

3   Cecil D. Elliott, 'The Variety of Scale', *Journal of Architectural Education*, (1963) pp. 35–37. Of the four kinds of scale Elliott identifies – Graphic, Personal, Building and Conceptual – this chapter intends to address all four simultaneously.

4   Samuel Wyld, *The Practical Surveyor, or Land-Measuring Made Easy*, London, 1725, p. 111.

5   Dorit Tanay, *Noting Music, Marking Culture: the Intellectual Context of Rhythmic Notation, 1250–1400*, Holzgerlingen, 1999.

6   Raymond Nicyper, *Scale Drawing: Graphics Underlay Guides*, Westport, 1973.

7   Both the ancient Egyptians and the Greeks probably had scale rules. The drawings

inscribed in the wall of the Temple of Apollo at Didyma identified by Lothar Hassel-berger show a column drawing with the width at full scale while the height is at one-sixteenth scale (the number of fingers in a foot). Roman bronze fixed-proportional compasses have been uncovered from the beginning of the Christian era. H.W. Dick-inson, 'A Brief History of Draughtsmen's Instruments', *Transactions of the New-comen Society*, 27 (1949–1951) pp. 73–83, 73. A fixed-proportion bronze Roman compass at the British Museum is pictured in O.A.W. Dilke, *Mathematics and Mea-surement*, London, 1987, frontispiece. Gordon Higgott, 'Book Review, Maya Hambly, *Drawing Instruments 1580–1980'*, *Journal of the Society of Architectural Historians*, 49, 1 (March 1990) pp. 111–112.

8   Flemming Johansen, *Statues of Gudea Ancient and Modern, Mesopotamia Volume 6*, Copenhagen, 1978, p. 10.

9   Maya Hambly, *Drawing Instruments 1580–1980*, London, 1988, p. 115.

10   Andrea Palladio, *Four Books on Architecture*, trans. by Robert Tavernor and Richard Schofield, Cambridge, 1997, I.13, p. 19.

11   Vincenzo Scamozzi, *L'idea della architettura universale*, Venice, 1615, Parte Prima, p. 73.

12   Christy Anderson, *Inigo Jones and the Classical Tradition*, Cambridge, 2007, p. 98.

13

> In every country there are different measures according to the place and things measured. As the thing is more precious, so the measure is larger or smaller even with a measure of the same name and properties, as, for instance, the braccio. The braccio for measuring wood is longer than that for wool. The braccio for wool is longer than that for velvet. ... The braccio is longer in Rome than in any other place. ... Perhaps this is because the braccio took its origins from large men. Since Rome was still the largest city, perhaps they wished to accord [with this greatness].
>
> (Filarete, *Treatise on Architecture*, trans. by John Spencer, New Haven, 1965,
> I. 4r, p. 9)

For the renaissance measures, see: William Parsons, *Engineers and Engineering in the Renaissance*, Cambridge, 1967, Appendix B, 'Measures of Length', pp. 625–635.

14   Palladio shows scales in twenty-two of the drawings in his treatise:

> For ease of comprehension and to avoid the time and tedium which would be inflicted on the reader were I to describe the dimensions of every part in minute detail, I have indicated all the dimensions in the designs with numbers.
> (Palladio, *Four Books on Architecture*, IV. 6, p. 221)

15   Sebastiano Serlio, *Sebastiano Serlio on Architecture, Volume One, Books I–V of Tutte L'Opere D'Architettura et Prospetiva*, trans. by Vaughan Hart and Peter Hicks, New Haven, 1996, Bk. III, p. 187.

16

> 'I will not discuss [the villa plan's] measurements because since it is in propor-tion, the experienced architect will be able to plan the size of one place accord-ing to the wishes of his patron, and having made it so many feet – or other measure – all the other parts of the building can be deduced.
> (Serlio, *On Architecture*, Bk. III, p. 242)

17   Serlio, *On Architecture*, Bk. III, p. 127.

18   Sebastiano Serlio, *Sebastiano Serlio on Architecture, Volume Two, Books VI and VII of Tutte L'Opere D'Architettura et Prospetiva*, trans. by Vaughan Hart and Peter Hicks, New Haven, 2001, *Extraordinary Book*, p. 462.

19   Leonard Digges, *A Geometrical Practical Treatize named Pantomentria, divided into three books: Longimetra, Planimetra and Stereometria*, London, 1591.

20 Samuel Wyld, *The Practical Surveyor or, the Art of Land-Measuring Made Easy*, London, 1725, with notes by David Manthey, Arlington, Virginia, 2001, pp. 6, 199.

21 P.D.A. Harvey, *Maps in Tudor England*, London, 1993, p. 8.

22 H.W. Dickinson, 'A Brief History of Draughtsmen's Instruments', *Transactions of the Newcomen Society*, 27 (1949–1951) pp. 73–83, 81. Maya Hambly, *Drawing Instruments 1580–1980*, London, 1988, p. 115.

23 John Robertson, *A Treatise of such Mathematical Instruments as are usually put into a portable case*, facsimile of the third edition, Arlington, Virginia, 2002 [1775].

24 'In one of the corners at the bottom, make a Scale equal to that by which the Plott was laid down, adorning it with Compasses, Squares, Ovals & c.' (Wyld, *Practical Surveyor*, p. 113).

25 Edward Worsop, *A Discoverie of Sundrie errours and faults daily committed by Landemeaters, ignorant of Arithmetike and Geometrie written Dialoguewise*, London, 1582, n.p. Worsop's student in this dialogue proclaims that: 'I have seene the like lines, and compasses set in mappes, but I never understood what they meant till nowe. ... The opening and extending of the compasses upon the scale [is] the application of the compasses to the scale.'

26 Anonymous, Map of the British Isles, *c.*1534–1546, British Library, Cotton MS. Augustus 1.i.9, reproduced in P.D.A. Harvey, *Maps in Tudor England*, London, 1993.

27 Mark Girouard, *Robert Smythson and the Elizabethan Country House*, New Haven, 1983.

28 W.M. Minifie, Architect, *A Text Book of Geometrical Drawing for the use of Mechanics and Schools,* Baltimore, 1849, p. 28.

29 H.W. Dickinson, 'A Brief History of Draughtsmen's Instruments', *Transactions of the Newcomen Society*, 27 (1949–1951) pp. 73–83, 81.

30 The scale should be written on every drawing, or the scale itself should be drawn on the margin. ... the paper itself contracts or expands with every atmospheric change, and the measurements will therefore not agree at all times with a detached scale; and, moreover, a drawing laid down from such a detached scale, of wood or ivory, will not be uniform throughout, for on a damp day the measurements will be too short, and on a dry day too long. Mr. Holtzapffel has sought to remedy this inconvenience by the introduction of paper scales; but all kinds of paper do not contract and expand equally, and the error is therefore only partially corrected by his ingenious substitution of one material for another.
(W.E. Worthen, editor, *Appleton's Cyclopedia of Technical Drawing, embracing the Principles of Construction as applied to Practical Design*, New York, 1889, p. 49)

31 Thomas E. French, *A Manual of Engineering Drawing*, New York, 1918, p. 37 (emphasis in original) and see pp. 21–22. Frederick Newton Willson, *Theoretical and Practical Graphics, an Educational Course on the Theory and Practical Applications of Descriptive Geometry and Mechanical Drawing*, New York, 1898, pp. 16–17.

32 Micromégas uses a diamond microscope to see the diminutive human that he calls, like bacteria, 'a little animalcule in academic dress'. Gulliver was studied by the giants with a 'Magnifying-Glass' (Jonathan Swift, *Gulliver's Travels, Complete, Authoritative Text with Biographical and Historical Contexts, Critical History and Essays from Five Contemporary Critical Perspectives*, edited by Christopher Fox, Case Studies in Contemporary Criticism, New York, 1995, pp. 108, 111).

33 Libeskind knowingly borrowed the title *Micromegas* for a series of his architectural drawings. Daniel Libeskind, *Micromegas, Symbol and Interpretation. Cranbrook Academy of Art*, Zurich, 1981.

34 Swift, *Gulliver's Travels*, p. 42. Vaughan Hart, 'Review, *Gulliver's Travels*, Jonathan Swift: Case Studies in Contemporary Criticism', *Utopian Studies*, 22 March 1998.

35   Swift uses architectural elements to provide an understanding of human scale in describing Gulliver as unable to ascend a stair with risers that are six-feet tall (Swift, *Gulliver's Travels*, p. 93).

36   *The Hunting of the Snark*, on the other hand, did have a map that showed only ocean (i.e. was blank) and included a scale, but one that was without any numerals (Lewis Carroll, *The Hunting of the Snark*, London, 1974).

37   Voltaire gives the Earth's circumference as 126,249,600 Paris feet, which are 0.78" longer than English and explains that 'from that alone may be derived the whole system of attraction' (Voltaire, *Letters Concerning the English Language*, Oxford, 1999 [1733], p. 69).

38   'M. Picart's clarification of the meridian corrected earlier efforts by showing there are seventy English miles to one degree of latitude' which was described by Voltaire as 'sublime verity with the aid of a quadrant and a little arithmetic' (Voltaire, *Letters*, p. 69).

39   Robert Hooke, *Micrographia, or Some Physiological Descriptions of Minute Bodies made by Magnifying Glasses with Observations and Inquiries thereupon*, London, 1655.

40   Lisa Jardine, *The Curious Life of Robert Hooke, The Man Who Measured London*, New York, 2003. One of Hooke's innovations was the double-hung window. Stephen Inwood, *The Forgotten Genius: the Biography of Robert Hooke 1635–1703*, New York, 2003.

41   Voltaire, *The Elements of Sir Isaac Newton's Philosophy*, trans. by John Hanna, London, 1738, p. 23.

42   Hooke believed a researcher needed constant and fruitful interaction between Baconian fact and Cartesian theory. Stephen Inwood, *Forgotten Genius*, p. 60.

43   Robert Hooke, *Micrographia, or Some Physiological Descriptions of Minute Bodies made by Magnifying Glasses with Observations and Inquiries thereupon*, London, 1655.

44   After returning to his own kind from the land of the giants, Gulliver found that ordinary-sized men appeared to him as 'Pigmies' (Swift, *Gulliver's Travels*, p. 142).

45   André Robinet, *Système et existence dans l'oeuvre de Malebranche*, Paris, 1965, p. 12, cited in Nicolas Malebranche, *The Search after Truth, Wherein are treated the Nature of Man's Mind and the Use He Must Make of It to Avoid Error in the Sciences*, trans. by Thomas Lennon and Paul Olscamp, Cambridge, 1997 [1674–1675], p. viii.

46   To understand better what we should judge concerning the extension of bodies on the basis of the testimony of our eyes, let us imagine that from a quantity of matter the volume of a ball God has made a miniature earth and sky, and men upon this earth having the same proportions observed in the larger world. These tiny men would see one another, the parts of their bodies, and even the little animals that might bother them, for otherwise their eyes would be useless for their preservation. It is obvious on this supposition, then, that these tiny men would have ideas of the size of objects quite different from ours, since they would regard their world, which is but a ball to us, as having infinite space, more or less as we judge the world we are in.

Or, if it is easier to conceive, suppose that God created an earth infinitely more vast than the one we inhabit, such that this other earth would stand to ours as ours stood to the one we were just speaking about in the preceding supposition. [Assuming god preserved the same proportions]. ... It is ridiculous to suppose that they see things as having the same size as we see them.

(Malebranche, *Search After Truth*, pp. 29–30)

47 Nicolas Malebranche, *Search After Truth*, p.28.

48 Jenk Bos, *Redefining Geometrical Exactness: Descartes' Transformation of the Early Modern Concept of Construction*, New York, 2001.

49 For example, if you use a scale of 1" = 10' and the actual measurement on the drawing happens to be 3½", you do not say that the particular line is three and one-half inches; rather, read the measurement as 35 feet.

   (John Traister, *BluePrint Reading for the Building Trades* Carlsbad, California, 1985, p. 119)

50 Filarete, *Treatise on Architecture*, p. 81.

51 Rosalie Osmond, *Imagining the Soul: a History*, Stroud, 2003.

52 Leon Battista Alberti, *On Painting*, trans. by Cecil Grayson, London, 1991, p. 53, Bk. 1, 18. According to Rykwert *et al.*, Alberti probably knew Protagoras from Diogenes Laertius, *De vitis philosophorum*, IX, 51. Of Protagoras' surviving fragments, the most famous is the *homo-mensura* (man-measure) statement (DK80b1): 'Of all things the measure is man, of the things that are, that [or "how"] they are, and of things that are not, that [or "how"] they are not.'

53 Similarly, Swift, a friend of Bishop Berkeley, emphasizes that 'nothing is great or little otherwise than by Comparison'.

54 Marco Frascari, 'The Compass and the Crafty Art of Architecture', *Modulus* (1993) pp. 1–14. L.R. Shelby, 'Medieval Masons' Tools II. Compass and Square', *Technology and Culture*, 6, 2 (Spring 1965) pp. 236–248. The Greek mythical inventor of the compass is Perdix, nephew of Daedalus (Diodorus Siculus, IV.76; III. 58).

55 W.M. Minifie, *A Text Book of Geometrical Drawing for the Use of Mechanics and Schools*, Baltimore, 1849, p. 28. Frederick Willson, *Theoretical and Practical Graphics, an Educational Course on the Theory and Practical Applications of Descriptive Geometry and Mechanical Drawing*, New York, 1898, p. 12. Thomas E. French, *A Manual of Engineering Drawing*, New York, 1918, pp. 22–23. Greek words for compass include *diabetes* meaning walking or stepping across.

56 I wish to express appreciation to the Soane Museum for allowing me to examine the walking stick. Soane purchased it believing that it belonged to Sir Christopher Wren, but it was actually made much more recently. Review: Maya Hambly, 'Drawing Instruments', *Journal of the Society of Architectural Historians*, Vol. 49, No. 1, Gordon Higgot (March 1993) pp. 111–112.

57 Swift, *Gulliver's Travels*, p. 115.

58 Marco Frascari, 'The Body and Architecture in the Drawings of Carlo Scarpa', *RES* 14 (Autumn 1987) pp. 123–142.

59 Claude Bragdon, *Frozen Fountain, Being Essays on Architecture and the Art of Design in Space,* New York, 1924.

60 This idea also appears repeatedly in the famous logician, Charles Dodgson's writings:

  And then comes the grandest idea of all! We made a map of the country, on the scale of a mile to the mile! Have you used it much? I enquired. It has never been spread out yet, said Mein Heer, The farmers objected: they said it would cover the whole country and shut out the sunlight! So we now use the country itself, as its own map, and I assure you it does nearly as well.

   (Lewis Carroll, *Sylvie and Bruno Concluded,* New York, 1893)

61 At the time that scaling was changing from walking the compass to merely measuring from a rule, Neutra recalled:

  In the year 1900, Adolf Loos started a revolt against the practice of indicating dimensions in figures or measured drawings. He felt, as he often told me, that such a procedure dehumanizes design. 'If I want a wood paneling or wainscot to be of a certain height, I stand there, hold my hand at that certain height, and the carpenter makes his pencil mark. Then I step back and look at it from one point and from another, visualising the finished result with all my powers. This is the only human way to decide on the height of a wainscot, or the width of a window.' Loos was inclined to use a minimum of paper plans; he carried in his head all the details of even his most complex designs, and prided himself on being an architect without a pencil.

(Richard Neutra, *Survival Through Design*, New York, 1954, p. 300)

The cultural context of design and the corporeal dynamism of drawing as the foundations for the imagination of construction

Qi Zhu

Introduction

As instruments that reveal the imagination of construction, the architect's drawings are intricately grounded on two critical underpinnings: the cultural context of design and the corporeal act of drawing. This idea is explored by contrasting the role of images as tools and the nature of mimetic images. Plato criticizes the utility of mimetic images as contrary to reasoning. However, he endorses images as devices to mediate between experience and intellect. In the medieval icon paintings of Christ, portrayed to attract the onlooker to enter the divine realm through imagination, images are employed as instruments stirring the onlooker's imagination. In Chinese culture, similar kinds of figurative images are illustrated as methods to raise imagination, suggesting a meaning beyond that represented. The twelfth-century Chinese architectural drawings are contextually analyzed with twelfth-century Chinese architectural paintings to elaborate on how the imagination of construction is revealed through drawings and their details. Quite often, details such as mortise and tenon joints that are neglected in the paintings are meticulously arranged in the drawings to induce the observer's imagination of the construction technique.

The two critical underpinnings associated with architectural drawings – the cultural context of design and the corporeal dynamism of drawing – are examined by comparing two Chinese reconstructions of Agostino Ramelli's drawing, *Crankshaft Well Windlass* (1588), with the Ramelli original. This study concludes that the exhibited architectural drawings – displayed as final outcomes and static visual objects – are removed from the foundations on which the original imagination of construction was formed. They tend to be regarded as mimetic images rather than as instruments of the imagination of construction. However, when the critical observer makes the effort to redraw the exhibited drawings and reconnect with the cultural context of design and corporeal act of drawing, the drawings become vastly richer for imaginative exploration.

There are two approaches to drawing an imagined moon. The first directly sketches a mimetic image – a circle or crescent to imitate its visual contours. The second renders clusters of clouds leaving a round or crescent un-drawn area amidst the clouds to evoke the imagined form.[1] The context and the action of drawing the 'clouds' create the rudimentary environment for the final realization of the moon. The role of architectural drawings is analogous to the latter approach which reveals imagination in stages rather than as a direct outline. Architectural drawings are devices for the architects to compose the 'clouds', step-by-step, eventually leading to the visualization of the imagined construction. This function of architectural drawings is elucidated by Stan Allan as 'the drawing as artifact is unimportant, it is rather a set of instructions for realizing another artifact'.[2] Given the prescribed relationship between architectural drawings and the imagination of construction, the two critical underpinnings associated with drawings – the cultural context of design and the corporeal dynamism of drawing – become paramount in the process toward imagination and conceptualization of a design in absentia.

A recent phenomenon is the growing enthusiasm for exhibiting or preserving architectural drawings as valuable artefacts. Displayed as imitable images and the end results of a process, architectural drawings become detached from the original flow of their cultural contexts and their corporeal creation. Besides the loss of their utility as instruments, they transform into contextually indistinct and static snapshots. Just as the imagination of the moon becomes obscured when the supporting clouds are erased, the imagination of construction becomes invisible when the displayed architectural drawings disengage from their design contexts and the dynamic act of drawing them. They alone cannot recollect the embedded constructive imagination. Instead, the act of redrawing initiates a journey into the original design imagination. It concludes by proposing to re-enter the constructive imagination of the exhibited drawings through redrawing.

Mimetic images versus images as tools – and their relationship with imagination

According to Plato, significant differences exist between mimetic images that duplicate nature and images used as tools for reasoning. Mimetic images are reproached because they have no substance except to produce imitative copies from a copy. In Book X of *The Republic*, Plato builds his argument with the example of three abstractions of a bed. The first represents the essence or ideal form of the bed, which is created by God as a result of reasoning. The second is a physical copy of God's bed fabricated by the carpenter. The third is a visual image of the carpenter's bed drawn by the painter.[3] The last of the three is the most inferior since it is farthest removed from the true object and hence requires little effort of reasoning. For Plato the act of imagination is synonymous with the act of making mimetic images, the nature of which is imitative and devoid of direct contact with the essence of things or truth.

However, Plato realizes a great paradox in his criticism of images or imagination: he resorts to creating mimetic images or imagination of beds in readers' minds to prove his reasoning. To justify his contradiction, Plato distinguishes 'the legitimate function of images', as that in which they are 'never treated … as ends in themselves. They serve rather as instruments for mediating between sensible experiences and rational intelligence'.[4] The practice of using images as devices extends into medieval times when images and the aroused imagination did not always serve as the vehicle for reasoning – rather they were used to open up a world of spirituality. The typical medieval icons of Christ were customarily painted to reveal the imagination of divinity, de-emphasizing any visual resemblance. When closely examining the eyes of Christ, they are not portrayed as staring out with feelings or immense power, but as expressionless. The emptiness of the eyes and the emotionless facial expression encourage the onlooker to gravitate toward the divine realm through the imagination. The icon brings the viewer from the representational into the imagined.[5]

Similar contemplation around the use of images as tools for attaining comprehension beyond the represented is deeply rooted in Chinese culture. An image that contrasts with the Christ icon shown below is the eighth-century drawing of the legendary scholar, Fusheng, by Wang Wei in *Fu Sheng Shou Jing Tu* (*FSSJT*).[6] According to the conventional explanation, *FSSJT* describes the story of Fusheng who memorized the classics burnt by the Chinese first emperor, and taught these memorized works to the later Han rulers. The scholar sits next to a small table where the scholar's ink-stone and ink-tainted brush are placed. One hand holds a blank scroll, while his other hand points to it. Both hands extend out to the edge of the table, ready to pass on the lost knowledge. Yet further observation reveals a deeper meaning beyond the representation. The scholar's body is extremely withered, yet his head is drawn disproportionately

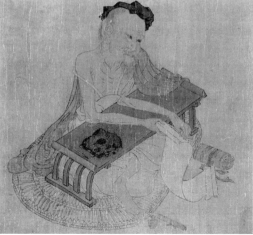

Left: *Christ the Pantocrator*, Anonymous. Right: *Fusheng Handing out the Classical Canon* (伏生受经图) by Wang, Wei 王维, eighth century.

large and round – a cultural profile that indicates attainment of the ultimate enlighten-ment of a Taoist. Fusheng's eyes, instead of following his hand pointing to the blank scroll of paper, mindlessly glimpse into the future with an out-of-this-world expression. The image, using the story of Fusheng as a metaphor, possibly discretely mirrors the painter's own life experience. It functions not just as mimetic delineation but as a device for the observer to delve into – meditating toward a contemplative realm.

Architectural drawings are not mimetic portraits of absent buildings

Architectural drawings are images that serve as tools for architects to imagine the con-struction of their buildings as part of the continuous flow of their design practices. They reveal the imagination of construction through a complex unfolding process rather than representing the frozen mimetic depiction of the absent building. These drawings are different from paintings about architectural subjects, known as *Jie-hua* in the tradition of Chinese painting. *Jie-hua* literally means the painting made with the aid of the *Jie*-ruler, which guides the line-brush to draw straight and parallel lines. The term *Jie-hua* was first theorized in the Northern Song period by Guo Ruoxu in his treatise *Tu Hua Jian Wen Zhi* (1074).[7] He comments on this genre of painting as a technical process, accurately illustrating the image of a building:

> When one paints wooden construction, calculations should be faultless and the linear brushwork should be robust. … How can one paint construction if he does not understand about Han Halls, Wu Halls, beams, columns and brackets, ridge purlins, cross-beams, king-posts … ?[8]

The faultless calculation and the thorough knowledge of the building elements are therefore critical in generating the correct duplicate of the building. *Xuan He Hua Pu*, another Song dynasty treatise about architectural painting, is tinted with a similar tone. *Xuan He Hua Pu* states:

> When painters took up these subjects (buildings, boats, oars, and chariots) and completely described their formal appearance, how could it have been simply a question of making a grand spectacle of terraces and pavilions, of doors and windows? In each dot or stroke one must seek agreement with actual measurements and rules. In comparison with other types of painting, it is a difficult field in which to gain skill.[9]

These writings exemplify not only the tendency toward exquisite precision in Song architectural paintings, but also position them as mimetic copies of buildings rather than as instruments to aid the imagination. The surviving masterpieces illustrate this tendency. The city gate, for example, is portrayed in the early-twelfth-century painting, *Going up the River on the Qing Ming Festival* (see the figure below, left portion), with the finest details and a great exactness, providing an impressive panorama for the

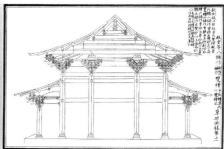

Left: *Going up the River on the Qing Ming Festival* (清明上河图) **by Zhang, Zeduan** (张泽端). **Right:** *YingZaoFaShi illustration.*

human activities. However, *Jie-hua* painting generally renders the final image of the characteristic architecture rather than revealing how the buildings are made.

Contemporary to these treatises about *Jie-hua*, the Song court also published a building manual with illustrations. The illustrated drawings, not granted as artworks, serve a different purpose. They take the viewer to the imagination of the making of buildings and their elements. The building structures are not drawn in axonometric overview, but in sections (see the figure above, right portion). The imagination of construction is embedded in the carefully delineated details of the drawing. For example, the columns drawn on the section have vertical plumb lines in the center. At the top, the plumb line crosses a square where it needs to be mortised to allow the transverse beam tenon to rest. At the bottom, another square indicates two constructional possibilities: a transverse threshold for receiving the door; or a special technique of carving out part of the bottom of the wooden column to minimize its contact area with the stone column base to prevent erosion and provide sufficient ventilation.[10] These details in the drawing serve as instruments for the realization of the imagined construction. If the architectural drawings are tools in a process of disclosure, this process is grounded on both the cultural context of design and the corporeal act of drawing.

The cultural context of design and its relationship to the imagination of construction

The cultural context of design as the foundation for the imagination of construction is illustrated by examining drawings developed in one culture that have been contextually translated by another. The altered cultural context distinctively amends the imagination of construction.

In the early seventeenth century, under the sponsorship of the Jesuits in China, the Chinese artisans re-carved Agostino Ramelli's drawing of *Crankshaft Well Windlass* (1588) on a wood block. The 1627 reproduction was in the folio called *Novel Apparatus from the Far West*, initiated by the Scholar–Bureaucrat Philip Wang Zheng (1571–1644), a disciple of the Jesuit Schreck.[11] There are many modifications in the

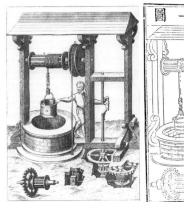  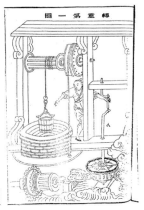

Left: *Diverse et Artificiose Machine* (1588), Figure LXXXV.
Middle: Anonymous Chinese artisan, 1627.
Right: Anonymous Chinese artisan, 1726.

Chinese re-carved version. The continuity of the mechanical movement, which the Ramelli drawing intends to convey, was not grasped by the Chinese artisans. The cutaway line on the ground originally used to present the otherwise invisible underground structure was re-imagined by the Chinese artisans as magical and miraculous floating clouds. This re-interpretation is often viewed as resulting from the lack of understanding of the western concept of perspective and the conventions of engineering representations.[12] However, the differences reveal more than misconceptions. The human figure in Ramelli's print uses one hand to rotate the crank to initiate the movement, while the other hand stabilizes the rising bucket – the final outcome of the movement. Yet in the Chinese translation, the figure rests one hand on the crank while he uses the other hand to point toward the bucket in the distance, highlighting the novelty of the apparatus to suit the purpose of the publication as describing imaginative instruments from the Far West. In *Gu Jin Tu Shu Ji Cheng*, a Qing dynasty encyclopedia of 1724, another artisan tries to decipher his predecessor's woodcut copy of Ramelli's mechanics. The second reconstruction was produced about a hundred years after the earlier copy. The new translator used his imagination to rationalize his predecessor's emphasis on novelty. The clouds that replaced Ramelli's cutaway lines on the ground were portrayed this time as fluttering waves to suit the more conventionally imagined Chinese water well.[13] Through these examples, the imagination of construction can be seen to derive from the factual experience of the author conditioned by the cultural context of design. Similarly, architectural projects are grounded on a wide variety of cultural contexts, providing both the foundation and the boundary for the imagination of construction.

The corporeal act of drawing and its relationship to the imagination of construction

In addition to the cultural context of design, there are also variations in the corporeal act of making between Ramelli's original engraving and the Chinese redrawn version.

Ramelli's drawing is printed from an engraved copper plate. The common engraving technique uses a burin or graver with a sharp fine point. The thumb and forefinger guide and push the burin across the surface of the plate. This action carves out thin strips of metal and leaves slim furrows in the plate's surface for the ink to fill. This technique allows the engraver to compose a variety of shading-tones or chiaroscuro to represent depth. The use of chiaroscuro to render depth is consistent in Ramelli's print (see the figure on page 84). The surfaces of the wooden posts receding into the distance are shaded darker with denser carvings and more in-fill of ink than on the frontal surfaces. Similarly, the depth of the water well, the curved-in surface of the bucket, and the oblique surface of the foreground free-standing mechanical parts are all represented with chiaroscuro. Naturally, the depth of the underground pit beneath the cut-away lines is shaded black, except for the exposed mechanical parts buried within.

By contrast, for the Chinese artisan's redrawn copy of Ramelli's original copper plate print, the medium used was the woodblock and the wood engraver. Traditional Chinese woodblocks are made from plank-wood cut along the grain. An even, close-grained and relatively hard wood plank was preferred. With denser grain, more precise carving can be achieved and more press-runs can be endured.[14] Yet correctly choosing the hardness or softness of the wood plank is important. If the wood plank is too hard, it will be difficult to carve. If too soft, it will be prone to wear after just a few presses. Due to the nature of the wood plank and the wood-carving technique, the tonal gradations are limited. Instead, outline drawings are widely used. However, chiaroscuro is not unknown in China, although it is assigned a different meaning. For example, in landscape painting, the technique of shading the surfaces of the stones with different parts of the ink-brush is utilized to represent different textures of the rugged surfaces of the stones. Shading in Chinese culture is a conventional technique to represent texture rather than depth. Clearly, the Chinese artisan scrutinized the chiaroscuro represented in Ramelli's print when it was redrawn. The shading-tone was likely construed by the artisan as representing textures. If the shading-tone on the receding surfaces of the column posts is taken as the 'texture' of the posts, it makes sense for the artisan not to shade them since in reality the front and side surfaces of the post appear to possess the same texture. The inside surface of the water, well-shaded by Ramelli, also appears construed and substituted as texture, i.e. as several courses of bricks. The bucket in Ramelli's print is metal with two thin metal hoops on the top and bottom. Yet the Chinese artisan again replaced it with the texture of a Chinese bucket made of three equal strips of curved wood (see the figure on page 84). When the Chinese artisan meditated on the dark area below the well encircled by zigzag lines, he may have construed it as a peculiarly textured surface, or a novel form of 'ground'. Therefore, the corporeal understanding of this information as suggested by his familiar medium of representation swayed him to represent the cut-away lines on the ground as mystical billowing clouds – a 'texture' for the 'novel ground'. The wood carving media and their interactions with the bodily senses conferred on the Chinese artisan alternative forms of imagined reality. Thus the corporeal act of drawing can be seen as critically grounding the Chinese artisan's imagining process.

Conclusion: redraw, redraw and redraw

If the cultural contexts of design and the corporeal act of drawing form the foundations for the imagination of construction, then the ungrounded passive gazing upon conventionally exhibited drawings proves inadequate to divulge this deeper imaginative process. Since exhibited drawings are normally taken as artworks or as end results in themselves, they are often isolated from both the original flow of their cultural contexts and the corporeal act of making the drawing. Just as the imagination of the moon becomes obscured when the supporting clouds are erased, the imagination of construction is invisible if isolated from its two critical underpinnings.

However, the act of redrawing can initiate a journey into the original architectural imagination. The aim of redrawing, or re-creation, although inevitably a process of re-interpretation, can also be to open the thoughts and actions of the observers toward a mutual dialogue with design contexts as well as the corporeal dynamisms embodied in the drawings.

As analyzed above, the Chinese artisan corporeally replaced Ramelli's imagined reality of the seventeenth-century European culture and technology with the eighteenth-century Chinese correspondences, leading to dramatically different forms of imagined construction. If we discard the notion of right or wrong interpretation, the Chinese artisan's act of redrawing has merit in the sense that it is not a visual mimetic copy of Ramelli's print, rather it offers the artisan the tool to imagine the 'novel apparatus' through his own bodily experience of each stroke presented in the original. The act of redrawing opens the dialogue of the observer's imagination with that of the original author. When the critical observer takes up a pencil to decode the exhibited drawing, the drawing becomes vastly enriched for exploration. Through the action of redrawing, the critical observer will open a sensory inquiry into a bountiful sphere of imagination to discover and experience. As Carlo Scarpa stated:

> If I want to see things, I do not trust anything else. I put them in front of me, here on paper, to be able to see them. I want to see, and for this I draw. I can see an image only when I draw it.[15]

Notes

1 The two ways of drawing the moon were articulated by the Chinese philosopher Feng, YiuLan (冯友兰) in arguing 'the defiance to direct definition' in traditional Chinese aesthetics and thinking. Gao, Chen-yang (高晨阳), Zhong Guo Chuan Tong Si Wei Fang Shi Yan Jiu (中国传统思维方式研究), Jinan, Shandong Da Xue Chu Ban She, 1994, p. 59.
2 Allen, S., Practice: Architecture, Technique and Representation, G+B Arts International, 2000, p. 32.
3 Plato, Plato's Republic. Indianapolis, Hackett Publishing Company, 1974, pp. 240–241.
4 Kearney, R., The Wake of Imagination: Ideas of Creativity in Western Culture, London, Hutchinson, 1988, pp. 91–92, 101–102.

5 Ibid., pp. 6–8.

6 Xun, J., *Xie Gei Da Jia de Zhong Guo Mei Shu Shi,* Beijing, San Lian Chu Ban She, 1993, p. 103. *Fusheng Handing out the Classical Canon* (伏生受经图) by Wang, Wei 王维.

7 Chung, A., *Drawing Boundaries: Architectural Images in Qing China*, Honolulu, University of Hawaii Press, 2004, p. 10.

8 Quoted from Chung, A., translation, ibid., p. 10.

9 Quoted from Chung, A., translation, ibid., p. 11.

10 This technique is still in practice in Japan. See Brown, S.A., *The Genius of Japanese Carpentry: the Secrets of a Craft*, Kodansha International, 1995, p. 94.

11 Edgerton, S.Y.J., *The Heritage of Giotto's Geometry*, Ithaca, Cornell University Press, 1993, p. 272.

12 This image was also described in Edgerton, S.Y.J., *The Heritage of Giotto's Geometry*, Ithaca, Cornell University Press, 1993, p. 273.

13 This image was also described in ibid., p. 280.

14 Chia, L., *Printing for Profit: the Commercial Publisher of Jianyang, Fujian (eleventh–seventeenth century)*, Cambridge, Harvard University Press, 2002, pp. 30–31.

15 Frascari, Marco, *Architectural Synaesthesia: a Hypothesis on the Makeup of Scarpa's Modernist Architectural Drawings*, 2003.

Architecture's twinned body

Building and drawing

Federica Goffi

Introduction

In today's practice of architecture, the problem of 'drawing' is the problem of 'building', both are perceived as final ends. Mistaking the temporal nature of architectural work as being 'eternally unchangeable', they have become fixed 'models' of their own image, projecting onto each other an unchanging vision of reality. Prior to this contemporary understanding, the building was a perpetually unfinished entity, capable of being worked and reworked including through the media of drawing.

The proliferation of photo-realistic computer-generated images – enhancing 'literal' representations – produces a typical dilemma when looking at drawings, regarding whether the image is computer-generated or a photograph.

Reality and imagination are treated as mirror images. Virtual pre-figurations become 'contract-documents' to be thoroughly fulfilled; meanwhile, the 'accidents' of the making are removed from the design process. Temporally speaking, 'drawings' no longer project an image of process but a processed image portraying an 'eternally' unchangeable vision of reality.

The unending 'process' of making, i.e. time, is evinced from architecture, producing its disembodiment. The denial of the process of change implies that buildings/drawings perpetuate a fixed image, facing the problem of assuring continuity despite and/or within change.

The problematic relation of drawing and building is paralleled in a mid-thirteenth-century fiction about the 'king's two bodies'. This fiction, which survived well into the Renaissance period, concerns the problems of continuity of a divine monarchy with the death of the human king or queen and it was meant to resolve problems of continuity and identity concerning the 'state'.

Abducting the 'king's two bodies' within architecture lays the foundations for a theory of architecture as a form of imagination in 'absentia'. During the transformation of the building, the drawing makes discernible the intangible presence of the building's sempiternal body, acting as a 'substitute'. Drawings are produced in an 'in-between' condition, making 'visible' and accountable for a transformation that is 'invisible' when looking in the present condition, at the building.

The twinned body of architecture

The 'natural body' of the king, whose life was bounded within time, was twinned with the 'political body' of sempiternal existence. When the king dies, the 'political body' reigns *in absentia*, and will soon reincorporate in the natural body of the next king. The 'continuity' of the Crown is allowed by the continuous existence of the political body.

The effigy provides material representation to the invisible 'political body' acting as 'substitute'. The invisible nature of the 'twinned persona' becomes visible during funerary rites when the demised king (body natural) and the effigy (sempiternal body) are displayed together.[1] Carlo Ginzburg underlies the role of effigies in controlling the traumatic event of death and the changes associated with it: 'On the one hand the "representation" stands in for the reality that is represented, and so evokes absence; on the other, it makes that reality visible, and thus suggests presence.'[2]

Architecture is a two-bodied entity. The 'body natural', i.e. the physical building and its twin, the 'sempiternal body', i.e. the drawing, stand in a relationship of signifier and signified. The building's external appearance and essence are both represented in the drawing, the twin persona of the building.

Leon Battista Alberti (1404–1472) expresses that not only the appearance of the building but also its 'form', i.e. the essence of the thing signified, are conveyed through drawing.[3] The drawing has the potential to reveal not just likeness but presence, not just body but soul in terms of similitude by means of representation. Vitruvius connects drawing with the word 'idea', i.e. 'form' or 'essence'.[4] The 'form' of a thing – defined by Plato as the 'essence' (Greek *eidos*) or nature of something[5] – provides continuity despite the changes that invariably happen to its physical appearance.

Tiberio Alfarano's 1571 ichnography of Saint Peter's as true 'form' and the two bodies of architecture

Evidence of the twinned body of architecture can be found in a 1571 hand drawing ($117\frac{1}{2}$ cm $\times$ $66\frac{1}{2}$ cm),[6] by Tiberio Alfarano[7] representing the Basilica of Saint Peter's in the Vatican during its Renaissance renovation. The renovation of the 'Old' temple, i.e. the 'natural body', initiated by Pope Giulius II in 1506, leads over a period of 120 years, to a complete renewal. Change is a traumatic event controlled through the media of drawing, in its role of 'twinned body'. Tiberio Alfarano's manuscript '*De Basilicae Vaticanae antiquissima et nova structura*',[8] complements the drawing and the title of the manuscript states the content and significance of the work. Alfarano portrays the '*Forma Sacrosanctae*' or the 'true form' of Saint Peter's Basilica,[9] i.e. not a literal figuration but rather an epiphany of essence.

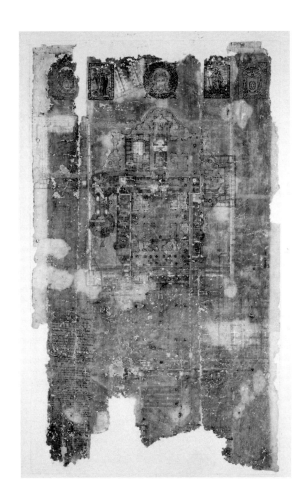

Tiberio Alfarano's 1571 hand-drawn ichnographia of the plan of the Vatican Temple.

At the time of Alfarano's drawing, the New and the Old Basilica coexisted, joined by the *'Muro Divisorio'* erected by Antonio da Sangallo in 1538. The renovation works were far from completion. Despite that, this drawing escapes chronological classifications claiming an 'a-temporal' interpretation of the Basilica's substance.[10] The adjective 'sacrosanct' refers not only to its being the most Holy but also to the inviolability of the essence portrayed in the drawing. The drawing's description reads: *'Haec est integra ichnographia antiquissimi Templi Sancti Petri Apostolorum Principis Romae in Vaticano'* – the Latin adjective *'integra'* refers to the intactness of the Temple, implying an idea of conservation and completion.

A 'literal' reading of the drawing suggests the presence of Old Saint Peter's within the New. A 'physical' footprint of the Old temple made of truncated columns and walls is preserved under the New.[11] The physical superimposition of the New Basilica onto the vestiges of the Old is reflected in the making of the drawing generated by 'layering'. Alfarano 'added' Michelangelo's *ichnographiam* above that of the Old Temple, overlapping and gluing on the outlined plan a cut-out of Etienne Duperac's print reproducing Michelangelo's plan.[12] The superimposed plans allow a reading of the physical and metaphorical relationship between them. The presence of Veronica's veil in this drawing, i.e. the true image (*vera icona*) of Christ, attributes to the 'ichnography' the value of 'iconic representation', having the potential to reveal not just likeness but presence. Alfarano reinforces that he delineated only 'one' drawing (*unoque folio perstrinxi*[13]) tracing the 'ichnography' of the temple, which, like the word's etymology suggests, possesses iconic qualities. The analysis of Veronica's iconography and its placement within this drawing is the hinge to revealing the presence of the 'twinned body'. This Veronica reflects the double nature of Christ as both 'human' and 'divine'. The saviour is crowned with thorns representing Christ in his human attributes. The Holy Face is surrounded by an 'evergreen garland' made by intertwined leaves of laurel and oak. The wreath is the Christian symbol of immortality.[14] Laurel's evergreen foliage traditionally symbolizes eternity. Oak was not only the tree from which Christ's cross was made, but it also symbolizes endurance and the strength of faith and virtue. The Veronica is composed by re-assembled cut-out prints glued onto the paper.[15] The surrounding evergreen garland is a separate xylographic fragment added to circumscribe the veil. This highlights Alfarano's process of 'invention'[16] not relying specifically on iconographic tradition in assembling the fragments forming Veronica's icon.

Evidence of the mystical body, i.e. a corporation concept of Church,[17] can be deduced by other iconographic elements. According to Augustine, the '*corpus Christi mysticum*' – i.e. the Church – was made by Christ as the 'head' and by the archbishops, cardinals and all the clergy representing the 'members' of the Church's body. The apostle Paul wrote, 'He put all things in subjection under His feet and gave Him as head over all things the church, which is His body, the fullness of Him who fills all in all' (Ephesians 1:22–23).[18] The 'body natural' of Christ was referred to as '*corpus verum*' or 'true body', while the 'mystical body' was synonymously indicated by the notion of '*corpus fictum*', '*corpus imaginatum*' or '*corpus representatum*' (represented body).[19] The 'true body' and the 'represented body' are joined in Alfarano's plan – following Alberti's dictum – both '*forma et figura*' of the building are present in the drawing. He delineates the Basilica as a corporeal and spiritual entity, i.e. a duality of body and soul (*corporalibus spatiis* and *spiritualis Ecclesia*). Alfarano's representation of the basilica's corporeal appearance ('*beati Petri materialis Ecclesia*') becomes the 'outward' sign of the 'inward' presence of the spiritual Church. The relationship between the two is one of *similitude*, not likeness.[20]

The gold-leaf pochee of Old Saint Peter's walls – rendered with a procedure similar to that used for illuminated books miniatures[21] – demonstrates the 'sempiternity' of the old Basilica and indicates the presence of the 'mystical body', i.e. the 'spirit'. The undercoating of 'Armenian bole' marking the edges of the gold-leaf walls signifies the presence of the 'material body' of the church in its bloodily sacrifice. The three-figured deesis formed by Saint Peter and Saint Paul flanking Veronica's veil in the top portion of the drawing is essential in delineating the presence of the 'represented body'. This scheme is borrowed from pictorial tradition going back to the first twenty years of the sixteenth century.[22]

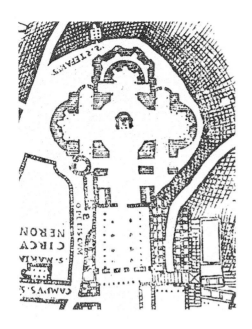

Leonardo Bufalini,
Plan of Rome, 1551.

Ugo da Carpi's altarpiece for Veronica's chapel (*c.*1525) is likely to have been a direct referent for Alfarano's three-figured deesis. This composition however has an eastern origin and a much older tradition that goes as far back in Rome as the thirteenth century. Such is the case with Saint Peter's votive icon of the Serbian Queen Mother Helen in Rome. Here a medallion of the Holy Face surmounts the double portrait of Peter and Paul.[23] Alfarano's use of the language of icons inscribes his 'iconography' within a long-standing tradition according to which only the simultaneous presence of both Peter[24] and Paul allows for a representation of the Church of Rome.[25] In addition, 'marking' in the plan the tombs and altars dedicated to church 'members' completes the representation by making visible the invisible 'mystical body'. The old cross-formed plan was a burial place, literally representing the corporate body.

The insignia of Pope Gregory XIII and Cardinal Alessandro Farnese to the far left and far right – i.e. the Vicar of Christ and the Archpriest of Saint Peter's respectively[26] – 'portray' the present moment (1572) in Church history. Veronica's icon stands in a relationship of head to body with the Basilica's footprint. The Holy Face crowned with the imperishable wreath is the visible 'head' of the Church;[27] the 'body' becomes visible through the figuration of the basilica's footprint combining old vestiges and new elements. The contextual representation of Old and New temple can be explained through an understanding of Veronica's veil and its symbolic transparency. The transparency of the veil allows contemplation '*ad faciem*'. Gazing 'beyond' the eye transcends the visible penetrating beyond the two-dimensional appearance of the object into a metaphysical dimension.

Metaphoric transparency allows the gazing of Old Saint Peter's vestiges concealed underneath. Had this 'plan' been understood as 'horizontal cut', i.e. a literal description of above-ground level, the result would have been similar to what Leonardo Bufalini represented – twenty years earlier – in his 1551 plan of Rome. Bufalini demonstrated the 'result' of the cut-and-paste process, i.e. two half plans joined by the shared *Muro Divisorio*. Alfarano's drawing is a representation of 'process'. The 'composite body' is the result of a transformation where two bodies, natural and sempiternal, simultaneously coexist and intertwine.

The relationship between the Old and New Basilica is similar to that between the 'natural' and the 'sempiternal' body. A 'footprint' of Constantine's Basilica – made by truncated columns and walls – has been revealed by archaeological excavations during the 1940s. The wreath surrounding Veronica's veil is the sign revealing the 'sempiternal' body: the New 'central' plan 'circumscribing' Old Saint Peter's rising above the vestiges of the old. This iconic drawing through its symbolic 'transparency' unmistakably provides access to an invisible world 'beyond'. The drawing conceived as iconic representation is the instrument revealing the hidden presence of Old Saint Peter's. In this relationship of above/below the connection between New and Old basilicas can be explained in terms of two bodies, the natural and the sempiternal. The width of the main nave of New Saint Peter's corresponds to that of the Old, allowing the preservation of the old main nave *'intacta'*.[28] The New main piers fall outside the outer perimeter enclosing the old main nave and transept. The two west piers are located above the shoulders of the cross, outside Old Saint Peter's body.

The old 'ichnography' reveals, predicts and generates the new. Veronica's icon is a reminder of this 'multi-temporal' value of the drawing. The drawing's gaze is directed in two directions: looking towards the past refers to memory while having simultaneous pre-figuration of what has yet to come. Veronica's cloth is not just the memory of Christ's face but also the epiphanic revelation of his 'future presence'.[29] The retrospective and prospective character of the design process can be experienced through the intermediacy of the drawing.

Similar to what happens during funerary rites where the body natural and the sempiternal body are displayed together, funerary monuments portray the natural body and the sempiternal one together. The tomb of Innocent VIII (1484–1492), executed between 1492–1493 and 1497–1498 by Antonio Pollaiolo (c.1432–1498), portrays the effigy of the dead pope supine and lifeless on a sarcophagus under the sempiternal body, represented in corporeal liveliness above. This is the only funerary monument 'translated' from the Old into the New basilica.[30] Six years before the 1626 completion of the Basilica, the position of the two bodies was inverted.[31] The 'sempiternal body' was now above the 'natural body'. This inversion is symbolic of the relationship between Old and New basilica; the vestiges of Old Saint Peter's lie now below the New temple's resurrected body.

Tomb of Innocent
VIII executed
between 1492–3 and
1497–8 – Antonio
Pollaiolo
(1432–1498).

Vasari's fresco in the Sala dei Cento Giorni, Rome, 1546: the role of drawings in the process of change

The two bodies of architecture become visible in Giorgio Vasari's (1511–1574) fresco *Paul III inspecting the rebuilding of Saint Peter's* in the Sala dei Cento Giorni, Palazzo della Cancelleria executed in 1546 (see figure below). Pope Paul III (1534–1549) on the left is being presented the ichnography of the New Temple by the personifications of Lady Architecture, Painting, Sculpture and Geometry. Vasari represents Saint Peter as 'body' as well as 'drawing' and 'building'. The reclining figure to the lower right surrounded by putti has been identified as a representation of the Vatican Hill and the six hills of Rome.[32] The reclined figure though can be interpreted as a representation of Saint Peter as Vicar of Christ. This figure holds with the right hand a Papal Umbrella while with the left arm embraces a Papal Tiara, symbolizing the papacy. The three crowns on the *Triregnum* represent the triple power of the Pope as father of kings, governor of the world and Vicar of Christ. The Papal Umbrella is the sign of dignity usually carried by the Pope's 'substitute' during the transition period between the death of a Pope and the election of a successor. This seems to allude to this

Giorgio Vasari, 1546.
Paul III Inspecting the Rebuilding of Saint Peter's. **Sala dei Cento Giorni, Palazzo della Cancelleria, Rome.**

'transition' phase involving the substitution of the old temple with the new. Six putti mend the head of Saint Peter while at the same time crowning him with laurel wreath symbolizing eternity. The mending of the head alludes to renovation work started in the apsidal area. The reclined figure can be interpreted as a personification of Saint Peter's basilica symbolizing transformation and renovation into sempiternity.

The 'drawing' is identified as the medium where the analogy between 'body' and 'building' takes place. The gesturing of the key figures underlines that. There is no direct comparison of the 'building' with the 'body' of Peter. Such comparison happens through the drawing's intermediacy. Lady Architecture points with her right hand at the personification of Peter, while holding a compass pointing downward and an L-square alluding to the 'physical' measurements of the body and to a translation of its presence into the building/drawing. The 'geminate' body of architecture becomes visible in the gestures of the Pope simultaneously pointing at the drawing and at the building under renovation.

During the transformation process, the demised building and the drawing-effigy are displayed together. The 'drawing' – i.e. the second body – acts as a substitute envisioning the future by demonstrating the Basilica's body as 'whole'. The drawing is the medium projecting the imagination into the dimension of sempiternal time and allowing a vision of the absent resurrected body.

Conclusions: architecture never dies

Architectural drawings no longer instruct on how to construct, but have become prescriptive. Image forming is conceived as the visualization of a final product. This kind of representation is a pre-figuration of literal appearance but not an epiphany, i.e. monstrance of 'presence'. Iconographic drawing is not a final drawing or a literal one providing a photographic image but, rather, a program of intentions to be revealed – in time – through making. Architecture is a two-bodied entity. The 'body natural', i.e. the physical building and its twin, the 'sempiternal body', i.e. the drawing, stand in a relationship of signifier and signified. The building's external appearance and essence are both represented in the drawing, the twin persona of the building.

A drawing so conceived allows the imagination to grow and develop rather than be fixed. The process of building – whether drawing or building – is not just imposing an idea on material but growing through it so that material influences the result rather than merely receiving it. The retrospective and prospective character of the design process can be experienced through the intermediacy of the drawing. The drawing should articulate the dialogue between the pre-existent and the future design; something that does not happen in today's practice where 'as-builts' – in the form of measured drawings – and design drawings are kept separate. 'Rejoining' these two temporal conditions through 'metaphoric transparency' allows for a real 'trans-formation' of the building entailing continuity of identity. 'True form' – in Renaissance drawings – is not literal figuration of one's appearance. Drawing is epiphanic demonstration, providing a moment of sudden revelation and insight into the essence of a building. The role of drawings is central in the ritual shaping of the 'memory of the future'.

Notes

1 Royal effigies were displayed during funeral rites for the first time in England in 1327 (Kantorowicz, 1981).

2 Ginzburg, 2001.

3 It is the function and duty of lineaments, then, to prescribe an appropriate place, exact numbers, a proper scale, and a graceful order for whole buildings and for each of their constituents parts, so that the whole form and appearance of the building may depend on the lineaments alone.

(Alberti, 1997, I, 1, 4–4v)

4 Vitruvio, *De Architectura*, Book I, 2, 2 (1997).

5 Plato, *Republic*, 1998.

6 The drawing, currently preserved in the AFSP in the Vatican, located within Veronica's pier, is mounted on a wood board. The drawing was restored by Mario Tiburzi, a master restorer from the BAV, in 1992–1993 (Notiziario Mensile della Basilica di San Pietro Anno VI, Gennaio 1994, N.1, p. 2).

7 Tiberio Alfarano, born in Gerace, was Beneficiary Clerk of Saint Peter's Basilica from 1567 until 1596 when he died. Very little is known of his life before arriving at Saint Peter's. By 1544, Alfarano was in Rome and by 1556 he lived in a house within the Basilica's precincts (Cerrati, 1914).

8 The manuscript was donated in 1582 to Pope Gregorius XIII (BAV, Vatic. Lat. 9904).

9 Alfarano provides three summaries of the original manuscript, entitled: *Forma sacrosanctae Basilicae Beati Petri Principis Apostolorum a Tiberio Alpharano descripta cum catalogo rerum celebrium ut facile quisque per elementa alphabetica et numeros omnia dignoscere posit* (BAV, Barberini lat. 2362; Cerrati, 1914).

10 Michelangelo's dome was completed in 1590. In 1607, Carlo Maderno won the competition for the addition of the eastern arm. New Saint Peter's was consecrated in 1626.

11 Apollonj Ghetti *et al.*, 1951.

12 Alfarano used the roman Palm (22.3422 cm) as unit measure. The plan is at the scale of 1:385 (Silvan, 1992).

13 Alfarano, 1582, 1914.

14 Saint Paul I Corinthians 9:24–25.

15 Barbara Iatta, Director of the Gabinetto delle Stampe (BAV), identified Veronica's veil as a 'bulino' (February 2006).

16 Monsignor Vittorio Lanzani, Delegato della Fabbrica di San Pietro, explained that the reference to Veronica's icon is purely symbolic and that it does not belong to the rigorous iconographic tradition (February, 2006).

17 Kantorowitcz, 1957, Ch. V, I, pp. 194–206.

18 The 'Church' as 'corpus Christi' was represented through organological metaphors denoting the unity of the head and members into one body. This metaphor goes back to Saint Paul and was incorporated into Augustine's theory of the Church (Grabowski, 1957).

19 The Doctrine of transubstantiation expressed in the Dogma of transubstantiation (1215) officially designates the Eucharistic body as 'corpus verum'.

20 Just like with the Eucharist, the visible signs are bread and wine, the inward invisible reality is the presence of Christ. The problem of representation is resolved by means of similitude, not likeness.

21 *Notiziario Mensile della Basilica di San Pietro*, Anno VI – Gennaio 1994 – N.1.

22 Morello, 1993; Belting, 1984.

23 Belting, 1994.

24 The visible head of the mystical body of Christ was the Roman Pontiff.

25 Morello, 1993, p. 156.

26 He was the head of the Congregation of Cardinals overseeing the renovation (Robertson, 1992).

27 The Crown and the 'mystical body' were comparable entities (Kantorowicz, 1959).

28 From the Latin *intactus*, from *in* – 'not' + *tactus,* past participle of *tangere* 'touch'.

29 Memory thus had a retrospective and, curious as it sounds a prospective character. Its object was not only what had happened but what was promised. Outside of religion, this kind of consciousness of time has become remote to us.

(Belting, H. 1994)

30 Pinelli, 2000.

31 Readon, 2004.

32 Robertson, 1992.

Bibliography

Leon Battista Alberti, *On the Art of Building in Ten Books,* translated by Joseph Rykwert, Neil Leach and Robert Tavernor, MIT Press, 1997 [1452].

Tiberii Alpharani, *De Basilicae Vaticanae antiquissima et nova structura*, introduction by Michele Cerrati, Tipografia Poliglotta Vaticana, 1914 [1582].

B.M. Apollonj Ghetti, A. Ferrua, E. Josi and E. Kirschbaum, *Esplorazioni sotto la Confessione di San Pietro in Vaticano eseguite negli anni 1940–1949*, Tipografia Poliglotta Vaticana, 1951.

Hans Belting, *Likeness and Presence: a History of the Image Before the Era of Art*, University of Chicago Press, 1994.

Sible de Blaauw, *Cultus et decor. Liturgia e architettura nella Roma tardoantica e medievale: Basilica Salvatoris, Sanctae Mariae, Sancti Petri*, 2 vols, Citta' del Vaticano, 1994.

Pavel Florensky, *Iconostasis*, St Vladimir's Seminary Press, 1997.

Stanislaus Grabowski, *The Church: an Introduction to the Theology of St. Augustine*, St. Louis and London, 1957.

Federica Goffi

Carlo Ginzburg, *Wooden Eyes: Nine Reflections on Distance*, Columbia University Press, 2001 [1998].

Anthony Harvey and Richard Mortimer. *The Funeral Effigies of Westminster Abbey*, Boydell & Brewer, 2003.

Ernst Kantorowitcz, *The King's Two Bodies: a Study in Medieval Political Theology*, Princeton University Press, 1981 [1957].

Giovanni Morello, *Vatican Treasures: 2000 Years of Art and Culture in the Vatican and Italy*, Electa, 1993.

Antonio Pinelli, *The Basilica of St. Peter in the Vatican*, Edizioni Panini, 2000.

Plato, *Republic*, Oxford University Press, 1998.

Wendy Readon, *The Deaths of the Popes*, McFarland & Company, Inc., Publishers, 2004.

Clare Robertson, *Il Gran Cardinale Alessandro Farnese Patron of the Arts*, Yale University Press, 1992.

Vitruvius. *The Ten Books on Architecture*, Dover Publications, 1960.

Translucent and fluid

Piranesi's impossible plan

Teresa Stoppani

Introduction

In the mid-eighteenth century, Giovanni Battista Piranesi's oeuvre produced a fierce visual attack that unsettled, once and for all, the stability of the classical language of architecture. Neither theoretical treatise as intellectual manifesto (Alberti), nor self-promotional catalogue of innovative architectural designs (Palladio), the strength of Piranesi's work resides in its being a graphic visual manifesto: his re-conception of architecture operates through a series of powerful images, which still remain active and resonate today in contemporary architectural discourse and practices.

Reconsidered as a variegated and non-contradictory whole, Piranesi's work proposes a new idea of space. Reading and reactivating the urban space in a critical dimension, it explores the spatial and temporal complexity of the 'difficult complications, alternations, and superpositions' (Deleuze and Guattari) of the different forces at work in the space of the city.

Between 1741 and 1743, Giovanni Battista Nolli prepared his famous *Topografia di Roma*. The Nolli plan is all about clear distinctions, lines that divide, coded representation of scaled and measurable elements. Its lines are peremptory, solid black ink conceals the articulation of private spaces. In the same years, Piranesi's works proposed a city made of fragments that become available materials, can be dislocated, manipulated, cloned and endlessly mutated. They are used to inhabit – rather than form, define or control – the experimental space of an impossible Rome, in which the historical city is almost entirely dissolved and replaced by the extraordinary congestion of fragments. Both spatial and temporal relations are constantly renegotiated on an uncontrollable fluid ground that defies any Cartesian measurements and opens up possible definitions of surface as space.

Translucent and fluid

'Translucent and fluid' is an allusive title. It intends to place this chapter in relation to both its object (or plurality of objects) and to its ways of approaching it. The object is – in a mediated and indirect way – the idea of the city and the treatment of the city (Rome) in Giovanni Battista Piranesi's etchings. The approach intends to situate itself not in the ambit of the urban studies or in the history of the representation of the city, but in the context of those critical works in the theory of architecture that operate (in particular, but not only) between history (Manfredo Tafuri) and criticism (Jennifer Bloomer).

'Translucent' is used by Jennifer Bloomer[1] in relation to Piranesi's plan of the *Ampio e Magnifico Collegio* (1750), which she reads as a partly transparent horizontal section that veils and at the same time suggests – screens – possible depths and three-dimensional expansions. Here the plan of the 'building' is not a given and non-negotiable solid starting ground, but a precarious sectioning surface, thinner than the paper it is impressed upon. 'Fluid' refers to Manfredo Tafuri's analysis of the spatiality of Piranesi's *Campo Marzio dell'Antica Roma* (1762).[2] For Tafuri

> the 'triumph of the fragment' ... dominates the formless tangle of the spurious organisms of the *Campo Marzio*. ... [the *Campo Marzio*] takes on the appearance of a homogeneous magnetic field jammed with objects having nothing to do with each other. ... [this produces] a kind of *typological negation*, an 'architectural banquet of nausea', a semantic void created by an excess of visual noise.[3]

Here with 'translucent' and 'fluid' I do not refer to the *Collegio* or the *Campo Marzio*, but to other works that preceded the *Campo Marzio* anticipating, outside the defined format of the plan (of a building or a city), the dissolution of space that characterizes the *Campo Marzio*. Tafuri emphasizes the chronological progression of the dissolution of form in Piranesi's work, form the architectural object and its representation in the *Carceri* (first state *c.*1750, second state *c.* 1761) and in the *Collegio*, to the city in the congested and yet fluid urban field that is the *Campo Marzio*. Here I focus instead on the transitional phase of Piranesi's work on Rome, contemporary to the first state of the *Carceri* and to the *Collegio*.

Piranesi's Rome, beyond the representation of the present and the reconstruction of the past, is a site of experimentation for the production of a new idea of space. This project is modern: while it uses both broken and (re)invented elements of classical Rome, it does not speak its language, constructing instead a chaotic proliferation of fragments, partial overlaps and broken axes as a tool of urban design. And while it breaks from the rules of the classical order of the city, this project is also far removed from – and far ahead of – the statically ordered (functional zoning) and dynamically infrastructured (transportation) city of the Modern movement. It is this crucial difference that the young Le Corbusier does not understand, or refuses to see, remaining critically dismissive of this 'other' possibility for the modern city, which threatens the making of his own 'radiant' city 'of tomorrow'.[4]

> All the reconstructions of Piranesi, the Rome plan, and the tight-rope com-
> positions that have so dreadfully served the Ecole des Beaux Arts are
> nothing but porticoes, colonnades and obelisques! It's crazy. It's ghastly,
> ugly, imbecilic. It is not grand, make no mistake about that.[5]

Le Corbusier sees only objects in Piranesi, and fails to consider the fluid space in
which they float, an inconvenient open question for both classicism (including its
Beaux Arts epigones) and for Le Corbusier's 'tomorrow'.

Re-reading Piranesi

Suspended, unresolved, conveniently ignored by the Modern, instrumentally and
reductively appropriated by architectural postmodernism, the questions opened by
Piranesi's past still (and again) offer grounds for investigation to critical architectural
thinking. In particular, a contemporary re-examination of Piranesi's critique of the classical language of architecture and of urban space may suggest a reading that, going
beyond the crisis of languages, marks the current shift in architecture from the definition of form to the ongoing workings of its materiality. A re-reading of Piranesi's work
allows the identification in the crisis of the classical, the possibilities already at work of
an architecture of becoming: an architecture beyond form, which works with change
and materiality.

Relegated by historical circumstances to operate mostly on paper, mainly
through the medium of copper engravure, Piranesi's work produced through its images
a graphic denunciation of the status of architecture at the time. Free to experiment on
paper, Piranesi explored the limits of the classical language of architecture, taking it to
its extremes with the production of paroxystic and impossible spaces that defied and
contradicted the well-established notions of type, composition, proportion that regu-
lated the canons of architecture. Piranesi uses that language, applies the rules of the
architectural orders and breaks them to empty them of their meaning and symbolic
value. He applies the rules of representation to go beyond representation: the spaces
he represents are at times impossible; the medium of representation and its conventions are challenged; the space of representation, detached from that of material production, becomes the space for the production (construction) of ideas. Perspective, in
particular, is used to represent impossible 'interiors', be they building interiors or urban
interiors; the idea of section – including the plan as horizontal section – is challenged
and redefined. If the work is confined to operate within the limits of architectural
representation, its effects go well beyond representation. Piranesi's images represent,
and in representing they construct, a new notion of space – open, infinite, changing,
smooth, dynamic – that still occupies the efforts and attention of contemporary architectural and, more in general, spatial practices.

Piranesi's work opens architecture's space to the possibility of constant
redefinition. His challenges to the classical language produce critical effects that

question not only the possibilities of language as such, but address the very making of space in architecture. The questions raised by Piranesi over two-and-a-half centuries ago remain unanswered, and are still at work in contemporary critical architectural practices that attempt to redefine the notion of architectural space in dynamic terms. For this reason, Piranesi's work has been repeatedly addressed by different discourses beyond traditional art and architecture historiography, and has been used every time to challenge established canons, certainties or disciplinary divisions. From film theory (Eisenstein), to literary criticism (Yourcenar), from architectural critical history (Tafuri), to architectural design (Allen, Eisenman), to – more recently – critical theory operating between literature and architecture (Bloomer),[6] different forms of discourse have addressed Piranesi's work as an ongoing construction of relational space rather than a defined object of investigation. Problematic and unresolved, the issues at play in Piranesi's disruption and critique of space remain still active, and of special relevance within a contemporary dynamic reading space.

Forms and forces (and the city)

In their theorization of the smooth and the striated in *A Thousand Plateaus*,[7] Deleuze and Guattari describe the sea as the smooth space par excellence: space of traject-ories rather than points, space of lines of movements that connect rather than divide, directional space rather than metric or dimensional. Filled by events more than by formed things, the sea is intensive space, *spatium* rather than *extensio*. The city is, instead, the space of the striated: measured, controlled, subdivided and known. But of course the difference is never so clearly distinguished, no space is all smoothness, no space is all striation. And while the sea undergoes striations, the city is indeed the space of complexity and co-presence of the smooth and the striated. What defines and determines the striation of the city, what differentiates it from the space of the sea, is mainly the nature and treatment of its *surface*. It is in the nature and in the definition of the surface that problems begin and complexities unfold. It is the surface of the city that is striated: a space in which 'one closes off a surface and "allocates" it according to determinate intervals, assigned breaks', while in the smooth 'one "distributes" oneself in an open space, according to frequencies and in the course of one's *crossings*'.[8]

It is on the grounds of this distinction, and of the ambiguities and contami-nations that it implies, that it is possible to propose a re-examination of the making of the space of the city in Piranesi's oeuvre, his etchings of a surveyed, measured, but also reinterpreted and reinvented Rome. Deleuze and Guattari's understanding of smooth space and striated space and their idea of smooth voyage allow the re-opening of Piranesi's critique of the classical language of architecture and of urban space in a direction that is still active today. Deleuze and Guattari repeatedly maintain that a clear distinction of smooth and striated spaces is possible only in theory, while they are always manifested in a mixture of both. Originated from an initial striation, the city is in fact such a mixture, combining in its orders always both kinds of spaces. The 'Roman' works of Piranesi all but reveal this intrinsic nature of the urban space. Piranesi's Rome and its surroundings, a multiple city made of past and present, never exist as a resolved, flat, static plane, but always 'become': dynamic, layered, fragmented, they work on a surface that is an ambiguous space of tension, never possibly resolved by a dividing line (the black figure on the white ground of the Nolli plan). It is for its treatment (or making) of space that Piranesi's work remains significantly placed in architecture, dangerously and provocatively suspended between the classical language and its rupture, between an enclosed urban space and the proliferation of the formless – not only on an outside defined and excluded by walls, but also within, inside, underneath the actual and visible structured order of the city. It is therefore possible to re-engage the modernity (in the sense of a topical and contemporary criticality) of Piranesi's work, for its reading and reactivation of urban space in a critical dimension. Piranesi can therefore be reconsidered not only as a critic of the classical order of architecture, but as an interpreter of the conflicts already embedded in the order of the historical city, before its contemporary explosion. Over two-and-a-half centuries ago, Piranesi was already exploring the spatial and temporal complexity of the 'difficult complications, alternations, and superpositions'[9] of the different forces at work in the space of the city.

The smoothing voyage

> To think is to voyage. . . . What distinguishes [smooth and striated] voyages is neither a measurable quantity of movement, nor something that would be only in the mind, but the mode of spatialization, the manner of being in space. . . . Voyaging smoothly is a becoming, and a difficult, uncertain becoming at that.[10]

Beyond the specifics of the occasion, the type of the building, the scale and the kind of representation – view of the city or city plan, plan or perspective of an interior space – Piranesi's works always introduce a tension in the system of classical space, be it that of the city or of the building. Unsettling classical orders, presenting architectural interiors that are always incomplete and never quite defined in their limits, inventing structures of centripetal and possibly infinite expansion, representing a city of proliferating fragments, Piranesi introduces the notion of 'movement' as common denominator of his oeuvre. Architecture will never be still again. And the movements staged in it are of different orders.

In their definitions of smooth and striated spaces, Deleuze and Guattari offer a possible reading of space in terms of movement. Space is not defined by the figures that it produces or by the objects that occupy it, but by the forces that are at play in it. Space is thus characterized by the movement that occurs in it, by 'voyage' rather than stasis. Smooth and striated natures do not occur in different places, are not mutually exclusive, do not take shape; they coexist, not in the form that the space takes, but in the kind of movements that occur in it: in the voyage. The complications and mixtures of smooth and striated spaces always bring into play 'dissymmetrical movements', 'differentials of speed, delays and accelerations, changes in orientation, continuous variations'.[11] The smoothness of a space does not reside in its objects or in its resolved composition, but in the movements that read, inhabit, *incur* in it.

In Piranesi's case, the objects and the language he employs remain apparently classical, elements of an established tradition of a rediscovered antiquity. But their composition, rather than repeating given paradigms, produces unresolved tensions and triggers an explosion of fragments that question the validity of any established order. It is through smooth movement, by introducing 'nomadic transit in smooth space' into the striated space of the explored classical city and its architecture, that Piranesi unsettles their authority and the legitimacy of their origin, setting uneasy grounds for an architecture that operates as (self-)critical discipline.

To do so, Piranesi uses the tools of his work, the unbuilt architecture of the drawing and the etching, the plan and the view: lines, cross-hatching, infill, shading, chiaroscuro are used to define the constituent elements of his spaces and to characterize the inhabitants of these spaces. The nature of a space is thus determined by the movements that operate in it, and these occur on two levels in Piranesi's images. On the one hand, his use of the techniques of representation – the structure of the image, the perspectival construction, the drawing and etching techniques – constructs spaces that upon careful examination often reveal themselves to be incomplete, impossible or distorted; and they are represented by a line that moves – draws, scratches, etches, incises – at different speeds, with different levels of precision or intentional blur. On the other hand, often unusual or inexplicable presences populate his images: objects, props, machines, human beings and indefinable creatures are, more than 'accessories', complements to the architecture and integral parts of the structure of the space represented in the image. Movement, in other words, is not literally represented, but it is thought, suggested by the construction of the lines and by the inhabitation of space – by inanimate objects, machines or living creatures.

No figure no ground (the Nolli plan)

Between 1741 and 1743, Giovanni Battista Nolli prepared his famous *Topografia di Roma*, published in 1748. In these years Piranesi collaborated with Nolli to prepare a reduced version of the plan (the so-called *Small Nolli*) accompanied by views of Roman monuments and monumental sites. The small plan, containing an alphabetically ordered table of contents, is intended to both accompany the *Large Nolli* and/or be an independent – and cheaper, and therefore commercially more viable – publication.

The Nolli plan is the fundamental documentary representation of Rome, based on first-hand surveys but also incorporating the wealth of mapping efforts and productions that had previously represented and codified the city. For its clarity and accuracy, the Nolli plan becomes 'the' plan of Rome, to which we still turn today for an understanding of the historical city. And yet this plan is not only a representation, but also a clear editing project of exclusions, omissions and rectifications.

Beyond its object – Rome – the Nolli plan is also a fundamental element of reference and definition in urban cartography. Representation, in it, is always not only the result of the gathering, preparation and presentation of information, but also an explicit decision (*de-cidere*, in the sense of division). Nolli's plan results from a scientific survey, it unifies and systematizes the existing, it produces an order, a taxonomy. Space is divided and divisible, measured for archaeological, commercial, political and land-revenue purposes. It defines a whole – closed and finished – and its parts – finite and commensurable. It is a project of striation. It reconciles the semi-lost and broken antiquity (in darker shade) with the present baroque edifice (lighter) in one temporarily established frozen form. The Nolli plan operates at a (relatively) fixed level to cut its horizontal sections. With equal precision – peremptory more than accurate – the lines in the Nolli plan divide and conceal. The plan represents public space, while it obliterates or hides the private. Urban interiors, stairs, courtyards of palaces are assigned to the public, and therefore represented in white. But the further articulation of the complex urban space that Rome is, is reduced to a series of peremptory thresholds. There is no room here for grey areas.

In his analysis of the articulation of spaces in Piranesi's *Campo Marzio*, Peter Eisenman points out that

> the Nolli plan has today become the icon of an architectural fundamentalism which calls itself New Urbanism. It represents an idea of original truth, of a moment in time that uses this moment in the eighteenth century as a badge of authenticity to authorize work in the present. The Nolli map was a literal projection of Rome as it was in the eighteenth century. On the other hand, the *Campo Marzio* has little to do with representing a literal place or an actual time. The *Campo Marzio* is a fabric of traces, a weaving of fact and fiction.[12]

Here I want to suggest that in his contribution to the *Small Nolli* plan, Piranesi anticipates the 'fluidity of space'[13] of the *Campo Marzio*. In the small plan, Nolli is responsible for the reduced version of his own cartography, while Piranesi is to surround it with a series of views of Rome. Piranesi's perspectival renderings, arranged around Nolli's plan, anticipate a breaking of the urban space and a reconstructed fictional continuity that does not find any correspondence in Nolli's work, but produce an 'other' space. Nolli measures (scale plan), orientates (compass rose), perimeters (city walls), distinguishes – at the territorial scale between built and unbuilt, *urbs* and *ager*; at city scale, between public and private as ground and figure, flattens, reducing everything to the plane of a theoretical horizontal section at ground level. On the margins of the *Small Nolli* plan, Piranesi reassembles an impossible Rome of Baroque and antique monuments, whose reinvented proximity is made possible by the distortion and composition of multiple perspectives. The given order of the city here is destroyed, in favour of a synoptic and partial view that clashes and jams together different times, scales, speeds of movement. Their new composition, defiantly juxtaposed to Nolli's 'correct' but obliterated plan, seems to challenge the distinction of public and private: converging perspectives construct intimate spaces instead of illustrating linear axes, angled views let interior private spaces show through. The elements of the Classical and the Baroque Rome are here glued together in a soft muddy ground offered by the broken antiquities: collapsed structures and abandoned fragments, half-sunk remains of ancient buildings, the mud that swallows them, the minuscule quasi-human creatures that populate lightly (floating, surfacing) this soft ground. Piranesi's lines – thin, broken, rapid, multiple – confuse, unite, combine elements in a soft and changing space that anticipates the 'fluidity of forms' (Eisenstein) of the *Carceri*. The views by Piranesi accompany the Nolli plan, but they anticipate, with their multiple and fragmented perspectives, what Piranesi will do a few years later, with his plan of a fantastic Rome in the *Campo Marzio dell'antica Roma*.

On the margins of Nolli's figure/ground projection, Piranesi insinuates another way of conceiving, thinking, recording the city. It is what Eisenman calls, in the *Campo Marzio*, the 'figure/figure urbanism', which 'does not give primacy to the ground as an original instance or datum. Rather, the ground becomes and interstitial trace between objects, which are also traces in both time and space.'[14]

The Nolli plan presents a series of deliberate and strong choices, expressed with equally strong graphics. The representation of the city, limited to the plan, is defined by strong oppositions: solid and void, private and public, black and white.

Giovanni Battista Piranesi, Antichità Romane, Vol. I. Tav. XIII Fig. I. Colonna Antonina. Detail.

There is no room here for any indecision, for the interstitial, for what Piranesi represents as a muddy and never perfectly flat ground, for the space of overlaps, admixtures and continuities that, beyond architectural Modernity, anticipates the contemporary city.

Notes

1   Bloomer, 1993. See, in particular, 'Construction Two: La Pianta di Ampio Magnifico Collegio', pp. 87–107.
2   Tafuri, 1987 (1980).
3   Ibid., p. 35.
4   Both 'radiant' and 'of tomorrow' refer to the titles of two key works on urbanism by Le Corbusier: *Urbanisme*, Paris: Editions G. Crès & Cie 1924 (translated in English as *The City of To-morrow and its Planning*, New York: Payson & Clarke, 1929) and *La ville radieuse*, Paris: Vincent Freal, 1933 (translated in English as *The Radiant City*, London: Faber, 1967).
5   Le Corbusier, Fondation Le Corbusier, Boite B.N., *c.*1919. Quoted in Manfredo Tafuri, ' "Machine et Mémoire": the City in the Work of Le Corbusier', part 1 in *Casabella*, 48, 502, May 1984; part 2 in *Casabella*, 48, 503, June 1984. Also in H. Allen Brooks (ed.), 1987, pp. 203–218.
6   In film theory: Sergei M. Eisenstein's 'Piranesi, or the Fluidity of Forms', translated into English first in *Oppositions* 11, 1978; now in Tafuri, *The Sphere and the Labyrinth*, pp. 65–90. In literary criticism: Marguerite Yourcenar, 'The Dark Brain of Piranesi', in *The Dark Brain of Piranesi and Other Essays*, Henley-on-Thames: Aidan Ellis, 1985, pp. 88–128. In architectural critical history: Manfredo Tafuri, ' "The Wicked Architect": G.B. Piranesi, Heterotopia, and the Voyage' and 'The Historicity of the Avant-Garde: Piranesi and Eisenstein', in Manfredo Tafuri, *The Sphere and the Labyrinth*, pp. 25–64. In architectural design: Stan Allen, 'Piranesi's *Campo Marzio*: an Experimental Design', *Assemblage* 10, 1989, pp. 70–109. In critical theory, working between literature and architecture, in Jennifer Bloomer, *Architecture and the Text*.
7   Deleuze and Guattari, 1988 (*Mille Plateaux*, 1980). In particular '1440: the Smooth and the Striated', pp. 474–500.
8   Ibid., p. 481; my emphasis.
9   Ibid., p. 481.
10 Ibid., p. 482.
11 Ibid., p. 482.
12 Eisenman, 2006, p. 40.
13 To paraphrase Eisenstein's 'Piranesi, or the Fluidity of Forms'.
14 Eisenman, 2006, p. 40.

Bibliography

Stan Allen, 'Piranesi's *Campo Marzio*: an Experimental Design', *Assemblage* 10, 1989, pp. 70–109.

Jennifer Bloomer, *Architecture and the Text: the (S)crypts of Joyce and Piranesi*, New Haven and London: Yale University Press, 1993.

G. Deleuze and F. Guattari, *A Thousand Plateaus: Capitalism & Schizophrenia*, London: the Athlone Press, 1988, p. 482.

Peter Eisenman, *Feints* (Silvio Cassarà, ed.), Milan: Skira 2006.

Sergei M. Eisenstein, 'Piranesi, or the Fluidity of Forms', *Oppositions* 11, 1978. Republished in Tafuri, *The Sphere and the Labyrinth,* pp. 65–90.

Luigi Ficacci, *Piranesi: the Complete Etchings*, Cologne: Taschen 2000.

Teresa Stoppani, 'Voyaging in Piranesi's Space: a Contemporary Re-reading of the Beginnings of Modernity', *Haecceity Papers*, Vol. 1/issue 2, Spring 2006, "What Now Architecture?", pp. 32–54. Online, available At: haecceityinc.com (accessed: 1 October 2006).

Manfredo Tafuri, *The Sphere and the Labyrinth: Avant-Gardes and Architecture from Piranesi to the 1970s*, London and Cambridge, MA: MIT Press, 1987 (1980).

Manfredo Tafuri, ' "Machine et Mémoire": the City in the Work of Le Corbusier', in H. Allen Brooks (ed.), *Le Corbusier: the Garland Essays*, New York and London: Garland, 1987, pp. 203–218.

John Wilton-Ely, *Piranesi: the Complete Etchings*, Cologne: Alan Wofsy Fine Arts, 1992.

Marguerite Yourcenar, 'The Dark Brain of Piranesi', *The Dark Brain of Piranesi and Other Essays*, Henley-on-Thames: Aidan Ellis, 1985, pp. 88–128.

Contemplating the unfinished

Nicholas Temple and Soumyen Bandyopadhyay

Introduction

This chapter considers the unfinished as a cultural and historical idea, in the light of the contemporary pre-occupation with the finished state as the only viable mode of representation. In our age that gives overwhelming priority to the manipulative techniques in image production – with their affectations of unalterable completion – it is extremely difficult to find situations where the processes of emergent form can be 'measured', experientially, through momentary encounter or contemplative observance. Without the ambiguity that the unfinished furnishes in human experience, as we witness for example in a building under construction or the performance of an incomplete symphony, the receptiveness to new possibilities is prematurely circumvented for the sake of efficiency and constancy.

The enquiry raises questions about whether certain examples of the past can give us a better understanding of how to envisage change in the contemporary city, beyond the precipitous constructs of virtual reality and their surplus of promotional images. The examples chosen for discussion, that include a study of the ruin in early-sixteenth-century Rome and the 'fabricated' ruin in Le Corbusier's India, may at first seem arbitrary. Whilst taken from very different historical periods and geographical locations, we believe these examples reveal something critical about the role of the unfinished in the architectural imagination. This concerns a common underlying theme: the notion of the unfinished as a 'redemptive' metaphor that invokes a future world of potential reconciliation.

At the heart of this study is our belief that the demise in the creative role of the unfinished in contemporary architecture and in culture is symptomatic of a more general impoverishment of historical understanding of urban life. In our desire to 'embrace' the completed artefact, or at least its semblance, architectural production closes avenues for potential dialogue with its historical setting.

Flux versus stasis

In Michel Jeanneret's book, *Perpetual Motion*, the author claims that order in the Renaissance was guided by a perpetual state of becoming, by which notions of the unfinished constituted a cultural condition for reinvention and rediscovery.[1] He highlights how literary and artistic ideas were in a continual state of flux, whereby emergent form resists a premature state of completion or fixity.

Whilst Jeanneret's assertion reveals a crucial aspect of Renaissance thinking, it only partly explains the motivating forces that influenced artistic creativity. A survey of the drawings of Leonardo da Vinci indicates a more complex situation. On the one hand, Leonardo represents, in his studies of landscapes and animals, the turmoil of divine creation. These convey the unfinished state as a rich reservoir of embryonic forms that are conducive to cross-fertilisation and translation, the basis of mimetic and analogical thinking. At the same time, however, Leonardo also sought to codify the natural order, as expressed in his studies of pictographs.[2] The relation between both modes of conceiving the divine order could be considered in relation to the terms *natura naturans* ('creating nature') and *natura naturata* ('created nature'). For the former, nature is construed as an active agent – or impulse – that governs all life. In the case of the latter, however, nature has reached its final purpose (*telos*) and therefore becomes mere effect.[3]

What we see in the two aspects of Leonardo's work is a desire to preserve nature's abundance through the structures of representation. This capacity to 'codify' the divine order finds expression in Leonardo's preliminary drawing for the *Adoration*. Here, the gridded pavement takes on the function of a calibration – or 'caging' – of space, above which float gesturing figures unanchored to the terrain that lies beneath. The tension between both reveals something significant about Renaissance views of order; the desire to capture nature's movement – its creative *anima* – in the net of pictorial space. We are given here a sense of Leonardo's search for mathematical or geometric exactness in the face of nature's perpetual transformation.

This progression 'towards' a concrete world underlies the experience of the unfinished in the Renaissance that assumes culture itself as a 'work-in-progress'. At the heart of this principle is the expectation of a Golden Age when the 'fullness of time' will redeem the destructive forces of temporal existence. Expressed in the writings of humanists, this expectation was tempered by pessimism about the prevailing conditions of human existence. Whilst condemning papal Rome as an equivalent to Babylon, Giles of Viterbo, chief spokesman to Julius II, also saw the city re-emerging as the second Jerusalem.[4] Giles and his Pope believed that the shadow of Babylon could be erased by instigating Church reform through the renewal – or *renovatio* – of the Classical/Biblical past.

The search for ways of measuring the progress of this ambitious enterprise was evident in building work. At a time when the remains of Classical antiquity were being rediscovered and surveyed, the understanding of the ruin as a metaphor of future possibilities gave impetus to the quest for a Golden Age. This meaning was largely mirrored in the guarded optimism of Giles that the Catholic Church could rise above the iniquities of the present.

The redemptive implications of the ruin acquired unparalleled symbolic importance during the construction of the new St Peter's Basilica, begun under Julius II (1503–1513). The building site became the subject of a number of detailed drawings by Maerten van Heemskerck. In these, as Christof Thoenes suggests, the very idea of sin takes on tangible significance.[5] In reference to Heemskerck's drawing of St Peter's from the north, Thoenes observes:

> The gigantic building seems quite frail here, as if collapsed, already ancient; the weathered walls, partly covered, partly bare, are strewn with holes for scaffolding and are raked with furrows and grooves. … If Martin Luther and others compared Rome with Babel, then the association with the great tower and its collapse must have been unavoidable, a "common proverbial example of Superbia rebelling against God."[6]

Only by completing the project can the taint of sin be mitigated and ultimately redeemed. This idea forms the underlying theme in the *Disputa* fresco by Raphael in the Stanza della Segnatura. We witness here, in the form of tiers of hemicycles, the assembly of angels, prophets, saints and Church fathers centred on Christ enthroned. Oriented towards St Peter's Basilica, the fresco's composition alludes to a large apse, evoking the form of the actual Basilica. This is underlined by the presence of a large plinth wall in the fresco, located on the right-hand side of the altar. It is conceivable that this wall was intended to represent part of the western apse of the new St Peter's Basilica, as it was being constructed during Raphael's execution of the fresco. Hence, the *Disputa* could be interpreted at one level as a building site in which the juxtaposition of gesturing figures and building work serves as a measure of the progression *towards* salvation. At the same time, the monolithic wall also evokes the Holy Tabernacle – the Old Testament precursor to the Christian *ecclesia* – since the concordance between Old and New Testaments pervades the fresco's iconography.[7]

There is another construction, on the left-hand side of the altar and located in the background, as if to balance this architectural feature. Partly surrounded by scaffolding, the scene incorporates the construction of a curved ramp (right side), whose ascending passage is abruptly terminated. To understand the possible symbolic meaning of this scene, it is necessary to examine the standing figures positioned immediately in the foreground. Heinrich Pfeiffer claims that the figure, on the extreme left, leaning over a rail with back turned to the altar and left hand gesturing towards an open book, is Donato Bramante.[8] His attention to the book seems to be momentarily interrupted by a youthful standing figure to his right who is pointing to the monstrance on the altar that forms the focus of the fresco. Pfeiffer claims that this scene refers to a daring proposal put forward by Bramante to Julius II; to reorient the new St Peter's Basilica on the north–south axis so that it would align with an ancient obelisk (visible in the Heemskerck drawing), that originally formed part of the earlier Circus of Caligula. According to popular belief, the orb at the apex of the obelisk contained the ashes of

Disputa (Disputation over the Blessed Sacrament). Raphael (1483–1520). Vatican, Stanza della Segnatura.

Julius Caesar.[9] Alignment between Basilica and Obelisk was probably inspired by Bramante's desire to promote Julius II as the '2nd Caesar'.[10] In turning his back to the altar, Bramante is demonstrating his rejection of what Giles of Viterbo preached: 'Man must be changed by religion not religion by man.'[11]

This argument leads one to construe the possibility that the unfinished structure in the background was intended as the symbolic antitype to the monolithic wall on the right-hand side. Given the allusion to Rome as simultaneously Jerusalem and Babylon, in the writings of Giles of Viterbo (one of the humanists incidentally who is credited with conceiving the iconography of this fresco), could we not construe that the scene represents the construction of the Tower of Babel – or at least a stage in its erection left in limbo in acknowledgement of Bramante's own *conversio* through his reorientation to the altar? In so doing, the vanity underlying Bramante's audacious proposal is measured against the vanity of humanity generally, as it is constituted in the Tower of Babel.

From what has been presented so far in the chapter, it seems clear that the unfinished in Renaissance culture served as a crucial symbolic device for invoking humanity's search for redemption through renewal. In this initiative the ruin was not seen as a nostalgic relic of some bygone age, but rather as a mechanism for facilitating future possibilities.

Evocative fragments and the 'obsolete in reverse'

Jeanneret's enquiry into the unfinished as a cultural phenomenon has important implications far exceeding the particular worldview of the Renaissance, as a reading of Le Corbusier's Mill Owner's Association (MOA) building in Ahmedabad, India, will now argue. Corbusier's sketches during his Indian visits were complex fragments recording hitherto un-encountered experiences, yet their incompleteness was replete with the possibilities of connections. The extreme fragmented nature of his text entries, with suggestive connections codified in symbols (e.g. '+', '−', '=') and the occasional under-lined emphasis on phrases and words created a multi-planar cubist text, simultaneously finite and prosaic, yet evocative and poetic, liberating space from the confines of stagnant words,[12] making it difficult not to misread the most prosaic of entries as poetic text.[13] Of particular interest is the manner in which Le Corbusier strove assiduously to reconcile the quasi-mythical with the mathematically charged fragments to arrive at a unique encompassing poetics, as if the latter was the resultant of a mysterious alchemic transformation.[14]

Equally engaging was his treatment of the architectural 'image' appropriate for the newly independent country, where he sought to embody the ambition of the future in the 'incomplete'. While arguably such a conception emerged out of an enduring presence in his mind of the Acropolis and the Indian ruins, a crucial distinction lay in his treatment of the future, affirming Vladimir Nabokov's view that 'the future is but the obsolete in reverse'.[15] Together with the conscious employment of fragments, his Ahmedabad projects made use of the conception of the ruin as a powerful expression of a new future, created by collapsing and fusing the past and the future into a single space of a seemingly entropy-defying present.[16] By disrupting our longing for completeness, the incomplete holds within itself both an enhanced indication of what it could become, a result of our mind's projective cast into the future, as well as a sense that it has always been.

Ruin

The Ahmedabad projects express diverse notions of the ruin. The *brise soleil* appears to have its early manifestation – so it has been suggested – in the unfulfilled Carthage project of 1928.[17] Paradoxically, it is in his observation of life of the Indian poor that we detect its other origin, in an artefact of everyday use nearing obsolescence: the tattered curtain. It provided the basis for the eight vibrant perforated tapestries of the High Court in Chandigarh, as well as the *brise soleil* in Ahmedabad. The connection – at least in Le Corbusier's mind – between the *brise soleil* and the fragile piece of fabric offering 'an Indian [brand of] Héraclite comfort'[18] points to the essentially 'extra-architectural' nature of the screen and parallels the origin of Indian architecture itself, in the rock-cut caves of western India – in which Lutyens failed to find any architectural merit, at all.

MOA and Sodhan House are overt embodiments of this idea of the *brise soleil* as ruin, both exploring further how this condition weaves into, expands or even interrupts the day-to-day inhabitation of these buildings. At MOA the facade breaks down to create a rusticated cavernous zone of transition, made even more rugged through the strong Ahmedabad sun, recalling the dark hollow beaconing of the Karle cave entrance. At Karle, nature and the essentially incomplete character of human intervention overlap, fused further by the play of light, a quality the early Romantic etchings so appropriately captured. Equally Romantic is Le Corbusier's MOA, for not only does his screen anticipate a gradual reclamation by nature (through the vegetation within the *brise soleil*), but it itself displays the paradoxical qualities of fragility, but also depth and density.

Beyond, a vertical concrete plane deliberately obstructs direct view by rising through the double-height entrance space, with a rectilinear aperture positioned along the centre line of the ramp that leads up to the entrance, forcing visitors to re-orientate themselves to access the central space. The orthogonal geometry set up by the facade extends inwards flanking this space, which overlooks the river from an elevation. Another screen – a much shallower and delicate one – frames the view of River Sabarmati. Together with what Frampton called the upper level 'minstrels gallery',[19] the space recalls Kailasha, cave XVI in Ellora, a representation of the celestial abode of Lord Shiva. In being lifted up the ramp and drawn into the central space, one is transformed into an object of ritual offering to the river, a holy rite practised on the banks of Indian rivers. To understand how precisely the redemptive space functions, one has to look into the role played by the ramp and the vertical plane, which, we would argue, plays a key role in a topographic fabrication that attempts to reconcile the opposition between the natural and the synthetic.

Fragments

The treatment of this theme of the 'inhabited ruin' extends inwards through the spatial organisation. The central space is orchestrated around a series of fragments or situated moments, articulated by the presence of a monolithic lift core and the positioning of three curvilinear elements: the reception desk, the table in the waiting area and the interlocking curved walls – a delicate, perhaps precarious embryonic adhesion to the voluptuous female body of the conference hall – holding between them the male and female toilets. While the tables designed in the manner of the roof cut-outs are indeed microcosmic representations, the male–female union seems to be indicative of two crucial mytho-religious themes: the creation myths relating to the churning (*manthana*) of the eternal sea that brought forth the nectar using the mythical serpents as the churning chord, and the penetrative union of the *linga* (phallus) and the *jyoni* (vagina) implicit in the phallic representation of Shiva.[20] That the 'churning rod' was a conscious conception is clear from its projection above the roof plane; this *axis mundi* appears to be held in place by the ground (which also includes the ground floor, below the main space, invisible and subordinated through its 'servant' programme). At roof level, a curious juxtaposition of the extended column and the projected incline of the conference hall roof lends itself to yet another reading of this central column: that of the shaft of a giant machine – perhaps a water mill – positioned carefully in proximity to the river.[21] This device, given his fascination with the rivers of India and notions of purity and sanctity,[22] was perhaps employed with a purificatory intent, in the manner that Lord Shiva – *neelakantha*, the one with a blue throat – drank the venom to purify the nectar. We are dealing with both a prosaic icon of productivity that lay at the heart of the city's wealth creation and a profound creative allusion, and the results (or products) of such actions. The cusped toilets, therefore, could be seen to be the key embryonic implantation instigating the reversal of obsolescence, contributing to the Indian project of *renovatio*.

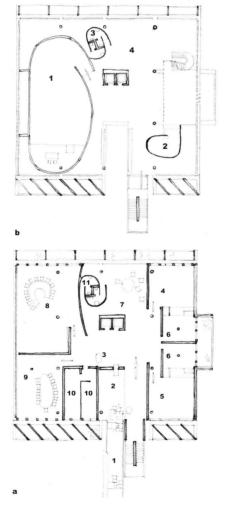

The Mill Owners' Association, Ahmedabad, India. Le Corbusier (1954). Plans. Entrance level (a): 1. Ramp, 2. Entrance hall, 3. Reception, 4. President's office, 5. Vice President, 6. Waiting area, 7. Sub-committee room, 8. Committee room, 9. Managing committee room, 10. Office, 11. Toilets. Upper level (b): 1. Meeting room, 2. Cloak, 3. Toilets, 4. Lobby. Drawn by authors after *Global Architecture* (*GA*) 37.

Reconciliation

The mediating role of the vertical plane positioned at the entrance is articulated through the aperture with its projected ledge focusing down the ramp. Through this ingenious device, the ritual passage turns back on itself to reorientate away from the river towards the city. The redemptive role of the central space with its mytho-religiously charged fragments is completed by the implied issuing forth of the nectar through this 'spout', embedded within which is the reconciled duality of purity and impurity (of water). Only now can one comprehend the pivotal role of his recordings of the 'water mill' of Amritsar or the aerial view of the sloping track for drawing water.[23] It has been argued how the interior of the building, with its stone-faced walls, stands in

The Mill Owners' Association, Ahmedabad, India. Le Corbusier. Entrance facade.

The Mill Owners' Association, Ahmedabad, India. Le Corbusier. Rear facade facing River Sabarmati.

**The Mill Owners'
Association,
Ahmedabad, India.
Le Corbusier.
Entrance foyer.**

contrast to the bold ruggedness of the exterior concrete.[24] The hand-finished paving slabs on the ramp, as well as the paving on the ground beyond, pick up the order of the interior stone facing and appear to bring it down in one uninterrupted fluid flow, a theme that also features in his treatment of the water channel in Sodhan House, which runs down from the roof in conjunction with a staircase, echoing the relationship between these two elements at MOA. The MOA's obsolescence is perpetuated by a questioning – perhaps even subversive – employment of Modernist programme, which expands its monumentality. The prominent positioning of the toilets cusped between the erotic curvatures within the main space interrogates the spatial hierarchy of served and servant spaces. To an extent, the move renders the surrounding programme obsolete, flushed out, as it were, with the flow.

Contemporary condition

In the highly sophisticated world of computer graphics, there is a growing assumption that the modes of architectural representation and the reality of built form can be merged as a continuum; that the way architecture is conceived as a possibility can be directly transcribed as a reality through the mechanical processes of digital graphics. This apparently seamless relationship is far removed from Robin Evans' assertion that in the traditional processes of architecture there exists a gap between drawing and building that requires the 'suspension of critical disbelief' in order for architects to successfully undertake a project.[25] Hence, the impossibility of providing in advance a complete determination of the final work is what gives, according to Evans, the architectural drawing its distinguishing quality. Like the drawings of Leonardo da Vinci, this gap provides a space in which creative ideas emerge through an embryonic process that does not assume clearly defined procedures or predictable outcomes.

As perhaps the last remnant of an explicit expression of making in our cities, the building site could also be considered as the principal vehicle for 're-activating' the notion of the unfinished as both a creative idea and as an architectural possibility. Indeed, if there still remains a way of experientially measuring change in our cities, then it is the building site that we need to examine. Reflecting upon the historical examples presented earlier, it is evident that the building site reveals deeply embedded redemptive meanings of urban renewal that extend beyond the specifics of construction. We allude here to the *Disputa* in which the act of construction always carries with it two potentially conflicting motivations; the desire to begin again at the expense of a prevailing tradition and the need to draw upon a background tradition. These meanings could be said to constitute a bridge between the past and an anticipatory future.

The opportunities of the unfinished manifested themselves in Chandigarh, evidenced in the most explicit manner within the grounds and periphery of the Capitol Complex. Here, urban design assumes that the city is in perpetual making, delivered through the continual experience and habitation of an embryonic urbanising intervention. In his many preparatory sketches of the Capitol, Le Corbusier aspired for reconciliation between the city and the surrounding Shivalik hills as a legitimising and redeeming gesture. This was achieved physically by thrusting the Capitol beyond the limits of the city and thus forcing a dialogue to take place. Equally engaging is the way in which the city eventually 'completes' itself by allowing for a surreptitious incursion of Nek Chand's Rock Garden – a microcosmic city of anthropomorphic and bestiary dwellers perched on the edge of the Capitol and contravening every rule set forth in the Chandigarh edict.

The enquiry has sought therefore to highlight the continually redefining relationship between the unfinished, or apparently obsolete, state of an architectural work, and its potency to generate new horizons of creative intervention. It is apparent in our age that the search for generality, and the big picture, has contributed to the emasculation of the particular. This issue is all the more acute in the design process where translation from drawing to building has shifted emphasis from the legibility of different forms of architectural representation (from thumbnail sketch to general working drawing) to a homogeneous schema of CAD lines and superimposed photographic renderings. Here, we are given the false impression of the manifold and often messy processes of design as a procedural matter, in which any signs of the unfinished are all-but-erased by the priority given to the uniformity of digital (and ultimately architectural) production. In the search for seamless continuity in architectural representation we are left without those signposts of ambiguity that once guided architectural thought to the defining moments of discovery.

Notes

1   Jeanneret, 2001, pp. 1–7, 29–49.
2   Popham, 1972, Ill. 115.
3   Biolostocki, 1963, pp. 19–30.
4   O'Malley, 1968, p. 103.
5   Thoenes, 2006, pp. 25–39.

6   Ibid., pp. 31–32.
7   See Pfeiffer, 1975. Pfeiffer equates Bramante with 'heretics' and Padovan Aris-
     totelians.
8   Pfeiffer, 1974, p. 89.
9   See Nichols, 1889, pp. 71–72.
10   Temple, 2006, pp. 110–127.
11   Martin, 1992, p. 285.
12   Le Corbusier, 1981–1982, sketchbook F27, p. 895.
13   Ibid., a programme brief in F25, p. 806.
14   Ibid., F24, p. 700; also E23, p. 694 and F24, p. 756.
15   Flam, 1996, p. 11.
16   Ibid., pp. 10–23 and 301–309.
17   Frampton, 1975, 2–5.
18   Corbusier, E18, p. 359.
19   Frampton, p. 4.
20   An indication of his awareness, in Corbusier, J36, p. 298.
21   Ibid., F24, p. 756.
22   Ibid., E23 p. 26; J35, p. 222; J37, pp. 366 and 368.
23   Ibid., H30, p. 1056 and E18, p. 346.
24   Frampton, p. 4.
25   Evans, 1997, p. 154.

Bibliography

Jan Biolostocki, 'The Renaissance Concept of Nature and Antiquity', in *The Renaissance and Mannerism: Studies in Western Art*, Vol. 2, Princeton: Princeton University Press, 1963.

Robin Evans, *Translations from Drawing to Building and Other Essays*, Cambridge, MA: MIT Press, 1997.

Jack Flam (ed.), *Robert Smithson: the Collected Writings*, Berkeley: University of California Press, 1996.

Kenneth Frampton, 'Le Corbusier and the Dialectical Imagination', *Global Architecture*, 37 (1975).

Michel Jeanneret, *Perpetual Motion: Transforming Shapes in the Renaissance from da Vinci to Montaigne*, Baltimore: John Hopkins University Press, 2001.

Le Corbusier, *Le Corbusier Sketchbooks*, London: Thames & Hudson, 1981–1982.

Francis X. Martin, *Friar, Reformer, and Renaissance Scholar*, Villanova: Augustinian Press, 1992.

Francis Morgan Nichols, *MIRABILIA VRBIS ROMAE: the Marvels of Rome*, London: Ellis & Elvey, 1889.

John O'Malley, *Giles of Viterbo: On Church and Reform*, Leiden: E.J. Brill, 1968.

Heinrich Pfeiffer, 'Raffaels Disputa und di platonische Theologie von Egidio da Viterbo', *Antiquity and Authority: Journal of the History of Ideas*, Vol. 27 (1974).

Heinrich Pfeiffer, *Zur Iconographie von Raffaels Disputa*, Rome: Università Gregoriana Editrice, 1975.

A.E. Popham, *The Drawings of Leonardo da Vinci*, London: Jonathan Cape, 1972.

Nicholas Temple, 'Julius II as Second Caesar', in Maria Wyke (ed.), *Julius Caesar in Western Culture*, Oxford: Blackwells Publishing, 2006.

Christof Thoenes, 'St Peter's in Ruins', in Michael W. Cole (ed.), *Sixteenth-Century Italian Art*, Oxford: Blackwells Publishing, 2006.

Le Corbusier's spirals

Figural planning and technique in architectural design

Antony Moulis

Le Corbusier's use of the spiral figure in his architectural plans raises issues of meaning in relation to architectural drawing as a medium for design. Scholarship suggests that Le Corbusier's use of the spiral as a plan form is fundamentally an issue of symbolic currency – an expression of an ideal organicism for architecture.[1] Yet the spiral, drawn as a plan form, has obvious uses and effects beyond this purely symbolic meaning. These uses and effects, described by Le Corbusier through his commentaries, concern possibilities for experience through architecture, the efficiency of circulation spaces and construction techniques, and the efficacious extension of programme through properties of form. The fact that the character of a specific graphical figure, spiral or other, can be matched by an architect to particular programmatic demands in this way is hardly surprising; it is a fundamental technique of the architectural design process, one that is implicit in the architect's act of drawing. However, the workings of this technique can easily be overlooked, as attention is given to general properties of figuration, beyond a clear and direct consideration of the figure's explicit usefulness to the architect as part of a design process.

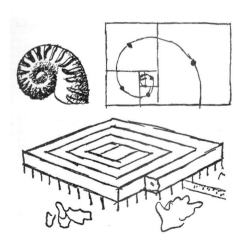

Museum of Unlimited Growth: diagrams and sketches.

In Le Corbusier's work, the process of attributing architectural effects to the spiral figure as a plan can be seen as a sophisticated technique in its own right, a building up of knowledge over time leading to new discoveries about the implications of its use. These discoveries are based on the act of drawing and redrawing the spiral through an extended sequence of 21 projects that leads from the Villa La Roche of 1923 through various iterations of the Spiral Museum type to the Venice Hospital of 1964.[2] As surprising as the myriad uses of the spiral figure is the regularity of its use over the career of the architect. From 1923 onwards, and excluding the period of the war, there is no more than a three-year gap to the start of another project involving a spiral plan. This remarkable consistency suggests that the spiral plan was an on-going project of the studio, which reads in retrospect like a single line of inquiry, a type of design research through the media of drawing into the possibilities of architectural figuration.

The project commonly identified as the initial version of the spiral type is the Mundaneum museum of 1928, with its distinctive ziggurat form based on a three-dimensional spiral. However, the spiral is tried much earlier, in the design development of three 1920s villas – Villa La Roche-Jeanneret (1923), Villa Meyer (1925) and the Villa Savoye (1929). Signalled in each of these schemes is Le Corbusier's preoccupation with the spiral as an element that organises circulation or movement.

In the preliminary design drawings for the Villa La Roche-Jeanneret, there is a scheme for the project in which an elliptical plan form is set within a rectilinear entry hall volume. In the sketch views that accompany the plan drawing, it is shown that the elliptical form indicates a ramped circulation route, joining the first two levels of the building through the double-height volume. In the initial scheme for the Villa Meyer, there is also evidence of a spiral arrangement being tried out. The plan drawings show an unbroken ellipse positioned at the centre of each level, which connects rooms situated around it. The ellipse indicates a spiral ramp travelling through all the levels of the plan to the roof garden. In this initial scheme, the spiral is more dominant over the overall arrangement than was the case in the La Roche-Jeanneret project, though it does not yet become the whole of the plan.

In an early sketch drawing for the Villa Savoye, a spiral stair is positioned at the centre of the plan in an ellipse-shaped enclosure. The use of the spiral does not dominate the plan in this version of the project, but its use does indicate a type of circulation arrangement that is pursued and developed through to the final version. In the final version of the scheme, the spiral appears twice, in an access stair – and more famously – in the form of the villa's central ramp leading from the ground to the roof garden. Le Corbusier himself portrays the ramp as creating a spiral route passage through the building in his commentary on the villa in the *Precisions* lectures.[3]

It is clear that the architect deploys the spiral graphic to form circulation routes. The type of circulation or movement created coincides with the architect's *promenade* concept – the idea that architecture is experienced as an unfolding event generated by a body that turns as it moves through space. In short, the spiral can be understood as a generator of the *promenade*.

In the Mundaneum museum project, the spiral figure as circulation (and as *promenade*) emerges more strongly, becoming the entire arrangement of architectural space. This museum is essentially a three-dimensional spiralling ramp enclosing a hidden interior volume – an arrangement that can be seen as a direct development of the ramp idea used in the Villa Savoye, which was being designed concurrently with the Mundaneum, but here distilled and expanded to monumental effect.

Le Corbusier's interest in the spiral form as a generator of circulation and, more particularly, of bodily movement, is clearly described in the plan drawings of the project published in the *Complete Works*.[4] These drawings feature incidental lines (diagrams of circulation) that describe the direction of movement through the arms of the spiral plan. In a part-plan, even more serpentine movement is shown, as the wide ramping space is broken up by freely arranged partitions. Again, this project reveals itself as an intriguing variant of key conceptual elements that produced the Villa Savoye. In the villa, the promenade space of the ramp is clearly separated from peripheral functional spaces, which are orchestrated in accordance with the concept of the free plan. In the museum the free-plan arrangement is utilised within the *promenade* space of the ramp and not distinctly of it, creating a labyrinth-like effect by inverting their relationship.

In 1931, Le Corbusier proposed a scheme for a Museum of Contemporary Art for Paris. The core of the architect's proposal was the creation of a building that had the ability to be easily extended over time. The plan, a square spiral, was the key factor in facilitating continuous extension or growth, allowing the possibility of constructing the arms of the museum in stages as funding from donors became available. In terms of its overall form, the 1931 museum is based upon the earlier scheme for the Mundaneum. The major difference between them is that, in the 1931 scheme, the spiral figure is deployed in the one horizontal plane rather than as a three-dimensional form – as if the enclosed spiralling ramp of the World Museum was collapsed downward and had formed itself into one layer of space.

The next iteration of the spiral plan comes in 1939 with the project for a Museum of Unlimited Growth. With this project the architect identifies, in retrospect, the trajectory of his research of the spiral plan, writing that this project is continuous with 'a series of studies over a period of ten years'.[5] Here, there is a further observance of the spiral/*promenade* as the organising principle. However, there is another type of plan figuration brought into the arrangement, a series of four axes organised as a pinwheel and overlaid on the spiral that the architect calls a swastika. The pinwheel figure emerges from a series of prior graphical and planimetric studies begun in 1935, yet it is not until the 1939 plan that the particular arrangement of figures (spiral and pinwheel) crystallises.

The specific role of the pinwheel figure as secondary circulation route is alluded to in Le Corbusier's commentary where he describes the pinwheel axes as producing the overall unity of the plan, necessary to 'correct' the labyrinthine tendencies generated by the principal spiral figured circulation.[6] Here the architect shows his interest in possibilities for experience through architecture, recognising what the spiral as plan would produce *as* experience.

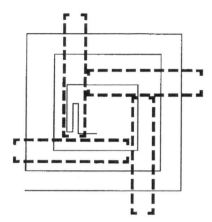

Museum of Unlimited Growth: diagram of plan figures.

While there are three built works that reproduce the figured plan of the Museum of Unlimited Growth more or less intact, a most intriguing development of the spiral/pinwheel plan figuration comes with Venice Hospital project of 1963. Here the plan image of the Museum of Unlimited Growth is multiplied, dissected and collaged to form the basis of a new serial structure. Further to this, the spiral-formed sections of the museum's plan are themselves cut out, replaced by orthogonal layout of wards, offices and patient rooms.

In making a case for the symbolic meaning of Le Corbusier's spirals, much critical attention has been drawn to the graphical analogy Le Corbusier makes between the form of the 1939 museum and spiral forms in nature and mathematics, yet these analogies seem like justifications of the plan rather than a broader acknowledgement of its generating devices. Most often, the spirals that appear in Le Corbusier's drawings are made as studies of circulation patterns and plans with freehand lines drawn over them to test movement paths, yet this fact has not received similar acknowledgement to the symbolic attributes later given to it by the architect and his critics.

Much of Le Corbusier's play with the spiral is through a technique that begins with the conversion of the graphic figure to an architectural plan without compromising its graphical quality. Once entered into the graphical space of architectural drawing, the figure reveals its 'inherent' properties as it is interrogated for its architectural uses. We might view this process today as a type of diagramming – the repetition of a specific figuration that is manipulated or extended into an architectural form in such a way that it provides an armature for specific programmatic demands. This technique is not just about an aesthetic preference for a certain shape or outline, it is about attaching architectural uses to a figure such that the figure might usefully serve architectural purposes.

In the case of Le Corbusier's work, what emerges is a remarkable 40 years of research into the broader architectural implications of the spiral, a gradual discovery of the possibilities in matching the figure to programmatic demands and architectural uses. This technique of figural planning might begin with the straightforward graphic

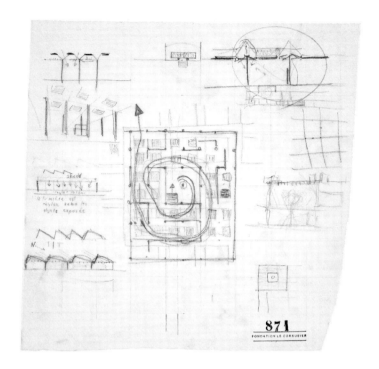

Pavilion des Temps Nouveau: plan and sketches.

act of forming a spiral, yet, like the axis in a nineteenth-century Beaux-Arts drawing, the spiral later becomes pre-conceptualised in terms of its architectural uses as its possibilities come to be understood as 'givens'.[7] Employing the spiral as a plan, time and again, we can imagine Le Corbusier applying this technique to produce modern concepts – concerns for function, circulation, construction, experience and the *promenade* – in much the same way as a nineteenth-century architect used the axis for the purpose of conceptualising *distribution, disposition, composition* and *marche*.[8] In both cases, the relations between the graphical figure, architectural concerns and the act of the figure's re-drawing provides a means to visualise and manipulate a complex set of architectural demands. In the end, Le Corbusier's choice of the spiral is more than a purely symbolic or aesthetic choice – it is one that recognises the implicit usefulness of graphical figures within the medium of architectural drawing, a technique that remains fundamental to contemporary practice.

Notes

1   The organic symbolism of the spiral figure in Le Corbusier's work is proposed by various scholars, including Stanislaus Von Moos, *Le Corbusier: Elements of a Synthesis*, William Curtis, *Le Corbusier: Ideas and Forms* and Kenneth Frampton, *Le Corbusier*.

2   Villa La Roche-Jeanneret (1923), Villa Meyer (1925), Mundaneum (1928), Museum of

Contemporary Art (1931), Bata Boutique (1935), University Campus, Rio de Janerio (1936), Centre of Contemporary Aesthetics (1936), Pavilion des Temps Nouveau (1936), Museum of Unlimited Growth (1939), Exposition Habitat 45 (1945), Urban Development, Saint-Die (1946), Exposition Synthèse Des Arts, Port Maillot (1949), Cultural Centre of Ahmedabad (1951), Tokyo Museum (1955), Etude d'urbanisation, Meaux (1957), Museum at Chandigarh (1957), Cultural Centre, Chad (1960), Museum of the Twentieth Century, Eirenbach (1963), Museum of the Twentieth Century, Nanterre (1965), Musee de lotissement (undated).

3   Le Corbusier, 1991: 136.
4   Le Corbusier, 1968a: 235.
5   Le Corbusier, 1968a: 238.
6   Le Corbusier, 1968a: 238.
7   As David Leatherbarrow notes in *The Roots of Architectural Invention*, axes in Beaux-Arts design practice were simultaneously recognised as instruments of projection (the means to describe built form) and instruments of composition (the means to orchestrate architectural effects).
8   *Distribution* described the apportionment of space according to programmatic requirements; *disposition* described the principal ordering of spaces; *composition* denoted the geometrical and spatial unity of the work; and *marche* referred to the organisation of building premised on the spectator's experience of an architectural and spatial sequence. See Mead, 1991, p. 110.

Bibliography

H. Allen Brooks (ed.), *The Le Corbusier Archive Vol. 1–32*. New York: Garland, 1982.

William Curtis, *Le Corbusier: Ideas and Forms*. Oxford: Phaidon, 1986.

David Leatherbarrow, *The Roots of Architectural Invention: Site, Enclosure, Materials*. Cambridge: Cambridge University Press, 1993.

Le Corbusier, *Precisions: on the Present State of Architecture and Town Planning*. Cambridge, MA: MIT Press, 1991.

Le Corbusier, *Complete Works 1910–1965*, London: Thames & Hudson, 1968a.

Le Corbusier, *Complete Works 1929–1934*, London: Thames & Hudson, 1968b.

Le Corbusier, *Complete Works 1938–1946*, London: Thames & Hudson, 1968c.

Le Corbusier, *Complete Works 1965–1969*, Zurich: Artemis, 1970.

Christopher Mead, *Charles Garnier's Paris Opera: Architectural Empathy and the Renaissance of French Classicism*, Cambridge, MA: MIT Press, 1991, p. 110.

Stanislaus von Moos, *Le Corbusier: Elements of a Synthesis*. Cambridge, MA: MIT Press, 1980.

Emergent realities

Introduction

In a recent book entitled *The Hand* by the physician and philosopher Raymond Tallis,[1] a claim is made for the origin of human consciousness in the opposability of the thumb and forefinger. The dawning awareness of agency brought about by the gradual instrumentalising of the human body is seen as the spark that ignited the subsequent development of fabricated tools and ultimately the 'big bang' of cultural evolution. If ontogeny does indeed recapitulate phylogeny in the development of human self-awareness, perhaps even the conception and healthy development of a building might still require a significant degree of input from the actions of the 'thinking hand'. As Malcolm McCullough has written in the book *Abstracting Craft*,[2] perhaps we are also on the verge of discovering new interfaces to the digital realm – ones that do not try to make the body 'disappear' into the screen but instead make full use of the intuitive grasp of space and materiality that is embedded into the very fabric of the body's perceptual and motor apparatus.

The second part of the book brings together chapters that are variously concerned with the possibilities and limits of the digital and moving image. By situating these various techniques in relation to historical debates on the nature of the 'real' and the 'ideal', each of the contributors addresses the problem of representing a three-dimensional world through a two-dimensional surface. Opening this section, Richard Coyne examines the phenomenon of mimicry in nature by considering the instinct towards camouflage and its often excessively wasteful consumption of energy. Historically, nature has been presented as the ultimate referent for art and architecture, no less so than in the revival of organicism that has accompanied recent innovations in digital architecture and the digital image. Coyne argues for a re-assessment of the role of representation from the point of view of Roger Caillois' biological insights into wastage, mimicry and darkness. Like several other contributors, Donald Kunze addresses the role of the body in the perception of architectural drawings. He does this through a complex and multi-layered investigation of the metaphorical power of the representational 'surface' in both cinema and narrative fiction. Drawing on the work of dramatists as diverse as Homer and Hitchcock, he illustrates the subtle rhetorical devices of concealment and delay by which 'meanings are created in advance of their arrival on the screen'.

In a more empirical investigation of contemporary film technologies, Mathanraj Ratinam sets out to test the limits of digital representation and the way it engages specifically with architectural practice. The chapter looks forward at the ways in which digital media are becoming capable of representing the more temporal aspects of architectural experience whilst also looking back to consider historical practices of architectural drawing. The chapter also links to the discussions in the first part of this volume on the nature of perspective representation and the various fraught relationships between two-dimensional images and three-dimensional forms. David Gissen uses the development of an 'air map' by the US Department of Homeland Security as a means to uncover a bio-political visual culture of ventilation and air movement in the representation of the city. By considering contemporary methods of 'drawing air' in relation to a broader analysis of 'vectored space', he emphasises the political economy that drives the way we understand architecture and urbanism. Christina Malathouni's chapter examines the potential of new computer graphics technology to represent novel configurations of form and space that cannot be realised in matter. By situating these developments within a historical perspective, the chapter also relates them to philosophical speculations on the status of the non-material realm. With specific reference to the early-twentieth-century writings of the American architect and stage designer Claude Bragdon, the current debate on the implications of new digital imaging techniques is seen as a symptom of the long-standing tension between idealist and materialist views of 'reality'.

Notes

1   Raymond Tallis, *The Hand: a Philosophical Enquiry into Human Being*, Edinburgh: Edinburgh University Press, 2003.
2   Malcolm McCullough, *Abstracting Craft: the Practiced Digital Hand*, Cambridge, MA: MIT Press, 1996.

Forms in the dark

Nature, waste and digital imitation

Richard Coyne

Introduction

Art imitates nature, according to Stoic philosophy (more precisely 'every art is no more than an imitation of the natural')[1] and some architectural polemicists.[2] Natural systems have long held artists and designers in thrall. Neo-organicism is rife within the putative field of digital architecture where digital media provide the means of realizing organic forms and processes modelled on evolution and genetics.[3] Conjectured architectural environments respond, learn, adapt and grow as if colonies of micro-organisms, corals and inter-breeding communities. In this chapter, I consider the divergent insights of Roger Caillois, in which this 'nature' as embraced in contemporary digital architecture is scarcely recognizable. Caillois' theories draw insights from unlikely natural phenomena, and counter the usual organicist claims that digital processes return us to the benign unity of nature, re-establish coherence between person and environment, provide models of emergent creativity, and models for seamless environments. Caillois is in the company of those descendants of Surrealism (Georges Bataille, Walter Benjamin, Paul de Man) who draw from nature the lessons of wastage, mimicry and darkness, each of which impinges on concepts of digital representation and the image.

Roger Caillois' article *Mimicry and Legendary Psychasthenia* directs attention to the adaptive characteristics of insect species.[4] Anthony Vidler has applied Caillois' insights to Etienne-Louis Boullée's creation of 'dark space'[5] and Elizabeth Grosz to the porosity of spatial boundaries, and the problematic relationships suggested by architecture, philosophy, gender and virtuality.[6] I have deployed Caillois' insights in a study of the uncanny in spatial representation.[7] Here I consider the application of Caillois' conjectures to the issue of computer imagery in detail, drawing on Claudine Frank's recent commentary and compilation of Caillois' papers.[8] Writing in the 1930s, Caillois' paper on mimicry and legendary psychasthenia, along with his paper on the praying mantis,[9] was an acknowledged influence on subsequent interpretations of Freud.

For Caillois, mimicry is a propensity found in all of nature, but most peculiarly in insect species that imitate aspects of their environment (other insects, plants, birds and rocks) ostensibly to ward off or escape predators, but apparently with effect in excess of immediate need. Although the ploy seems to be ineffective in some adaptations, it seems that nature's evolutionary, adaptive processes work towards mimicry, as if for the sake of mimicry itself, opposed to other strategies for survival.

Any student of contemporary genetics would have little difficulty explaining the apparent profligacy and extravagant mimetic displays in nature to which Caillois refers. Arguably, Caillois' understanding of biology fits more comfortably with the obsolete theories of Jean-Baptiste Lamarck, who conjectured that organisms inherit traits acquired somatically by their forebears, than with Charles Darwin's theory of fitness, survival and natural selection. But whatever the account of the mechanism, the phenomenon of mimesis in nature presents to our sensibilities as 'remarkable', itself evidence that psychology and biology are co-implicated in cultural production in ways yet to be exhausted.

Caillois sees the ability of certain species to mimic their environments as indicative of a disturbance in the perception of space for these species, and for us as we contemplate our own unavoidable commitment to mimicry. The creature that mimics a leaf is dislocated. It is at the mercy of its environment, rather than an agent of choice, and without the privileged position of an independent subject. This condition is also apparently manifested in human beings in the case of legendary psychasthenia: a psychological disorder characterized by phobias, obsessions, compulsions or excessive anxiety. It is ultimately a disturbance between personality and space. People with this condition apparently say they know where they are located but do not feel as though, or sense that, they are at that location. For Caillois, legendary psychasthenia exaggerates a condition intrinsic to all of us.

By this reading, the quest for representational realism, exhibited in various traditions of art, science and computer imagery, is already an indication of an aberrant condition, a strange relationship with our environment. We cannot avoid copying and mimicking other things (our environment, spaces, animals, machines, each other). Contrary to implying mastery and control, this tendency towards mimicry indicates their converse, a lack of control, a subjugation to the dictates of our environment. The propensity to mimic has the upper hand over independent agency and subjectivity, and is suggestive of disorientation. In this, Caillois tackles positivist science's all-embracing representational schemas, and, by projection, the idea of the complete digital model, and the chimera of the fully integrated CAD system by which every aspect of the design and construction of architecture is able to be represented and controlled. Under this critique, following Freud and Piaget, the presumption of control is consigned to the realms of infantile futility.

Clearly, the propensity towards photorealism in computer graphics is of a different order of technical and reflective sophistication than the cognitively bland instinct among insect species to look like twigs and leaves. But the biological mechanism is equally profound, and the strong implication of Caillois' polemic is that the ever-present impulse to visual mimicry is in excess of the *need* to reproduce the visual, sonic, tactile or structural properties of our environment. I will survey Caillois' three main themes as they relate to digital representation: wastage, mimicry and darkness.

Representation devours reality

Evolution favours the development of species traits, such as colourings, adornments and courtship rituals that have effloresced to a degree that seems to jeopardize other survival traits, for example by making organisms more visible to predators. Caillois is interested in the self-destructive capacity of such developments, a tendency towards 'dangerous luxury'.[10] Nature is wasteful. Apparently Phyllia are so successful in concealing their identity as insects that they mistake each other's wings for leaves and are known to mistakenly devour one another. In so far as there is a continuity between the life of insects and cultural production, there are resonances here with Freud's concept of the 'death drive'.[11] The profligacy of cultural production is well-presented in Thorstein Veblen's account of the bourgeois tendency to demonstrate power and wealth by showing how wasteful one can be (through conspicuous consumption), even when the wealth is not there,[12] and Marcel Mauss' anthropology of the potlatch, a demonstration of power to an ally by the wilful self-destruction of one's own resources (boats, houses, slaves), in lieu of a gift.[13] I expand on these themes in relation to digital media elsewhere.[14] By some readings, the propensity to wastage in architectural representation is manifested in ornamentation as a means of demonstrating excess capacity in building, and decadence as a condition of self-indulgent excess and decline on the path to self-destruction.

Applying Caillois' reading to film, the tendency to excess is manifested in the medium of digital representation. The entomological countenance of film involves exaggeration, an over-abundance of effects to the point of unreality to make the representations seem even more real than if human actors and physical sets, locations, pyrotechnics, vehicles and machines were involved. The medium develops as if on its own trajectory of improvement, to retain its capability to shock and over-excite the senses and to exceed what has gone before. Needless to say, this unbridled appeal to spectacle is often for the portrayal of conflict and destruction. This is spectacular film, but representations copy across media.[15] Film and computer games feed expectations of other media, such as the more prosaic depictions of architecture using computer animation. The now clichéd use of the ubiquitous 'fly-through' is one manifestation of this propensity towards unreal and excessive effect, as is the 'sensory-overload' presented through mass-media displays, dynamic signage and advertising in urban spaces.

It is commonly supposed that the danger of computer imaging is that we are fooled into believing that what we see is real, that consumption brings fulfilment, children are tempted to believe dinosaurs exist, or wrestle with giant gorillas, that buildings can float in mid-air, all colliding objects explode on impact, and that human lives can be dispatched without consequence. The counter-view is that the trajectory to excess of computer imagery moves us even further away from what we might regard as reality. As Jean Baudrillard points out, there is less danger that we develop false expectations of what reality offers than that such representations present to us as so blatantly false that we think this the only or quintessential presentation of false-hood.[16] We become inured to the unreality of day-to-day existence. Such spectacle leaves in its wake a strong conviction that what is not on the screen is in fact as real as anything can be. The digital representation masks the fact that what is being represen-ted is already a representation, and is permeated with unreality, no less so when we contemplate that many of the criteria we apply to digital falsities apply with greater consequence to life outside CGI (computer-generated imagery): going to war to assert democracy, fighting terror, torturing prisoners and presuming that in this media-saturated age it is feasible to keep secrets. The equivalent unreality of architecture includes the presumption that buildings last forever, economics 'taints' the essence of design, form follows function, architecture portrays forms in light, and the panoply of cultural aphorisms and 'myths' advanced in Roland Barthes' analysis of otherwise unquestioned cultural assumptions.[17]

The implications of Caillois' ento-thesis is that computer imagery is caught in a primal tendency towards excesses in representation that are inevitably manifested in destructive ways. This identification is not to counsel a retreat to 'authentic' modes of representation, but to advocate strategies that take untruth, subterfuge and play as endemic to cultural production. But digital media no longer find their most obvious real-ization in spectacular screen images. There is a counter-ento-tendency within digital media towards inconspicuous behaviour calculated to blend and render invisible.

Machines mimic their environment

Digital media are mimetic in several respects. The computer is deployed to create images, but is also itself presented as an image to be formed and re-configured. Com-mercially available laptops, mobile phones, cameras, navigation devices and countless domestic and office appliances attest to the plastic nature of the digital medium, that at times presents as a means of communication, organisation, entertainment, play or random creation. Software is a highly malleable medium, now abetted by various con-figurations of hardware, and the capability to hook components together. Designers and artists, even when inexpert in electronics, can fashion devices and environments to take on presentations as if working with malleable media, as evident in digital-installation designs that employ sound and movement sensors, projection and net-worked interconnections. The computer here participates in the full play of metaphor, the computer as typewriter, game board, theatre and canvas, a process assisted by the steadily diminishing visibility of the once-essential processor functioning. With miniaturisation, redundancy, and wireless connectivity, the industry is at a stage where microprocessors can be scattered like dust ('specks') across the environment.[18] Computers can be made to look and behave like almost anything we want, and they can also be rendered invisible.

Here the computer assumes something of the character attributed to insect species in Caillois' account. Ubiquity, seamless integration and embodiment have assumed the status of common currency in digital-media literature and research. Paul Dourish, for example, advocates 'tangible computing' where there are 'smoother and more natural forms of interaction and expression' that 'unify computational experience and physical experience', and that 'unify the physical and electronic worlds to create a blend which is more closely matched to our daily experience and abilities'.[19] The laudable aim of this blending signals a double effect. If our machines are to merge seamlessly with our expectations, and with us, then in the process we are bound to assume characteristics that blur our distinctiveness from the machine environment. This is the thrust of Donna Haraway's controversial machine–organicism and the well-publicized phenomenon of the human–machine hybrid known as the cyborg.[20] Insect-like, we blend into our machine environments.

Some Phyllia's leaf disguise is so convincing that their siblings consume them, with no apparent detriment to the gene pool and the proliferation of the species. Caillois' ento-metaphor recalls Marx's trope of the machine, in which, under capitalism, humankind is reduced 'by subdivisions of labour, which transforms the worker's operations more and more into mechanical operations, so that, at a certain point, the mechanism can step into his place'.[21] The play here is with consumerism as consumption, and ultimately consumption of the consumer-labourer by the machine. Identifying this danger need not endorse a retreat to some condition outside industrial production and consumer culture, but away from idealised understandings of representation, and towards a recognition that the inevitable impulse for mimicry is dangerous, and can be appropriated, enjoyed and configured, taking such characteristics into account. The putative architectures of intelligent buildings, responsive environments, invisible computing, ubiquitous communications, wearable devices, are not only benign, but hopefully present a series of dangerous and radical transformations on society and environment, with a challenge not least to the practices of the endangered species of architects, engineers, planners and geographers.

Dark sounds

The computer image is ostensibly a medium of light and of vision, in so far as we require projection to see its representations. Cultures of sound carry different connotations. McLuhan argued for an understanding of sound as the more primal medium, marshalling an engagement between person and environment.[22] It is with the sense of sight that we start to discriminate, divide the world, articulate and establish distance. Contrary to the language of vision, sound designers talk of sound in terms of enveloping, consuming and drawing us in.[23] (Moths are drawn to the light, although only by accident, as the light of the moon is meant to present a stable vector for navigation. If the light source is too close then the insect's trajectory inevitably takes the form of a lethal spiral. According to Connor, the spiral is a sonic form.[24]) Caillois does not address sound in his ento-myth, but deals with darkness. He observes that material objects remove light from our consideration, i.e. we become more aware of the material that reflects light than the immaterial light itself. Contrary to space infused with light, 'darkness is "filled", it touches the individual directly, envelops him, penetrates him, and even passes through him'. Quoting Minkowski, he notes: 'Dark space envelops me on all sides and penetrates me much deeper than light space'.[25] Here darkness, the absence of light, bears the character of sound.

Invisible and ubiquitous computing also bear similar traits to sound and darkness. In so far as ubiquitous computing invokes concepts of embodiment, engagement, and indiscriminate fusion, it presents as part of an immersive field, closer to the experience of sound and the dark.

It need not always be the case, but, unlike sound (and silence), darkness carries the connotations of a deficiency in sensory apparatus, dark practices, suspicion, risk, an absence of life. Caillois highlights the putative bleakness of these environmental spaces, as appropriated by the organism under the spell of mimicry. Spaces are dark, and penetrate and pass through us. Dark space envelops and penetrates deeper than light space. There is also a propensity towards reduced existence, the animate appears as the inanimate. Caillois relates this reduced experience to magic, which recalls Freud's argument about certain events exorcizing infantile beliefs, and invokes thoughts of the covert, and of night.[26] By this reading, mimicry is a dark practice, beyond the pale of rationality, subject to the exercise of suspicion. Digital representations participate in this shady art of mimicry. We can recast the issues of darkness by considering its equivalence in the sonic field. Darkness does not equate to silence, but the whole sonic field. Architecture's dark corners speak loudly of possibility.

Conclusion

If architecture is to imitate nature, then which nature? Architecture is already rightly concerned about the wastage of unsustainable building practices, and turns its back on concepts of nature as profligate and wasteful. The response to the wasted image requires greater nuance. Concepts of emergence, organic forms, patterns of growth and complex dynamic ecologies are suggestive of creation, but are prone to drift into the territory of romantic organicism, leaving aside nature's 'darker' aspects. As a design discipline, architecture is well placed to exploit metaphors of waste, mimicry and darkness, particularly as it contemplates its deployment of the digital image.

Acknowledgements

This work is supported by the Arts and Humanities Research Council. I am grateful to Bruce Currey for drawing my attention to Caillois' paper.

Notes

1   Marcus Aurelius, 1964.
2   Jencks, 1995.
3   Castle, 2004: 5; Wise, 2004: 54–63.
4   Caillois, 1984: 17–32.
5   Vidler, 1995.
6   Grosz, 2001.
7   Coyne, 2005a.
8   Frank, 2003.
9   Caillois, 1934: 23–26; Caillois, 2003.
10   Caillois, 1984, p. 25.
11   Freud, 1990a.
12   Veblen, 1998.
13   Mauss, 1990.
14   Coyne, 2005a.
15   Bolter and Grusin, 1999.
16   Baudrillard, 2001.
17   Barthes, 1973.
18   Arvind and Wong, 2004.
19   Dourish, 2001.
20   Haraway, 1991.
21   Marx, 1977.
22   McLuhan, 1962.
23   Kahn, 2001.
24   Connor, 2005.
25   Caillois, 1984, p. 30.
26   Freud, 1990b.

Bibliography

D.K. Arvind and K.J. Wong, 'Speckled computing: disruptive technology for networked information appliances', in *Proceedings of the IEEE International Symposium on Consumer Electronics (ISCE'04) (UK)*, September 2004.

Marcus Aurelius, *Meditations*, trans. M. Staniforth. London: Penguin, 1964, Manuscript from the second century AD.

Roland Barthes, *Mythologies*, trans. A. Lavers. London: Paladin, 1973.

Jean Baudrillard, 'Simulacra and Simulations', in M. Poster (ed.), *Selected Writings*, Cambridge: Polity, 2001.

J. David Bolter and Richard A. Grusin, *Remediation: Understanding New Media*, Cambridge, MA: MIT Press, 1999.

Roger Caillois, 'La mante religieuse'. *Minotaure*, 5, 1934.

—— 'Mimicry and legendary psychasthenia'. *October*, 31 (winter 1984), 17–32, first published in *Minotaure* in 1935.

—— 'The praying mantis: from biology to psychoanalysis', in C. Frank (ed.), *The Edge of Surrealism*, Durham, NC: Duke University Press, 2003, pp. 69–81.

Helen Castle, editorial to special edition on Emergence: Morphological Design Strategies (guest edited by Michael Hensel, Achim Menges and Michael Weinstock), *Architectural Design*, 74, 3 (2004), 5.

Steven Connor, *Edison's Teeth: Touching Hearing*. Online, available from: www.bbk.ac.uk/english/skc/edsteeth, 2001 (accessed 15 August 2005).

Richard Coyne, *Cornucopia Limited: Design and Dissent on the Internet*, Cambridge, MA: MIT Press, 2005a.

—— 'The digital uncanny: repetition, suspicion and the space of interpretation', in P. Turner and E. Davenport (eds), *Spatiality, Spaces and Technology*, Dordrecht: Kluwer, RAE 2007, pp. 5–18.

P. Dourish, *Where the Action Is: the Foundations of Embodied Interaction*, Cambridge, MA: MIT Press, 2001.

Claudine Frank (ed.), *The Edge of Surrealism: a Roger Caillois Reader*, trans. C. Frank and C. Naish, Durham, NC: Duke University Press, 2003.

Sigmund Freud, 'Beyond the pleasure principle', in A. Richards (ed.), *The Penguin Freud Library, Volume 11: On Metapsychology*, Harmondsworth, Middlesex: Penguin, 1990a, pp. 269–338, first published in German in 1920.

—— 'The "uncanny"', in A. Dickson (ed.), *The Penguin Freud Library, Volume 14: Art and Literature*, Harmondsworth, Middlesex: Penguin, 1990b, pp. 335–376, first published in German in 1919.

Elizabeth Grosz, *Architecture from the Outside: Essays on Virtual and Real Space*, Cambridge, MA: MIT Press, 2001.

Donna J. Haraway, *Simians, Cyborgs, and Women: the Reinvention of Nature*, London: FAb, 1991.

Charles Jencks, *The Architecture of the Jumping Universe, A Polemic: How Complexity Science is Changing Architecture and Culture*, London: Academy Editions, 1995.

Douglas Kahn, *Noise, Water, Meat: a History of Sound in the Arts*, Cambridge, MA: MIT Press, 2001.

Marshall McLuhan, *The Gutenberg Galaxy: the Making of Typographic Man*, Toronto: University of Toronto Press, 1962.

Karl Marx, 'Grundrisse', in D. McClellan (ed.), *Karl Marx: Selected Writings*, Oxford: Oxford University Press, 1977, pp. 245–387, written 1857–1858 and first published in German in 1941.

Marcel Mauss, *The Gift: the Form and Reason for Exchange in Archaic Societies*, trans. W.D. Halls, New York: W. W. Norton, 1990, first published in French in 1925.

Thorstein Veblen, *The Theory of the Leisure Class*, Amherst: Promethius, 1998, first published in 1899.

Anthony Vidler, *The Architectural Uncanny: Essays in the Modern Unhomely*, Cambridge, MA: MIT Press, 1995.

Chris Wise, 'Drunk in an orgy of technology', *Architectural Design*, 74, 3 (2004), 54–63.

Concealment, delay and topology in the creation of wondrous drawing

Donald Kunze

Introduction

The architectural drawing uses surface effects to set up, in the imagination, a symmetry between spaces of reception and locales of presentation. The drawing could be considered as a 'thinking machine' whose surpluses and gaps create openings for *ingenium*, metaphoric constructs that involve not just witty ideas but structural duets between subjects and objects, heres and theres, nows and thens. This graphic practice amounts to an 'anamorphic' mode of perception through concealment. To understand the drawing process, the study of cinema can provoke new angles of inquiry, particularly in the case of directors who 'storyboard' their plots, framing scenes as 'emblems'. In particular, Alfred Hitchcock's films provide ample evidence of dynamic anamorphosis on behalf of meanings that are created in advance of their arrival on screen. Hitchcock's intuitive and prescient use of the 'MacGuffin' – a gratuitous detail, which underwrites the audience's imaginative movement into the work of art – summarizes the wit of the architectural drawing as a strategy of concealment and delay.

Mad paper

Most projections eventually cease to be projections. This can be as simple a matter as intended, or unintended, destruction – holding a match to a map, or using a newspaper to wrap fish. The more interesting case is where this end is also the end, the limit, of the *idea* of projection. There's the funny situation of the country described by Jorge Luis Borges, where the rage for accurate maps led to drawing them at 1:1 scale.[1] The result was that this perfect map covered the whole country and consequently became useless. Borges may have simply intended to lampoon the correspondence theory of truth, but he raised an interesting question: what exactly would this 'end of representation' be like?

This question has occurred to thoughtful artists of other ages. John Donne felt that it was necessary to persuade the paper he used to write his poems to put up with the more extreme of his authorial ambitions. In his poem, 'To Mrs. M. H.', he wrote:

> Mad paper stay, and grudge not here to burne
> With all those sonnes whom my braine did create,
> At lest lye hid with mee, till thou returne
> To rags againe, which is thy native state.[2]

Donne's paper is apparently threatening to walk off the job; but, when instruments of representation rebel against their masters, aren't they simply living up to representation's claim to imitate life? If representation holds to its goal of exactitude, shouldn't it accept the unintended consequences of animated and empowered artifacts, which, once they gain a mind of their own, have other plans? Doesn't the 'end of representation', theoretically and anecdotally, involve the creation of a Golem, a Frankenstein's monster? 'Mad paper', when it gets really mad, rebels not just against the author but authorship in general; not just against a particular assigned role, but against the whole idea of intentionality in representation.

The Russian author of *Black Snow*, Mikhail Bulgakov (1968), suggests that this radical failure of intentionality might be more entertaining than what intentionality first had in mind. Having completed what he feels to be a bland novel, the novelist–narrator notices that the pages of his book have turned into a 1930s version of a video screen:

> I began to feel that something colored was emerging from the white pages. After staring at it and screwing up my eyes I was convinced that it was a picture – and a picture that was not flat but three-dimensional like a box. Through the lines on the paper I could see a light burning and inside the box those same characters in the novel were moving about. It was a delightful game and more than once I regretted that my cat was dead and there was no one to whom I could show these people moving about in that tiny little room.[3]

It is quite amazing that Bulgakov seems to have anticipated the age of the word processor, where the screen has taken over the job of the paper, sometimes as an intermediary, sometimes as an outright usurper. Mad pixels, stay!

The inside gap

To make this clear, let me try to define the function of this 'wondrous' artifact residing *inside* the representation process, the paper or pixels 'with an attitude'. An extreme but most definitive case would be the controversial 'Shroud of Turin', reputed to be the original cover of the prone corpse of Christ. Its cloth retains a direct transfer of what seems to be a body image. This ectoplasmic transfer collapses the sagittal distance of projection between representation and the represented. When the sagittal collapses, its related interests fail, such as the convention of authorial contrivance. No distance, no dissembling; hence, authenticity. But, is it possible to simulate this collapse inside the work of art, as a carefully laid trap? And, more importantly, can this 'end of representation', though purposefully planned, still lead to an experience of authenticity?

In Alfred Hitchcock's well-known film, *Vertigo* (1958), Scotty, a retired policeman recovering from a traumatic event involving falling, is doing a favor for an acquaintance, Gavin Elster, well-to-do owner of a ship-construction company. The magnate asks Scotty to follow his wife, Madeleine, who, Elster fears, is in danger of a nervous breakdown. She seems obsessed with the idea that she is the reincarnation of a long-dead *Latina*, Carlotta Valdez. Scotty agrees to take the job. He follows Madeleine around, spying on her as she sits in an art museum before Carlotta's portrait, spends time in the boarding house that was Carlotta's home, and takes flowers to Carlotta's grave. Finally, he intercedes in her attempted suicide beneath the San Francisco Bay Bridge. He is fascinated by the beautiful Madeleine and begins to half-believe in her fantasy. Now playing the role of the tragic lover, Madeleine leads Scotty to an old Spanish monastery. Because of his fear of heights, he fails to prevent her fatal jump from the bell tower. Scotty is devastated.

Weeks later, Scotty encounters a woman who bears a striking resemblance to Madeleine. He pursues and finally confronts her. Judy, a shop-girl living in a cheap apartment, is a tawdry version of Madeleine. Nonetheless, he is unable to relinquish his obsession. Judy reluctantly allows him to remake her in the image of the dead Madeleine. Scotty, however, discovers a piece of jewelry that had actually belonged to Madeleine – a ruby necklace just like the one in Carlotta's portrait in the museum. He realizes that the shop-girl was hired to play the part of the wife, enacting the presumed delusion by visiting the museum and cemetery and by attempting suicide to cover up the real murder of the real wife. Elster had established his innocence with the fake back-story of suicidal delusion. Scotty forces Judy to return to the monastery to replay the murder scene; this time the fake takes the fall.

The epistemology of *Vertigo* is quite complex. Analysis must begin with the recognition of the anamorphic functionality of the 'Judy–Madeleine' device. This is an 'appearance machine', which operates from inside *Vertigo*, sustaining all of its dramatic organisms. Judy is the artifact behind the created mask of Madeleine. Be careful, however. Madeleine is not a 'copy' of Elster's wife, but a creation made only to engage Scotty. She's like other Hitchcock creations, such as the spy, Kaplan, in *North by Northwest* (1959), a fictional invention of the CIA maintained to distract KGB spies. When an advertising executive, Walter Thornhill, is mistaken for Kaplan by the Russians, he can't prove his innocence because his double doesn't exist. This anamorph is 'pure' – not the distortion of some authentic original but the creation of the Real out of a durable difference. It is the distilled essence of the famous Hitchcockian 'MacGuffin' – a 'gratuitous' invention required to justify the audience's interest. In the case of *Vertigo*, the audience is Scotty.

To use a mathematical analogy, 'Judy–Madeleine' is an 'operator' with the same zero-degree status as Kaplan. In the main plot, she – or 'they'? (Isn't it time for James Joyce's 'twone'?) – facilitates the ruse of engaging Scotty to be the credible witness of Madeleine's 'suicide'. Elster can set up the death of his wife at the tower of the monastery because he knows in advance that Scotty will be traumatized by the climb up the tower stairs. Judy can step into the shadows just before the real wife is pushed out. The Janusian monster, Judy–Madeleine, is a dramatic device, but it's important to recognize the anamorphic function. Judy is able to play Madeleine in the main ruse, where her sophistication seems genuine. When Judy is discovered later, however, she can't scrub off her shop-girl persona. Her speech is common, her gestures rough. Despite our knowledge that she is in fact the original article, the *difference* is the anamorphic insulation that keeps Scotty from discovering the truth. Paradoxically, this failure establishes something like a 'super-identity' – a durable ideal of the self, based on a complete 'lack of substance'!

The anamorphic function oscillates between extreme 'off–on' settings. It has no mediating middle values, no compromise. It's either Judy or Madeleine. This is important, since the Judy–Madeleine machine keeps 'ruse plot' (Scotty in love with Madeleine) from crossing the 'restoration plot' (Scotty remaking Judy in Madeleine's image). Both plots can survive independently as long as the Judy–Madeleine machine is a 'square wave' that oscillates between two values without stopping at intermediate values.

The ruse plot (Madeleine's delusion) is basically a theatrical presentation designed to enchant Scotty. As an ideal audience, Scotty enters fully into the illusion of Madeleine. He is the very model of the 'hot detective', the one who loses perspective by foregoing detachment for direct interaction with the one he is paid to investigate. The 'Big Other', to use a term from Lacan, in this ruse plot is the hollow edifice of the murder scheme. By coincidence, the architectural model for this is the hollow square monastery tower with its interior labyrinthine stair.[4] Scotty's fear of falling is paralleled by the real wife's real exterior fall. When Judy slips up by wearing the same necklace she had used as 'Madeleine' in her visits to the museum, Scotty realizes that the basis of the 'plot' is hollow, that Madeleine 'does not exist', that Judy is and was the only Madeleine, constructed to assure his testimony at the inquest of Elster's truly dead wife.

The Madeleine–Judy machine works from the inside of these dramatic forms, works anamorphically, and is fundamentally *optical*. Throughout the film, Scotty finds Madeleine and Judy through windows, mirrors, and in museum portraits. She is constantly disappearing–appearing, slipping out, popping up. The theme of appearance is materialized in the jewel, the fake ruby necklace made up to resemble the one in Carlotta's portrait. It's a fake, but this only underscores its more powerful status as 'Real' with a capital 'R'! It's the surplus object *par excellence*, the item 'out of place' that sutures together both the ruse plot and the restoration plot. The Judy–Madeleine machine is the link and key to this suture.

The jewel is a stand-in, an objectification, of Judy, the shop-girl who is the hopeless fake but in fact none other than the authentic 'wife'. The term 'real fake' is best approached with Gilles Deleuze's idea of the *demark*, the sign that stands out, that does not fit into the natural order. Other Hitchcockian *demarks* include the monogrammed cigarette lighter in *Strangers on a Train*, the belt of the raincoat in *Young and Innocent*, the windmill turning backwards in *The Lady Vanishes*, or the downward-growing zinnias in *Rear Window*. One common quality that hints at the secret of the *demark* is what Michael Rifatterre called 'fictional truth' – a falsehood that, in the right context, becomes insuperably authentic. We're reminded of the combination of denial and truth that formed the authentic detail for Giovanni Morelli's theory of art authenticity – picked up by no less a figure than Sigmund Freud in his formulation of the idea of the unconscious use of the discarded detail as an indicator of psychic truth.

Just another nobody

The Madeleine–Judy machine works as a 'zero-degree' device. It creates an internal, anamorphic 'face' that establishes authentic identity ('whodunit') by undermining the whole question of identity in a radical way. There is no Madeleine just as there is no Judy, but together they are, as champions of non-existence, ladies of the night where, as Hegel would have put it, 'all cows are black'. The machine is a hinge between universal (the paragon of beauty, Madeleine) and the particular, Judy, the 'actual' flesh-and-blood actress hired to play Madeleine. The coupling of such a monstrous form in a single person is a form of antonomasia, the rhetorical figure of the name derived from a quality or a particular person. Hitchcock provides examples of each. In *The 39 Steps* (1935), an otherwise nameless performer is called 'Mr. Memory'. In the reverse direction, particular-to-universal, Hitchcock's famous device, borrowed from Angus McPhail, is the 'MacGuffin'. The figure of antonomasia shows the role of the name in mediating the universal and particular, the material and the ideal.

The issues of identity, name and antonomasia are not abstract. They arise in literature as questions of the non-person, the nobody, the stranger, the liminal being; in the shadowy background of myth and folklore are the traditions of the period 'between the two deaths' – journey between the death of the body and the final rest of the soul. These sources suggest that, for this crucial interval, blindness trumps vision; silence trumps speech; projection is collapsed and touch takes its place. This is where Truth itself speaks, but how?

Stereognosis, 'knowledge of the world through touch', can be represented only in terms of topography. An appropriately radical position would be to insist that this topography be forced to retain its experiential and temporal basis: a sequence of encounters encoded by topographical qualities of 'contingency', 'handedness' (left–right relations), and mirror-symmetry relationships (the face; the 'idiotic symmetry' of self-reference and recursion). Stereognosis might well be the official technical term for the failure of projective representation, and its official emblem might well be the Cretan labyrinth, the meander whose only variable is forward–backward – a reduction of space to the ultimate determination of facing.

Stereognosis, as we might expect, cannot be satisfactorily explained in projective terms. Analogies and examples fall short because they rely on what stereognosis precisely prohibits. Art teaches us, however, that stereognosis can be *experienced* in encounters that are structured by its logic. This means that the critic–theoretician must occupy the role of the audience and consider the *condition of the audience* as a constitutive ingredient for all theoretical constructs. This condition has been formalized through the syllogism known as the 'enthymeme'. In the zone where philosophy and rhetoric meet, we have the rhetorical syllogism, the 'If A is B and B is C then A is C' arrangement of propositions that Medieval logicians classified into nineteen forms, giving them such alluring names as 'Barbara' and 'Camestres'. The rhetorical syllogism, the enthymeme, treats the audience, like Donne's paper, as both mind and body, universal and particular. First: the audience is sitting in the auditorium thinking, 'now we are to watch something of some importance (or not)'. Second: the audience is disembodied and placed within the work – what film theorists who had read Lacan came to describe as 'suture', or localization of the audience inside a scene or character within the fictional representation.

The syllogism's classic form can be expressed using the 'calculus' of George Spencer-Brown, whose axioms could translate (and correct) Boolean logic into the terms of boundary crossings and 'calls'.[5] The complex sorites of Lewis Carroll can be dispatched quickly using Spencer-Brown's notation by identifying 'silent pairings' (B and B-cross in the figure below). The ruse of the interior face, the 'nobody', can be visualized through the function of the syllogism, where the middle term, B, stands for the audience's relation to the speaker and the speech. B and B-cross are the internal, self-silencing, self-referential Janusian audience; the 'antonomasia' that is simultaneously universal and particular.

Spencer-Brown's calculus uses one symbol, the angle, to represent both a boundary and, curiously, a 'call'. In art and literature, spatial divisions (entrapment, liminal crossings, temporal observations, etc.) are frequently coupled with the magical or ironic use of the name. Doors open with a magical word; an enemy is admitted under false pretences. For example, in the story of Narcissus, a mirror boundary undermines a case of self-identity and is tied to the punishment of Echo, whose desire is restricted to repeating the last word of the other (anacoluthon). An even more compact formulation can be found in the Homeric story of Odysseus's encounter with the Cyclops.

The Homeric tribe of Cyclopes was known for their lack of hospitality. Their name is the anthropological adjective for societies who, living in isolation, treated

The syllogistic form of the enthymeme, with the self-referential 'middle term', shown in the 'standard' and condensed calculus of George Spencer-Brown.

strangers as enemies or food and followed only the severe laws of their gods of the hearth. Odysseus wished to find out if the Cyclops Polyphemus could be persuaded to offer the Greeks the traditional host's gifts. Polyphemus refuted this thesis by imprisoning the Greeks inside his labyrinthine cave so that he might devour them at his leisure. The episode is structured by the witty tricks Odysseus employed to escape this cave prison. First, Odysseus blinded the one-eyed giant – possible only because the Cyclops had only one eye. Second, Odysseus presciently gave the Cyclops a fake name, telling him never to forget that 'Nohbdy' had blinded him. The literal-minded Cyclops accepted this pronoun as a 'particular' proper name (antonomasia), but his later use of it would be heard as a pronoun by his Cyclopean neighbours. This puts the Cyclops in the position of the audience, whose alternation between universal (consumer of artwork) and particular (element inside the work of art) is effaced in the suspension of disbelief. Whereas the audience voluntarily takes on this ignorance on behalf of the possible experience of art, the Cyclops is, involuntarily, ignorant of the difference. The third trick was a parody of hypotaxis, or subordination. The Cyclops counted his sheep by touch carefully as they were released each day to pasture, but the Greeks hung beneath the sheep. The sheep-men subverted the 'transitive order' of the cave by creating a 'monstrous' double the Cyclops could not detect.

'Topography' here involves not just the cave's transitive space in contrast to an 'intransitive' escape, but the common logic behind the tricks that form a tight sequence, a necessary order. Is there a connection linking these tricks and their common structure to travel space? The key lies in the 'internal mirror effect' provided by the enthymeme. The tricks were initiated with the shift from a visual to a tactile (stereognostic) basis, the blinding of the Cyclops. As a thoroughgoing literalist, the Cyclops had only one 'track' (= hearth or 'eye'), just as his cave had only one entrance and channel. The Cyclops' mono-logic was vulnerable to the sophistication of hypotaxis (subordination) in contrast to parataxis (one thing after another – the line of sheep). The 'middle term' of concealment, the antonomasia of 'Nohbdy', finished the game.

The meaning of 'Nohbdy' as a pronoun 'lay beneath' its use as a proper name, and so the antonomasia was 'silent' to the single-minded giant. The use of the name – particularly as an anacoluthon, where the last 'word' radically revises the meaning of preceding actions – and the theme of the 'nobody' comes in a single informative package. It is not for nothing that the Cyclops has (precociously) the fabled single eye of perspectival representation. As the enthymeme of the audience predicts, the central gap, the place of the nobody, is also crucially the place of the name; and the name is the key to a critical crossing or escape.

Odysseus shows the way for the audience, which is, like paper or pixels, always both itself and not itself, a 'Nohbdy'. The body sitting in the hard auditorium seat, coughing or staying quiet, must also be no-body, the correspondent soul transported into the fictional truth of the work of art. This quick and dirty solution to the famous 'mind–body problem' is actually something of a philosophical oddity, the formula of self-reference, a circular motion whereby the signifier, like Zeno's Achilles chasing the tortoise, never quite catches up with the signified, not because it's not faster and more mobile, easy to fold like the perfect representation, but because its time is of a different order, unable to synch up with the time of the represented, like a soundtrack that's a millisecond slower or faster than the moving lips of the characters in a cinema – an 'artifact' that reminds us that we're watching something artificial, imperfect, second-hand. For the drawing, this means that dialectic and time, not projective geometry, are generative and fundamental.

Topology and the logic of self-reference

Self-reference is easier to swallow when it's not an accident of production but something purposefully set to the service of rhetoric. This is when it becomes the basis of a joke, and hence the won-over affection of the audience, or the subject of ridicule, when the audience gets a good laugh at the expense of the speaker, accidentally or on purpose (cf. the political rally in Hitchcock's *The 39 Steps* or the auction scene in *North by Northwest*).

The audience as enthymemic body–soul is an audience between two deaths. The first death is separation of the soul from the body in the usual sense; the disembodiment initiated by imagination. The second is the 'death' brought about by the end of the artistic illusion, when characters either die or get married, if one follows the traditional formulas of tragedy and comedy. 'Between-the-two-deaths' is of course an anthropological stand-by: the interval of mourning set equal to the imagined journey of the soul in the underworld. Detached from funeral practice, it is the *katabasis*, the journey of the hero (originally meaning simply 'a dead person') in the same underworld, figured as a labyrinth, on a quest of retrieval (Hercules' recovery of Alcestis, Orpheus' rescue of Eurydice). In the everyday world, there is a simpler explanation: the escape of the subject by means of fantasy projection. Overwhelmed by the demands of the 'networks of symbolic relationships' – the real meaning of 'symbolic castration', not a symbolization of castration but a castration *by* symbols – the subject must 'de-realize' him/herself by entering into the *a-symbolic* realm of the Real.

How can fantasy projection, nothing less than the *locus* of art, be a-symbolic? There are various answers to this question: the 'demark' of Deleuze, the MacGuffin and nobodies of Hitchcock, the antonomasiacs of Homer and other ancient authors. When 'nobody's home', the puzzle, paradox and paranormal take over. Every road's a Möbius band, we know everything without knowing anything. Without a map, topology rules: we know the world through the left–right touch of the body (stereognosis) and we know the body through the a-logic of what Slavoj Žižek would call 'organs without bodies', or 'desire' liberated from the consensus of the *corp*-oration.[6]

Notes

1   Jorge L. Borges, 'On Exactitude in Science', in *Collected Fictions*, trans. A. Hurley, London: Penguin Group, 1998, p. 325.
2   John Donne, *c.*1607.
3   Mikhail Bulgakov, *Black Snow,* 1936–9, trans. Michael Glenny, 1968, p. 54.
4   References to Lacan in this chapter are general. For the standard introduction, see Jacques Lacan, *Écrits*, trans. Bruce Fink, New York: W.W. Norton & Company.
5   George Spencer-Brown, *Laws of Form*, London: Allen & Unwin, 1969.
6   Slavoj Žižek, *Organs Without Bodies: on Deleuze and Consequences*, New York: Routledge, 2004.

A digital renaissance

Reconnecting architectural representation and
cinematic visual effects

Mathanraj Ratinam

Introduction

How might emergent techniques of digital visualisation and representation enhance
the way we design architectural spaces? This chapter seeks to explore what architecture can learn from technologies developed in other fields, specifically considering the
potential application of cinematic visual effects for proposing architectural schemes.

There was a period in history when the field of visual effects was not
dominated by production houses in Hollywood, but sat clearly within the domain of
architecture. This chapter investigates how contemporary architecture can reclaim a
relationship to visual effects by looking back to the Renaissance and the Baroque and
looking forward to the innovative techniques used by production studios. The practice-
based research of this chapter is concerned with how visual-effects techniques used in
film might introduce more appropriate models for communicating architectural ideas.
The thesis is three-fold: first claiming the disciplinary relevance of an ocular-centric
approach, then expediently noting the time-saving technical advantages and, lastly,
promoting the phenomenological appropriateness of the moving image.

The research is particularly concerned with the area of visual effects that
focuses on ocular-centric techniques that begin, process and output in perspective
with little or no empirical input. By moving away from empirically measured methods
and towards a privileging of the view, we can use digital representation to critique
work in progress, indirectly enhancing the act of designing and the architectural
outcome. The significance of this interdisciplinary exchange lies not in the technological opportunities alone, for it is in this shift from analytical visualisation to interpretative representation that we can capture, investigate and explore the dynamic and
ephemeral dimensions of architectural space.

The relationships between film and architecture have been frequently
remarked upon, although much of this interest has focused on the literal depiction of
architecture within films. In these cases, architecture has often played a role in terms
of set design and scene backdrops, or as the subject in architectural documentaries.

Uninterested in the merely literal connections between the two disciplines, writers such as Juhani Pallasmaa[1] and Norman Klein[2] have discussed the ability of various film-making structures to convey an understanding of space and other ephemeral qualities shared by architecture. Pallasmaa and Klein concentrate on the poetics of representation and its cultural significance across disciplines. They both locate many of their thoughts not only in the overlap between architecture and film but in the moments when qualities from one discipline are able to transcend and even enlighten the other.

Aided by digital means, we have more recently seen a merging of the disciplines. Architectural practitioners such as Greg Lynn[3] and Lars Spuybroek[4] have explored and promoted techniques of film and animation that generate architectural forms which have also been widely explored in academia. But what about other relationships between film and architecture? Could animation have another role in the way it aids the architectural process?

This research project is framed by the broad question of critiquing and speculating upon the role of representation in architecture. In the specific case study recounted here, the aim was to investigate contemporary modes and techniques of digital representation, with a particular interest in those being employed by the visual-effects industry in cinema. The ambition was to re-appropriate these techniques to help to communicate architectural ideas whilst enquiring of their link to historical practices of architectural representation. Most importantly, the aim was to consider how a new approach could be used to critique a piece of architecture as the design develops, rather than communicate the outcome or, as formerly mentioned, be used to generate architectural form.

Digital panoramas and photogrammetry

To begin, two of these visual effects techniques need to be unpacked and explained before considering their involvement in the project and their relevance to architectural representation. There are two techniques that I have been investigating.

First, the most commonly understood and experienced are digital panoramas. These panoramas are made by digitally stitching together a series of photographic images of a scene that can be viewed through freely available software known as 'players'. Within the player there are a number of mapping methods used to project the panorama on what could be described as a room interior in which the viewer is located, and within which the viewer is able to rotate. The mapping, for the sake of the analogy, could be thought of as how the panoramic image would be wallpapered to the surface of the room. The projection method (and the shape of the room) can be spherical, cubical or cylindrical. However, there are no distinguishable differences when viewing a spherical or a cubical projection as their differences lie more in the production of the panoramas, as will be later explained.

The second technique, photogrammetry, has existed since 1851 as a technique for measuring objects from photographs.[5] The use of photogrammetry for architecture dates back to 1858 when the architect Albrecht Meydenbauer developed techniques to document buildings for preservation and rebuilding.[6] In simple terms, this can be thought of as reverse-engineering the technique used to generate a perspective view from a measured orthogonal drawing. As the photograph is a perspective with a central vanishing point, with basic information on the lens used to capture the image, measurements can be extracted through calculus. Digital advances have meant that photogrammetry has developed significantly whereby, using the same photographs, it is now possible for objects to be remodelled in a three-dimensional environment and textured. This method begins by collecting multiple images of the same object taken from different points of view. By locating common points in each of the photographs, such as the corner of a building or the edge of a window, one can position the photographs in space relative to the way they were taken. Once measurements are calibrated, a digital 3D model can be derived from the photographs and then the original photographs can be projected onto the 3D model to render its texture and describe its materials.

Visual-effects techniques and perspective

There is a strong connection between the visual-effect techniques of photogrammetry and panoramas – as well as Image Based Rendering[7] and 3D camera tracking[8] – and Renaissance investigations of perspective. What all the aforementioned techniques have in common, as with most techniques in visual effects, is that they are all ocular-centric techniques – as they begin with, develop through and output via perspective. Movie-making works entirely in perspective, as all images are captured through the lens, and for this reason almost all the technologies that have been developed for visual effects are based around the principles of perspective.

These contemporary techniques are arguably similar, and even derivative of, the investigations and debates around perspective that occurred through the Renaissance. The mathematics at the root of these techniques, in principle, is based on the same calculus. Digital methods employed in the visual-effects area in cinema, I would argue, are the contemporary digital perspective machines that Leonardo da Vinci, Brunelleschi and others were experimenting with in their time. In proposing this, I also take the position that such artists and architects were at that time also creating visual effects. One example of this is the vault of the nave decorated by Andrea Pozzo in Sant'Ignazio, Rome.

To help paint the vault, Pozzo developed and used his own *quadratura* technique whereby a candle would be placed in the space at eye level and above it, toward the ceiling, a grid constructed of string. The light from the candle would cast shadows from the string onto the ceiling, which would act as a guide to distort and transfer the fresco image to the surface of the architecture. When the eye of the viewer is located at the privileged position of the candle flame, regardless of the geometry that made up the ceiling, the image would fall into alignment. The ceiling would cease to be a

Ceiling of Sant'Ignazio, Rome, decorated by Andrea Pozzo (1684–1685).

painted image and would become an extension of the physical architecture, appearing to dissolve the ceiling and allowing the architecture to continue toward the sky.

The *quadratura* method used in Sant'Ignazio suggests two things. First, that the position of the flame and eye is significant to the technique and has a fixed position, and second, as the grid mesh was parallel to the floor and the image had a central vanishing point, the fixed position would need to be in the centre of the room in order to convincingly extend the geometries of the physical architecture into the painting. The *quadratura* method has a relation to both the viewer and the architecture that the viewer is within, as its repeated aim had been to extend the architecture beyond its physicality.[9] More specifically, in the case of the Sant'Ignazio, it appears to extend the ideology of the church by merging heaven and architecture through the fresco image.

This practice is still exercised heavily today, not so much in church and architecture, but in cinema and set design. The camera lens supplants the position of the eye, allowing the physically built set in the immediate foreground to extend to the painted and digital backdrops. This practice raises an important issue. Before the medium of film, visual effects used to sit clearly in the domain of architecture. This research is interested in how architecture can reclaim some of the techniques used in contemporary visual effects to better communicate architectural ideas. By re-appropriating contemporary techniques in visual effects, this research may also begin to test the limits of digital representation.

Digital model-making

The *quadratura* technique can help shed light on how contemporary representational practices in architecture can be improved. Currently, the technique used to create 3D rendered views of architecture and interiors follows a traditional and empirical process (see figure below). Beginning with a two-dimensional plan, one extrudes and constructs three dimensional forms. Textures are then scaled and applied to the surfaces. Thereafter, a camera is placed within the scene to render a perspective view. This approach to digital modelling comes from the legacy of physical model-making where the same process is used with cardboard and wood. Yet the ends of a physical model and a digital model, except in the case of digital prototyping, are very different. A physical model has the qualities of tangibility, massing, understanding the play of light and how materials react with each other, some of which are even measurable. But a rendering provides physically flat 3D views, often distorted beyond how we might really see the form and without influence of gravity.

This approach creates two problems. First, transferring the process of a physical model-making to digital modelling suggests that the digital is a more 'advanced' method for creating models when we know their roles in architectural representation to be distinctly different. And this leads to a larger crisis, as we've seen today, of digital models replacing physical models in the practice of architecture. The second problem concerns the empirical nature of producing digital models when the final output will be physically flat perspective views printed or displayed on a screen. In relying upon the technique used for creating physical models, the digital model is accurately measured during its construction but its results are not measurable. Both these problems suggest that, if the outcomes of a physical and digital model are very different, the process used to create a digital model should be reconsidered.

In the case of Sant'Ignazio the *quadratura* technique casts shadows onto a cylindrical vault with cuttings for the windows. But as the form of the ceiling can vary and still produce the same impression when viewed from the intended position, we can reconsider how the *quadratura* grid can also be altered to produce the same outcome. Working upon the same principal of shadow casting, rather than thinking of it as a grid of strings working as guides for the image, we can rethink the image as having been painted onto a glass lantern with the candle in the middle which would

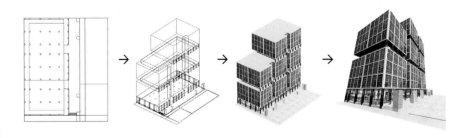

A conventional process of digitally modelling an architectural form.

also cast shadows onto the surrounding walls. The painting on the lantern is essentially a panoramic image running seamlessly around the lantern.

Constructing a panoramic image

To practice such an approach today, we digitally construct the panoramic image of the lantern by beginning, in this case, with a site. The City Square in Melbourne, Australia, has gone through a number of design changes. Because of its history, it appeared to be an appropriate testing ground for this technique and a suitable site for a new design. Digital photographs were taken from a fixed position that would tile together resulting in a spherical panorama (see the first and second figures below). Viewed through a player, one can pan, tilt and zoom in and out of the panorama. In zooming out as far as the player allowed, one can distort the image to present what appears to be a 2D-elevation view of the neighbouring hotel (third figure below). This is, in fact, a single-point perspective with the vanishing point located at the centre of the image. However, as the vertical and horizontal lines are parallel, it begs the question: if measurements could be extracted from this image, could it be considered a rendered orthogonal drawing?

Source images used for stitching together a panorama.

Preview stitch of panorama.

The sandy area in front of the hotel is the City Square and, in order to consider it as a site for a speculative intervention, the existing design needs to be cleared of the eucalyptus trees in the image. In removing the trees, the areas of hotel the trees occlude need to be painted back into the image. This can be done accurately by converting the spherical panorama to a cubical panorama, allowing the content of the image that needs to be painted back in to align with the grid of pixels that make up the image (first figure below). This is precisely for the purposes of cloning other areas of the image, such as the windows and brick patterns, over the pixels occupied by the trees (second figure below). Even in the cases where the hotel was in perspective, the facade can be perspective-corrected, retouched and distorted back into perspective (third figure below). When the editing is complete, the image is ready to be converted back to a spherical panorama for importing into a 3D-modelling and rendering program.

Once imported, the panorama is mapped, or wallpapered, onto the inside of a sphere and a camera is placed precisely at its centre. Essentially, this panoramic

Converting the spherical panorama to a cubical panorama (both unwrapped).

Digitally touching up the image to remove the vegetation.

Perspective correcting the facade in order to remove vegetation, then distorting it back into the original view.

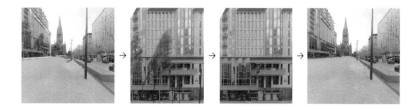

sphere is a digital recreation of the glass lantern and candle arrangement with the flame being replaced by the camera (first figure above). From the view of the camera, the image is aligned but, more importantly, the lens distortion has also been removed. To consider how an architectural proposal might be viewed within this environment, a modest design of an undulating grass surface is created and placed within the sphere to act as the intervention (second figure above). This design is orthogonal and measured, unlike the panorama which by its nature as a spherical image is highly distorted. Due to the removal of the lens distortion, the panorama and the 3D-generated design align in three-point perspective (third figure above). This arrangement is similar to both Sant'Ignazio, through the seamless merging of the physical geometry of the church in

Reconverted back to a spherical panorama, it is mapped to the inside of a sphere with a camera at its centre.

An undulating field of grass. This geometry is measured and modelled digitally in 3D.

The measured geometry of the grass field and the spherically mapped background cleanly align in three-point perspective.

the foreground and *trompe l'oeil* on the ceiling, as well as set designs for cinema with a physically built set close to the camera and the painted backdrop beyond it.

However, this is only a digital recreation of what appears in Sant'Ignazio. It is not a recreation of the experience of being within the church. In Sant'Ignazio, as one stares upward at the fresco painting with the horizon no longer within the peripheral view, one becomes partially unbalanced and the experience becomes dizzying. This dizziness, I would argue, is an essential part of the interaction with the *trompe l'oeil*, inducing the viewer into believing the painted extension of the interior and the fantasy it depicts. Such an ephemeral quality can never be recreated digitally. Nonetheless, the digital model presents opportunities otherwise unavailable in the physical world.

Allowing for movement

With examples such as Sant'Ignazio, the adventure begins when a viewer enters the space and sees the fresco painting overhead and continues walking until he or she has found the position it is intended to be viewed from, where the image and interior are aligned. From here, movement in any direction only causes the effect to collapse, but what if one could move into and occupy the space of the image? In the physical environment it would seem that this occupation of the image is impossible other than through the imagination. What I will explain below is how, through the deployment of specific techniques, this effect of occupying the image can be achieved digitally. Furthermore, this technique has so far only referenced a historic and physically practised method of representation, but from here on it begins to branch out to create a result that would be physically impossible.

By building what I will refer to as billboards in the digital sphere in place of buildings and geometry found in the panoramic image, these billboards can receive the same projection (or shadows from the candle, as it were) and would act as proxies for the painted geometry in the image. This, in effect, is crudely modelling within the interior space of the sphere what exists in the image mapped to the surface of the sphere. This allows the camera to move away from the centre of the sphere by allowing the billboards to create the necessary parallax to appear as if one was travelling through the image (see the first two figures on p. 156). In the case of this project, billboards were created for the hotel and for the church surrounding City Square. The question of the number of billboards is dependent on the level of detail and the intended trajectory of the camera. The foreseeable limit here is when the camera reaches the end of a billboard and intends to turn the corner; here it would be obvious that the hotel or church were not 3D models but merely painted backdrops. To work around this issue, multiple spherical panoramas could be used and calibrated, setting up the other facades of the

Billboards inserted within the sphere to represent the hotel and church are also textured with the same panorama as the background sphere. From the view of the camera at the centre, the billboards will appear camouflaged against the background sphere because they share the same mapping coordinates.

Frames from the animation as the camera travels away from the centre of the sphere. The billboards of the hotel and church create the necessary parallax, unlike the background sphere which would bow and distort.

buildings, to allow the camera to seamlessly travel throughout this digital *trompe l'oeil* (see figure below). Creating the billboards and mapping the projection onto them shifts the technique into the area of photogrammetry, but rather than using a planar projection as is traditionally the case, this technique uses spherical projection. When compared to the *quadratura* technique, both show relationships between image and geometry. However, as the *quadratura* technique was used to extend the physical architecture by way of the illusion created by the painted architecture, the photogrammetrical method I describe above aims to (re)build the space and geometry within the photographic image itself. Where Pozzo's technique continues the physical geometry into the image, this technique extracts the geometry from the image.

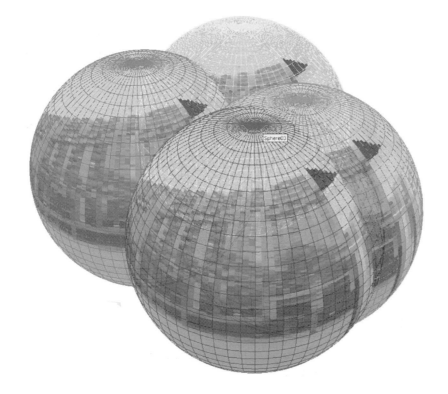

Multiple spheres can be compiled together to create a bigger scene for the camera to travel through.

Falling into the image

What has this achieved, and how has it improved the way we digitally model architecture? Technically, the research has generated a method of modelling a site and context without using any measurements as it was all developed in perspective. Whilst no measurements were used, it can nonetheless be scaled to conform to a measured design and provide a high level of accuracy. Any empirical measurements requiring calculation are handled by the software and not the operator, because the operator works entirely in perspective. Furthermore, this is a faster and more efficient method of modelling, taking a seasoned digital modeller a few days to complete, rather than a couple of weeks using the approach adopted from physical model-making.

For the discipline of architecture, the research provides a more experiential and immersive mode of communication, but at the same time an accurate digital site model into which to insert measured architectural propositions. In practice, this approach has the potential to shift the manner in which architects design and communicate their ideas in two ways. First, as the whole process is developed through perspective, it encourages modelling and considering the design through the view, rather than by measurements. Second, it allows for designs to be inserted into the sphere in much the same way as a physical site model. This creates opportunities for the design to be critiqued in relation to its context whilst the design develops, rather than simply rendering out the design outcome.

The digital technique I describe here begins to test the limits of digital representation and the way it engages specifically with architectural practice. It looks forward to speculate how digital representation can be more suited to architecture whilst looking back to consider its relation to historical practices of architectural representation. This, of course, not only questions the limits of digital representation but helps to debate the topic of perspective and the relationship between two-dimensional images and three-dimensional forms.

Finally, this method does not privilege any architectural form. Far too often, anything described as digital is thought of as being party to a particular type of architecture, namely blobs and other generative forms. This technique is not about generating architecture through representation or merely providing a means of representing the final design. Its aim is to help to critique the architecture in its context as it develops. In returning to Pallasmaa and Klein and the transcendence of qualities from one discipline to another, this research is not just an appropriation of visual-effects techniques for architecture, but a reclaiming of representational ideas and processes that had, historically, transcended from architecture to film.

Notes

1   Juhani Pallasmaa, *The Architecture of the Image: Existential Space in Cinema*, Helsinki: Rakennustieto Oy, 2001, pp. 7–10.

2   Norman M. Klein, *The Vatican to Vegas: a History of Special Effects*, New York: The New Press, 2004, pp. 10–12.

3   Greg Lynn, 'Animate Form', www.glform.com (accessed 15 January 2006).

4   Lars Spuybroek, 'NOX: Machining Architecture', www.noxarch.com (accessed 15 January 2006).

5   Michael Doneus, 'Introduction to Photogrammetry' www.univie.ac.at/Luftbildarchiv/wgv/intro.htm (accessed 10 June 2005).

6   Ibid.

7   Isaac V. Kerlow, *The Art of 3D Computer Animation and Effects*, New Jersey: John Wiley & Sons, 2004, pp. 167–170.

8   Ibid., p. 377.

9   Alberto Pérez-Gómez and Louise Pelletier, *Architectural Representation and the Perspective Hinge*, Cambridge, MA: MIT Press, 1997, pp. 58, 203–204.

Drawing air

The visual culture of bio-political imaging

David Gissen

With the rise of the modern state in the late eighteenth century, architects, engineers and urban planners developed an array of visual tools to image the movement of natural flows through space and their potential effect on the bodies of the citizenry. This bio-political visual culture extends from depictions of vast hydraulic landscapes to drawings that monitor the movements of 'miasmic' air in urban neighborhoods. Of the variety of bio-political imaging tools, the visual development of the ventilation sciences in architectural and urban thought presents a particularly rich and ongoing subject of analysis. Using the development of an 'air map' by the US Department of Homeland Security as a principal case study, this chapter examines the visual culture of ventilation and the relationship of contemporary methods of drawing air in the city to a larger ongoing analysis of 'vectored space'. Throughout the analysis, the chapter emphasizes the political economy that drives the way we understand architecture and urbanism to interact with this aspect of urban nature.

In 2002, the US Department of Homeland Security (USDHS) worked with the New York City Municipal Government and the computer-science division of the State University of New York, Stony Brook, to develop air maps of the Times Square District (TSD) of Manhattan.[1] The maps chart the vulnerabilities of this precinct to a bio-terrorist attack, part of a larger effort to armor the TSD from all potential terrorist threats. The choice of the TSD for this study reflects the sensitive role the precinct occupies in contemporary New York City. Re-developed and 'cleansed' of its sex trades and informal drug economy from the early 1980s to the mid-1990s, the neighborhood currently brings together prestige office development, retail, entertainment and media giants into one of the most populated tourist zones and highest grossing real-estate zones of any Western city. The air map (see the figure below) depicts the movement of a potentially harmful aspect of nature – air – moving through the TSD, an area of some 90 blocks and 850 buildings that also contains Rockefeller Center. The map's green vector streams represent the possible flows of air in and around the site and the potential movement of bio-agents through the area. In addition to the air map, the USDHS provided additional funds for scientists to study how the buildings in the area and buildings throughout New York City could be protected from potentially harmful air. The air map and the attending materials developed by the USDHS provide some tempting entries into examining the way air has been visualized in New York City. The mapping of air in the TSD is simply the latest effort to understand the trajectories of aerial danger in the city and the larger urban dangers of the contemporary global city. The federally financed air map and the attending materials developed by the USDHS also illustrate how this historical bio-political project intersects with contemporary efforts to restructure urban space. In the air map we see how a variety of urban agents imagine the interaction of the 'global' corporate city with an indifferent but potentially threatening form of urban nature.

The analysis of air in New York City begins with the establishment of the city in the sixteenth century. Dutch colonists were drawn to the site for its water access, but also due to what they described as the 'sweetness' of its air. As the colony grew into a substantial town of 1,000 people, colonists struggled to maintain what they had imagined to be a 'natural' cleanliness and health in the air of the pre-modern city. In approaching these problems, the directors of the growing settlement engaged in a discourse that was partially informed by Dutch folk knowledge and the ancient classical knowledge surrounding urban planning.[2] The employees of the Dutch

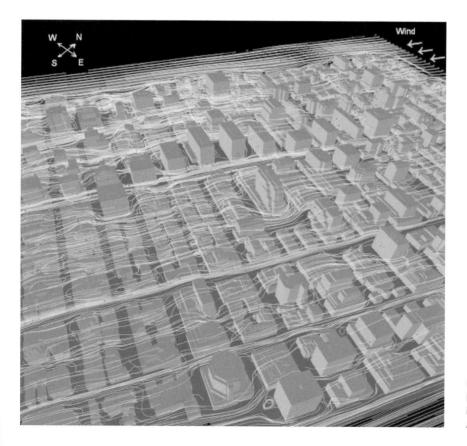

Urban Security Project, 'Streamlines in Times Square Area'.

West India Company, who formed the first European colony on Manhattan island, dealt with the problem of air quality by exploring the inter-relationships of manufacturing, housing, drainage and refuse sites. As the island settlement grew and was transferred to British rule, new conceptions of air and water were projected onto the island. In the eighteenth century, the British, New York-based engineer John Montresor engaged in a new approach to hydraulic and aerial issues in New York that emerged out of the European imperial project. Montresor developed the first representation of Manhattan illustrating the flow of water and air in and around the island's rivers with small arrows, often called 'vectors' (1766).[3] The map of Manhattan was used for the laying out of ports on the city's eastern side (it showed which way the trash flowed) and the harnessing of the river's hydraulic potential for the driving of machinery. Montresor based this map of New York, which was developed for engineering and military purposes, on the ideas of eighteenth-century British, French and Dutch engineers – the well-known work of Vauban, Delibor and Musschenbroek. These engineers developed powerful new imagery of water and air, and the formation of productive landscapes in colonial cities and metropoles.[4] Their treatises imaged vast territories pierced by a combination of aerial and hydraulic vector forces. In these early 'vectored treatises', sovereign-sponsored powers represented the harnessing of the flow of forces within precincts and territories for the purposes of manufacture, empire building or, in the case of Vauban, warfare. Although developed within the context of imperial sovereignty, these early treatises establish the visual language for a type of space we very much still occupy.

Beginning in the late nineteenth century, scientists and engineers in New York City employed the European techniques of vector analysis to solely analyse air at the urban scale. George Soper, the New York City municipal engineer, developed an entire vectored representation of the air within the New York City subway system (see figure below).[5] When the subway was completed, middle- and upper-class residents of the city feared that the presumably stagnant air in the subway would provide a site for the transmission of disease. Numerous New York residents refused to use the new transit system as it would require entering these underground spaces. The municipality hired Soper to demonstrate the motion of the underground air now swirling in the networked city, and the wide publication of Soper's maps allayed fears of the subway tunnels. Soper's maps depict the movement of air, but they also illustrate the increasing analysis of subject/nature interactions in the scientifically managed city. Analysts such as Soper used their skills to penetrate into the deepest zones of the city as an aspect of urban health-management schemes. The type of vectored analysis conducted by Soper of New York City's spaces extended into the core of the twentieth century and included depictions of the pollution from automobiles in the city's roadways and urban spaces; nuclear fall-out; the 'urban heat island effect'; and the potentially deadly weather that infrequently enters the city.

The air maps of the contemporary TSD extend from this scientific representation of air and cities, but they also relate to recent sociological analyses of this particular area and to the recent changes in the architectural and 'natural' character

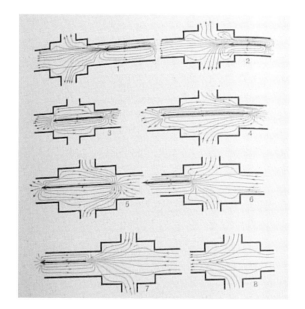

'Air Currents Set Up
by an Express Train
Passing Through the
Simplest Form of
Station in the New
York Subway'.

of the area. In the post-war period, the municipal government contracted analyses of the social, cultural and financial transformations wrought in the TSD – the heart of the Central Business District (CBD) of Manhattan. The city government was alarmed at the migration of real-estate capital away from the TSD and into the peripheries of the CBD. In the 1960s, several new buildings were completed within the neighboring Rockefeller Center and a massive influx of corporate building appeared in a ring surrounding the TSD. However, the TSD experienced an out-flow of real-estate capital, due in part to shifting tastes in entertainment and the suburbanization of cities. The area quickly became known as the 'foul core' of the city, where cheap real-estate attracted porn shops, massage parlors and burlesque theaters. In the late 1960s, the Lindsay Administration hired urban analysts who imaged the TSD as a neighborhood under decay that required massive re-structuring in order to serve the needs of the larger CBD and the larger city.[6]

The Midtown vice map, published in 1973, was the first city-financed moral geography of the area in the post-war period. The map documented porn shops, porn theaters and most nefarious 'massage parlors', which the city argued contained unlicensed masseuses who were merely prostitutes.[7] The map and the fear of crime, vice and disease that it represented fueled initial efforts to re-make the area. Between 1975 and 1985, numerous city officials argued that a 'new' TSD, with an influx of office towers, merchandise marts and hotels, would put in place 'good white collar professional uses … flood[ing] the place with thousands of middle-class pedestrians'.[8] Most of the initial efforts to re-structure the TSD failed, as the developers of office buildings favored office space in more sanitized locations in the peripheral CBD. However, in the early 1990s, with mayors David Dinkins and Rudolph Giuliani's invocation of a 'family-oriented city' and the brokering of a deal with the Disney Corporation to rebuild an entire one-block area of 42nd Street in the heart of the TSD, the precinct did indeed begin to shift demographically. From 1993 to 1998, theaters throughout the district were renovated, major corporations moved into the area and massive office buildings and hotels were built. Increasing police patrols of the area and the official harassment of the sex trades drove these businesses out and turned the TSD into one of the most heavily surveilled areas in the city. A map produced of the surveillance cameras looming out of the area's hotels, office buildings and retail stores (produced by the activist 'Surveillance Camera Players' group) demonstrates the pronounced shift of the new Times Square into a zone that is strictly monitored for crime in an effort to retain its current economic prosperity.[9]

With the area cleared of the sex trades by the late 1990s, developers and architects turned their attention to re-making the relationships between buildings, outdoor spaces and actual elements of nature – greenery, light and air – in the TSD, an area of urban re-structuring that often goes unnoticed in the recent literature. In addition to proposals in 1998 to remake the literal park-scapes in and around the precinct friendly to the tourists in the neighborhood, developers, architects and engineers employed green engineering concepts to the sites and buildings in the area. The Conde Nast Building and Reuter's Building began this trend by invoking some idea of a nature-friendly green architecture that would turn what was once a major sex vice center of the city into one of the most ironically 'green' business zones in the United States. These buildings that made up the new green Times Square promised some of the healthiest indoor air quality in a portion of the city that experienced and continues to experience some of the highest volumes of automobile traffic in the city.[10] Additionally, these buildings extended the moral geography of earlier efforts. In the most recent green skyscraper for the area, designed by Bob Fox Architect, the design team promised to create an office building that would exhaust cleaner air than that going into the building. Thus, the 'green skyscrapers' emerging in Times Square position office buildings as a cleanser of this particular precinct, thereby extending the earlier discourse.

The development of green skyscrapers in Times Square brought scientists into urban spaces to analyze air movements for low-energy air-conditioning equipment and for the enhancement of aerodynamically shaped passively ventilated structures. With the events of September 11th and the December 2001 anthrax attacks, the analysis and re-working of nature that was already in place in the TSD took on a more militant tone. In 2002, when the air map was commissioned, the scientists behind it were simply extending the scope of the air analyses in the precinct already underway in the name of green urbanism. With the invocation of paranoia behind these new images, they were also extending a larger understanding of the TSD's historically constructed vulnerability.

The air map was part of a three-stage project funded by the US Department of Homeland Security; separate teams of scientists erected computerized air-sampling equipment into the TSD to understand what might happen in the area in the event of a bio-terror attack. The resulting data from the air-sampling equipment enabled these scientists to depict how air moves through the site and how this air might carry some form of bio-agent (see figure below). The map tested the ability of computers to represent the complexity of air moving in the city, as well as the ability to predict the movement of bio-agents in urban space and into surrounding buildings. While the precise analytical results of the study are secret, the US Department of Homeland Security developed a series of guidelines with the US military, the American Society of Heating, Refrigeration and Air-Conditioning Engineers (ASHRAE) and select firms such as ARUP for the fortification of urban buildings from the potentially harmful contents of urban air. Differing from environmentalist images of buildings reaching out to their surroundings, these images show the office building as a fortress-like structure ready for a battle waged in the urban atmosphere. The guidelines suggest armoring HVAC equipment with impromptu sheds and locating ventilation equipment in upper floors out of 'harm's way'. In the existing literature, the military recommends a series of preventive equipment including irradiation machines, filters and devices that pressurize glass-skinned buildings that activate with bio-agent-detection sensors.[11]

The air map represents the latest analysis of urban air and its effects on the subjects of the city and the larger fears that are endemic to the TSD. But, in this analysis of the air map, we should explore one last feature of its visual culture. The air map also represents the latest episteme of governmentally produced links between urban

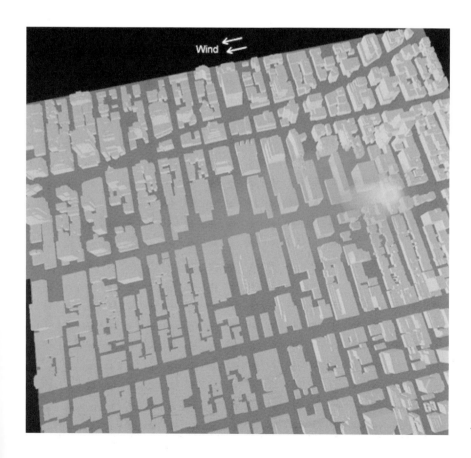

Urban Security Project, 'Plume in Times Square Area'.

nature and the urban body. All vectored images contain within their moving streams illustrations of relationships between bodies and 'produced nature', a variant of the phenomenon labeled 'bio-power' by Michel Foucault in the conclusion of his *History of Sexuality*.[12] Bio-power demands the state-maintenance of the citizenry as a form of biological life. It extends from the management of our births, deaths, ethnic and racial self-understanding. Manifestations of bio-power move through the earliest vectored images, illustrating links between subject/nature relationships under sovereign, bourgeois and local states. We see this in the images of vectored territories in the eighteenth century, vectored institutional buildings in the nineteenth century and the vectored urban networks of the nineteenth century. Each image produced within each vectored episteme articulates a space in which a form of power moves between an imagined subject, nature and governmental system.

Within this context of bio-power, the air map provides a vivid illustration of those emerging body/nature relations that are enacted in the spaces of contemporary urban re-structuring schemes. The rebuilding of urban cores into 'Class A' office space and family-friendly zones is one of the myriad ways municipalities have effected demographic transformations in the heart of post-industrial cities. The invocations of business needs, the moral and physical health of the tourist family and the 'pedestrian' are all used to justify the cleansing of urban neighborhoods. We see this at Times Square, Piccadilly Circus or Les Halles. But as municipal and federal governments encourage big businesses to locate in select neighborhoods of cities, they also look to these very businesses to participate in the maintenance of the body. The re-structured zones of the city articulate a new form of global bodily maintenance that is focused on the privatized sanitation of space; the maintenance of the employee's physical body by corporate entities; and the maintenance of the tourist body that enters these protected zones.

The US Department of Homeland Security's choice to study air in this precinct, the way air is studied in this precinct and the armoring of buildings suggested by the USDHS in the precinct illustrate how this new geo-political reality is reflected in the analysis of urban space. The TSD is not the most dense or vulnerable neighborhood in the city; however both the state and municipal governments have argued that it is a symbolic target due to its concentrations of business and media. Yet the continued scientific study of the vulnerabilities of the site and their suggested remediation have only increased the economic desirability of the site to these very same high-profile businesses. More literal mechanics of the map support this interpretative concept. For example, with its concentration on air from sidewalk level to three stories above the sidewalk, the air map suggests a concern with the literal three-story 'tourist epicentre' of the retail city and the pedestrian window-shoppers who are the life-blood of Times Square's economic future. Simultaneously, with its analyses of HVAC armoring and sophisticated defenses, the materials produced by the Department of Homeland Security suggest that the office building is the last line of national defense in the war on terror. In an almost Darwinian interpretation of urban form, this further suggests that non-high-tech buildings cannot adequately confront the geo-political realities that spaces such as the new Times Square provide to imagined combatants. Thus, the imagined subject/nature/space relations encouraged at Times Square tautologically entrench those urban processes that are remaking this and other city centers. As was done in the past, the local and national state sponsors the visualization of an urban nature, licensing territorial fantasies and desires.

With our discursive understanding of the mapping of air, our historical understanding of the goals of city officials to remake the TSD, and the geo-political realities that bring these aspects together in contemporary work, we realize that the air map presents us with an image of potentially hostile flows of air that only the continuation of urban processes already underway may confront. Only the current effort to re-build the TSD can adequately confront the indifferent air streams that move through the contemporary city. The air map represents the latest effort to map air and the city, but it also demonstrates how the rebuilding of the city, and the imagined inhabitants of this new city, require their own continuously reconsidered and customized relation to nature.

Notes

1 See 'Urban Security Project' and 'Urban Dispersion Project.' Online, available at: www.cs.sunysb.edu/~vislab/projects/urbansecurity/UrbanSecurity.html and urbandispersion.pnl.gov (accessed January 20, 2006).
2 See Duffy, 2005 and Kisacky, 2000.
3 See Cohen and T. Augustyn, 1997: 70–71.
4 See the numerous vectored images and descriptions in van Musschenbroek, 1751; De Delibor, 1737; and Le Prestre de Vauban, 1748.
5 Soper, 1908: 66.
6 Information on the decline of Times Square from Sagalyn, 2001: 40–67.
7 Sagalyn, 2001: 44.
8 Sagalyn, 2001: 81.
9 Surveillance Camera Players, 'Times Square Map.'
10 For a discussion of these buildings, see Gissen, 2002: 22–25.
11 See Barstow, 2001: 16; ARUP, 2004; NIOSH, 2002; and US Army Corps of Engineers, 2001.
12 Foucault, 1990: 135–159.

Bibliography

ARUP, 'Risk and Security for New York City Buildings: Report on a Roundtable Discussion,' September 21, 2004.
David Barstow, 'Envisioning an Expensive Future in the Brave New World of Fortress New York,' *New York Times*, September 16, 2001, p. 16.
Paul E. Cohen and Robert T. Augustyn, *Manhattan in Maps, 1527–1995*, New York: Rizzoli, 1997.
B.F. De Delibor, *Architecture Hydraulique*, 1737.
John Duffy, *A History of Public Health in New York City, 1625–1866*, New York: John Russell Sage Foundation, 2005
Michel Foucault, *The History of Sexuality*, New York: Vintage, 1990.

David Gissen, *Big and Green: Towards Sustainable Architecture in the 21st Century*, New York: Princeton Architectural Press, 2002.

Jean Kisacky, *An Architecture of Light and Air: Theories of Hygiene and the Building of the New York Hospital, 1771–1932*. PhD Dissertation, Cornell University, 2000.

Petrus van Musschenbroek, *Essai de physique avec une description de nouvelles sortes de machines pneumatiques, et un recueil d'expériences*, Leyden: Chez S. Luchtmans, 1751.

NIOSH, 'Guidance for Protecting Building Environments from Airborne Chemical, Biological, or Radiological Attacks,' May 2002.

Sebastien Le Prestre de Vauban, *The New Method of Fortification* (*le Nouveaux Méthode de Fortification*), London: S. and E. Ballard, C. Hitch, and J. Wood, 1748.

Lynn Sagalyn, *Times Square Roulette: Remaking the City Icon*, Cambridge, MA: MIT Press, 2001.

George Soper, *The Air and Ventilation of Subways*, New York: J. Wiley and Sons, 1908.

Surveillance Camera Players, 'Times Square Map,' Online, available from: www.notbored.org/timessquare-map.jpg (last accessed September 9, 2006).

Urban Dispersion Project, urbandispersion.pnl.gov (last accessed September 3, 2005).

Urban Security Project, www.cs.sunysb.edu/~vislab/projects/urbansecurity/UrbanSecurity.html (last accessed January 20, 2006).

US Army Corps of Engineers, 'Protecting Buildings and their Occupants from Airborne Hazards,' Washington, DC, 2001.

'Higher' being and 'higher' drawing

Claude Bragdon's 'fourth dimension' and the use of computer technology in design

Christina Malathouni

Introduction

The 'link between the embodied act of drawing and the perceptual experience of space', as suggested in *'The Real and the Virtual'* strand of the AHRA conference call, presupposes and refers to a certain model of the human in which the words 'embodied' and 'perceptual' are not only crucial but also implicitly demarcated as limited to 'the hand and the eye'. Yet, what happens if one accepts alternative conceptions of 'Reality', such as Idealist views that see the material world as a limited version of reality, or an illusion, and the role of our bodily senses as restricted and compromising? How would this affect our view of the 'self' and the balance between the two constituents of the assumed body–mind dualism? In such a case – and considering the highest potential of computer technologies, not merely CAD applications that follow the principles of traditional manual 'drawing' – would not the 'acquiescence and intangibility of digital data and screens' become a confirmation of our progression towards a 'higher' potential, a self surpassing its bodily limitations and our material world?

Moving along the axis of the work of the American architect Claude Fayette Bragdon (1866–1946) and mainly his interest in the concept of a spatial 'fourth dimension' and its associations to a 'higher' reality, this chapter will discuss the broader connotations of computer technology by reference to its potential to represent forms that cannot be realised in matter. Seen primarily through a historical perspective, such questions about the non-material, and the search for 'forms' and 'spaces' that may exist beyond the visible and tangible part of reality, will be appreciated as ageless and long-standing inquiries of mankind and not an exclusively contemporary phenomenon arising from the latest technological developments. Specific references to Bragdon's writings and recent experimentation in Virtual Reality will further support the main line of argument by illustrating that such associations between technological progress and metaphysical considerations are no mere speculation on the author's part.

Claude Fayette Bragdon and the 'fourth dimension'

Claude Bragdon lived and worked in New York State between 1866 and 1946. Based mainly in Rochester, NY, he practised architecture until 1923, when he moved to New York City and changed his career to theatrical design. A multifaceted and very energetic personality, Bragdon was involved in many other – artistic or otherwise – activities, such as theosophy, publishing, teaching, colour-music, and the so-called 'Song and Light Festivals'. At the same time, he was a prolific writer and lecturer on all these subjects – and yet more diverse matters – in his numerous books, articles and public talks.

In architecture, Bragdon never studied in an architectural school but instead was trained in a series of apprenticeships from an early age. He was initially influenced by the eclectic trends of his time, but soon became an enthusiastic admirer of Louis Sullivan's teachings. He shared Sullivan's view of ornament as a key feature of all architectural design and, at the same time, incorporated into his work functionalist principles alongside some very strong metaphysical foundations. However, Bragdon did differ from Sullivan in his use of geometry as the basis of the new ornamental mode, instead of the nature-based motifs used by Sullivan. In fact, it is the specific type of geometry that Bragdon employed for his new ornamental mode that makes his work particularly interesting, i.e. his use of fourth-dimensional geometry.

Claude F. Bragdon at his drawing board. Photograph dated June 1896

It was Bragdon's belief in mathematical laws governing the underlying order of the universe and his view of 'space' and 'time' as the 'two modes of consciousness'[1] that first attracted his attention to fourth-dimensional geometry; one subdivision of the 'New Geometries',[2] non-Euclidean and *n*-dimensional, the ground-breaking emergence of which, in the nineteenth century, supported the possibility of new types of 'space'. His strong theosophical beliefs further reinforced this turn to a spatial 'fourth dimension' as theosophy had appropriated the concept in order to denote a higher level of human development. So, despite its geometrical origins, Bragdon's interest in the 'fourth dimension' was, in effect, based on a much broader foundation: as with other artists and architects of the period,[3] this type of geometry appears to have offered Bragdon an 'umbrella' concept that recapitulated metaphysical considerations together with his quest for a systematic approach to the new design required for a new era.

[Representation in] form and [higher] reality

Bragdon employed projections of four-dimensional figures as the 'words' of his new ornament, and therefore named this 'Projective Ornament'.[4] Such projections of four-dimensional figures constitute representations of forms that appear to be possible to be conceived by the human mind but cannot be realised in matter nor perceived in their entirety by our bodily senses. Seen through this perspective, the use of such figures in design may offer the possibility of expressing such metaphysical concepts as a 'higher' existence. In more general terms, the emphasis that Bragdon attributed to the concepts of 'space', 'dimension' and 'form' in his quest for 'Reality' becomes clearer if one looks at Bragdon's view of 'dimensions' as a method fabricated by the human mind to come to terms with a concept as abstract and infinite as 'space'. In 1916, Bragdon wrote:

> Space is not measurable: we attribute dimensionality to space because such is the method of the mind. ... The so-called dimensions of space are to space itself as the steps that a climber cuts in the face of a cliff are to the cliff itself: they are not necessary to the cliff, they are necessary only to the climber.[5]

The significance of the concept of 'form', on the other hand, appears to be related to Carl Du Prel's 1885 *Philosophy of Mysticism*. In a key quotation included in Bragdon's 1913 *Primer of Higher Space*, Du Prel appears to relate the possibility of 'representation [in form]' with the distinction between 'the transcendental part of the world' and 'reality', or else, the 'perceived part' of the world.[6] And Du Prel continues:

> To the grub, working its way up to the surface of the earth, that surface is transcendental; to the caterpillar, the earth is real, and the free air transcendental; while to the butterfly, master of this added dimension, the threshold has again receded. ...

[...]

Arguing by analogy, everything which is to us transcendental exists nevertheless in some space. It is therefore possible that by an intention of consciousness we may be able first to apprehend, then to perceive as real, that which is now considered transcendental.[7]

Bragdon appears to summarise this association of 'form' and 'dimensions' with the distinction between the 'real' and the 'transcendental' by arguing that within the 'Higher Space Hypothesis', 'the difference between physics and metaphysics would become a difference of degree not of kind'.[8]

Depicting higher dimensions

Bragdon directly related his use of projections of four-dimensional figures into design, as outlined in his 'Projective Ornament', with the 'transcendental'. In his own words: 'Projective Ornament, derived as it is from Projective Geometry, is a new utterance of the transcendental truth of things'.[9] In fact, Bragdon also connected the method of 'projections' to metaphysical ideas, borrowed in this case from Eastern philosophies such as: 'the idea, old as philosophy itself, that all forms are projections on the lighted screen of a material universe of archetypal ideas: that all of animate creation is one vast moving picture of the play of the Cosmic Mind'.[10] However, this application of 'projection' in order to produce depictions of four-dimensional figures on the plane of drawing is not merely a way of associating such figures to 'higher' ideas; on the contrary, it is an inherent limitation of higher-dimensional figures.

The difficulty in visualising, or building in matter, higher-dimensional figures has always meant that all major proponents of the 'fourth dimension' have had to find roundabout ways of representing these figures within three-dimensional space. Usually such representations would be based on the use of sections or the method of folding down an n-dimensional figure into its $(n-1)$-dimensional components (or faces). Colour has also often been used to indicate different phases in a single object's representation. As becomes apparent from these alternative options, it has been necessary to associate the additional dimension with other visually recognisable features that exceed the strict definition of the concept of 'form' (that is, 'relations which [could] be expressed in terms of length, breadth and thickness'). In other instances, 'time' – or examples of 'change' which involve a temporal element and therefore 'might be regarded as significant of higher dimensionality', such as 'life, growth, organic being, the transition from simplicity to complexity, the shrinkage or expansion of solids' – have been associated with the existence of a higher spatial dimension; that is, 'time' is seen as 'an imperfect sense of space'.[11]

Higher dimensions and the use of computer technology

Bearing in mind all these inherent limitations of traditional 'drawing' techniques and media regarding the depiction of four-dimensional figures, the new opportunities offered by computer applications become evident. Not only do computers produce traditional depictions of such complex and innovative forms more effectively, they also offer the possibility of making 'drawing' – in its broadest sense – three-dimensional, animated and interactive.

Already since 1967 A. Michael Noll has generated visual displays of three-dimensional projections of rotating four-dimensional hypersolids [polytopes] by means of computer animation.[12] Not only were these displays produced more efficiently than manually executed drawings, but also offered the possibility of incorporating in such representations 'motion' or changing colours. Still, these early attempts did not go any further in relation to the theoretical principles underlying these techniques.

Virtual Reality (VR) has provided the opportunity for more advanced approaches to this question of representing higher-dimensional space. Joey Julien mentions research undertaken at the Electronic Visualisation Laboratory (EVL), a joint programme between the Department of Art and Design and the Department of Computer Science at the University of Illinois at Chicago.[13] As a specific example of the new objectives of such projects, one of the 'sub-cultural' goals in 'Getting Physical in Four Dimensions' (1994) was the provision of 'a more intuitive understanding of hyperspace [that] enabled users to physically interact with objects in four dimensions'.[14] In his own thesis, Julien adopts a similar position and aims at a development that would allow us to 'truly experience a visual sensation of a hypercube in [Henri] Poincaré's terms'. Julien's series of experiments examine the possibility of interacting with higher-dimensional solids in an intuitive, coherent and reproducible manner based on Poincaré's theories advocating that 'our visual, motor and tactile experiences are

Viewer/User in Julieta Aguilera's 'Unfolding Space' thesis exhibition at the EVL. Photograph dated 10th March 2006, taken by Daria Tsoupikova.

generated through associations between sensations and conditioned by personal experience and heredity'. Julien concludes that 'the next step is to investigate whether a user could actually learn the ability to navigate in four dimensions coherently'.[15]

In a more recent project at the EVL, Julieta Aguilera[16] attempted to 'augment reality in terms of structure and the relationship among its parts' by introducing the three-dimensional 'shadow' of a four-dimensional grid with which users/viewers would be able to interact. In effect, Aguilera attempts to enhance our sensual perception by following a path closely reminiscent of Julien's appropriation of Poincaré's theories. By integrating 'the dynamic abilities of the human body', Aguilera expands the notion of her main tool of the 'grid' to that of a 'dynamic grid'. As a consequence, she also extends our perception – as traditionally based on our five physical senses – to a more complex system by adding the parameter of our body motion. It follows that she sees 'gesture as dimension'[17] and, 'ultimately, the space becomes an adaptive structure tied to the structure of the body which allows us to inhabit higher dimensions in computer graphics'. Having already interweaved the concepts of 'form' and 'space', by means of the 'grid', which she suggests represents 'space', and having defined graphic design as 'based on the creation of visual paths that walk you through a given concept', she takes her arguments even further. She suggests that 'the motion of the person becomes the graphic element' and therefore makes it apparent how such new technological advancements 'challenge our assumptions about design and architecture altogether, opening up a world related both to language and space, which only exists with body actions'.

The potential of the new media as highlighted in Aguilera's project is even further expanded if one takes into account other VR experimentation that focuses on the use of senses other than vision. In addition, the possibility of the enlargement of the concept of 'drawing' – as an embodied experience inside the computer space, as suggested by Aguilera's 'Unfolding Space' – becomes even stronger when viewed in conjunction with Marcos Novak's discussion of 'Eversion':[18] Novak proposes that we 'import into ordinary space what we mine from the virtual' in order to escape the barriers of computer screens and make 'space itself . . . a screen upon which anything can be projected, not as a hologram but as a variation in density and material presence'.[19]

'Higher' drawing

As if directly associated with this debate about Virtual Reality offering the possibility to develop an intuitive understanding of higher-dimensional spaces, Bragdon related technological progress, and the availability of new representational media, with the ability of humanity's perception to evolve. As early as July 1910, in an entry to a notebook, Bragdon wrote about photography and 'moving pictures' as being the new media offering us the means to gain familiarity with the 'expansability and contractability of space'.[20] This is not the only reference in his writings that support our hypothesis that Bragdon would have approved of the use of computer technology in design. On

the contrary, Bragdon held technological progress in very high esteem and often associated the developments of his time with humanity's evolution and 'conquest of
space'.[21] In his autobiography, Bragdon referred to such phenomena in the same way
as they were perceived by the non-specialist, i.e. as 'magical' or 'miraculous', and
wrote – comparing his metaphysical considerations with the invention of the tele-
phone, cinema, and sound recordings:

> I am dealing ... with marvels and mysteries, but are they after all any more
> amazing than the familiar miracle of hearing in New York words spoken in
> London; of seeing re-enacted on a luminous screen some event which hap-
> pened elsewhere and perhaps long ago; or of listening to the living voice of
> a dead man?[22]

In November 1911, Philip Henry Wynne, a mathematician and one of Bragdon's close
friends and collaborators on the 'fourth-dimension' subject, also talked about 'marvels'
and associated these to a 'higher science'. He wrote: 'the real marvels ... appear to
the seeker in the great domain where the laws of thought and the laws of things rush
together – in the higher science where physics, mathematics, and psychology become
one.'[23] This 'higher science' revisits the idea of a body–mind dualism by in effect re-
phrasing the theories of Du Prel and Bragdon regarding 'representation in form' and
the transcendental and physics and metaphysics respectively. This is also evident in
the VR projects already referred to, and therefore these are seen as suggesting an
expanded notion of 'drawing'. In Aguilera's 'Unfolding Space' and Novak's 'Eversion',
advanced computer technologies enhance our 'perceptual experience of space' by reintroducing the human body in the process of 'drawing' which is now expanded into
the lived space, beyond any intermediate media, such as paper or computer screens.
Also, as Julien explains in his thesis, 'since the computer has no conception of the
nature of space, it is bound by the spatial metaphors and codified rule systems
contained within its programming';[24] or, as Novak writes about cyberspace, this
can actually achieve the 'literal placement of the body in spaces invented entirely by
the mind'.[25]

Bragdon relates the development of our space perception to the possibility
of our escape from the limits of material reality, towards an Ideal Reality. He points
out: 'In the fact of the limited nature of our space perceptions is found a connecting
link between materialism and idealism'. He subsequently adds (also making connections to religion, which will be omitted here): 'Thinking in terms of the higher we issue
from the tomb of materialism into the sunlight of ... idealism ... '.[26] As advanced computer technologies, such as VR, offer us possibilities of not merely 'thinking' but also
interacting 'in terms of the higher', it may be argued that this new type of 'drawing'
offers us the possibility of yet another 'removal of the boundary between representation and reality at the cost of the transcendental part of the world, and in favour of the
perceived part'.[27] Like new building materials and techniques, which enable the realisation of new architectural forms in matter, advanced computer technology may be considered as the development that can enable the 'realisation' of new, 'immaterial'

forms, unconstrained by geometrical systems applicable to our immediate physical world. In Bragdon's idealist world, such an 'acquiescence and intangibility of digital data and screens' would not have been a drawback from the 'tangibility and resistance of traditional media' but instead a positive development, leading us to the achievement of our 'higher' potential, and therefore also possibly named: 'Higher' Drawing.

Acknowledgements

This chapter is closely related to my doctoral research which has been generously funded by a full scholarship from the Greek State Scholarships Foundation and travel grants from the Society of Architectural Historians of Great Britain (Ramsden Bursaries) and the University College London Graduate School (Research Projects Fund).

Notes

1   Bragdon, 1910, p. 10.
2   The term 'New Geometries' used herein is introduced in Henderson, 1983, p. xx, n. 3.
3   On this subject see primarily Henderson, 1983.
4   Bragdon, 1972, pp. 61–62.
5   Bragdon, 1923, p. 22.
6   Carl Du Prel (*The Philosophy of Mysticism*, translated by C.C. Massey (2 vols), London: George Redway, (1885) 1889), as quoted in Bragdon, 1939, pp. 22–23.
7   Ibid., pp. 22–23.
8   Bragdon, 1923, p. 36.
9   Bragdon, 1972, p. 77.
10 Ibid.
11 Bragdon, 1939, pp. 24–26.
12 Noll, 1967.
13 See Julien, 1999, p. 50.
14 The 1994 project 'Getting Physical in Four Dimensions' was developed by Daniel J. Sandin, Milana Huang, Lou Kauffman, Joanna Mason and George Francis (see Sandin, 1994).
15 See Julien, 1999, pp. 30, 50. For references to Henri Poincaré's *La Science et l'Hypothèse* (Paris: Ernest Flammarion, 1902), see p. 27.
16 Aguilera, 14 April 2006. See also Aguilera, January 2006.
17 See Aguilera, 14 April 2006.
18 See Novak, 2002, pp. 309–323. Novak is a key figure in such a discussion given that he is considered to be the 'cyberspace' architect who has realised the dreams of those early-twentieth-century artists who first attempted to incorporate the 'fourth dimension' into their work (see particularly a comparison to the work of Kasimir Malevich in Clarke and Henderson, 2002, pp. 12–13). Furthermore, Novak's 'Eversion' is of significance in relation to Bragdon's 'Higher' Reality as Novak also makes associations to metaphysical considerations and 'invisible apparitions' such as 'spirits and ghosts, avatars and aliens, phantasms and specters' (Novak, 2002, p. 318).
19 Ibid., p. 323.
20 See entry dated 9 July 1910 in 'Manuscripts notes for Philos. of Architecture. 1909'

(notes dated 1909–1911), 36:5, Bragdon Family Papers A.B81, Department of Rare Books, Special Collections and Preservation, Rush Rhees Library, University of Rochester, NY (BFP).

21   Bragdon, 1923, pp. 126–128.
22   Bragdon, 1938, pp. 341–342.
23   Philip Henry Wynne to Claude F. Bragdon, 15 November 1911, 1:11, BFP A.B81.
24   Julien, 1999, p. 18.
25   Novak, 1991, p. 227.
26   Bragdon, 1923, pp. 154–155.
27   Du Prel, as quoted in Bragdon, 1939, pp. 22–23.

Bibliography

Julieta C. Aguilera, 'Virtual Reality and the Unfolding of Higher Dimensions', *Proceedings of the IS&T/SPIE's Electronic Imaging 2006*, San Jose, CA, January 2006. Online, available at: evlweb.eecs.uic.edu/core.php?mod=4&type=3&indi=287 (accessed 14 September 2006).

Julieta C. Aguilera, 'Unfolding Space', Thesis Project Documentation, Electronic Visualization Laboratory, University of Illinois at Chicago (unpublished), 14 April 2006. Online, available at: evlweb.eecs.uic.edu/core.php?mod=4&type=3&indi=298 (accessed 14 September 2006).

Claude F. Bragdon, *The Beautiful Necessity: Seven Essays on Theosophy and Architecture*, Rochester, NY: Manas Press, 1910.

Claude F. Bragdon, *A Primer of Higher Space, The Fourth Dimension* (to which is added *Man the Square, A Higher Space Parable*), London: Andrew Dakers Limited, 1939 (1913).

Claude F. Bragdon, *Projective Ornament*, Brighton, Seattle: Unicorn Bookshop, 1972 (1915).

Claude F. Bragdon, *Four-Dimensional Vistas*, 2nd edn, London: G. Routledge & Sons, 1923 (1916).

Claude F. Bragdon, *The Secret Springs: an Autobiography*, London: Andrew Dakers, 1938.

Bragdon Family Papers (A.B81; D.87; D.255), Department of Rare Books, Special Collections and Preservation, Rush Rhees Library, University of Rochester, NY, (BFP).

Eugenia Victoria Ellis, '*Ceci Tuera Cela:* Education of the Architect in Hyperspace', *Journal of Architectural Education*, 51, 1, September 1997, pp. 37–45.

Bruce Clarke and Linda Dalrymple Henderson (eds), 'Introduction', *From Energy to Information: Representation in Science and Technology, Art, and Literature*, Stanford, CA: Stanford University Press, 2002, pp. 1–15.

Linda Dalrymple Henderson, *The Fourth Dimension and Non-Euclidean Geometry in Modern Art*, Princeton, NJ: Princeton University Press, 1983.

Joey Julien, 'A cube is a cube is a cube is a cube ... or is it? An Investigation into the Feasibility of Interacting with a Four-Dimensional Hypercube in Immersive Virtual Reality', MSc Thesis Virtual Environments, University College London (unpublished), 1999.

Jonathan Rider Massey, *Architecture and Involution: Claude Bragdon's Projective Ornament*, PhD Dissertation, University of Princeton, 2001.

A. Michael Noll, 'A Computer Technique for Displaying *n*-Dimensional Hyperobjects', *Communications of the ACM*, 10, 8, August 1967, pp. 469–473.

Marcos Novak, 'Liquid Architectures in Cyberspace', in Michael Benedikt (ed.), *Cyberspace: First Steps*, Cambridge, MA: MIT Press, 1991, pp. 225–254.

Marcos Novak, 'Eversion: Brushing Against Avatars, Aliens, and Angels', in Bruce Clarke and

Linda Dalrymple Henderson (eds), *From Energy to Information: Representation in Science and Technology, Art, and Literature*, Stanford, CA: Stanford University Press, 2002, pp. 309–323.

Daniel J. Sandin *et al.*, 'Getting Physical in Four Dimensions' (EVL, UIC 1994). Online, available at: evlweb.eecs.uic.edu/core.php?mod=4&type=1&indi=104 (accessed 14 September 2006).

Critical dimensions

Introduction

One of the intentions of the Models and Drawings conference was to compare the role of the model with that of the drawing. In setting the conference theme, Marco Frascari interpreted the word 'model' in a specific way, using it to critique modes of representation where the imagination becomes stifled. The 'model-gaze' proceeds no further once it has settled on the object of enquiry (which might be an architectural drawing, model or text). In contrast, the proper architectural 'drawing' teaches the gaze 'to proceed beyond the visible into an infinity, whereby something new of the invisible in encountered'.[1] In this way, it opens up the imagination to possibilities beyond the immediately given.

Contemporary models of thought are rather suspicious of invisible things because they are supported by a materialist metaphysics, which only believes in what it can see. Higher dimensions of the material world are thus rendered invisible to its gaze. However, in *The Visible and the Invisible*,[2] Merleau-Ponty acknowledges the phenomenological presence of an invisibility which will forever prohibit the visible–material world from believing itself to be the only account of the world. In the heart of matter he starts to discern a second visibility: one that does not reinforce the immanence of matter, but one that creates a rupture between subjective and objective worlds. This second visibility is the invisible dimension that shapes formless matter and makes it into 'a something as opposed to a nothing': a glorified and particular living body as opposed to an indistinct and anonymous Being-in general.[3] This invisibility implies that the content of matter is higher that that of mere immanence and it prevents the model-gaze from settling upon its surface.

The intention of the contributions in this section was to develop some of the themes raised at the first AHRA International conference, *Critical Architecture*, held at the Bartlett School of Architecture in November 2003. In challenging the idle codification and canonisation associated with conventional model-type drawings, the chapters in this section address ways in which modes of representation can be critically discussed and/or used as critical design tools. The first four chapters discuss aspects related to drawing; the next two chapters discuss design projects and raise questions about the imagination of construction; the following two chapters discuss the role of language and text in the representation of architecture; and the last two chapters discuss aspects related to the perceptual experience of architecture. Collectively, these contributions expose new insights about the way modes of representation are used and discussed in architecture and thus, albeit in a different way, they critically expand or open up something new of the invisible.

With reference to a permanent installation by the artist Janet Hodgson within the Land Securities' Whitefriars Development in Canterbury, Jane Rendell, in her chapter 'Seeing time/writing place', considers differences in how architects and archaeologists draw space and time according to their particular disciplinary perspectives and procedures. The discussion compares archaeological drawings, which attempt to see time, with a number of contemporary architectural drawings, which attempt to spatialise time. Rendell describes Hodgson's work as a critical spatial practice where an 'indexical representation of a location is inscribed back into that site, in order to raise questions about how the decisions we make in the here-and-now influence the construction of architectural spaces', and she associates this practice with Freud's Mystic Writing Pad. The chapter raises questions about how we make decisions about what to remember and what to forget about the past, and how we assign value to matter.

Judith Mottram, in her chapter 'Marks in space: thinking about drawing', questions why significant value is assigned to hand-made or craft-based drawing processes compared to digital-imaging technologies. Corresponding to the shift away from drawing as a core pedagogical component in art courses, there has been an increasing valorisation of drawing. With reference to the visual theory of J.J. Gibson's 'ecological optics', she speculates about the enduring attraction of drawings.

In 'Drawing lines of confrontation', Catherine Hamel discusses architectural drawing through the theme of 'confrontation'. Accepting that the space of architectural translation is never unobstructed or neutral, but instead subject to interpretation, selection, preference and judgement, Hamel discusses the productive potential of drawing lines of confrontation. Through the theme of exile and with reference to geographical and political lines of confrontation, she reveals contrasting aspects of confrontation. Within these conditions, Hamel argues that the drawing acts as a site of ongoing negotiation and she encourages receptivity towards the process of emergence and unfolding, that the drawing allows.

Jonathan Hill's chapter 'Weather architecture, weather drawing' starts by discussing various meanings of the word 'design', tracing it back to the fifteenth century and exploring the subsequent transformation of meaning during the eighteenth century. It addresses the implications for the way architects draw and design, and it considers the limitations associated with each understanding. With reference to eighteenth-century garden design, and influenced by John Locke's theory that ideas are dependent upon experience, Jonathan Hill explores the relationship between architecture and weather. Moreover, he suggests that if architects are to respond to the changeability that the perception of weather–architecture implies, they will have to transform the way they draw and thus the way they design.

Picking up on this theme, in his chapter 'Drawing on light', Sam Ridgway addresses how the material presence of architecture is conceived 'in' and 'of' light. Influenced by the writing and teaching of Marco Frascari, Ridgway advocates a poetical and ontological understanding of construction. He discusses how this understanding has influenced his teaching in architectural construction and in the design of his private house in Adelaide.

Bradley Starkey's chapter, 'Post-secular architecture: material, intellectual, spiritual models', inverts the conference theme and turns from 'drawings' back to 'models'. It questions why architectural models are under-theorised in architectural discourse compared to drawings, and it advocates the process of design-by-making as a way of drawing forth ideas. The discussion refers to Bradley Starkey's design project. Comprising a material levitating model, this design critiques the secular basis of contemporary models of thought by examining the division and dissociation between material and spiritual dimensions.

Whereas the first four chapters in this section examine drawing, the next two discuss text and language as the subject of critical investigation. While drawing is accorded considerable value as a medium of architectural representation, the specification is considered to be a mere supplement to drawing, indeed the specification is not considered to be a representation at all. In her chapter 'Specifying materials: language, matter and the conspiracy of muteness' Katie Lloyd Thomas argues that the consequence of this is that the materiality of architecture 'disappears as the invisible medium of representation' since it is not included as an object of representation in the drawing. By examining the role of language in describing materiality, Katie Lloyd Thomas gives critical attention to the architectural specification. She compares the language of the specification with the proême's of French poet Francis Ponge, discussing both in terms of how they represent, reflect and/or transform the materials to which they refer. In doing so she expands the conceptual possibilities of the architectural specification.

Drawing upon the work of Benjamin, Bachelard and Lacan, in her chapter 'Architecture as image-space-text' Betty Nigianni discusses the role of visuality in spatial experience beyond conventional optics. Counter to the divisions resulting from Cartesian perspectivalism, Betty Nigianni suggests a more discursive relation between subject and object. With reference to the poem 'Tale of a Tub', written by Sylvia Plath, she discusses the implications of a more textual rather than visual representation and suggests diverging possibilities for architectural representation, where the priority of 'surface' is replaced by the metaphor of the 'interface.'

In her chapter 'Acts of imagination and reflection in architectural design', Peg Rawes discusses the role of the imagination in reflective thinking and spatial experience. Rawes explains the distinction between Kant's notion of 'reflective judgement' and cognitive reasoning, where the former is a special kind of embodied thinking that involves the imagination. She argues that Kant's theory is interesting for architects because it reinforces the importance of the designer's ability to think 'reflectively' in the production of aesthetic and technical judgements. Through a discussion of geometry, Rawes reveals the operation of embodied reflection in the process of drawing, and she argues that geometric thinking and geometric relationships are inherently connected to the designer's reflective and aesthetic powers. Furthermore, with reference to a discussion of an experience of *The Weather Project* by Olafur Eliasson at the Tate Modern, she argues that the imagination intrinsically underpins the designer's personal experience of architectural and urban space.

In the last chapter of this section, the discussion of spatial perception is expanded. Katja Grillner discusses the role of distraction in the perceptual experience of architecture. With reference to the author's two recent writing and spatial installation projects and drawing on the work of Walter Benjamin, she discusses the critical and political function of distraction. Counter to normative reviews of contemporary architecture, which avoid notions of distracted use, her installations advance the idea of the 'distracted critic', who detects what is happening in the corner of perception. Grillner believes that it is necessary to address distraction if we are to produce an architectural criticism of relevance to contemporary conditions.

Notes

1   Conference Call for Papers, Marco Frascari, *Models & Drawings: the Invisible Nature of Architecture*, University of Nottingham, 2003.
2   Maurice Merleau-Ponty, *The Visible and the Invisible*, Alphonso Lingis (trans.), Evanston, IL: Northwestern University Press, 1964.
3   See Philip Blond (ed.), *Post-Secular Philosophy: Between Philosophy and Theology*, London: Routledge, 1997, for an expanded discussion.

Seeing time/writing place[1]

Jane Rendell

Introduction

This chapter is an essay commissioned by art consultant Samantha Wilkinson to accompany the publication of 'The Pits' (2005), a permanent installation by artist Janet Hodgson, within the Land Securities' Whitefriars Development, Canterbury. It started life as a conversation that took place between Janet and myself as we walked through her work – the embedding of an archaeological drawing of a site into the stone paving of that site's new public square – the focal point of an almost-to-be-completed shopping centre. At the start of her project, the site was an archaeological dig, and archaeological drawings became the key influence for the making of 'The Pits'. In this chapter, in order to consider how drawings represent space and time differently, according to their particular disciplinary perspectives and procedures, I explore the artwork from an interdisciplinary perspective, discussing how the work operates across art, archaeology and architecture. In the first part I discuss how archaeological drawings are attempts to 'see time' and to create, from the material fragments excavated in a site, an understanding of the chronology and sequence associated with the history of a place. I compare this to the way in which certain contemporary architectural drawings spatialise time, creating new ways of drawing narrative and event. In the second part, I argue that, by focusing on the archaeological process of retrieval, 'The Pits' asks us to consider the relative value of material items, from those we treasure to those we throw away. The work uses its title to draw attention to its position at the heart of a new shopping centre; here the re-making of a drawing raises questions of its site in terms of cultural context and architectural production and reproduction.

As Janet Hodgson and I walked through her new work in the centre of Canterbury, we shared a delight in the precise way the lines of the drawings met across paving junctions, and at how the words beneath our feet seemed at times to be somehow out of place:

**Janet Hodgson,
'The Pits' (2005)
Canterbury.**

Animal burrow
Area not e.c. further as within 3 m of edge of site/pile
Truncated by
Pile cap cannot dig beneath obviously

Very quickly it became clear that Hodgson was entranced by archaeological draw-ings. She described the scene of the site to me as a working dig, divided by a grid of ropes, each archaeologist excavating their own small square plot, revealing objects and spaces through the removal of earth.[2] To her, an artist, this inversion of the traditional sculptural act seemed strange, and for me, with my architectural training, this process reversed the other activities of a building site, where architec-ture is produced through the accumulation of material components, rather than their removal.

Hodgson's fascination was not so much with the archaeological practice of removal, since this is not so different from the work of a conceptual artist like Michael Asher who removed architectural elements of the gallery, or a more contemporary artist such as Rachel Whiteread whose practice has become one of making absence present, but with how archaeologists draw time.[3] Hodgson described another scene to me, this one in the archaeologists' office, where the small drawings produced by indi-viduals on site were placed next to one another in order to establish chronological sequence.

The patterning of the drawings inscribed in Hodgson's memory, which she then described to me, I in turn discussed with some archaeologists. They responded: 'Ah! Yes! That sounds like a stratigraphic matrix.' A matrixial stratigraph, I immediately mis-remembered the phrase. To a non-archaeologist, but someone interested in images and marks that are both spatial and temporal, this was magic; caught up with excitement, I started to research, to discover that the inventor of the matrix, Edward Harris, describes it in terms of 'seeing time':

> In the simplest of terms, but dealing with that most complicated of ideas, namely, *time*, the Matrix is a new type of calendar, which allowed archaeologists for the first time, to *see* the stratigraphic sequences of complex sites. Calendars and clock faces are two of the few ways in which we can 'see' absolute time, for since it has no physical reality, but is inherent in most things, it must be translated to a diagrammatic form to be understood as a schedule or sequence ... [4]

For archaeologists, the purpose of stratigraphy is to establish time.[5] In the Harris Matrix, each layer is drawn as a box, the boxes are then positioned next to each other to correspond with the 'superpositional relationship of their deposition'; this allows a temporal relationship to be made between all the strata in a site (see the figure below). This process is not uncontroversial in archaeological practice, it appears; as Michael Shanks explains, the Harris Matrix questions the logic of understanding a site through geological layers, and instead suggests a form of diagram that maps the interface between deposits:

> There are different ways to map the archaeological site. There is the obvious planned survey. But also the stratigraphic matrix, a type of diagram invented by Edward Harris, and in its modifications a cornerstone of British field excavation. This form of diagram does not represent the layers of deposits of a site but deals with their volumes by reduction to the concept of interface – the dividing line between deposits, or conversely their surfaces. The task of excavation is one of establishing these interfaces.[6]

The conventions of the architectural drawing in professional practice – plans, elevations and sections – tend to show space as a horizontal or vertical slice in one moment in time. Three-dimensional drawings, such as the axonometric and isometric, produce an artificial view of a building, from a standpoint impossible to achieve in 'real' life, while the perspective may be drawn from one, or perhaps two, fixed positions. As part of the architectural specification package, drawings are made with the intention of allowing the competing contractors to cost a project and later provide the instructions for what needs to be built. These drawings are representations of space rather than time, but there are of course more conceptual architectural drawings rooted in a more critical tradition, which attempt to draw time, such as 'event' in the work of Bernard Tschumi, or story-telling and narrative in the projects of cj lim.[7] Recent explorations of the diagram in architecture argue for visual practices that are temporal as well as spatial, and a number of practitioners have investigated through images and

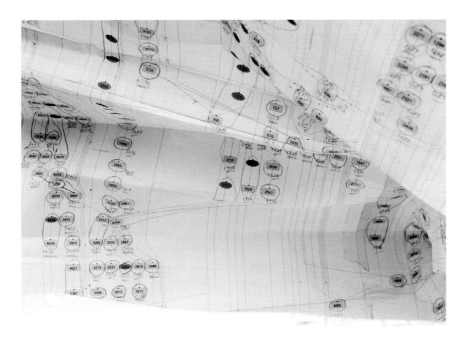

A matrix drawing, courtesy of Canterbury Archaeological Trust.

words the gradual changes to space over time through the design process and possible future occupations of a building.[8]

Despite the fact that, in the architectural office, drawings are produced by more than one person and altered over time, they tend to be presented as the work of a single architect, with careful attention paid to the removal of all but the final layer of lines. (Preceding the advent of computer, the roughened patches on pieces of tracing paper provided material evidence of the reworking of a drawing over time.) The archaeological drawing process sounded to me rather more collaborative, part of a collective investigation into a site, rather than instructions for the production of a complex artefact. It is interesting to note, then, that while archaeology is currently excited about the creative potential of its own modes of investigation, with fieldwork described as a 'mis en scene' examined in terms of performance and theatre, architecture is investigating how the drawing can be a site of theoretical exploration as well as a codification for the production of space.[9]

Hodgson chose to inscribe the archaeologists' drawings into the york stone slabs set as a landscaped element in the new shopping complex designed by Chapman Taylor and built by Land Securities in Whitefriars, Canterbury. Since each drawing is composed of lines that travel across several slabs, to produce such an inscription demanded an amazing degree of precision, and careful collaboration between the artist and the sub-contractor, MSS of Leeds. This kind of slow and painstaking task does not necessarily sit comfortably with the prioritisation of speed on many fast-track building sites. It is important, therefore, to acknowledge the key role that the invisible web of conversations plays in producing the relationships of trust and mutual respect required to make a work of such finesse.

Hodgson has an ongoing interest in time and history. Her 1999 installation 'History Lesson' for the Bluecoat Gallery, Liverpool, involved simultaneous projections in different parts of the space of 17 hours of video recording the fictional re-enactment of the everyday life of the building in its previous incarnation as a Victorian school. The work does not attempt to re-stage history 'as it really was', but rather explores historical knowledge as an ongoing reconstruction in the present, located somewhere between fact and fiction. The life-size video recordings of the building being decorated to look like a typical Victorian school are projected back into their original position at the same scale. At each site of projection you see the time it took to construct another time – the past – one possible version of history. It is not physically possible to view all these times together, and even if you could see all the images, the result would not simply be simultaneous – a moment in time – or sequential – time passing. As characters in Victorian costume move from one scene to another, intermingling with decorators and painters, the time depicted is complex and layered, what you see slips in and out of making sense, more like memory.

A more recent work, 'Time Machine', has, through several incarnations in different sites, continued to develop Hodgson's interest in time and space, deepening and complexifying her understanding of their interconnections in relation to a number of sites. In 2002, 'Time Machine' was shown in a number of locations in Canterbury. The works were composed of video projections on the inside and/or outside of various shop windows and a construction based on the time machine in George Pal's 1960 film version of H.G. Wells' *Time Machine* (1895) was fabricated from cardboard boxes which once contained digital commodities. The video projection makes temporal play of the fashion sequence from the film slowing down and speeding up the sequence in which a mannequin is dressed in outfits from different eras.

When the 'Time Machine' travelled to the Oakville Galleries in Ontario in 2004, it transformed into a new work, 'Here and There, Then and Now', a response, in part, to Hodgson's fascination with the architecture of the gallery. She discovered that Oakville Galleries, constructed in 1922, was a copy of another building in Toronto and that both these architectural structures were influenced by the work of British architect C.F.A. Voysey, in particular Spade House in Kent, England, designed as a commission for H.G. Wells. Voysey's design work could be described as 'Arts and Crafts', and his architecture connected to William Morris' aspiration for a new society paradoxically influenced by looking backwards to a romantic view of medieval England. 'Here and There, Then and Now' consisted of installations in three rooms, including the time machine and two new video compositions. In one room, we see through the window a man dressed in an upper-class Edwardian costume wandering at leisure through an idyllic garden setting, and in another room, images of architectural settings from these other sites are projected back into the gallery at the same scale. At first, the view from the window seems to suggest a romantic escape, but finally the character viewed 'out there' in the garden appears 'in here', on our side of the window, in front of us in the same room. As in 'History Lessons', we are asked to consider aspects of the distant in the near, but where the earlier work made us conscious of the past in the present, in this more recent work, the emphasis is less on time and more on space. Hodgson's exploration of time in terms of history has evolved into an investigation of relationships that are as much about location and dislocation as they are about what was, what is and what might be. Wells' utopian visions are historically sited and brought into relation with the Arts and Crafts' tendency to project the past into the future, but at the same time, we are asked to think about locations that are absent, but which form the model for those that are physically present.

The archaeological processes at work in Whitefriars seem to coincide with Hodgson's desire to see many times at once, perhaps informing her decision to inscribe the site with drawings of the holes the excavations revealed, bringing the past into the present, as an ongoing creative construction, alongside the on-site production of future architectures. The specifics of process as well as disciplinary attitude are key here. Following my understanding of the Harris Matrix, it is the very act of drawing – the representation of spatial relationships – that allows one to see time. For the archaeologists at work in Whitefriars, this drawing involves first recording parts of the site and then repositioning these drawings spatially in order to respond to a question particular to archaeology: 'how is time spatially ordered in this particular place?' Hodgson draws time, in line with her approach to making an art that is critical as well as site-specific, something I have described elsewhere as a critical spatial practice, in this case (as in the works involving video projections described earlier) an indexical representation of a location is inscribed back into that site, in order to raise questions about how the decisions we make in the here-and-now influence the construction of architectural spaces.[10]

Writing place

> The Mystic Pad is a slab of dark brown resin or wax with a paper edging; over the slab is laid a thin transparent sheet, the top end of which is firmly secured to the slab while its bottom end rests on it without being fixed to it. This transparent sheet ... consists of two layers, which can be detached from each other except at their two ends. The upper layer is a transparent piece of celluloid; the lower layer is made of thin translucent waxed paper. ... To make use of the Mystic Pad, one writes upon the celluloid portion of the covering-sheet which rests on the wax slab. ... a pointed stilus scratches the surface, the depressions upon which constitute the 'writing'. ... If one wishes to destroy what has been written, all that is necessary is to raise the double covering-sheet from the wax slab by a light pull ... The close contact between the waxed paper and the wax slab at the places which have been scratched (upon which the visibility of the writing depended) is thus brought to an end and it does not recur when the two surfaces come together once more. ... The surface of the Mystic Pad is clear of writing and once more capable of receiving impressions. But it is

easy to discover that the permanent trace of what was written is retained upon the wax slab itself and is legible in suitable lights. Thus the Pad provides not only a receptive surface that can be used over and over again, like a slate, but also permanent traces of what has been written, like an ordinary paper pad: it solves the problem of combining two functions *by dividing them between two separate but interrelated component parts or systems*. But this is precisely the way in which ... our mental apparatus performs its perceptual function.[11]

How do sites get marked through time? If we were to make an analogy between a site and a subject, then we might imagine a place to hold traces in a way similar to the Mystic Writing Pad. We would expect, then, to be able to see and touch the remains of only some past actions. How do archaeologists decide what to remember and what to forget? How do they know what to look for, what to keep and what to reject? Archaeologists are trained to seek out what passes as invisible to the rest of us, to know the difference, for example, between seemingly identical clumps of earth, to discern those that have been disturbed by human action and those that have not. It is not necessarily a matter of age or of material worth in today's terms that makes an archaeologist value one object, notice one process, rather than another, but importance is placed on whether this object or that process allows something new to be known about how we understand the past.

As I discovered at a recent conference on archaeology and architecture, debates are ongoing concerning the items that are found in pits and what they might tell us about human habitation.[12] Are pits places where precious items are stored, perhaps over time in nomadic periods, or locations where rejected things were thrown – pots and flints as well as organic refuse? The use of pits for rubbish or waste certainly does not appear to be constant, but, rather, depends on historical period. There seems to be some agreement that in the Middle Ages the pits in back gardens were used for unwanted objects, but in times further away, in the Neolithic period for example, interpretations are less certain. Some research has shown that fragments of the same pot may be found in several pits, indicating a type of action that in today's terms is not easy to explain. Anthropologist Mary Douglas' much-quoted phrase 'dirt is matter out of place' comes to mind here, as I realise that the decisions made about what to treasure and what to discard depend on historical period but also location.

A brief browse in the windows of the new shops in the Whitefriars redevelopment reveals a glittering array of clothing, jewellery and shoes. The life span of these items – from purchase through use and on to the landfill site – will be staggeringly brief. What would a Neolithic person make of an archaeological dig that revealed the depths of a landfill site or even a fragment of Hodgson's work? Of all the drawings the archaeologists made in and of this place, including those of a rare and ancient street, here in this new pleasure house of commodity consumption, Hodgson chose to inscribe only the drawings of the rubbish pits back into the site.

What does this say as a cultural comment? At this point it is worth referring to another artwork that has used the insertion of text into site as a way to critique past actions, present processes and future occupations. For the redevelopment of Federation Square in Melbourne, artist Paul Carter was commissioned to make a work for the main plaza. 'Nearamnew' (2001) is a text-based piece developed in collaboration with Lab architecture studio. American political scientist Morton Grodzin's comparison of the organisation of federal systems of government with the layers of marble cake provided the starting point for the work. The project consists of three elements: a whorl pattern manifest throughout the plaza, eight surface figures located along the force lines of the swirl and eight federal texts engraved into the surface figures. Carter likens these to the three layers of federal government – global, regional and local.

The word 'nearamnew' is derived from a local word, 'narr-m' in pidgin, meaning 'the place where Melbourne now stands'. Pidgin is a language that has been described as a 'contact zone', the kind of place that would operate as an un-fixed site in James Clifford's terms and, for Homi Bhabha, as a contested hybrid space. Carter's interests lie in the writing of place, between site-identification and self-identification, and between place-naming and name-placing. His aim for the project was 'to rename, and thereby to bring into being, a new place'.[13]

This renaming occurs not by simply positioning a word in a site, but also through the various ways in which each reader produces a space through their own embodied reading of the place. Through the use of various fonts, scales and spacings, differences are constructed, for example, between the federal text written in a cramped 'generic bureau grotesque font' and the 'ur-letters' of the larger-scale surface figures that appear more like images.[14] At each of the three scales, the reader is offered a different reading experience and alternative understanding of the site, raising questions concerning the ownership of land in the political history of Australian government.[15]

Hodgson chose to title her work 'The Pits', so marking Whitefriars with information the site already contained concerning its own lost past and buried topography. Numerical figures indicate the depths and dates of historical layers, lines gesture to the holes beneath the surface, and there are also the asides, the notes the archaeologists made perhaps only to themselves, that are now writ large upon the site. This renaming of a place operates to bring the hidden indentations of the site, Freud's marks on the resin of the Mystic Writing Pad, into visibility. While one can easily pass through the work and experience it as visual pleasure, it is possible to look more closely, to read it as an image and, at closer quarters, as a text. Such forms of embodied reading allow different negotiations with the past of Whitefriars and the selection of rubbish as a historical act. Hodgson's decision to name the work 'The Pits' draws attention to insignificant past actions and asks us to remember the objects that those who came before chose to throw away: actions and objects not usually recognised as the stuff of history.

It is possible for words and drawings inserted into a site to construct meaning in a number of ways. They may point to what is no longer there, but also question what is here, using the ambiguity of language to contradict as well as overemphasise. One reading of 'The Pits', then, takes the term to describe directly what was present but is now hidden beneath the surface – the pits of the past revealed by the archaeological dig. Another reading, taking 'The Pits' as a colloquialism, suggests that this is rubbish. However, it is also possible that 'The Pits' is referring to its context; compared to the rubble that we know exists under the paving slabs, the brand new items for sale in the shops surrounding the work are clearly *not* rubbish, but on the other hand commodities do get treated as if they are rubbish. It is not clear, nor is it meant to be, which of these interpretations Hodgson intends; rather, she is asking us to think about the ways in which we assign value to matter.

Connections have been made by many between the dream work of psycho-analysis, the role of the Freud's talking cure in the excavation of the unconscious, and the processes of archaeology, a discipline involved in a physical as well as concep-tual and analytic uncovering of the past. So it was interesting for me to find the archae-ologist Michael Shanks using the term 'traum werk' (translated into English as 'dream-work') as 'something of a (tongue-in-cheek) reference to Freud's notion of dream-work – How disparate (and often fragmentary) components get linked in the cultural imaginary'.[16]

By inscribing archaeological drawings into the paving, Hodgson reinscribes the past back into Whitefriars – 'The Pits' provides a way of 'seeing time'. Akin to the dream-work that also excavates aspects of history that have lain repressed, Hodgson's actions visibly trace an unwanted memory of the site – 'The Pits' provides a way of 'writing place'.

Notes

1   This chapter was first published as Jane Rendell, 'Seeing Time/Writing Place', in Janet Hodgson, *The Pits* (a work commissioned by Land Securities in partnership with Canterbury City Council), SWPA Publishing, 2006, pp. 28–37. It is republished here with the kind permission of Samantha Wilkinson and Janet Hodgson. The book, which includes essays by the commissioner and archaeologists and full documenta-tion of the making of the artwork, can be purchased from Insite Arts by contacting publishing@insitearts.com.

2   The dig at Whitefriars in Canterbury is referred to as 'The Big Dig' on the website. See www.canterburytrust.co.uk/archive/bigdig01.html (accessed May 2005).

3   For Michael Asher see, for example, 'September 13–October 8, 1973, Galleria Toselli, Milan, Italy' and 'March 20–April 10, 1976, The Clock Tower, Institute for Art and Urban Resources, Inc., New York', in Asher, 1983, pp. 125 and 88. For Rachel Whiteread see, for example, 'Water Tower', New York (1998) and 'Holocaust Memor-ial', Jüdenplatz, Vienna (1995). See Neri, 2000 and *Rachel Whiteread*, 1997, p. 31.

4   See www.harrismatrix.com/history.htm (accessed May 2005).

5   Renfrew and Bahn, 2005, pp. 244–5.

6   Michael Shanks. See traumwerk.stanford.edu/~mshanks/traumwerk/index.php/strati-graphic%20matrix (accessed May 2005).

7   See, for example, Tschumi, 1996 and www.cjlim-studio8.com (accessed May 2005).

8   See muf, 2001 and Till and Wigglesworth, 2001.

9   See Shanks, 2002 and traumwerk.stanford.edu/~mshanks/writing/indexPDF.html (accessed May 2005). See also Hill, 2003.

10　For a discussion of the term 'critical spatial practice' in relation to works of art and architecture, see Rendell, 2006.
11　Freud, 2001, pp. 229–30.
12　Beadsmoore, Garrow and Knight, 2005.
13　See Carter, 2001, p. 138.
14　See Carter, 2001, p. 144.
15　See Carter, 2001, p. 137.
16　See traumwerk.stanford.edu/~mshanks/traumwerk/index.php (accessed May 2005).

Bibliography

Michael Asher, *Writings 1973–1983 on Work 1969–1979*, written in collaboration with Benjamin H.D. Buchloh, Halifax: Press of Nova Scotia College of Art and Design and the Museum of Contemporary Art, Los Angeles, 1983, pp. 125 and 88.
Emma Beadsmoore, Duncan Garrow and Mark Knight, 'Neolithic Spaces and the Material Temporality of Occupation', paper at *Connected Space*, McDonald Institute, Cambridge, 14–15 May 2005.
Paul Carter, 'Arcadian Writing: Two Text into Landscape Proposals', *Studies in the History of Gardens and Designed Landscapes*, 21, 2 (April–June 2001): 137–47.
Sigmund Freud, 'A Note Upon the "Mystic Writing-Pad" ' [1925], *The Standard Edition of the Complete Psychological Works of Sigmund Freud*, v. XIX (1923–1925), translated from the German under the General Editorship of James Strachey, in collaboration with Anna Freud, London: Vintage, 2001, pp. 227–32.
Jonathan Hill, *Actions of Architecture: Architects and Creative Users*, London: Routledge, 2003.
muf, *This is What We Do: a muf Manual*, London: Ellipsis, 2001.
Louise Neri (ed.), *Looking Up: Rachel Whiteread's Water Tower*, New York: Public Art Fund, 2000.
Jane Rendell, *Art and Architecture: a Place Between*, London: I.B. Tauris, 2006.
Colin Renfrew and Paul Bahn (eds), *Archaeology: The Key Concepts*, London: Routledge, 2005.
Michael Shanks, 'Towards an Archaeology of Performance', 2002. Online, available at: traumwerk.stanford.edu/~mshanks/writing/indexPDF.html (accessed May 2005).
Jeremy Till and Sarah Wigglesworth, *9/10 Stock Orchard Street: a Guidebook*, London: 2001.
Bernard Tschumi, *Architecture and Disjunction*, Cambridge, MA: MIT Press, 1996.
Rachel Whiteread, British Pavilion, XLVII Venice Bienalle (1997), Venice, 1997.

Websites

www.canterburytrust.co.uk/archive/bigdig01.html (accessed May 2005).
www.cjlim-studio8.com (accessed May 2005).
www.harrismatrix.com/history.htm (accessed May 2005).
traumwerk.stanford.edu/~mshanks/traumwerk/index.php/stratigraphic%20matrix (accessed May 2005).

Marks in space

Thinking about drawing

Judith Mottram

Introduction

There is something about everyone's interest in drawing that both appeals and irritates. Is it the directness of drawing that is valorised, in its ability to provide a pure trace of the hand of the artist? If so, how are we meant to engage with drawings that are merely a tool for communicating instruction? It could be suggested that the value attributed to the 'hand of the artist' is sometimes overblown, with inconsequential doodles receiving excessive commendation for minimal communication. This chapter discusses drawing practices from a range of disciplines and explores the values attributed to the act of making marks and its outcomes. With reference to the 'ecological optics' of J.J. Gibson, theories about the enduring attraction of drawing are discussed. The contemporary context for drawing is one in which digital tools have removed the imperative to develop accurate representations within art and design training. Despite this, audiences continue to be interested in looking at drawings.

This contribution was conceived as a catalogue text for the exhibition *Marks in Space* that presented a broad range of approaches to drawing by sculptors and other drawers whose practice occupied two- and three-dimensional spaces, in an attempt to provide a context for questioning some of these issues. In conclusion, it is suggested that the learning embodied in craft skills, which developed over many hundreds of years, and which is enshrined in many of the heuristics of art and design training, are now in danger of being jettisoned as digital tools become the norm. A significant challenge ahead will be the development of mechanisms for re-thinking the skills we need to develop to represent and imagine future scenarios.

The context of drawing

Drawing is an activity that has various uses in contemporary life. It is a tool usually associated with artists and designers, particularly in respect of their initial 'working out' of an idea for an artwork or the design for a more utilitarian object, or when attempting to grasp how parts combine to form a whole. Drawings are made for buildings, both as initial sketches and the more developed image for use in construction. Drawings are also made by those people involved in a variety of other professions, such as those made by the surgeon, the rugby coach or the forensic psychologist. All of these types of drawing are clear in their objective of mapping out or exploring the relationships between entities, whether using projection systems or more diagrammatic methods. Drawings also become objects of attention in their own right, such as in exhibitions.

The means by which drawings may be made, and consensus on just what might be counted as a drawing, has been extending to include those made in three dimensions, images generated through computers, and others that do not result from conscious human activity. It has been suggested that the ability to generate drawings through advancements in computer technology is part of the reason why there has been increased interest in this activity over the past ten years. Eames proposes that 'were we not faced with a somewhat myopic attitude towards the visual arts and computing there would not be the intuitive and renewed interest in the practice of drawing'.[1] Whatever the reasons for the apparent increase of interest in drawing, technological advances as applied to other realms of human enquiry have enabled significant progress to be made in understanding various aspects of human activity. It may be that the turn to drawing is a turn to the known in the face of the inexplicable.

Drawing was previously the bedrock of training in university and art-school courses in fine art (including painting, sculpture, printmaking and, more recently, installation and new-media practices). In the UK, these courses generally grew out of the diplomas in art and design that originated in the Victorian art and design schools. The central focus on drawing had built upon the conceptions of the proper training of artists that originated with the atelier and academy systems. However, a shift in the content of the curricula delivered within fine-art courses has taken place since the advent of digital tools in the mid-1980s. Drawing, along with other 'hand skills', has lost its central position as a core skill. The increasing use of digital imaging, and in particular the increased access to moving-image programs, has seen students move away from the use of simple and direct means of mark or image-making. The diagram is about as good as it gets, as a tool for specifying for fabrication. These shifts, away from the manipulation of stuff, away from manual dexterity, mirror the increasingly diverse actions and activities that may now be presented as art objects, and the increasing emphasis on being (like an artist), rather than doing (like an artist).

At the same time as this move away from drawing as a central course component, there has been a steady stream of events that explore, valorise or celebrate drawing. There has been the development of a discrete field of academic enquiry through conferences such as *Drawing across boundaries*[2] and the online journal, *Tracey*.[3] There has also been a clear sense of an emerging strand of interest among curators. For the publicly funded exhibition providers like the Hayward Gallery, putting together exhibitions of drawings by major artists from the 1600s to the present day, drawing largely from collections such as that of the British Museum, has been an effective means of providing historical exhibitions.[4] The *Jerwood Drawing Prize*[5] has become an established element of the annual competition and exhibition cycle, and even the Royal Academy had a special focus on drawing in its 2004 summer exhibition.[6] Despite the decline of engagement with drawing within the art schools, drawings do appear to have an enduring interest for gallery and museum audiences.

The exhibition *Marks in Space*[7] sought to explore the different ways in which drawing operates in relation to contemporary sculptural form. With an emphasis on linearity, it presented sculptural objects themselves as spatial drawings, alongside drawings within three dimensions that generate sculptural space. Relationships between sculptural and architectural objects with their installation instructions and plans were exposed, and the information specifications implicit in the linking of 3D computer imaging and rapid prototyping were made explicit. We intentionally presented some drawings constructed as functional diagrams for the construction of art works, downplaying them as objects in their own right – these parallel the notion of architectural representations as 'models' for imitation. Installation plans and working drawings by Dan Graham, Tony Goddard, Susan Hiller and Richard Long exemplified this approach. We wanted to remind the audience that these models or functional representations often get re-codified after initial use. These typologies were presented alongside more established notions, of drawing as a process to develop or explore sculptural form, or to envisage objects in space, such as in the work by Ed Allington. We included examples of how new technologies were enabling the seeing of the previously unseen, through Eugenia Fratzeskou's animated drawings exploring the application of Boolean algebra to renderings of geometric form, and Stephan Gec's animation of the Apollo–Soyuz Test project. As a background to the exhibition, the following discussion was developed to consider some more generic issues about drawing and to attempt to explain why drawing is still intriguing.

The directness of drawing

What is meant by saying that the value of drawing might be in its directness? The answer could be that drawing provides a very simple means of presenting the outcome of perceptual or cognitive effort that generates a record that can be apprehended by vision. The construction or making of the drawing might take time, but there is no temporal delay in experiencing the outcome. The drawing may be complex, and some elements may not be immediately discernible, but it can be apprehended in one go. We have not yet thought of the implications of what is being drawn. It is important to distinguish for a moment between drawing something from observation, and drawing something from imagination, or from a set of instructions, or in response to a set of other stimuli. Do we know what happens when an artist, or for that matter a non-artist, is in the process of drawing? And whatever is happening during that process, is there any difference if visual stimuli are present, or if verbal or numerical stimuli are used, or if the stimulus is solely within the resources of the drawer?

The trace of the artist's hand

The idea of drawing being a trace of the hand of the artist (for now, take 'artist' as whoever is making the drawing) seems to come attached to a notion that this trace, this expression by the individual making the mark, has some intrinsic value. Why might this be so? Is there some magic attached to marks made by humans, or to those made by animals, or the way water 'draws' lines across sand, or the strata laid down by geological forces? There certainly is the potential for delight, or aesthetic responses, to all of these things, yet perhaps they are not of the same class. Let's pick up on that perceptual or cognitive effort of the artist, as distinct from the observer, in that they are both making and seeing the results of that making. We can distinguish between the two sorts of effort to some extent by thinking about visual perception as particularly associated with the act of receiving stimulus, and the cognitive as more knowing or understandable apprehension. It may be suggested that the cognitive is called upon more in relation to drawing from non-visual stimuli (verbal, numeric or imaginary) that require processing into visual outcomes. However, it must be remembered that both perceptual and cognitive effort are actually very interrelated, and that in the process of making the drawing, as in the process of seeing the drawing, they act in tandem, informing each other to build up the comprehension of what is being seen, or drawn.

So why is the trace of the hand of the artist such a powerful concept in relation to drawing? It is worth extending the idea to include consideration of the value that is attached to the hand-made in other areas of human activity as well, particularly those where the media employed retains marks, impressions or other visual evidence of the application of tools to materials. One explanation might be that we know some talented person has made the marks that we are viewing – we are attributing value by association. That presumes that there is foreknowledge that the object of attention has been subject to physical manipulation by a person of esteem within the field in question. This explanation does not, however, deal with those instances where value is attributed for the first time.

Empathy and tenderness

A more plausible explanation, and one that comes through in David Hockney's short essay on the Rembrandt sketch of a family teaching a child to walk,[8] is that we can empathise with the effort made by the artist in making the marks. I would suggest, in fact, that it is more like a mimetic impulse, where the viewer mentally mimics the looking and mark-making carried out by the artist. Maybe we can recognise implicitly the mental activity that occurred when Rembrandt was looking at the milkmaid's arm carrying the full pail (or remembering it), and the transaction that occurred between his eyes, brain and hand to make the marks with ink and brush. Hockney said; 'I'm looking at the marks and I can feel his arm.' He went on to say that 'When I look at these marks, I know a Chinese master of the seventeenth century would recognise instantly that this drawing was the work of a master.' But despite these clues, Hockney appears to stress more that the importance of drawing is in its capacity for tenderness, and that the 'trace of Rembrandt's hand is still alive'. It is as if he feels the need to use emotion to explain the power of this particular earlier drawing, and to account for the enduring interest in drawing as such a simple tool for communication.

Visual thinking

We can take the idea of the mimetic impulse further, to account for both the appreciation of the viewer for the handmade, and for the power of drawing as a tool for 'visual thinking' for the artist or designer. For the viewer, the resonance, or even recognition, of marks that they themselves might have made, in response to particular stimuli, could be giving rise to the response of recognition. The instinct to match shapes or marks, whether actual with actual, or actual with imagined, could be seen as one of those 'hard-wired' aspects of the human perceptual system from the perspective of evolutionary biology. So, even if art or craft activities are not learnt, there will be residues of understanding the impressions or marks that can be made in clay, by charcoal, or by the use of hand-held tools. This is a fairly simplistic account for the value given to the hand-made, but if we look further at the 'visual thinking' idea in relation to what is understood about how we see, further reasons for the importance of drawing becomes evident.

The idea that drawing is an act of visual thinking for the artist and designer is fairly widespread. Allen Jones, in the discussion of the reasons behind the decision to focus on drawing in the 2004 Royal Academy Summer Exhibition,[9] said that 'We look at drawing as visual thinking and we want the work we're showing to get as close as possible to that creative act, to that point where the eye, hand and heart meet.' This statement raises two questions: what is happening during visual thinking, and what is actually happening during the creative act of drawing? Accounts of vision developed over the past fifty years suggest some pretty persuasive models that seem to account both for drawing from observation and for drawing from other resources.

The particular ideas on vision that appear to provide a plausible explanation for the power of drawing as a tool for making sense of the world include the propensity within various visual systems for discriminating edges or boundaries, theories about 'invariants' and 'affordances', and the identification of 'picture primitives'. A very direct link appears to exist between elements commonly found in drawings – line, tonality, depiction of proportional relationships, and boundary representations – and these basic components of visual perception. It could be argued that drawings effectively provide us with a fairly concise arena in which we are able to perceive visual information.

Through drawing, the drawer is able to translate the seen, or make visible the imagined, through economical means that reflect the fundamental building blocks of vision. We tend to recognise a line, or a discernible contrast between one tone and another,[10] as shorthand for distinguishing between two areas. Boundary recognition then enables the discrimination of shapes, which may or may not conform to those that are familiar. An understanding of those 'invariant'[11] aspects of the visible world allows us to account for unfamiliar representations, to which further understanding is provided by the meanings, or 'affordances', that the perceived forms or environments have for the viewer. This approach to understanding vision draws upon the 'ecological optics' of J.J. Gibson,[12] which could provide the basis for explaining the enduring utility of drawing as an active tool for thinking, and as an effective source of information. Ramachandran suggests that the effectiveness of outline drawings and sketches is explained by a combination of the 'peak shift principle' – where 'supernormal' stimuli, or accentuation of characteristic features, lead to more vigorous responses – with the tendency to group perceived features together until they are 'readable'.[13] He refers to Zeki's proposal that the artist's ability to 'abstract the 'essential features' of an image and discard redundant information is effectively mirroring 'what the visual areas them-selves have evolved to do'. Although his 'eight laws of aesthetic experience' rest on such suppositions that 'feature binding' leads to the sensation of 'reward' or aesthetic pleasure, his argument has internal logic, evolutionary rationale, and apparently fits current understanding of neurophysiology. In terms of trying to understand the direct-ness of the appeal of drawings, these ideas seem to provide a rather more fruitful starting point for our notions of the 'aura' of the artist being transmitted through the marks they made.

The creative act of drawing

As to what is happening during the creative act of drawing, the above discussion has given us some clues about the identification of salient features. These might be taken from an observed visual world or visual field,[14] and we could assume that what happens then is that they are reduced, or abstracted, to form the picture primitives of the drawing. That this process parallels what the visual system has evolved to do gives support for current views that creativity itself is a normal human activity. Instead of the idea of the artist as a person possessing a special gift, it has been suggested that notable creative contributions are made not by the specially gifted, but by those who have been able to operate in the optimum conditions to stimulate that innate cre-ativity. Knowledge, personality type, learning style, motivation, deliberate practice and environment can all play a part in setting up these optimum conditions.[15] And the short answer for what is happening during the creative act is that problems might be solved, such as how to convey the weight of that pail and the strain on the milkmaid's arm, or new problems may be discovered. What I'm not sure of is the extent to which the heart has a role to play in this.

Learning to draw again

Recent scientific enquiry in psychology and neuroscience appears to indicate that these disciplines are starting to provide fairly convincing reasoning to explain the background to certain heuristics of art and design training. However, this new thinking is not part of the disciplinary knowledge of art and design, and much of the legacy of the guild, academy and industrial revolution training models have already been abandoned. It could be suggested that knowledge acquired by humanity over the course of evolution, through activities like making art, is being forgotten within its base discipline just as we are starting to understand how and why we are able to be creative in this way. New explanations for vision, for creativity, and probably for other human functions, are starting to reflect behaviours that were once commonly known and understood as central to training artisans. Deliberate practice had been a cornerstone of artistic training, from the ateliers of the Renaissance until the latter part of the twentieth century. Cognitive science now sees deliberate practice as one of the conditions for creative activity. However, over the past thirty years, emphasis on task repetition has declined in the art schools and it is now not so common for those trained in the visual arts to be able to execute a coherent drawn representation. The ability to engage intelligently with materials, to process them from natural form through to another state, is also being lost. The expertise of the artisan has been subsumed by a professionalising that is severing tactile engagement with the materials of the disciplines, in favour of the ability to promote the representation of the individual as a simulation of the artist as a cultural commentator rather than representer. It may be argued that the skill of accurate rendition by drawing is no longer required, as digital representations can be captured with ease. But what we can do is to follow up those clues of interest or valorisation, to find out more about why we respond so positively to the outcomes of certain practices, and then think again about how these can be re-incorporated within disciplinary practices to effect new opportunities for creative action, instruction, representation or commentary.

Notes

1   Eames, 2000.
2   Mottram and Whale, 2000.
3   Sawdon *et al.*, n.d.
4   For example, Martin, 1995; Petherbridge, 1991.
5   *The Jerwood Drawing Prize*, London. Wimbledon College of Art.
6   *Royal Academy Illustrated 2004: a selection from the 236th Summer Exhibition*, London: Royal Academy of Arts, 2004.
7   Mottram and Ayers, 2004. The exhibition included works by: Edward Allington, Atkinson Design Associates and Goddard Manton Architects, Alain Ayers, Andrew Bannister, Judith Cowan, Cathy de Monchaux, Richard Deacon, Eugenia Fratzeskou, Anya Gallacio, Stephan Gec, Liam Gillick, Dan Graham in collaboration with Haworth Tomkins Architects, Graham Gussin, Susan Hiller, Simon le Ruez, Richard Long,

Cornelia Parker, Keir Smith, Pak Keung Wan, Jenny West, Annie Whiles, Alison Wilding, Richard Wilson and Daphne Wright.

8   Hockney, 2004: 54.

9   Jones, 2004, quoted in Greenberg, 2004: 48–51.

10   Hubel and Wiesel discovered that the visual cortex of cats and monkeys contains specific cells that are responsive to lines and edges and it has been suggested that this implies that 'perception of certain basic features of the world is unlearned', or 'wired into' the nervous system. See Gordon, 1997: 224.

11   'Invariants' have been described as 'higher-order properties of patterns of stimulation which remain constant during changes', whether those changes are movement by the observer, changes in the environment around the observer, or a combination of these. See Gordon, 1997: 190.

12   Gibson, 1979.

13   Ramachandran and Hirstien, 1999: 15–51.

14   For a discussion of the differences between the visual world and the visual field, see Willats, 1997: 172–173.

15   Sternberg and Lubert, 1999: 11.

Bibliography

Angela Eames, 'From Drawing to Computing and Back Again', in Judith Mottram and George Whale (eds), *Drawing Across Boundaries*, Loughborough: Loughborough University School of Art and Design, 2000 (CD-ROM).

J.J. Gibson, *The Ecological Approach to Visual Perception*, Boston: Houghton Mifflin, 1979.

Ian E. Gordon, *Theories of Visual Perception*, Chichester: Wiley, 1997.

Sarah Greenberg, 'Kitchen Confidential', *The Royal Academy of Arts Magazine*, 83, summer 2004.

David Hockney, 'Life Drawing', *The Royal Academy of Arts Magazine*, 83, summer 2004.

The Jerwood Drawing Prize, London. Wimbledon College of Art. Online, available at: www.wimbledon.ac.uk/jerwood (accessed 8 September 2006).

Michael Craig Martin, *Drawing the Line*, London: The South Bank Centre, 1995.

Judith Mottram and Alain Ayers, *Marks in Space: Drawing and Sculptural Form*, 13 July to 24 October 2004, The Usher Gallery, Lincoln.

Judith Mottram and George Whale (eds), *Drawing Across Boundaries*, Loughborough: Loughborough University School of Art and Design, 2000 (CD-ROM).

Deanna Petherbridge, *The Primacy of Drawing*, London: The South Bank Centre, 1991.

V.S. Ramachandran and William Hirstien, 'The Science of Art', *Journal of Consciousness Studies*, 6, 6–7, 1999.

Royal Academy Illustrated 2004: a Selection from the 236th Summer Exhibition, London: Royal Academy of Arts, 2004.

P.J. Sawdon *et al.* (eds), *Tracey*, Loughborough: Loughborough University School of Art and Design. Online, available at: www.lboro.ac.uk/departments/ac/tracey/index.html (accessed 8 September 2006).

Robert J. Sternberg and Todd I. Lubert, 'The Concept of Creativity: Prospects and Paradigms', in Robert J. Sternberg (ed.), *Handbook of Creativity*, Cambridge: Cambridge University Press, 1999.

John Willats, *Art and Representation*, New Jersey: Princeton University Press, 1997.

Drawing lines of confrontation

Catherine Hamel

Introduction

In architectural production, the drawing of lines is generally aimed at clarifying ideas of space, a graphic progression towards resolution in form. In this context, to draw is often reduced to an act of neutral transmission. Building on Robin Evans' assertion that in translating architectural ideas from drawing to building there is no neutral space through which ideas travel unobstructed, this chapter explores the productive aspect of this distortion in drawing's role to confound and question as opposed to resolve.

The space of translation is a landscape to be invented on which thought traces paths. One such path marks lines of confrontation. Lines of confrontation unite what they divide. They clarify. They distort. Drawing lines of confrontation is a seemingly simple act of demarcation, of geographic knowledge, of staging where opposing contexts, opposing ideologies meet. In drawing, there is confrontation. To confront is not always a hostile act. To confront is also an act of comparison, of consideration. Drawing lines of confrontation in architecture is explored through the experience of exile and translation. Experiences where the act of crossing borders can never be complete. Though momentary, the potential of the ongoing negotiation rests in the awareness of conditions that get overlooked; of comfortable assumptions that become stale.

Drawing lines of confrontation

In a world in which very little is constant, fixed or permanent, becoming anchored by trusting a system and savouring its mechanistic pleasure is a welcome relief for many. A system provides stability with predictable sequences, each part of a carefully patterned curve that forms the neat trajectory of beginnings, developments and ends. There is striking persistence to allow the priority of the systems formed to precede their need and relevance. The principle of absolutes fears contamination. It is a fear that all distinction will be lost should one category come into contact with another. But contact exists, even if it is precarious when not ignored. If a precarious pause cannot be coded, it does not mean that it does not exist. In refusing to be contained, it surpasses the discourse that regulates it as a system. Differentiation invites confrontation in highlighting opposition. In drawing distinction, conflict concedes to the slightest overlap. It is a moment of comparison that highlights the link as opposed to the rupture. Confrontation tapers choice towards selection. It is an acceptance of constraints, an attempt at resolution, towards precision. But the act of confrontation does not necessarily produce clarity or resolution. Sometimes a moment is all that is needed, a moment that 'allows us to bask in the luxury of doubt, the experience which offers us the potential to see far beyond out short sighted certainties'.[1]

A line of confrontation is a term used to denote frontlines of war. The nature of war lies in the claim of borders: physical, cultural, social, religious, economic. The outcome is a series of demarcation lines that denote territorial claims. Some of these lines confronted are physical, others psychological, many are carved on the lens of the viewing eye. A line of confrontation is not a single concept. It is something political, dynamic, contested.[2] It can be a site of resistance or a symbol of defeat. It can also be a collaborative effort by sides to define space, something open for negotiation. Lines of confrontation do not always forge themselves through space as a rigid line of defence or attack. These geographies do not only form the topography of the territory of war but of human lives that cast their shadows on the landscapes. Constantly changing, they form shifting boundaries, forcing people to draw up continuously shifting maps of their world to form their mental geographies.

In representing the space of war, lines of confrontation delineate a burdened space reduced to the thinness of a graphic line. The Beirut Green Line exemplifies but one of many demarcation lines that score the earth. It is a line that separated the city of Beirut for sixteen years during the war in Lebanon (1975–1991). According to some, this 'green line', as it was known, was a term borrowed from military mapping vocabulary. A more populist view traces the name to the relentless vegetation that took over the asphalt and ruins:

> The growth of this wild life that choked many of the streets and buildings was fuelled by years of ruptured water pipes and overflowing drains until it became a dangerous urban forest planted with mines and unexploded shells hidden in the roots and foliage.[3]

In the complexity of such abstraction and simplification, where such a space is condensed to near extinction in the thinness of the line that gets portrayed on a map, there is confrontation in 'tracing a shifting threshold'[4] between the limited knowledge given by representation and the realities and impact of the space. The extreme conditions of the frontlines of war point at the limitations of architectural representation. A seemingly simple fissure between two sides reveals a much more complex tug of war with many supporting roles. What is of interest are the traits the act of drawing share with lines of confrontation. In speaking of drawing lines of confrontation in architecture, the confrontation referred to is not one of aggressive opposition. It is the collision between modes of expression and experience that can never be perfectly matched. The reverberation of a collision is more interesting than the obvious explosion. To confront is not always a hostile act. To confront is also an act of comparison, of consideration.

The context where a boundary becomes a path, where a line exhales and appropriates space, is Robin Evans' 'space of translation' in his essay, *Translation, From Drawing to Buildings*. Evans asserts that, in translating architectural ideas from drawing to building, there is no neutral space through which thought travels unobstructed. Although in principle translation is an attempt at transferring information as accurately as possible, precision is not achieved. A discrepancy exists between the original version and its counterpart. How much of a discrepancy depends on how observant one is, how much of the connective tissue one wishes to save or decides to sever. Translation, deemed to be an exercise in accuracy, is elusive. To translate only what is fixed does not make for precision.

In translation, implications and nuances of meaning are abundant. The translator is faced with interpretation and selection, preferences and judgements. Choice is a constant companion. Like a musician plays a score, a translator can play his intent. Nuances are highlighted, subtleties ignored and the outcome is altered. The space of translation is one of deviation. It is contested, dynamic, political.[5] This world of potential is a landscape to be continuously invented. Unlike traditional landscapes where a single viewpoint is imposed, active landscapes receive the density and continuity of the world. They are layered, ready to be constructed, ready to be excavated. Always in the making, they are open-ended and untidy.[6] Their space is a changing one where contradictions coexist and conditions of transformation appear as a norm.

The difficulty of translation is exemplified by the exile. The exile is defined as such because of a forced crossing over a border. A border often begins as a line of confrontation and settles into a line of distinction that differentiates and segregates. It is not so much a movement across the border as much as a crossing into the expansive space that the experience entails. Though the crossing may seem finite and directional, the passage is an act that is never complete. Julia Kristeva describes the experience of living in a border space as 'a standing invitation to some inaccessible, irritating journey'.[7] It is a common experience of forced displacement. An unresolved existence oscillating between the dangerously manipulative memories of a lost place and the difficulty of adaptation to new cultures and their accompanying space. It is a rich existence that defies the comfort of stale meaning. Nothing is clearly understood. Life relentlessly demands to be reinterpreted from a different point of view, in a different language. It is also a solitary existence among the ghosts of all that is silenced by the nature of translation. One can flee this irritation, 'not through levelling and forgetting, but through the harmonious repetition of the differences it implies'.[8] The confrontation can be lightened up by constantly coming to it, more and more swiftly. It is not a question of maintaining perpetual transience. This inaccessibility can take root, intensely, but temporarily. Sometimes certain, it knows nevertheless that it is passing by.[9] Translating oneself across a border is an ongoing and delicate balance between loss and discovery. Past experience does not always find itself heard, yet new textures and visions emerge in the new context, through a new vocabulary. The difficulty of translation and the accompanying transformation are also its bittersweet offering; a new world to be explored, more secrets to be discovered.

Architecture is predominantly brought into existence through drawing, with the future of the idea lying 'in the hope of being drawn, in the struggle to rework it and to offer it back through the structure of the work itself, a process which finds its destination through drawing, redrawing, drawing out, drawing towards.'[10] Drawing is an act that is difficult to define:

> whether drawing is approached as a general set of material conditions (such as unique works on paper), or techniques (such as line or mark making), or functions (such as preparatory or investigative tactics) the practice of drawing resists, or is indifferent to reductive definitions.[11]

The emphasis on a concise definition of drawing often falls on what has been excluded. The words persistently point at what has been forgotten in what has been said. In the introduction to the exhibit *Just My Imagination*, an exhibit with the intention to challenge and expand the idea of drawing, David Merritt states the he 'endeavours to make a virtue of contingency, exchanging the imperative *drawing is* ... for an open and provisional drawing as ...'[12] He adopts Michel Serres' words and settles on drawing as 'a barrier of braided links that leaks like a wicker basket but can still function as a dam'.[13]

Such a barrier does not merely exist between one condition and another. It unites what it divides. It clarifies, it distorts. There is selection as to what seeps through and what is dammed. Yet fluid, the exchange is not directional and is ongoing. Drawing, then, blurs and delineates, excludes and includes, contests and accepts; in expressing, it suppresses. It is not limited by medium, technique or intent. Recognising drawing as a site of ongoing negotiation within this ebb and flow, it becomes an act that challenges segregation and the parcelling of thought. The act of crossing defined limits can never be complete. One persistently exists between conditions, oscillating, perpetually crossing, perpetually drawing.

The persistence of the drawn line is a deliberate act of constantly searching the boundaries of our world. To define something is to mark its boundaries, to outline its edge.[14] Differentiation and perception are strongly linked. To create order out of multiplicity, to make distinction within flow, entities are separated in order to be seen: 'Separating entities from their surrounding is what allows us to perceive them, to distinguish what we attend to and what we ignore.'[15] We draw lines of distinction in the construction of our world: lines that are rigid, aggressive, imposing; Lines that can be subtle, delicate, wondering. Vulnerable lines turn drawing into a 'questioning process that challenges one's assuredness, intentions and assumptions'.[16] The paths we draw through the space of translation are lines of confrontation, lines that can dispel the boundaries imposed. In his essay 'Exactitude' in *Six Memos For the Next Millennium*, Italo Calvino states 'that the real work consists not in the definitive form, but in the series of approximations made to attain it'.[17] Drawing as a leaking barrier is defective and fragmentary. In an attempt to trace the 'successive displacement of thought',[18] drawing 'always says something less with respect to the sum of what can be experienced'.[19] The lines 'point at something more. And we are always searching for something hidden, or merely potential, following its traces whether they appear on the surface.'[20]

        In architectural production, the drawing of lines is generally aimed at clarify-
ing ideas of space, a graphic progression towards resolution in form. This act is often
reduced to a neutral transmission of information between different systems. The
density of the fluid world of spatial experience is muted, anchored and jammed into
rigid lines and inert surfaces. Without undermining the importance of precision – the
plan, the section, the detail, all drawn with exactitude – without denying that at
the later stages of design one is held accountable for every line made, it is important to
learn to trust in the unfolding of the idea, to be receptive to the growth of the image,
to allow the drawing to lead, but at the same time be able to select, discard or
further build upon uncovered possibilities. To do so, one has to allow half-resolved
forms, which in their ambiguous state may provoke alternate possibilities.[21] The
experience invoked might be one of uncertainty comparable to a sense of organized
disorder. Paths might lead nowhere, suggestions not pursued as strange combinations
and associations of ideas emerge, hints teasingly dropped.[22] Edward Hill likened
drawing to courting an idea. Courting is a confrontation that involves comparison,
consideration, negotiation.

        In the process of drawing away from experienced reality, abstraction is the
basis of interpretation and expression in the process of forming architecture.[23] To
abstract is to select, to select is to make a choice, to choose one thing is to disregard
others. In the simple process of selection, ideological positions are revealed. How and
what we represent betrays how we see, what we value, what we condone. When
lines of distinction become lines of confrontation, even momentarily, they cut through
isolated objects to search out the evasive relations between things. Like a successful
sketch, which is more than an inflexible outline that rigidly maintains the full periphery
of an object, the secret lies in the openness of the malleable line that searches,
breaks, pauses. Its success lies in conceding to its limitations and embracing its ability
to evoke by supplying sufficient definition without providing a complete depiction.

Drawing lines of confrontation is to surrender to the moments when transmission is disrupted. To surrender is an active act to choose passivity. A precarious pause that gives up resistance to drawing's role to confound and question as opposed to resolve.

Notes

All drawings by Catherine Hamel.

1   Valenzuela, 1991, p. 81.
2   Bender, 1993, p. 276.
3   Angus and Maluf, 1996, p. 8
4   Merritt, 2005, p. 11.
5   On the political power of translation as an act of both intellectual ability and moral worth, refer to Paz, 1987, pp. 15–22.
6   The concept of active landscapes in based Barbara Bender's 'landscapes in motion', where she states:

> If we understand landscape to be the way in which people understand and engage with the material world around them, then landscapes are always in process, potentially conflicted, and uneasy. They are never preordained because our perceptions and reactions – though they are spatially and histori-cally specific, are unpredictable, contradictory, full of small resistances, and renegotiations. Which bit of ourselves we bring to the encounter also depends upon the context, as neither place, nor context nor self stay put, things are always in movement.
>
> (Bender and Winer, 1991, pp. 3–4)

7   Kristeva, p. 4.
8   Ibid., p. 3.
9   Ibid., p. 4.
10   Whiteman, 1990, p. 7.
11   Merrit, 2005, p. 12.
12   Ibid., p. 11.
13   Michel Serres, 1983. p. 75. The original image was used in comparing living organ-isms and information systems.
14   'Indeed, the word *define* derives from the Latin word for *boundary*, which is *finis*' (Zerubavel, 1991, p. 2).
15   Zerubavel, 1991, p. 1.
16   Basha, 1996, p. 10.
17   Calvino, 1988, p. 77.
18   Merritt, 2005, p. 11.
19   Calvino, 1988, p. 75.
20   Ibid., p. 77.
21   Hill, 1966, p. 37.
22   Hannoosh, 1992, p. 6.
23   Peter, 1985, p. 1.

Bibliography

Gavin Angus and M. Ramez Maluf, *Beirut Reborn: the Restoration and Development of the Central District*, New York: John Wiley & Sons, 1996.

Regine Basha, *Diary of a Human Hand*, Montreal: Gallery of the Saidye Bronfman Centre for the Arts, 1996.

Barbara Bender, 'Stonehenge – Contested Landscapes (Medieval to Present Day)', in Barbara Bender (ed.), *Landscape: Politics and Perspectives*, Oxford: Berg, 1993.

Barbara Bender and Margot Winer (eds), *Contested Landscapes: Movement, Exile and Place*, New York: Berg, 1991.

Italo Calvino, *Six Memos For the Next Millennium*, Massachusetts: Harvard University Press, 1988.

James Corner (ed.), *Recovering Landscapes: Essays in Contemporary Landscape Architecture*, New York: Princeton Architectural Press, 1999.

Robin Evans, *Translations from Drawing to Building and Other Essays*, Cambridge: MIT Press, 1997.

Maggie Helwig (ed.), *Speaking in Tongues: PEN Canada, Writers in Exile*, Banff: The Banff Centre Press, 2005.

Michele Hannoosh, *Baudelaire and Caricature: from the Comic to an Art of Modernity*, University Park: Pennsylvania University Press, 1992.

Edward Hill, *The Language of Drawing*, New Jersey: A Spectrum Book, 1966.

Julia Kristeva, *Strangers to Ourselves*, New York: Columbia University Press, 1991.

Philomena Mariani (ed.), *Critical Fictions: the Politics of Imaginative Writing*, Seattle: Bay Press, 1991.

Donald Meinig (ed.), *The Interpretation of Ordinary Landscapes: Geographical Essays*, New York: Oxford University Press, 1979.

David Merritt, 'Drawing as ... ,' in David Merritt and Kim Moodie, *Just My Imagination*, London: Ontario Council for the Arts, 2005.

David Merritt and Kim Moodie, *Just My Imagination*, London: Ontario Council for the Arts, 2005.

Rievel Netz, 'Barbed Wire', *London Review of Books* (20 July 2000).

Ben Nicholson, *Appliance House*, Cambridge: MIT Press, 1990.

Octavio Paz, *Convergences: Essays on Art and Literature*, trans. Helen Lane, New York: Harcourt Brace Jovanovich, 1987.

Alberto Pérez-Gómez and Steve Parcell (eds), *Chora: Intervals in the Philosophy of Architecture*, Volume 2, Montreal: McGill-Queens University Press, 1996.

Frank Peter, 'Architecture and Abstraction', *Pratt Journal of Architecture*, 1 (Fall 1985).

Wellington Reiter, *Vessels & Fields*, New York: Princeton Architectural Press, 1999.

Michel Serres, 'The Origin of Language', *Hermes, Literature, Science, Philosophy*, Baltimore: John Hopkins University Press, 1983.

George Steiner, *After Babel: Aspects of Language and Translation*, Cambridge: Oxford University Press, 1975.

Luisa Valenzuela, 'The Writer, the Crisis, and a Form of Representation', in Philomena Mariani (ed.), *Critical Fictions: the Politics of Imaginative Writing*, Seattle: Bay Press, 1991.

John Whiteman, 'Drawing Towards Building', in Ben Nicholson (ed.), *Appliance House*, Cambridge: MIT Press, 1990.

Eviatar Zerubavel, *The Fine Line: Making Distinctions in Everyday Life*, New York: The Free Press, 1991.

Weather architecture, weather drawing

Jonathan Hill

Introduction

The conception of design established in the Italian Renaissance has a number of failings. First, it suggests that creativity is a one-way street and fails to recognise the creativity of the user and others involved in the conception and production of architecture. Second, it assumes that as ideas emanate from the architect to the user, so does the critical. Third, it promotes the superiority of the intellect and denigrates the manual, material and experiential.

Design as it was first conceived relies on a fiction, both interesting and stimulating, that a building can be like a drawing. Acknowledging the uncertainties of weather and the subjectivity of perception, eighteenth-century garden design recognises, however, that they are often very different. The original meaning of design, as the drawing of a line and the drawing forth of an idea, remains valuable to architectural practice and research as long as its limitations are acknowledged and tempered by the eighteenth-century understanding of ideas as provisional and dependent on experience at conception and reception. Whether a building is understood to be critical depends on the user as much as the architect, and users' perceptions of architecture are not necessarily consistent because the conditions in which we experience architecture are not consistent. In the first half of this chapter I discuss what drawing means to the practice of architecture. In the second half, focusing on the relations between architecture, perception and weather, I discuss what drawing fails to comprehend.

Drawing the architect

Before the fifteenth century, the status of the architect was low due to association with manual labour and dispersed authorship. Of little importance to building, the drawing was understood to be no more than a flat surface and the shapes upon it were but tokens of three-dimensional objects. The Italian Renaissance introduced a fundamental change in perception, establishing the principle that the drawing truthfully depicts the three-dimensional world, and is a window to that world, which places the viewer outside and in command of the view. For the first time, the drawing became essential to architectural practice.

The command of drawing unlocked the status of the architect. Interdependent, they affirm the same idea: architecture results not from the accumulated knowledge of a team of anonymous craftspeople working together on a construction site but the artistic creation of an individual architect in command of drawing who designs a building as a whole and at a remove from construction. Thus, the architectural drawing depends on two related but distinct concepts. One indicates that drawing is an intellectual, artistic activity, distant from the grubby materiality of building. The other claims that the drawing is the truthful representation of the building, indicating the mastery of architects over building production.

The histories of the architect and the drawing are interwoven with that of design. The term 'design' comes from the Italian *disegno*, meaning drawing, suggesting both the drawing of a line on paper and the drawing forth of an idea. Dependent on the assumption that ideas are superior to matter and, thus, that intellectual labour is superior to manual labour,[1] *disegno* enabled architecture, painting and sculpture – the three visual arts – to be recognised as liberal arts concerned with ideas, a position they had rarely been accorded previously.

The sixteenth-century painter and architect Giorgio Vasari was crucial to the promotion of *disegno*. In *The Lives of the Most Eminent Painters, Sculptors and Architects* (1550), he presents painters, sculptors and architects as heroic figures, laying a foundation for the cult of artistic genius. Vasari also formed the first collection to value drawings as original works of art, the *Libro de' Disegni*, and in 1563 founded the first art academy, the *Accademia del Disegno* in Florence. A model for later institutions in Italy and elsewhere, it enabled painters, sculptors and architects to converse independently of the craft guilds and replaced workshop instruction with education in subjects such as drawing and geometry. *Disegno* is concerned with the idea of architecture, not the matter of building. Leon Battista Alberti notably states: 'It is quite possible to project whole forms in the mind without recourse to the material.'[2]

In the new division of labour that occurred in the fifteenth and sixteenth centuries, design was distanced from construction and the construction site. Alongside the traditional practice of building, architects acquired new means to practise architecture: drawing and writing. To affirm their status as exponents of intellectual and artistic labour, architects began increasingly to theorise architecture in drawings and books. Sebastiano Serlio[3] and Andrea Palladio[4] are notable early exponents of this tradition, Le Corbusier[5] and Rem Koolhaas[6] more recent ones.

Often a design does not get built, and an architect must be persuasive to see that it does. Sometimes a building is not the best way to explore an architectural idea. Consequently, architects, especially influential ones, tend to talk, write and draw a lot as well as build. The relations between the drawing, text and building are multidirectional. For example, drawing may lead to building. But writing may also lead to drawing, or building to writing and drawing. If everyone reading these words listed all the architectural works that influence them, some would be drawings, some would be texts, and others would be buildings either visited or described in drawings and texts. Studying the history of architecture since the Italian Renaissance, it is evident that researching, testing and questioning the limits of architecture occurs through drawing and writing as well as building.

Ideas and appliances

The history of design from the fifteenth century to the twenty-first is not seamless, however, and a significant departure occurred in the eighteenth century, when the meaning of both design and ideas changed somewhat.

Opposed to utility, the classification of the fine arts – notably poetry, music, painting, sculpture and architecture – is primarily an invention of that century. Associated with utility, the design disciplines that proliferated due to industrialisation, such as product design, are categorised as applied arts at best. In the Renaissance, a form was synonymous with an idea.[7] But, especially since the nineteenth-century codification of formal type, a form can be less about ideas and more about production.[8] Painters and sculptors discarded design once it became associated with collective authorship and industrial production. Among the fine arts, which include the three visual arts, only in architecture is the term 'design' regularly referred to today. Many people associate design with the newer design disciplines, which affects how architectural design is understood. But in the discourse of architects, the older meaning of design – drawing ideas – and the newer meaning of design – drawing appliances – are both in evidence.

For architects, from the fifteenth century to the twenty-first, design can draw forth an idea. In the Italian Renaissance, an idea was understood as universal and superior to matter. But in *Essay Concerning Human Understanding* (1690), John Locke argues that ideas are dependent upon experience,[9] countering the assumption that knowledge is certain and universal and undermining the distrust of the senses in Renaissance theory.[10] In 1757, David Hume adds: 'Beauty is no quality in things themselves: it exists merely in the mind that contemplates them; and each mind perceives a different beauty.'[11] Consequently, perception is subjective and changeable. Any change in the weather, the time of the day or the position or mood of the viewer can affect perception, so that even an object seemingly as solid as a building may not seem the same from one moment to the next. Focusing attention on subjectivity transformed the visual arts, its objects, authors and viewers. No longer was architecture a cohesive body of knowledge dependent on universal proportions. Since the eighteenth century, design may draw forth an idea that is provisional and dependent on experience at conception and reception.

In the eighteenth century, associated with personal and political liberty, the design and appreciation of picturesque gardens – 'ambiguous objects' in which ideas and meanings are relative – developed alongside the increasing value given to subjectivity.[12] The picturesque tradition celebrates ambiguity because it is appropriate to the recognition that perception is subjective and changeable. The original meaning of the Italian term 'pittoresco' is a method of laying on paint in bold and irregular strokes to depict not a detailed copy of nature but something closer to the experience of nature.[13] For eighteenth-century advocates of the picturesque, the status of garden design as an art depended on its relations with landscape painting, but the garden was not equivalent to the painting. Thomas Whately, author of *Observations on Modern Gardening* (1770) states that 'Gardening ... is as superior to landskip painting, as a reality is to a representation', adding that paintings are 'studies, not models' for gardens.[14] The picturesque garden was designed the way it was experienced, by a figure moving across a landscape: 'The spot from whence the view is taken is in a fixed state to the painter, but the gardener surveys his scenery while in motion,' writes Humphry Repton in 1794.[15] Valuing the subjectivity of the architect and the user, the uncertainties of the weather and seasons, and with less regard for orthogonal drawings, eighteenth-century garden design was a significant departure in the practice of the architect.

Natural weather

A recurring theme in architectural discourse states that the house is the origin and archetype of architecture, the manifestation of its important attributes.[16] The most noted example is the primitive hut, for which the Roman architect Vitruvius is 'the source of all the later speculation'.[17] But a more familiar and idyllic image of the primitive hut, compatible with the eighteenth-century concern for origins, appears in the frontispiece to Marc-Antoine Laugier's *An Essay on Architecture*, 1753, depicting four tree-trunks supporting a pediment of branches.[18]

Banister Fletcher writes that 'Architecture ... must have had a simple origin in the primitive efforts of mankind to provide protection against inclement weather, wild beasts and human enemies'.[19] Increasingly since the seventeenth century, the house is a private home synonymous with the self, providing psychological as well as physical protection. Robin Evans writes: 'There was a commonplace analogy in seventeenth-century literature that compared a man's soul to a privy chamber, but it is hard to tell now which became private first, the room or the soul. Certainly, their histories are entwined.'[20]

Defined by its separation from the world outside, the home is assumed to be the most secure of environments. The apparent stability of the home may provide gratification but it can also, simultaneously, create anxiety because the home can never be safe enough. David Sibley notes that 'Nature has a long historical association with the other',[21] while Mark Cousins remarks:

> people ... ask nothing of the house in architectural terms, except that it be
> sealed away absolutely successfully from any natural process. ... There is

no reason why the window cannot be fixed the next day, or the next week. But it simply follows from the degree of psychic investment which people have made in respect of the building's integrity, that it must be fixed at four in the morning.[22]

Its opposition to weather historically defines architecture. In an early demonstration of linear perspective, made between 1413 and 1425, Filippo Brunelleschi depicted the square around the baptistery in Florence. But, rather than draw the sky, he silvered part of a wooden panel so that it was seen in reflection, and a different sky was always present.[23] Brunelleschi's demonstration seems to confirm the opinion that weather is outside architectural representation and outside architecture. But an alternative interpretation indicates the importance of weather to architecture. Uncertain and changeable, weather makes architecture more ambiguous, expanding its potential for creative and multiple interpretations.

Ambiguity is a quality rarely attributed to the critical. In art since the early twentieth century, shock is often the agent of the critical and the artist its author. Shock may help to promote new architectural ideas and spaces. But it wears off quickly and is comparatively ineffective, as most buildings are experienced not once but many times when they are not the focus of attention. As the user's experience depends on complex juxtapositions of many moments and many conditions, whether a building is critical may depend not on instantaneous shock but enduring ambiguity, the ability to appear ever-changing, resist resolution and remain open to interpretation.

The value of ambiguity and its association with weather was occasionally recognised in the Italian Renaissance. Leonardo da Vinci's fascination for the effects of weather is wonderfully expressed in the title of his painting *A Town Over-whelmed by a Deluge*, c.1515. Leonardo credits Sandro Botticelli for noticing that 'various inventions are to be seen' in a building stain[24] and identifies similar potential in weather: 'I have in the past seen in clouds and walls stains which have inspired me to beautiful inventions of many things.'[25] Attention given to the effects of weather and weathering is, however, an architectural tradition developed principally from the eighteenth-century picturesque, which held particular fascination for the genius of the place in all its manifestations and ruins as indicators of the passage of time.[26]

In 1849, John Ruskin writes:

For, indeed, the greatest glory of a building is not in its stones, or its gold. Its glory is in its Age ... it is in that golden stain of time, that we are to look for the real light, and colour, and preciousness of architecture.[27]

Ruskin reserved praise for ageing due to the effects of nature rather than the appearance of ageing, as in the newly fabricated picturesque ruin, and regretted the effects of industrialisation. But his symbiosis of architecture and nature counters the assumption that weather is either a problem or a resource:

The idea of self-denial for the sake of posterity, of practising present economy for the sake of debtors yet unborn, of planting forests that our descendants may live under their shade, or of raising cities for future nations to inhabit, never, I suppose, takes place among publicly recognised motives of exertion … God has lent us the earth for our life; it is a great entail. It belongs as much to those who are to come after us, and whose names are already written in the book of creation, as to us; and we have no right, by nay thing that we do or neglect, to involve them in unnecessary penalties, or deprive them of benefits which it was in our power to bequeath.[28]

Man-made weather

Eighteenth-century picturesque gardens proliferated in conjunction with parliamentary land enclosures, which transformed open land into regular fields defined by hedges and walls, creating larger estates. Caught between the exploration of subjective experience and promotion of objective reason, the eighteenth century established two conflicting concepts of weather. In one, evident in the picturesque and developed by Ruskin, weather is associated with the pleasures of perception. In the other, Enlightenment reason conceives weather as just another resource to be manipulated. Through the study of glaciers, plants, grape harvests and other natural phenomena, eighteenth- and nineteenth-century empirical science questioned the long-held assumption that climate was unchanging and divided according to zones. Empiricism replaced a static world with one understood as fluid. As Lucian Boia remarks: 'Man was becoming the dynamic factor through his ability to modify climate and to alter existing natural balances as he pursued his own projects.'[29] The principle that weather is not a condition to be either feared or favoured but one to be manipulated increasingly came to influence the history of architecture.

With rudimentary drainage, open fires and candle lighting, the eighteenth-century house was no more successful as a climate modifier than one centuries before. By contrast, the emergence of new technologies such as gas lighting, the water closet and central heating ensured that the nineteenth-century house provided a more comfortable domestic environment. In 1907, for the first time, the pioneer of air-conditioning, Willis Havilland Carrier, guaranteed the environmental conditions within a building.[30] The term 'air-conditioning' was devised not by Carrier but by a competitor, Stuart W. Cramer, in 1904. For many years, Carrier used a more poetic and appropriate term: 'man-made weather'. In *Towards a New Architecture* (1927), Le Corbusier often mentions architectural solutions to environmental concerns.[31] As early as 1915, he proposed a universal 'neutralising wall' to isolate inside from outside, its materials either transparent or solid as required.[32] Depending on the external climate, either hot or cold air was to circulate in the gap between a double membrane, maintaining the internal temperature at a constant 18°C wherever the building's location.[33]

Electromagnetic weather

Today, threats to the home arrive by new means and old. Physical barriers – such as doors and walls – are less likely to keep the outside outside and the inside inside. While means to exclude natural weather increase, electromagnetic weather flows in and out of the home via the phone, television, radio and computer, extending the permeability of architecture. Unlike natural and man-made weather, electromagnetic weather is generated inside as well as outside. Anthony Dunne and Fiona Raby write that 'electromagnetic weather, oblivious to damp proof membranes, effortlessly passes through, saturating everything'.[34] Identifying and naming the worst excesses of the electromagnetic landscape, they write that 'The rapid expansion of uses for the electromagnetic spectrum has resulted in a new form of pollution, or electrosmog'.[35] Consequently, they argue that the 'challenge today is not to create electronic space, but electronic-free space'.[36] In 1998, Dunne and Raby proposed a Faraday Chair, an enclosed day bed to counter the flow of electronic information. The physicist Michael Faraday invented the Faraday Cage in 1836 to shield a room from external electrical fields. Faraday indicated that the charge of a charged conductor – in his experiment a room coated in metal foil and earthed – is dispersed across the exterior and does not enter the interior. The Faraday Cage is used to protect electronic equipment from electrostatic discharges, such as a lightning strike. Dunne, however, proposes its wider application:

> I realised that today all space is electronic, and that the challenge to designers is to create an 'empty' space, a space that has not existed for most of the century due to the explosion of uses for the electromagnetic spectrum.[37]

Military weather

Culminating the developments initiated by eighteenth-century empirical science, the principle that weather is a resource to be exploited led to its deployment as a military weapon in the second half of the twentieth century. For example, the 1940s discovery that pure silver iodine sprinkled into clouds stimulates precipitation encouraged the US military to employ 'cloud seeding', as in a CIA plan to destabilise the Cuban economy by seeding clouds before they reached the Cuban sugar crop. In response to such tactics, the UN General Assembly passed Resolution 3264 in December 1974, which led to the 'Prohibition of action to influence the environment and climate for military and other purposes compatible with the maintenance of international security, human well-being and health'.

Weather architecture

The assumption that weather and architecture are distinct is unconvincing. First, because the terms 'architecture' and 'weather' are imprecise intellectual constructs through which we comprehend and create our world. Second, because very little weather is only natural. But weather's relationship to architecture, and the discredited assumption that it is a resource to be manipulated, has assumed added significance since the mid-twentieth century because of changing attitudes to the environment, informed by publicity given to climate change. Climate-change research takes account of temperature fluctuations up as well as down. Global warming may occur when carbon dioxide and other gases such as nitrous oxide and methane concentrate in the atmosphere to prevent long-range radiation escaping into space, creating a greenhouse effect. A means to focus criticism on the free-market economy and question the isolationist policies of countries and corporations, global warming can also be understood as a modern-day manifestation of a tradition that includes the biblical flood, in which human failings are threatened by environmental catastrophe. Rather than weather as a resource to be exploited, critics of global warming recognise the co-existence of the environment and its occupants. Critical awareness of the weather, its causes and effects, is a valuable basis for architecture because, in all stages of building, it recognises the co-existence of architecture with its immediate and wider environments, leading to action against climate change, for example. Such knowledge has undoubted benefits but weather's other great asset to critical architecture is its potential to focus attention on the ambiguities of perception.

Richard Gregory writes that 'visual and other perception is intelligent decision-taking from limited sensory evidence. The essential point is that sensory signals are not adequate for direct or certain perceptions, so intelligent guesswork is needed for seeing objects.'[38] Consequently, permeated by memory and experience, 'perceptions are hypotheses. This is suggested by the fact that retinal images are open to an infinity of interpretations.'[39] Binding design to perception focuses attention on the 'capacity to perceive one perceiving'[40] and encourages critical awareness of the spaces we inhabit.

Weather drawing

Whether on a drawing board or a computer screen, the principles of the architectural drawing today are largely the same as those established in the Italian Renaissance. The purpose of such a drawing is to accurately describe an object, not to explore the fluctuations of weather, memory and perception. In the eighteenth century, there was no significant transformation in drawing equivalent and appropriate to the transformations in understanding. If architects are to belatedly exploit the architectural potential of perception suggested by the picturesque, they must either discard or transform the way the draw, and thus the way they design.

Notes

1   Plato, *Timaeus, Critias, Cleitophon, Menexenus, Epistles*, trans. R.G. Bury, Cambridge, MA: Harvard University Press, 1929, p. 121.

2   Leon Battista Alberti, *On the Art of Building in Ten Books*, trans. Joseph Rykwert, Neil Leach and Robert Tavernor, Cambridge, MA, and London: MIT Press, 1988, p. 7. First published as *De Re Aedificatoria*, *c*.1450, trans. J. Leoni, as *Ten Books on Architecture*, 1726.

3   Sebastiano Serlio, *Sebastiano Serlio on Architecture*, vol. 1, books I–V of *Tutte l'opere d' architettura et prospectiva*, 1537–51, trans. Vaughan Hart and Peter Hicks, New Haven and London: Yale University Press, 1996.

4   Andrea Palladio, *The Four Books on Architecture*, trans. Robert Tavernor and Richard Schofield, Cambridge, MA: MIT Press, 1997. First published as *Quattro Libri dell' Archittetura* in 1570.

5   Le Corbusier, *Towards a New Architecture*, trans. Frederick Etchells, London: Rodker, 1927.

6   Rem Koolhaas, *Delirious New York: a Retroactive Manifesto for Manhattan*, Rotterdam: 010, 1994. First published in 1978.

7   The Renaissance was named in recognition of the revival and reinterpretation of Classical antiquity, notably Plato's claim that all the things we perceive in the material world are modelled on the ideal 'forms' of a divine geometry. See Plato, *Timaeus*, p. 121.

8   Alberto Pérez-Gómez, *Architecture and the Crisis of Modern Science*, Cambridge, MA: MIT Press, 1983, pp. 302–11.

9   John Locke, *Essay Concerning Human Understanding*, ed. Peter H. Nidditch, Oxford: Clarendon Press, 1975. First published in 1690.

10   Marsilio Ficino, letter to Giovanni Cavalcanti, quoted in Albert Hofstadter and Richard Kuhns (eds), *Philosophies of Art and Beauty*, Chicago: University of Chicago Press, 1964, p. 204.

11   David Hume, 'Of the Standard of Taste', in *Selected Essays*, Oxford: Oxford University Press, 1993, pp. 136–7.

12   Manfredo Tafuri, *Theories and History of Architecture*, trans. Giorgio Verrecchia, London: Granada, 1980, p. 84.

13   Caroline van Eck, ' "The Splendid Effects of Architecture, and its Power to Affect the Mind": the Workings of Picturesque Association', in Jan Birksted (ed.), *Landscapes of Memory and Experience*, London: Spon, 2000, p. 247.

14   Thomas Whately, 'From *Observations on Modern Gardening*', in John Dixon Hunt and Peter Willis (eds), *The Genius of the Place: the English Landscape Garden 1620–1820*, London: Elek, 1975, p. 62. First published in 1770. Whately uses the Old English term 'landskip'. Its original meaning was a picture of the land, not the land itself.

15   Humphry Repton, *The Art of Landscape Gardening*, 1794, quoted in Yves-Alain Bois, 'A Picturesque Stroll around Clara-Clara', *October*, 29, Summer 1984, p. 43.

16   Vitruvius, *The Ten Books on Architecture*, trans. Morris Hicky Morgan, New York: Dover, 1960, pp. 38–9. First published as *De Architectura* in the first century BC.

17   Joseph Rykwert, *On Adam's House in Paradise: the Idea of the Primitive Hut in Architectural History*, New York: Museum of Modern Art, 1972, p. 105.

18   Marc-Antoine Laugier, *An Essay on Architecture*, trans. Wolfgang and Anni Herrmann, Los Angeles: Hennessey and Ingalls, 1977. First published as *Essai sur l'Architecture* in 1753.

19   Banister Fletcher, *A History of Architecture on the Comparative Method*, London: B.T. Batsford, 1924, 7th edition, p. 1.

20   Robin Evans, 'Figures, Doors and Passages', *Translations from Drawing to Building and Other Essays*, London: Architectural Association, 1997, p. 75.

21   David Sibley, *Geographies of Exclusion: Society and Difference in the West*, London: Routledge, 1995, p. 26.

22   Mark Cousins, 'The First House', *Arch-Text*, no. 1, 1993, p. 37.

23   Hubert Damisch, *A Theory of /Cloud/ Toward a Theory of Painting*, Stanford: Stanford University Press, 2002, pp. 123–4; Robin Evans, *The Projective Cast: Architecture and its Three Geometries,* Cambridge, MA: MIT Press, 1995, p. 133.

24   Leonardo da Vinci, *Leonardo on Painting: an Anthology of Writings by Leonardo da Vinci*, ed. Martin Kemp, trans. Martin Kemp and Margaret Walker, New Haven and London: Yale University Press, 1989, p. 201.

25   Da Vinci, *Leonardo on Painting*, p. 222.

26   Whately, 'From *Observations on Modern Gardening*', p. 305.

27   John Ruskin, *The Seven Lamps of Architecture*, New York: Farrar, Straus and Giroux, 1984, ch. VI, X, p. 177. First published in 1849.

28   Ruskin, *The Seven Lamps of Architecture*, ch. VI, X, p. 180.

29   Lucien Boia, *The Weather in the Imagination*, London: Reaktion, 2005, p. 42.

30   Huguet Silk Mills, Wayland, NY.

31   Le Corbusier, *Towards a New Architecture*.

32   First devised for the Villa Schwob, La Chaux de Fonds, 1915. Reyner Banham, *The Architecture of the Well-tempered Environment*, London: Architectural Press, 1969, pp. 156–63.

33   Quoted in Banham, *The Architecture of the Well-tempered Environment*, p. 160. First published in 1930.

34   Anthony Dunne and Fiona Raby, 'Notopia: Leaky Products/Urban Interfaces', in Jonathan Hill (ed.), *Architecture – The Subject is Matter*, London and New York: Routledge, 2001, p. 102.

35   Anthony Dunne and Fiona Raby, *Design Noir: the Secret Life of Electronic Objects*, London/Basel: August/Birkäuser, 2001, p. 21.

36   Dunne and Raby, *Design Noir*, p. 26.

37   Anthony Dunne, *Hertzian Tales: Electronic Products, Aesthetic Experience and Critical Design*, London: Royal College of Art, 1999, p. 105.

38   Richard Gregory, *Eye and Brain: the Psychology of Seeing*, Oxford: Oxford University Press, 1998, p. 5.

39   Gregory, *Eye and Brain*, p. 10.

40   James Turrell, in Richard Andrews and Chris Bruce, '1992 Interview with James Turrell', in Richard Andrews (ed.), *James Turrell: Sensing Space*, Seattle: Henry Gallery, 1992, p. 48.

Drawing on light

Sam Ridgway

Introduction

This chapter describes the central role Marco Frascari's deliberations on *Lume Materiale* (material light) have played in both an introductory construction course for students of architecture and the design of a small house in suburban Adelaide. In both, the aim has been to emphasise the important architectural objective of embodying the intangible in the tangible. Frascari has played a major role in challenging the prevailing rational and instrumental view of architectural construction. Instead, he articulates an alternative understanding, revealing construction materials and techniques to be culturally embedded and profoundly ontological. Influenced by his early professional and teaching experience with Carlo Scarpa, 'The Tell-the-Tale Detail,'[1] a phenomenological exploration of the role of architectural details published in 1984, was written as a means of introducing the idea that construction embodies the fundamental meanings of architecture, into the design studio at the University of Pennsylvania. 'The *Lume Materiale* in the Architecture of Venice,'[2] published in 1988, explores the spiritual dimension of construction by focusing on the Venetian phenomenon of *Lume Materiale*.

The current division between design and construction (mind and body) in both the architectural profession and the academy makes it unusual to hear the word imagination used in relation to construction. Creativity and imagination are more commonly associated with design, and construction with technical proficiency, extensive knowledge of building products and economic level-headedness. In schools and the profession, construction knowledge is generally applied in an instrumental fashion to designs conceived in the design studio or the director's office. Materials and techniques of construction are considered to be neutral objects and systems from which buildings are assembled, and there is a tendency to rely heavily on product manufacturers to provide technical advice regarding standard detailing. In schools of architecture, the drawing forth of an alternative pedagogy that revitalises the imagination of construction requires us to address its current under-theorisation.

Teaching lightness

My interest in reconceiving the currently dominant, instrumental mode of construction teaching began with research towards a Masters degree during the early 1990s that transformed my naive desire to create an industrialised building system into a deeply sceptical, Heideggerian critique of such systems. My conclusion that they represented the possible annihilation of much that is good in architecture led me to question an architectural education that still nurtured the possibility of such technological utopias. Despite the spectacular demise of modernism and the subsequent loss of status afforded to the architectural profession, due in large part to the failings of its physical fabric, in our school and, I suspect, in many others, construction was still being taught at that time in an instrumental fashion as a set of neutral materials and techniques that could be applied to designs conceived independently in the design studio. The bifurcation of knowledge into matters of mind (design): creativity, innovation and imagination; and matters of body (construction): knowledge of building products, construction techniques and structures, was profound. This was reinforced by a major restructuring of the programme from one five-year professional degree into two, three-year undergraduate degrees, the first dealing with theory and the second with practice. This was later changed to a three-plus-two-year structure. 'Body' knowledge was largely untheorised and lacked historical, cultural, social or philosophical context. There was an understanding that construction should be taught in a linear, technical and encyclopaedic fashion, starting with so-called 'simple' building techniques, domestic timber framing for example, and progress to more technically complicated buildings. The notion that construction could play a generative role in design or that the material embodiment of design ideas held the key to their meaningful presence was not on the agenda.

In the mid-1990s I was appointed to the School and given the task of teaching our first-year, introductory course in construction. My aim was to re-conceive this knowledge so that it would become part of the way students think about design rather than a separate and technical category of skills that must be then integrated into the design studio. In this way I hoped to move considerations of materiality from the periphery of architectural imagination (and pedagogy) to the core and to provide a means of augmenting the traditional method of conceiving a building through attention to form and plan only. While the worthy goal of increasing students' knowledge in this area is common, it is usually implemented in an instrumental fashion resulting in more courses and more assessable construction content in studio projects. My approach was instead to address the supposed neutrality of materials and building techniques. Paradoxically, for a course focusing on the materials of architecture, this meant beginning with theoretical texts rather than with simple building techniques, something that some of my colleagues found quite alarming. Starting with texts, however, provides a very different entry point for instruction in construction, signalling that 'basic' knowledge is an understanding that construction embodies significant meaning. Texts provide an immediate antidote, for example, to the facile notion that discourse concerning architectural production can be reduced to what Dalibor Vesely has described as 'the merit of technical efficiency versus that of aesthetics.'[3] One of the most effect-ive pieces of writing I have found to introduce an alternative understanding of architec-ture's material nature to students is Marco Frascari's article 'The *Lume Materiale* in the Architecture of Venice.'

Published in 1988, '*Lume Materiale*' describes a phenomenological constru-ing or interpretation of the materials of architecture, where, as Frascari writes: 'stones change themselves in light through architecture and architecture exists because of light.' This 'ontological storytelling of architectural events' depicts a method of con-structing buildings from 'palpable material light' (*lume materiale*), 'something born in the materials of construction and imprisoned in the body of an edifice as the mind is imprisoned in the body.' 'A tangible essence of architecture which can be used as a touchstone for the discovery of the true nature of the substances composing a constructed world.'[4] The poetic core of this article is developed from the truism that without light there is effectively no architecture and without architecture there is no light:

> A mound of stones, a splendid Venetian home, a wonderful Byzantine dome, and the most extraordinary Greek temple are the same inert matter without light. Conversely, there is no light without the architectural material which makes up the constructed world.[5]

Frascari's story about light as a building material centres on the Ca'Dario, a Venetian Palace built by the diplomat Giovanni Dario between 1487 and 1497. In an inscription on the facade, Dario dedicates the building to 'the genius of the city' (*Urbis Genio*), thus defining it as a celebration of the city rather than as a personal aggrandisement. Frascari reveals the importance of place and culture in his story about building with light by quoting a Byzantine inscription taken from the Archbishopric Chapel in Ravenna: 'Light is either born here, or imprisoned, reigns here in freedom.' This enig-matic inscription can be interpreted to mean that all cultures build light into their archi-tecture differently through the use of colour, shadow, overhangs, ornament, weatherings, detailing, composition of facades, use of light reflecting or absorbing materials, interior day lighting, sun penetration and so on. When cultures mix, as they do in Venice, Ravenna and Adelaide, architecture begins to embody this diverse revela-tion of *lume materiale*. It does not matter whether it is local or imported, once built-in it 'reigns ... in freedom.' In relation to the Ca'Dario, Frascari points out that it is a

> hybrid – or 'monstrous' – building ... a combination of bold, Gothic ele-ments, Tuscan traditions, Lombardic decorations, and Byzantine memories. ... Ca'Dario is an expression of the multi-faceted culture of Venice. ... an extraordinary hybrid that combines the architecture of the West and the East with the influences of Greece and Rome.[6]

The article goes on to describe in detail several of the key features of the Ca'Dario, including the circular stone and Venetian glass patens that 'can imprison light' and the 'maternal' marble skin of the upper storey made of reused *gallio antico*, a yellow marble from Numidia. In relation to these details, Frascari writes that 'lume materiale … is a rich substance producing a tangible built poetry out of elemental knowledge.'[7]

From the beginning, my construction course established itself as equally concerned with theory and practice. The four journal articles that for the last several years have been the required reading for the course, of which 'The *Lume Materiale*' is one, immediately establish that this is not theory in the current techno-rational sense of theory providing rules in advance of practical action.[8] Rather, it is in the ancient Greek sense of the pairing of *theoria* and *praxis*. As Adrian Snodgrass points out in his article, 'On Theorising Architectural Education,' for the Greeks, *theoria* did 'not precede or stand apart from *praxis* but participated in it.'[9] The crucial and distinguishing aim of this course is to propose an alternative to technical construction theory based on experimentation, calculation and quantification and, instead, to reconceive theory in the mode of *theoria*, as construction knowledge that can participate in the design process. Bringing to the fore the phenomenological and ontological nature of making buildings allows practical knowledge to inform the design process that, as Donald Schön has shown, must at its best deal with 'complexity, uncertainty, instability, uniqueness, and value conflicts.'[10] At its worst, design may be technically competent but fail at a cultural or environmental level. The current instrumental conception of construction theory conforms to the 'criterion of 'efficiency,' which is defined exclusively in terms of utilitarian, quantitative and, increasingly, monetary outcomes.[11] The inability or unwillingness of students to apply or integrate this technical knowledge into a design studio that may be operating in a very different theoretical mode can cause problems and is the source of much discussion. Teaching more construction and insisting on more assessable construction content in design projects does not address the underlying cause of the problem. The moment the word 'integration' is used in relation to construction knowledge and the design studio, it signals that there is a conceptual and structural separation between the two that is unlikely to be resolved by force![12]

'The *Lume Materiale*' offers an elegant means of allowing construction knowledge to transcend the prevailing impasse created by instrumental thinking and to participate in design. The collective revelation that beginning construction students have when reading and presenting this article during tutorial sessions is that there is, for them, a quite new and exciting way of conceiving the material presence of a building 'in' and 'of' light. While they often find the writing difficult, this in itself makes the eventual understandings more lasting and more influential. Its poetic and multi-layered nature allows students to work at many different levels, from issues of interior day lighting to matters of colour, reflectance and shadows to the more complex notion of the cultural specificity of *lume materiale*. The uniquely architectural nature of the building knowledge this article reveals, the fact that 'architecture is co-existent with light' and that an 'architectural presence exerts itself' through light seamlessly correlates theory and practice. Students naturally translate theoretical notions into practical construction decisions; there is no boundary between construction knowledge and the design process. Further, students are unavoidably confronted with one of the most fundamental and continually evolving but often illusive tasks of our profession – that of embodying the intangible in built form. Frascari, for example, refers to the trans-formative process of spinning molten glass on a wheel to make the circular patens that are embedded in the facade of the Ca'Dario as the casting 'of a new tectonic figure', 'that perspicuously presents the colloidal nature of glass.' These thick coloured glass elements participate actively in the 'giant marble puzzle' of the building's facade, liter-ally trapping light and making it a 'material of construction.' The explicit nature of this example leads to further insights as to how other materials, details and elements, both on the facade of the Ca'Dario and other buildings, 'are defined by a piercing light, which engraves their lines and sublimates them to a symbol of repose, certitude and solemnity.'[13]

The major project for the course requires students to 'design' a 'construc-tion' that exemplifies or reveals some aspect of the theoretical material they are working with. In particular, this means an exploration of light, weathering, detailing or *techné*. Because all the articles are presented and discussed in tutorial groups, there is often a significant cross-over between the theoretical interests revealed through each model. The project is to design the construction of a $6 \times 6 \times 6$-metre cube building and to make a model of this at the scale of 1:20. This is inspired by and loosely adapted from the Cooper Union cube exercises under John Hejduk and is assessed according to how it resolves and reveals programmatic, theoretical and construction knowledge. Importantly, for the beginning student, the strict size requirement of the model removes complicated formal and planning deliberations, allowing them to focus primarily on con-struction. Form recedes as a background against which materiality can show up. A simi-larity does exist with the original exercise and that is that the form and size of the building, smaller by 40 per cent, tends to prescribe its possible uses. Too small for a house, its simple volume is conceived as a retreat, library, music room and so on. As a challenge to students to think about the relation of place and building, the constructions are site-specific, the design and modelling of which is the first exercise of the course. Importantly, 'The *Lume Materiale*' offers a profoundly phenomenological interpretation of Venice as the cultural, urban, luminous and ontological place of the Ca'Dario. Frascari explains that, in both painting and construction, 'the Venetians rejected the search for a rationalization of site in favor of a phenomenology of site.'[14] A positivist interpretation of the use of the yellow Numidian marble on the building's facade, probably pillaged from sites around Venice, for example, would be that it was due to issues of site access, limited space, distance from the quarry and cost. A phenomenological interpretation might be that it was the consequence of the Venetian understanding of the 'maternal' nature of weathered materials in the construction of a marble '*cosmesis*' to cover bare brick walls. Frascari's text is a good example of how this student project tries to distin-guish itself from the notion of 'homogenous space as the place of modernity' referred to by Perez-Gomez in his introduction to the reissue of the *Education of an Architect*. This construction course attempts to begin the education of students into 'someone who knows where he or she stands, becoming responsible for a personal *making* in view of the dilemmas of contemporary culture, understanding *why* one makes (and *what* one accepts as an ethical task), and not only how.'[15]

Constructing lightness

It is in the context of devising and teaching this course that I began designing a house for my wife and I to live in, situated on a small suburban site in Adelaide. Listening to student presentations of 'The *Lume Materiale*' in tutorial sessions over several years, helping tease out issues and bring the discussion back to local architectural examples, I developed a deeper understanding and appreciation of this phenomenological inter-pretation of light. The starting point that makes this building possible was an attempt to understand the site in terms other than the purely rational, in particular to interpret and reveal the local light conditions. Much of our training leads us to read sites in terms of what can be measured and calculated: orientation, dimensions, solar access based on sun angles, prevailing winds, the direction of the best views, vehicle and pedestrian access points, slope of the land and so on. Sites are also economically ratio-nalised and the buildings designed for them conceived as commodities, the dollar value of which is known in advance of their construction. It is almost impossible not to be drawn into this cycle of commodification. As architects, however, it is worthwhile contemplating how to introduce a non-instrumental reading of site phenomena into our design process that distinguishes what we do from other design professionals. This may help to divert attention away from a shallow obsession with economic value only, and more successfully deal with issues of dwelling on the Earth in a specific place.

From the beginning I was drawn to the site partly because of its wonderful light, especially the late afternoon, golden light that streams from the west and is particularly striking because of the site's elevation and its proximity to the nearby Ade-laide Hills. While a detailed discussion of place is beyond the scope of this chapter, it is worth noting that the building, in particular its western stone wall, was constructed to embody and reveal the particular local light conditions as a background against which the practices of habituation are played out. Of course it is difficult to counter the claim that it is merely pushing itself and the phenomena of the site forward in the modern sense as spectacle, and it is true that it reveals the movement of the sun throughout the day and the passage of the seasonal light conditions more explicitly than a tradi-tional house. In Heideggerian terms, however, this disclosive characteristic is 'prim-ordial' in nature. In other words, it 'discloses the embodied understanding that we already have of things in the world.'[16] As Frascari writes in the *Lume Materiale*: '[t]his palpable material light, however, is free to express itself, and rules the construing of architectural events posited by the material resolution of elements and the detailing of construction.'[17]

As I lived nearby, I visited the site often and I began to conceive the build-ing in terms of both technical practicalities and in response to the light conditions. The initial design concept was simply to develop two, two-storey masonry facades, one to the west and one to the east that would contain and protect a more delicate, timber-framed and timber-clad body from the prevailing weather. The timber body is quite open to the north and therefore penetrated deeply by the winter sun. The masonry was a response to the suburban context of the building but also, especially in the western facade, a means of developing a paradoxical lightness. That is to create a 'light construction' using heavy materials, thus highlighting the true, joyful nature of lightness. This is in contrast to the current inexorable move towards lightweight buildings. To quote Frascari:

> [t]he prevailing commonplace – a theoretical doxa – is that constructions are increasingly becoming lighter. However, it is just an illusion of lightness since buildings present heavy and distressing inenarrable tales. Consequently a gentle image of architecture, an idealized tale of joyfully, lightly-conceived architectural bodies and images, is no longer the paradoxical motor of successful and delightful structures.[18]

I always imagined that the western facade that faces the street and the western light would be made of stone. Of course all materials are revealed and transformed in light but to me there is a special affinity between stone and light. Stone is a natural material, literally pieces of the planet that have been quarried and shaped to reveal an inner substance. Standing up a wall of stone to the light and the sun is a primal act of dwelling on the Earth as much as it fulfils the need to suitably clad a suburban house. After some deliberation, I chose a honey-coloured sandstone from Basket Range in the Adelaide Hills that had traditionally been used in houses around Adelaide for many years. The concept was still to simply cut large blocks of stone, to try to get as much colour variation as possible and to randomly lay the blocks so that the eye would be drawn to the detail of the wall as much as to its entirety. I realised later that even such a simple idea about colour variation was problematic because, as I soon learned, the stone-supply industry is geared to providing as uniform (neutral) a product as possible.

When the time came to finally resolve the stone detailing of the western elevation, a concern I had about the scale of the blocks being too large for the building

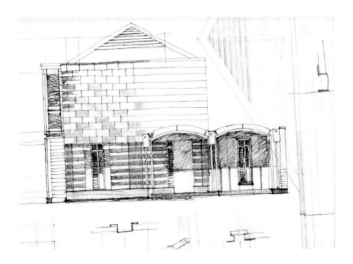

Design sketch.

Working model.

Sample stone blocks.

and the street encouraged me to rethink this elevation. I suddenly realised that I could enhance the light effects on the wall without creating a direct reference to classical or traditional buildings. I wanted the building to face the future and make a stand against the inane sprawl of poor quality, high energy, reproduction buildings that are appearing all over suburban Adelaide. I made a quick cardboard model and was really excited with the results. I realised immediately that there was a way of achieving this detail by using a variation of an existing stone cutting technique (see figure below). In relation to the reuse of stone elements in the Ca' Dario that had been pillaged from abandoned sites around Venice, Frascari suggests that they were transformed 'by technical operations proper to stone work, producing tectonic figures of wonder and ingenious variety in contrast to the purely functional aspects of the built artefact.'[19] Of course fifteenth-century Venice is a rather different story to twenty-first-century Adelaide, but nevertheless I felt that somehow this idea had translated itself across time and was capable of creating something that was very forward-looking and site-specific but still powerfully connected to the past. I'm not sure what tools and techniques were used to cut and shape the stone for the Ca' Dario, but nowadays stone is cut primarily using water-lubricated diamond-tipped oscillating and circular saws and it is relatively easy to cut one face of a block on an angle either by adjusting the saw blade or by sitting each block in an angled jig and then running it through the saw. Despite this, because it stepped outside the normal practice of the cutting yard that specialised in producing reproduction facades for new houses, it caused many problems and delays.

In conclusion, I am reminded of Carlo Scarpa's statement quoted by Frascari in 'The Tell-the-Tale Detail' that, 'in architecture, there is no such thing as a good idea. There is only expression.'[20] I had many sleepless nights wondering what the 'expression'

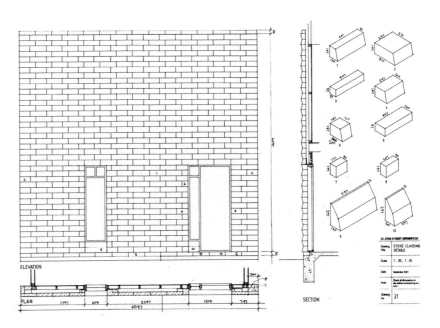

Stone cladding details.

The crinkled stone facade reveals local light and the daily movement of the sun.

of this wall would be and how it would be received by the neighbourhood! I was worried that it was 'a good idea' only and that its paradoxical lightness would in fact be 'inenarrable.' These fears started to recede when I travelled to the stone-cutting yard to look at the samples and knew immediately that the idea and the expression were sound. This was confirmed on the exciting day when the first five courses of blocks were laid. Most people understand immediately that it has something to do with light. Others see it as ripples on water; one asked if it was to become a waterfall. Several have thought the facade was made of timber which, having been through the dramas and difficulties of making it out of stone, initially astonished me but on reflection I welcomed this interpretation as part of a rich process of signification (see figure below). In this short chapter, I have concentrated only on a story about light. Simply put, this building is my attempt to stand against the prevailing technological view of everything; to step aside from the off-the-shelf mentality where we are supposed to create something original and creative from building products designed by product designers not architects. It is my attempt to respond to the fact that we dwell on the Earth in a specific location within a moving universe. It tries to say something about the simplistic notion that lightweight buildings are light buildings. But most of all, it is just an attempt to make a joyful, serene building that faces the future while acknowledging a rich architectural past.

Notes

1   Frascari, 1984, 22–37.
2   Frascari, 1988, 137–145.
3   Vesely, 1995, p. 44.
4   Frascari, 1988, p. 138.
5   Frascari, 1988, p. 138.
6   Frascari, 1988, p. 140.
7   Frascari, 1988, p. 141.
8   The other three journal articles are Meagher, 1988, 158–164; Frascari, 1984, 22–37;
     Leatherbarrow and Mostafavi, 1992, 116–123.
9   Snodgrass, 2000, p. 90.
10   Schön, 1983, p. 14.
11   Snodgrass, 2000, p. 91.
12   For a lengthy discussion of integrating technical knowledge into the design studio,
     see *The Journal of Architectural Education*, 51, 2 (November 1997). See also
     Ridgway, 2003, 152–163.
13   Frascari, 1988, p. 143.
14   Frascari, 1988, p. 144.
15   Pérez-Gómez, 1999, pp. 14–19.
16   Hill, 2002.
17   Frascari, 1988, p. 137.
18   Frascari, 2002, 1–11.
19   Frascari, 1988, p. 141.
20   Frascari, 1984, p. 29.

Bibliography

Marco Frascari, 'The Tell-the-Tale Detail,' *Via*, 7 (1984).

Marco Frascari, 'The *Lume Materiale* in the Architecture of Venice,' *Perspecta*, 24 (1988).

Marco Frascari, 'A Light, Six-Sided, Paradoxical Fight,' *Nexus Network Journal*, 4, 2 (2002):
      1–11. Online, available at: www.nexusjournal.com/Frascari_v4n2.html (accessed
      7 March 2006).

Glen Hill, 'Out of Place in the Landscape: Questioning the Rhetoric of Place,' *Additions to
      Architectural History*, XIXth conference of the Society of Architectural Historians, Aus-
      tralia and New Zealand, Brisbane (2002).

David Leatherbarrow and Mohsen Mostafavi, 'On Weathering: a New Surface Out of the
      Tracks of Time,' *Daidalos*, 43 (1992).

Robert Meagher, '*Techné*,' *Perspecta*, 24 (1988).

Alberto Pérez-Gómez, 'Education of an Architect: Unravelling a Point of View, 1999,' intro-
      ductory essay to the reissued original exhibition catalogue, *Education of an Architect:
      a Point of View – The Cooper Union School of Art & Architecture 1964–1971*, New
      York: The Monacelli Press, 1999.

Sam Ridgway, 'Construction Knowledge and the Design Studio: the Question of Integra-
      tion,' *Architectural Theory Review*, 8, 2 (2003).

Schön, *The Reflective Practitioner*, New York: Basic Books Inc., 1983.

Adrian Snodgrass, 'On Theorising Architectural Education,' *Architectural Theory Review*, 5, 2
      (2000).

Dalibor Vesely, 'Architecture and the Question of Technology,' in Martin Pearce and Maggie
      Toy (eds), *Educating Architects*, London: Academy Editions, 1995.

Post-secular architecture

Material, intellectual, spiritual models

Bradley Starkey

Introduction

In 'Translations from Drawing to Building' Robin Evans observes that, unlike sculptors or painters, architects do not work directly with the object of their labour but work towards it through intervening media.[1] Drawings, texts and models are used to develop and communicate design information in the architectural design process. Whereas architectural drawing and writing have been subjected to architectural theorisation, however, architectural models have tended to escape analysis. Likewise, architectural theorists use the modes of drawing and writing to theorise their work, but they rarely use the architectural model as a critical or theoretical tool. Models are more likely to be used for descriptive purposes in the design process. The lack of critical attention focused on the model as a medium of architectural representation is surprising. In *The Book of Models*, Chris Dillon writes that 'we are often unaware that our methods, values and modes of action are themselves ideological. They are particular theoretical positions of which we are unaware but which we unconsciously support.'[2]

      Architects commonly adopt the assumption that forms of architectural mediation are ideologically neutral. Compared with models, however, the 'methods, values and modes of action' associated with drawings and texts are more consciously and critically understood. The scope of this chapter is to critically investigate aspects of the architectural model. After an initial exploration of the meaning of the term 'model' itself, it will discuss the displaced status of architectural models in relation to architectural theory. It argues that, whilst drawings have been accorded intellectual status, models have been more closely associated with the realm of the material.

      With reference to the strategies of 'immediacy' and 'hypermediacy', the chapter will discuss the ideological performance of descriptive models and, with reference to a levitating architectural model constructed by the author, it will suggest an alternative role for the model in architecture. The chapter concludes by relating architectural models with models of thought. Contemporary models of thought are constructed upon assumptions that promote materiality rather than spirituality. With the intention of advancing the idea of the post-secular, the levitating model offers a tentative interpretation of what a contemporary reappraisal of the spiritual in architecture might be.

The architecture of models and models of architecture

In an attempt to understand the architecture of models, it is helpful to refer to a classification system that was proposed by Marcial Echenique in the late 1960s, which aimed to identify the characteristics of different model types.[3] The system plotted model types within a cubic space defined by three dimensions: what the model was made for; what the model was made of; and how the model engaged with time. In relation to the first dimension, models could be made for 'descriptive', 'predictive', 'exploratory' or 'planning' purposes. In relation to the second dimension, models could be made of either 'materials' or 'concepts'. Material models were further sub-divided into either 'iconic' or 'analogue' types, and conceptual models were further sub-divided into text-based or mathematically based types; and in relation to the third dimension, models could either establish 'static' or 'dynamic' temporal relationships. Different permutations of the three dimensions generated multiple model types.

Within this system, a model was defined as being a representation of reality 'where representation is the expression of certain relevant characteristics of the observed reality and where reality consists of the objects or systems that exist, have existed, or may exist'.[4] In *The Book of Models*, Chris Dillon adopts a similar understanding of the term when he writes that 'whenever we attempt to speak, write or otherwise represent aspects of our experience and understanding of physical reality we are entering into a modelling relationship with the world'.[5] John Monk reinforces this definition when he writes that a model is a thing or concept that 'stimulates people to give accounts that could also be triggered by the object being modelled'.[6]

Whilst these applications of the term advance our understanding of what a model can be, they each define the term in relation to the notion of an observed external or original reality, where the model is a description or representation of that reality. The application of the term within everyday language, however, suggests another type of modelling relationship.

Multiple meanings of the term 'model' are currently in circulation. It can refer to an object that is made to represent another object (usually at a different scale); a system or theory that describes attributes of some aspect of reality; or an object used in testing a final product. The term can also be used to refer to a person or object serving as an example to be imitated by another; a person who acts as the subject for an artist or who is used to display clothes; and it can also be used to refer to a specific style of a particular item (i.e. make and model of a car). From its etymological roots in the Latin term *modus* and *modulus*, it also has connotations of proportion and measurement.[7] Across these diverse nuances of meaning it is useful to distinguish between models that describe aspects 'of' something else, and models that act as an example or standard 'for' something else. Whilst the former type is limited to the representation of reality, the second type has the potential to generate reality.

When architectural practitioners, teachers or students talk about models in the context of design, pedagogy and practice, the word is generally understood to refer to a particular model type. Counter to the multiple typologies generated within Echenique's cubic system, and to the multiple applications of meaning in everyday language, the application and understanding of the term within architecture is reductive. Since the eighteenth century, architectural discourse has predominantly interpreted the term to mean an original that should be imitated, as in a small-scale representation of a building.

Model theory

Diana Agrest has written that architecture is produced through three modes: drawing, writing and building.[8] While she promotes the value of writing and thus legitimises architectural theory as a generator of architecture, she also undervalues the role of the model. Agrest does include the model as a possible fourth mode of production; however, she includes it as a footnote rather than within the main text, and this implies that there is a displacement between the status of the architectural drawing, text or theory and the status of the architectural model.

The marginalised status of the architectural model can be traced back to the Italian Renaissance when the emergence of design as a distinct and specialised discipline began to be associated with the process of drawing, and disassociated from the materiality of building. During this period, changes in building procurement meant that the design of a building had to be documented before its construction. Prior to this, design information would have been orally transmitted, from the mind of the master mason to the craftsmen working on site, without detailed construction drawings. With building procurement in the Middle Ages, the design and supervision of building was fused with the materiality of building, but in the Italian Renaissance a division in labour emerged that separated design and supervision from building. Architects became distanced from the materiality and manual labour of craft-based work and configured their practice on intellectual terms.

While architects used both drawings and models to communicate design information in the Italian Renaissance, drawings were, in time, accorded a higher intellectual status and were therefore of greater strategic significance to architects. The process of making a model required skill but the handling of matter and models was messy work and therefore was carried out in the workshop. In contrast, drawings could be made in the 'gentlemanly' space of the study. The process of drawing was perceived to be equivalent to the process of writing, doing mathematics or philosophising. Drawings were associated with the intellectual, and came to be a recognised medium through which architects could elevate their minds and, consequently, the status of the profession. Conversely, models were more closely associated with the material and were therefore accorded a lower status.

Communicating and generating design ideas

Architectural models exist somewhere between the realm of ideas and the physical materiality of buildings. They are typically used in the design process as a complement to drawing and it is often stated that architectural models are easily understood by those without architectural training or experience in spatial thinking. For this reason, models are often made to communicate design proposals to the public or for competition entries.

While models are frequently used to 'communicate' design ideas, they are rarely used to 'generate' them. Architectural models are usually made after a building has already been conceived which, since the Italian Renaissance, has usually occurred through the process of drawing. In 'Translations from Drawing to Building', Robin Evans writes: 'Drawing in architecture is not done after nature, but prior to construction; it is not so much produced by reflection on the reality outside the drawing, as productive of a reality that will end up outside the drawing.'[9]

Architecture is brought into existence through drawing, where the subject matter or building exists after the drawing, but not before it. In this way architectural drawings are predictive in that they describe a reality that does not yet exist. Evans' statement is less true of the conventional architectural model, however, and while it is recognised that drawing has the potential to bring ideas into existence that do not exist prior to drawing, the subject matter for descriptive architectural models already exists in drawn form prior to construction. For descriptive architectural models, then, Evans' statement might be re-written thus: 'Models in architecture are not constructed after nature, but after drawing.' However, to restrict model-making to descriptive rather than generative functions reinforces the assumption that attributes drawing with intellectual status elevated above the material.

Unlike the medieval master mason directly engaged with the materiality of building, modern-day architects exercise a remote control over building dealing primarily with drawings, models and texts. In *The Book of Models*, Rolf Hughes uses the terms 'mediated' and 'unmediated reality' to distinguish between the mediated realities created by drawings, models and texts and the unmediated realities to which they relate.[10] The terms are appropriate because they acknowledge that mediated realities do not simply represent aspects of an external original or reality, but they also construct particular realities of their own. In this way, drawings, models and texts are hybrids. Hughes writes: 'When we talk about these models our account will be a "hybrid", using words associated with the model alongside words associated with the object being modeled.'[11]

Immediacy and hypermediacy

In their book entitled *Remediation*, Jay David Bolter and Richard Grusin identify two strategies towards the perception of mediated reality as 'immediacy' and 'hypermediacy'.[12] Immediacy refers to forms of mediation where the presence of the medium is perceived as invisible or transparent. Virtual reality, for example, strives towards immediacy where the mediating presence of the computer interface is invisible so as to fully immerse the user in a virtual world without distraction. Linear perspective also promises immediacy through the transparency and invisibility of the surface of the painting, which dissolves and presents the viewer to the scene beyond. Bolter and Grusin write: 'It is important to note that the logic of transparent immediacy does not necessarily commit the viewer to an utterly naive or magical conviction that the representation is the same thing as what it represents.'[13] Whilst the viewer is not completely deceived by immediacy, however, 'the user is no longer aware of confronting a medium, but instead stands in an immediate relationship to the contents of that medium'.[14]

Whereas immediacy assumes the transparency or neutrality of the act of representation, hypermediacy acknowledges and visibly expresses the presence of the medium. The strategy of immediacy constructs the illusory perception of direct access to a contact point with unmediated reality, whereas the strategy of hypermediacy acknowledges and expresses its indirect, hybrid and thus mediatory role.

At one level, huge discrepancies exist between the realities of architectural models and the complexity of buildings. Given the differences between them, one would expect architectural models to be perceived as hypermediatory. However, this is rarely the case and the totality, three-dimensionality, manoeuvrability and/or physicality of architectural models encourages the assumption that the model 'is' the building. The perception of architectural models as ideologically neutral and as offering a perceptual immediacy with the buildings that they represent has become deeply embedded within architecture. John Monk writes that

> a model or set of models or genre provide the way in which specialists, such as engineers, make sense of reality. To join a profession like engineering involves becoming so familiar with a set of models that the models provide the way in which someone orders their view of reality.[15]

By implication, the same can be said of architectural models.

The construction of immediacy

With reference to empirical research, Bolter and Grusin explain that the strategy of immediacy is a culturally constructed form of deception or illusion. Photographs and linear-perspective drawings were shown to participants who were unfamiliar such media. They write:

> For the Westerners, photography and linear-perspective drawing are media that are constructed as transparent. The images are transparent, however, only because Westerners have already learned to overlook, or 'look through,' the conventions that they appear on paper and offer a static, monocular view. When the same images were handed to the African

subjects, they were at first experienced as hypermediated. Some of the subjects had never seen paper before, so that the very idea of paper carrying an image was foreign to them. After that initial phase, when the subjects had adjusted and could read the images 'properly,' the media would still not necessarily be transparent in our sense, because the African subjects would not have had the opportunity to build the collective response that Western culture now has to perspective painting, photography, and realistic film.[16]

Architectural models are perceived as transparent and ideologically neutral because they are understood within an architectural culture that has been conditioned to 'look through' or to 'overlook' the hybrid materiality and hypermediate reality of the model. Disturbingly, this suggests that architects may be unknowingly ordering their view of reality through deceptive and illusory media.

Abstract models

In the *Production of Space*, Henri Lefebvre is critical of the way in which architects work with abstractions. He says that the architect's space (along with the space of other experts such as that of urbanists and planners) is a space of calculations and intellectual abstractions rather than a space of living subjects. He writes:

> Within the spatial practice of modern society, the architect ensconces himself in his own space. ... This 'conceived' space is thought by those who make use of it to be 'true', despite the fact – or perhaps because of the fact – that it is geometrical: because it is a medium for objects, an object itself, and a locus for the objectification of plans.[17]

For architects, the potential problem of immediacy is that it encourages the assumption that the abstract reality created by the model (drawing or text) is synonymous with the unmediated reality within which it is intended to be projected. To use Lefebvre's words, it 'forgets that space does not consist in the projection of an intellectual representation'.[18] The three-dimensionality, physicality, manoeuvrability and totality of architectural models increases the tendency for them to be perceived as synonymous with the building. Mediated realities are never synonymous with unmediated realities, however, and architectural models are always, but in different ways, abstract and partial. Models can never present a one-to-one relationship in all aspects and dimensions. John Monk writes:

> A model cannot trigger all possible stories about the modelled object so a model is in some way specialised and limited. Of course if all the accounts of the model and the object being modelled were the same then the objects would be indistinguishable and we might even conclude that they were the same object.[19]

Whether the abstracting tendencies of architectural models is problematic in the way that Lefebvre claims is dependent upon whether their mediatory role is acknowledged and used knowingly, or whether the strategy of transparent immediacy is uncritically and unconsciously assumed. In relation to drawing, Jonathan Hill has written:

> To contradict Lefebvre, the architectural drawing does have a positive role if [the] differences and similarities [between the drawing and the building] are acknowledged, and used knowingly. All practices need an articulate language to develop complex ideas and propositions before or without their physical application. The drawing is a means to explore ideas, to develop theories, to speculate on matter and use, and a space in which to dream and research.[20]

Building a model

This discussion of models establishes a theoretical context for the author's design-based research. This section will now refer to an architectural model constructed by the author. The model comprises a floor slab and a transparent plane. The floor slab is constructed out of medium-density fibre-board and measures 700 × 1950. Thirty-five holes are drilled into the board in a grid pattern; each hole has a nickel-plated neodymium iron boron disc inserted into it. The discs are glued into position to flush with the top surface of the board and the board is laminated with a mirror, which is cut to flush with the perimeter of the floor slab. The transparent plane is cast out of clear polyester resin and measures 340 × 1200 × 10. With the length of the plane notionally divided into three, an elliptical mound is centred on one of the dividing lines (see the first figure below). The mound is not solid and has the same thickness as the plane so that a continuous smooth surface is created, integrating both plane and mound. Centred on the other notional dividing line is a rectangular void measuring 110 × 260 (see second figure on next page). Thirty-five nickel-plated neodymium discs are embedded within the thickness of the resin in the same grid pattern as the discs in the floor slab.

**Bradley Starkey,
Post-Secular Model,
2005.** *Mound.*

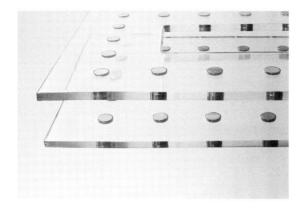

**Bradley Starkey,
Post-Secular Model,
2005. *Void.***

Neodymium iron boron is the most common form of high-energy magnetic material. With a Bhmax range of 207 to 326 kJ/m³, it has a high energy-to-unit volume performance. A powerful magnetic field is created above, within and below the floor slab but to the naked eye the field is invisible. The magnets are not visible either. The transparent plane is positioned parallel to the floor slab with the neodymium disks vertically aligned and the plane levitates (see figures below).

**Bradley Starkey,
Post-Secular Model,
2005. *After Rainfall.***

**Bradley Starkey,
Post-Secular Model,
2005. *Drifting Sand.***

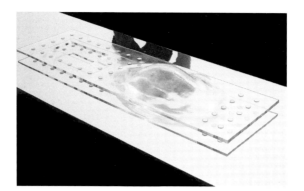

Bradley Starkey,
Post-Secular Model,
2005. *Reflection*.

The floor slab is open and accessible from all sides, and the void between the floor slab and the levitating plane frames the horizon (see figure below). The mirrored surface produces a reflection of the levitating plane and doubles its apparent height of levitation. The mound is reflected in the floor slab and a transparent cocoon-like enclosure is created; one half is formed by the internal surface of the mound; the other by its reflection. The neodymium discs in the levitating plane are also reflected in the floor slab and allude to the existence of the hidden magnets. However, they do not occupy the same location. The real magnets are located directly behind the surface of the mirror; the reflected magnets appear to be located deeper down.

This exercise in design-based research implements the process of 'building a model', rather than the more conventional and familiar process of modelling a building. The significance of building a model is that it allows the construction of a speculative space in which to generate design through research and through the process and materiality of making. Consequently, the research outcome is not solely focused on the production of a model 'of' architecture. Rather, the process itself becomes a model 'for' architecture and it suggests a mode of production where the model is used to generate design ideas through the materiality of making. The status of the architectural model is thus elevated above mere descriptive or predictive functions. Predictive models all-too-often result in predictable buildings, where the building is projected as a scaled-up version of the architect's model. The technology of the levitating architectural model referred to in this chapter cannot simply be scaled up and the model therefore adopts a critical stance, informing architecture in multiple and diverging ways.

Bradley Starkey,
Post-Secular Model,
2005. *Framing the
Horizon*.

Post-secular architecture: material, intellectual, spiritual models

This chapter has discussed the architectural model in terms of material and intellectual dimensions, and it has argued that the model has not been accorded equivalent intellectual status to the drawing. By using the model as a critical research tool, and one that is capable of generating rather than merely describing design ideas, the architectural model can integrate a hybrid synthesis of material and intellectual dimensions.

In contemporary western culture, however, both material and intellectual dimensions are ultimately validated by a materialistic metaphysics. Contemporary models of thought are constructed upon hypotheses that are predominantly secular and rational and which ultimately promote materiality rather than spirituality. Furthermore, western culture has generally defined the spiritual in opposition to the material, and as transcending the material world. Material things, such as works of art, buildings and architectural models have generally been located in the material world and therefore disassociated from the spiritual. Commenting on the relationship between art and divinity in the Middle Ages, but still widely reinforced by contemporary models of thought, Moshe Barasch has written:

> The divine is immaterial; it has no definite, specific forms; it is invisible. The work of art, on the other hand, is by necessity material; it has definite, specific forms; and it is completely rooted in the realm of the visible and tangible, in the field of sensuous experience.[21]

Post-secular reinterpretations of philosophy have recently emerged, however, and they suggest a contemporary reappraisal of the spiritual.[22] In advancing the idea of the post-secular within architecture, the author has built an architectural model that is not completely rooted in the material world, but instead levitates above it. The levitating model represents the author's interpretation of what a contemporary reappraisal of the spiritual in architecture might be.

Notes

1   Evans, 1997, pp. 153–193.
2   Dillon, 1998, p. 51.
3   Echenique, 1970, pp. 25–30.
4   Echenique, 1970, p. 25.
5   Dillon, 1998, p. 49.
6   Monk, 1998, p. 40.
7   Perez-Gomez and Pelletier, 1997, p. 106.
8   Agrest and Allen, 2000, p. 164.
9   Evans, 1997, p. 165.
10   Hughes, 1998, pp. 11–31.
11   Hughes, 1998, p. 13.
12   Bolter and Grusin, 1999.

13   Bolter and Grusin, 1999, p. 30.
14   Bolter and Grusin, 1999, p. 24.
15   Monk, 1998, p. 44.
16   Bolter and Grusin, 1999, pp. 72–73.
17   Lefebvre, 1991, p. 361.
18   Lefebvre, 1991, p. 200.
19   Monk, 1998, p. 40.
20   Hill, 2003, p. 174.
21   Barasch, 2000, p. 52.
22   Blond, 1998.

Bibliography

Diana Agrest and Stan Allen, *Practice: Architecture, Technique and Representation*, London: Routledge, 2000.

Moshe Barasch, *Theories of Art: From Plato to Winckelmann*, London: Routledge, 2000.

Phillip Blond (ed.), *Post-Secular Philosophy: Between Philosophy and Theology*, London: Routledge, 1998.

Jay David Bolter and Richard Grusin, *Remediation: Understanding New Media*, Cambridge, MA and London: MIT Press, 1999.

Chris Dillon, 'Constructs and Deconstructs', in Rolf Hughes and John Monk (eds), *The Book of Models: Ceremonies Metaphor, Performance*, Milton Keynes: Open University, 1998, pp. 49–67.

Marcial Echenique, 'Models: a Discussion', *Architectural Research and Teaching*, 1:1 (1970), pp. 25–30.

Robin Evans, 'Translations from Drawing to Building', in *Translations from Drawing to Building and Other Essays*, London: Architectural Association, 1997.

Jonathan Hill, 'Hunting the Shadow: Immaterial Architecture', *Journal of Architecture*, 8:2 (2003), pp. 165–179.

Rolf Hughes, 'Second Nature: Philosophy & Performance, Metaphors & Models', in Rolf Hughes and John Monk (eds), *The Book of Models: Ceremonies, Metaphor, Performance*, Milton Keynes: Open University, 1998, pp. 11–31.

Rolf Hughes and John Monk (eds), *The Book of Models: Ceremonies, Metaphor, Performance*, Milton Keynes: Open University, 1998.

Henri Lefebvre, *The Production of Space*, trans. D. Nicholson-Smith, Blackwell: Oxford, 1991.

John Monk, 'Ceremonies and models', in Rolf Hughes and John Monk (eds), *The Book of Models: Ceremonies, Metaphor, Performance*, Milton Keynes: Open University, 1998, pp. 33–47.

Alberto Perez-Gomez and Louise Pelletier, *Architectural Representation and the Perspective Hinge*, Cambridge, MA and London: MIT Press, 1997.

Specifying materials

Language, matter and the conspiracy of muteness

Katie Lloyd Thomas

The architectural drawing replicates a prevalent but limited conceptualization of material as matter. Here the use of language in the poems of Francis Ponge and in the architectural specification open up possibilities for a more properly architectural understanding of materials.

Introduction

In his work *Incidents of Mirror-Travel in Yucatan* (1969), the artist Robert Smithson set up twelve identical mirrors in the ground of nine very different sites in the Yucatan. For Smithson, the mirrors stood in for the eyes of the artist, and reflected particularly the material and temporality of the landscapes in which they were placed. The perfect blue of the Gulf of Mexico sky, swarms of swallowtail butterflies caught momentarily as they flew over a gravel heap, the sluggish movement of river mud as it slowly crumbled over them.[1]

A photograph of each 'displacement' and Smithson's accompanying text are all that document this work. The reflections are literal absences in the images – white holes – but Smithson finds them similarly difficult to capture in text. 'Ideal language,' he wrote, could only capture the mirrors as 'ongoing abstractions'.[2] Their duration and physicality evaded representation.

Materiality and time are also notoriously difficult to capture in orthographic drawing; an ongoing abstraction in which only the form of building appears and the material is nothing but the emptiness between the lines; the unblemished whiteness of the paper or the infinite blackness of the screen. It was not just the reflections which Smithson could not describe. The mirrors themselves displayed, he wrote, 'a conspiracy of muteness concerning their very existence'.[3] Ordinary mirrors, such as the ones he used, are perfectly and evenly silvered, and polished into disappearance. This is of course the case for all mediums of representation – their contribution to the production of meaning or content is intended to go unseen.

Smithson's project provides a number of starting points for this chapter. It reveals some of the tensions between ideal and material that occur in any form of representation. And, despite the limitations that the artist encounters, he or she tries to find a way through them by using language where the image fails. Most importantly, it lends us an easily recalled example of a form of representation – here the travelling mirrors – which, like the orthographic drawing, remains constant whatever its object.

In this chapter I identify and discuss an alternative strategy to the travelling mirrors, in which the form of representation does not necessarily remain constant but, instead, deflects in response to its objects. Here we might imagine that Smithson brought a different set of mirrors to each of his sites – some greener perhaps, others cloudier, another set curved and so on – and as a result their specific materialities would be visible at least in relation to the others. This is the intentional strategy of the French poet Francis Ponge whose project was to speak 'on the side of things'. It is also, I hope to show, the (unintentional) strategy used in the architectural specification to make possible distinctions between materials – as individuated from each other and between their various roles in construction. While Ponge's medium is the 'proême' as he called it, rather than the clause of the specification, it also attempts to describe the physical world using written language. While some of Ponge's subjects could be called 'materials' – anthracite, the pebble or soap, and at a stretch wind or moss – many are manmade or natural objects – the door, the crate, the oyster, the mimosa – and even persons – the gymnast. They do not map neatly onto the materials (and components) of the specification – concrete, plasterboard, glass (locks, cavity ties, u-bends), but as in the specification, Ponge takes very particular care to distinguish one from the other, and to find language that is adequate to the specificity of each.

In architecture, the task of describing materials is left to language, both in the notes and annotations on drawings and in the specification, which contains no photographs, drawings or diagrams.[4] Indeed, for the team who designed the National Building Specification (NBS) – the standardized version of the specification that was introduced in the UK in the 1970s and now prevails – the distinction between drawing and language was crucial. John Carter, an executive member of a committee who pre-pared an early feasibility study, considered it was essential 'to trace a boundary between drawings, quantities and specification' and that certain information was 'better expressed in words than graphically'.[5] Colin McGregor, one of the team who produced the original NBS and worked on it right up until his recent retirement, reiterates:

> You cannot draw a concrete mix for example. Carter is right (and we have been plugging this message since the beginning) that design intent cannot just be expressed on drawings … much of the design must be expressed non-graphically.[6]

While the drawing represents form using geometry and is valued in itself, the specification is merely a 'supplement' to the drawing and is not usually considered a representation at all.[7] So material disappears as the invisible medium of representation is not included as an object of representation in the drawing, and where it does finally appear, in language, it is considered outside critical attention, nothing more than a 'practical', 'legal' or 'technical' document. This neglect of the specification might be considered the third 'conspiracy of muteness' surrounding material in architectural representation.

Ponge was himself interested in the relationships between artistic and technical disciplines. In 1954 he was commissioned by the Électricité de France to write a prose piece that would persuade architects to make more use of electricity and incorporate it into their designs.[8] He saw himself as 'a technician of language' acting as 'an intermediary' between two categories of (intelligent!) technicians – the architect and the electrician. The role of the text would be perhaps as 'a spark leaping between two opposite poles, separated by a hiatus in the expression only the elimination of the logical link allowing the spark to flash'. His work was, he wrote, 'conceived in two instalments, the first ... distinct from the other' which was to be 'wholly technical'.[9] Perhaps this image of a technical and poetic text side-by-side lends a precedent to this study of the specification in relation to Ponge's poetry.

Specifying materials: a plurality of mirrors

In Jacques Derrida's interpretation of Husserl's account of hearing oneself think, he concludes that a medium of representation must be at work (for if it was not present, how would our own speech come back to us as expression?). He imagines it as a mirror that does not intervene in the representation and must then be 'without colour of its own'.[10] Modernist art across the disciplines has been particularly concerned with bringing the colourless medium into visibility. Just as paint and gestures have been foregrounded and canvases have been slashed in the visual arts in order to make the medium visible, some architectural theorists have explored the fleshiness of the line or the graphite smudge in architectural drawings.[11] Likewise, in literary practice, there have been countless experimentations with the materiality of the text, from Mallarmé to Derrida. Language poetry and visual poetics in particular understands the word as material; it has a history and has been produced, and has a material presence on and in relation to the page.[12]

Ponge is not a typical writer of this modernist enterprise, but in his concern to find correspondences between his texts and the objects they describe, he does draw attention to the materiality of both. For example, in his poem 'Les Mures' – 'ripe blackberries' – he plays on the similarity of the inkiness of the printed text and the black juice of the fruits:

> In the typographical thickets that go into the making of a poem, along a road that leads neither beyond things nor to the mind, certain fruits are formed by an agglomeration of spheres, each filled with a drop of ink.[13]

While these lines succeed in connecting the absent blackberries to the printed text in front of us, the materiality of the text that they evoke is limited to that of the substance which gives the words presence (as voice does in spoken language). For Ponge, this strategy would limit the use of adequation to objects that shared qualities with type. Here, material is other to meaning or form, and, like Husserl's mirror, it is the by-product of any representation. It is matter conceived in a negative relation to form and as such it is only ever singular.

Ponge's mirror poem 'Fable' is also concerned with the material of the medium of representation – the 'silvering' that always intervenes in the reflection – but in it he finds a range of means within its language to express this.

> Fable
> Par le mot *par* commence donc ce texte
> Dont la première ligne dit la vérité,
> Mais ce tain sous l'une et l'autre
> Peut-il être toléré?
> Cher lecteur déjà tu juges
> Là de nos difficultés. . . .
>
> (APRÈS sept ans de malheurs
> *Elle brisa son miroir*)
>
> Fable
> By the word *by* then starts this text
> Whose first line tells the truth,
> But this silvering beneath the one and the other
> Can it be tolerated [borne/allowed]?
> Dear reader, already you can judge
> From this our difficulties. . . .
>
> (AFTER seven years of misfortunes
> *She [it] broke her mirror*)[14]

Looking at the poem in greater detail a number of lines of symmetry become apparent:

1	By		the word *by*
2	By the word *by* then starts this text		Whose first line tells the truth,
3	Beneath the one		and the other

Since Ponge addresses the reader directly, a fourth line of symmetry could also be drawn between:

| 4 | The poem | | and the reader |

Ponge reminds us of the mirror's physicality that always exists between the object and its reflected image in the line 'but this silvering beneath the one and the other'. In the first line we see how this silvering is not able to produce an ideal reflection.[15] We can imagine 'the word *by*' as the reflection of 'By'. Spoken out loud, the two 'by's sound the same and reflect truthfully, but in their written form, as they appear materially on the page, they are different, one italicized, one capitalized. In addition, the two 'by's are not used in the same way – the first has meaning in the sentence (it is a signifier) while the second refers only to the word as sign. The act of reflection produces a transformation, not a copy, and is a fabulation, as the title of the poem suggests.

In 'Fable' the silvering cannot be tolerated, it cannot be allowed, for as soon as it appears (as when it begins to flake on a mirror) the mechanism of reflection is revealed and no longer neutral. The silvering is exactly that which disrupts ideality – whether of mirrors or spoken and written language – and finally causes the mirror to break.

'Fable' comments on the impossibility of a pure copy or representation, and draws attention again to the 'silvering' of the mirror and the language of the poem which both makes the representation possible and intervenes in it. But 'Fable' uses a very different set of techniques to 'Les Mures' to render the mirror visible. It does not simply substitute, for example, a black type with a reflective silver one to suggest the mirror, but uses the way we move through a reading of the poem to constitute its materiality, thus reconfiguring the relationship of the language to the object. Thus the 'material' of each poem is different, and resists reduction to matter as the carrier of meaning. We might then say that Ponge works with 'materials' (in the plural) as opposed to matter.

This differentiation is also achieved in the language of the specification. Although the specification is now divided into sections titled with letters of the alphabet, and this might suggest equivalence between them, a closer look reveals that even within the same section the forms of definition vary from clause to clause.[16] Clauses do not merely repeat with the names of different materials of their preferred properties substituted. They completely reconfigure, describing quite different aspects of the material. Here concrete is defined through its dimensions, as if in a drawing:

> Make up to required levels under concrete beds and pavings with approved brick hardcore *broken to pass a 75mm gauge*[17]

When it is to be made up on-site, how the concrete is made becomes its defining characteristic:

> *Mix A* – one part cement to seven parts all-in aggregate *to pass a 38mm sieve*
> *Mix B* – one part cement to seven parts all-in aggregate *to pass a 19mm sieve*
> The concrete shall be prepared in an approved mixer, or delivered to site ready mixed to BS 5328: 1981, with only enough water added *to give a good workable mix*[18]

Here the concrete is considered in terms of its constituent parts which themselves cannot be fully explained in terms of substance and dimension. The amount of water is specified in relation to workability, thus bringing the experience and judgement of the fabricator into the definition.

In order to specify concrete, a number of different definitions must be used, that consider it through quite different frames. In the case of stone we see how the definition changes between natural and cast stone:

F21   **NATURAL STONE ASHLAR WALLING/DRESSINGS**

To be read with Preliminaries/General conditions.

TYPES OF WALLING/DRESSINGS

110   ASHLAR _____ .

–   Stone:

–   *Name (traditional):* _____ .

–   *Petrological family:* _____ .

–   Colour: _____ .

–   Origin: _____

–   Finish: _____ .

–   Supplier: _____ .

–   Quality: Free from vents, cracks, fissures, discoloration, or other defects adversely affecting strength, durability or appearance. Before delivery to site, season thoroughly, dress and work in accordance with shop drawings prepared by supplier.

–   Mortar: As section Z21.

–   Mix: _____ .

–   Sand: _____ .

–   Other requirements: _____ .

–   Bond: _____ .

–   Joints: Flush.

–   Width: _____ mm.

–   Pointing: _____ .

–   Features: _____ . [...]

F22   **CAST STONE ASHLAR WALLING/DRESSINGS**

To be read with Preliminaries/General conditions.

TYPES OF WALLING/DRESSINGS

110   CAST STONE _____ .

–   Cast Stone Units:

–   *Manufacturer:* _____ .

–   *Product Reference:* _____ .

–   Absorption: As clause _____ .

–   Compressive strength: To BS 1217.

–   Cube strength:

Average (minimum): _____ .

Single (minimum): Not less than _____ .

–   Finish: _____ .

–   Colour: _____ .

–   Mortar: As section Z21.

–   Mix: _____ .

–   Sand: _____ .

–   Bond: _____ .

–   Joints: Flush.

–   Width: _____ .

–   Pointing: _____ .

–   Other requirements: _____ .[19]

The clause for natural stone specifies its source. It is identified by geographic origin and its geological classification. The cast stone, however, which is produced, not simply extracted, is identified by a manufacturer and reference.

By using different forms of definition, the specification is able, like Ponge's poetry, to differentiate between materials, and does not treat materials as substitutable. Such a differentiation at the level of language enables materials to appear *in* language, and in their plurality. The language of the specification may then offer a way of writing architectural materials that escapes their conceptualization as instances of matter.

Specifying materials: the performings of mirrors

Perhaps in part because we imagine them filling the white blanks of the drawing, it is easy for architects to think of materials as surface effects that are quite substitutable. In their arguments about form and matter, philosophers of hylomorphism also assume materials to be substitutable. Bronze is the typical material used to demonstrate the concept of prime matter, for it can be melted down to be transformed into any form, and is in itself formless. In fact, it is the particular plastic properties of bronze that make it exemplary. A statue made of charcoal would disintegrate into a pile of useless dust if we tried to transform its shape. When Aristotle shows that a sphere can be made in any material we will not doubt him, but he does not consider the properties of its material. A ping pong ball may have formal similarities to a cannonball, but it is clearly distinguished by the properties of its material and the way it behaves.

In 'Fable', Ponge makes the mirror appear – but he also brings the operations of the text – printed and spoken – to our attention at the same time. We are confronted at once with the mirror through its operations and with the means of its representation. Ponge does not really describe the mirror or the reflections as a representation might. Instead, the text performs the operations of the mirror. Ponge makes the text reflect, and produce reflections as a mirror does. He draws the reader's attention to the act of reading, by addressing them directly, by playing between the text as spoken and as written, and by literally bouncing you around the text. In the second line he sends you back to the first. The last word names the mirror so you return to the start to review the poem in the light of this information and so on. We might say that the text enacts the object and language becomes something other than a simple mirror.

In his long poem 'Faune et Flora', Ponge finds a relationship between the voicelessness of words and letters in themselves and that of plants:

> They have no voices. They are all but paralyzed. They can only attract attention by their postures.
>
> For all their efforts to 'express' themselves, they merely repeat the same expression, the same leaf, a million times ... they think they're breaking into a polyphonic canticle, bursting out of themselves.[20]

The text itself repeats lines and phrases, adequating the replication of the leaves Ponge is interested in, and drawing our attention more to the rhythm and repetition of the language than to its meaning. Ponge concentrates on what poem, plant and mirror do, finding ways of using language that could correspond to his object without necessary recourse to its appearance or form. This strategy of enactment involves a shift from the thinking about objects as formed and inert to considering them in terms of the ways they act in time.

The specification (at least since the 1930s, and increasingly since the 1960s) also reveals an emphasis on the material's behaviour, as opposed to its appearance, as we saw in the clause for cast stone that identifies absorption and compressive strength. Surprisingly, perhaps, my trawl through the NBS revealed only a couple of examples where the material's appearance is described – one concerning knots in wooden floorboards, and another about the texture of brushwork for intumescent paint – hardly a major issue for architecture. A whole range of performance factors, such as thermal and acoustic transmittance, solar and light control or resistance to thermal stress, may be important for a material such as glass:

> ### H10   PATENT GLAZING
> *371   HEAT CONSERVATION*
> –   Average thermal transmittance (U-value) of patent glazing: _____
> *391   SOLAR AND LIGHT CONTROL*
> –   Glazing panes/ units: Must have:
> –   Total solar energy transmission of normal incident solar radiation (maximum): _____ .
> –   Total light transmission (minimum): _____ .
> *401   THERMAL SAFETY*
> –   Glazing panes/ units: Must have adequate resistance to thermal stress generated by orientation, shading, solar control and construction.
> *411   ACOUSTIC PROPERTIES*
> –   Sound transmittance: Minimum weighted sound reduction index (Rw) within 100 to 3150 Hz frequency range to BS 5821–3: _____ .
> –   Location: _____ .[21]

While the architectural drawing defines what is static and permanent in the building, the specification understands both the materials of the building and the object they construct as constructions in themselves that are put together in specific ways, and have a life that precedes and exceeds the moment of their articulation in the specification. They even have a duration while on-site (including endless clauses from very early on and increasingly, obsessively, about protecting materials on-site, plaster in specially built dry sheds, covers on timber floors once laid and so on), and after they have been built in terms of how they will perform – preventing a certain sound transmission, protecting from fire for a certain time and so on.

The hylomorphic schema sets form up as active and matter as merely inert. Within its terms of reference, matter does not act and is outside duration. This was perhaps the limit that Smithson could not get beyond when he tried to describe the mirrors themselves. Ponge's strategy of enactment, and the performance specification understand materials in their capacity to act, and therefore in time. Thus these documents provide an alternative concept of the material that is able to embrace their constitution and their capacity to continue to effect, long after the building process is complete.

A language of materials

Clearly the specification must also be more 'properly' read along Foucauldian lines as an institutional product that in turn replicates the institution.[22] And indeed, as the use of the NBS becomes standard practice and has yet more dominant reproductive power, many of the ambiguities and peculiarities of the specification that have been mentioned here are being ironed out. According to McGregor, the NBS is intended now to describe 'work in place', i.e. the finished result rather than the process of achieving it.[23] The recently digitized version of the NBS allows you to 'fill in the blanks' from a list of given choices, reintroducing the principle of materials as substitutable. By making the insertion of customized clauses extremely cumbersome, it reinforces standard practice and restricts other possibilities.

But if we always pass over the specification because it is 'just' a technical or legal document, we maintain the 'conspiracy of muteness' concerning materials in architecture. Despite its poetry, Ponge's language is extremely precise, even dry, and strives for objectivity that he is also aware can never be achieved:

> [L]yricism in general disturbs me. That is, it seems to me that there is something too subjective, a display of subjectivity which appears to me to be unpleasant, slightly immodest. I believe that things – how can I say it – that emanate from your subjectivity should not be displayed. Naturally, one never does anything but that.[24]

In this way, it lends itself to a comparison with the technical language of the specification which, in turn, may be read as an open text. But there is more at stake in this parallel reading than a poeticizing of the specification. I hope to have made a case for some conceptual possibilities the specification might offer. Where Smithson's mirror travels hold up identical mirrors to a myriad of sites, the specification, in common with Ponge's prose poetry, uses language in a variety of ways to hold up different mirrors to different materials, even to the same materials taking up different roles in the building process. In this way, I suggest, the language of the specification is a medium in which 'materials' in the plural can be described as opposed to 'matter' in the singular. And if we look closely at the language of materials, we discover that its definitions move beyond the concept of inert, passive matter; they are defined as active and temporal. Although the drawing treats material through the prevalent hylomorphic model – as that which is formed – the specification offers a version of materials that cannot be contained by the concept of matter and reveals its inadequacies. In the specification we begin to identify a model of materials that is properly architectural and more adequate to the discipline.

In his 'Text on Electricity' Ponge suggests that there may be productive relations between architecture 'electricity' and poetry. Here a literary analysis of a technical text challenges the 'conspiracy of muteness' concerning materials in architecture and, through these strange operations, finds ways to think about materials that escape their confinement to a concept of matter.

Notes

Thanks here to Martin Mulchrone and Jim Randell at DLG Architects, to John Gelder and Colin McGregor at the NBS, and to Andrew Leach for their responses to my questions and to the RIBA archive for access to their specifications.

1   See Smithson, 1996, pp. 119–133. For the most interesting discussion of material and mirror in Smithson's work see Shapiro, 1995.
2   Smithson, op. cit., p. 122.
3   Ibid., p. 124.
4   There is no one 'specification', and when I use the term it is in the most general sense and normally means 'as we use now in the UK'. In the eighteenth-century specifications, layout drawings are sometimes included in the document, and in later examples one does sometimes see sketches – usually marginalia and 'outside' the text. Whether the diagrams and drawings that appear as hyperlinks in the online NBS are inside or outside the text is a more complex question!
5   Carter, 1969, p. 760.
6   Colin McGregor, email correspondence with the author, 14 February 2005.
7   Bowyer, 1985, p. 9.
8   See Leach, 2002, pp. 35–49 for a fascinating discussion of this text.
9   Ponge, 'Text on Electricity', http:www.electronetwork.org/articles/ponge, transcribed from Ponge, 1979, pp. 156–212.
10 This discussion of Husserl's argument in *Ideas I* follows Jacques Derrida's interpretation. Derrida suggests that Husserl uses a mirror analogy to account for this medium, but that this mirror must be ideal. See Derrida, 1973, p. 118.
11 See her collaborative project enlarging the lines of an ordnance survey map in Ingraham, 1991, p. 69 and Justine Clark's piece on the material 'underside' of the drawing, *Smudges, Smears and Adventitious Marks*.
12 See, for example, Silliman, 1995.
13 *Selected Poems*, 1998, p. 15. Translation of this poem by C.K. Williams.
14 Translation based on Sorrell's, 1981, p. 118, with minor changes.
15 Here I disagree with Sorrell's analysis that this line 'offers perfect symmetry' (op. cit.).
16 The alphabetic structure of the specification has its origins in an earlier division into trades, and eighteenth-century specifications are divided by the storeys of the building.
17 Jack Bowyer, op. cit., p. 55.
18 Ibid., p. 57.
19 NBS, 2004, F21, F22.
20 Op. cit., p. 71. Translation of this poem by Margaret Guiton.
21 NBS, op. cit., H10.
22 For an excellent summary of these issues, raised particularly in the work of Michel Foucault and Gilles Deleuze, see Lecercle, 2002.

23   Colin McGregor, email correspondence with the author, 6 March 2006.
24   Ponge, interview in Gavronsky, 1969, p. 37.

Bibliography

Aristotle, *Metaphysics*, trans. Hugh Lawson-Tancred, London: Penguin, 1988.

Jack Bowyer, *Practical Specification Writing*, London: Hutchinson and Co., 1985

Jack Carter, 'National Building Specification', in *The Architects' Journal Information Library*, 19 March 1969.

Justine Clark, *Smudges, Smears and Adventitious Marks*. Online, available from: www.architecture.auckland.ac.nz/publications/interstices/i4/THEHTML/papers/clark (accessed 30 April 2004).

Jacques Derrida, *Speech and Phenomena*, trans. David Allison, Evanston: North Western University Press, 1973.

Serge Gavronsky, *Poems and Texts: an Anthology of French Poems, Translations and Interviews*, New York: Random House, 1969.

Catherine Ingraham, 'Lines and Linearity: Problems in Architectural Theory', in *Drawing Building Text*, Andrea Kahn (ed.), New York: Princeton Architectural Press, 1991.

Andrew Leach, 'Electricity, Writing, Architecture', *Mosaic*, 35/4 December 2002, pp. 35–49.

Jean-Jacques Lecercle, *Deleuze and Language*, Basingstoke: Palgrave-Macmillan, 2002.

NBS, *National Building Specification: Standard Version (Update 38)*, London: RIBA Enterprises Ltd, 2004.

Francis Ponge, *The Power of Language: Texts and Translations*, ed. and trans. Serge Gavronsky, Berkeley: University of California Press, 1979.

——— *Francis Ponge: Selected Poems*, Margaret Guiton (ed.), London: Faber and Faber, 1998.

——— 'Text on Electricity'. Online, available from: www.electronetwork.org/articles/ponge (accessed 8 October 2006).

Gary Shapiro, *Earthwards: Robert Smithson and Art After Babel*, Los Angeles: University of California Press, 1995.

Ron Silliman, *The New Sentence*, New York: Roof Books, 1995.

Robert Smithson, *Robert Smithson: the Collected Writings*, Jack Flam (ed.), Los Angeles: University of California Press, 1996.

Martin Sorrell, *Francis Ponge*, Boston: Twayne Publishers, 1981.

Architecture as image–space–text

Betty Nigianni

Introduction

A poem by Sylvia Plath provides a basis for contemplation on the intertwining relations between 'space', 'image' and 'text' and on how they might inform architectural representation in a critical way. Departing from a framework that sees an essentially empathetic and inter-productive relation between space and the subject, this chapter discusses the engagement of architectural representation with visuality and textuality, reconsidered, however, through a poeticising subjectivity. Drawing from Benjamin, Bachelard and Lacan, I argue that the role of visuality in spatial experience should be reconsidered beyond conventional optics, but instead in terms of 'images' that derive from psychic activity. In this sense, 'image' refers to an endowment of architectural space with a subjective quality; visuality, therefore, implies a certain creative engagement with the object. Such a perspective holds interesting implications for architectural representation. From a 'text' to be 'read', something to be gazed at from a certain viewpoint, architecture becomes something that interacts with the subject, making impossible its representation in the conventional sense. There is no 'reality' to be represented, but an ongoing interaction between 'object' and 'subject', 'architectural space' and 'user', producing each time a different 'textuality' that allows meaning to be reconstructed over and over; and so a different 'spatiality' that provides a terrain for the subject's transformation. I then suggest that architecture is rethought as a 'hybrid' created out of materiality, narratives and psychic space – what I call 'image–space–text'; and that architectural representation does not simply recreate, but rather creates that hybridity. Engaging with a variety of sources, such as the visual arts, film or literary narratives, could be a way to do this. By addressing the subject's reality and somehow weaving it into the design process, architectural representation will make critical architecture possible.

Accepting an empathetic and inter-productive relation between space and the subject, this chapter discusses the involvement of architectural representation with visuality and textuality reconsidered through subjectivity and poetic imagination. 'Tale of a Tub', a poem 'written from the bathtub' by Sylvia Plath[1] accompanies, interrupts, highlights, juxtaposes the discussion. The poem is, however, not analysed or interpreted. I have not treated the poem as a 'representation' in the conventional sense, but as a framework, which enabled my reflections to develop. As the chapter sets out to argue, representation cannot be limited to the re-creation or interpretation of a reality; to represent is essentially to create new spaces for critical experience and practice.

Architecture as image–space–text

Current visual theory and practice have been much preoccupied with a reconceptualisation of vision and visuality, and have stressed the necessity of postmodern representation to go beyond the 'objective', focused modernist vision, to embrace issues of subjectivity. Critiques of modern models of representation have specifically attacked 'Cartesian perspectivalism', mainly for its separation of subject and object, which renders the first transcendental and the second inert, recreating a bipolarity of subject and object that sustains metaphysical thought, empirical science and capitalist logic;[2] as visual theorist and artist Victor Burgin argues, 'the image of the convergence of parallel lines toward a vanishing point on the horizon became the very figure of Western European global economic and political ambitions'.[3] Critics of perspectivalism rejected the consideration of perspective as empirically true and universally valid, and instead they tried to demonstrate how it is a 'symbolic form', inconsistent and discontinuous as any other model of representation. A concern about sight as a historical and social fact has therefore developed; as art critic Hal Foster argues, there has been an effort 'to 'socialise vision' and to 'indicate its part in the production of subjectivity'.[4] In addition, drawing from the Lacanian dialectic of the gaze, a thinking on vision's own production as part of intersubjectivity has further contributed to that dialogue.

In this context, vision and visuality have been addressed as involving – if we were to make any distinctions – body, psyche and mind together. Although a difference between the two terms has been sustained, with vision related to sight as a physical operation, and visuality considered as a social construct related more to mental images rather than to what is visible to the eye, that difference has been constantly challenged. In The Visible and the Invisible, Maurice Merleau-Ponty recognised the guide of Plato's 'idea' in the eye and made a point about mental images originating in the realm of the senses; inspired by Merleau-Ponty, Jacques Lacan in his turn stressed the importance of the role of visual images in the workings of the human mind.

Such a rethinking of vision and visuality has inevitably been integrated with a rethinking of spatiality. If perspective is but a model of perceiving and constructing the world, then there is more than perspectival space. Instead of the universal and stable entity envisaged since the Enlightenment, space has been gradually reconsidered in terms of the subject's experience and production; from the Kantian a priori, it has moved closer to the Freudian extension of the psyche.

> The photographic chamber of the eye
> records bare painted walls, while an electric light
> flays the chromium nerves of plumbing raw;
> such poverty assaults the ego; caught
> naked in the merely actual room,
> the stranger in the lavatory mirror
> puts on a public grin, repeats our name
> but scrupulously reflects the usual terror.[5]

Walter Benjamin observed a connection between the human mind and architectural space through a form of 'photographic' image.[6] In *A Berlin Chronicle*, he recollects his childhood memories of Berlin largely as *tableaus*, 'street images' as he names them. These are snapshots of the physical fabric of the city invested with a personal sense of meaning.[7] For Benjamin, visuality has an important part in the process of coming to terms with space and it is formed by a kind of, in his own terms, 'unconscious optics':[8]

> Nothing prevents our keeping rooms in which we have spent twenty-four hours more or less clearly in our memory, and forgetting others in which we passed months. It is not, therefore, due to insufficient exposure time if no image appears on the plate of remembrance. More frequent, perhaps, are the cases when the half-light of habit denies the plate the necessary light for years, until one day from an alien source it flashes as if from burning magnesium powder, and now a snapshot transfixes the room's image on the plate.[9]

This imprinting of architectural spaces onto the mind, similar to the camera's 'snapshot', is not dependent upon the physics of conventional optics: buildings are experienced as a series of pictures taken out of a deeply personal photographic album.

'Image' plays a vital role in Gaston Bachelard's thinking on architectural space. Bachelard sees spatial experience as being formed by 'images' with a localising quality that come before thoughts and out of psychic activity.[10] In *The Poetics of Space*, rooms, even chests and drawers, are dreamed, imagined or remembered; spatial experience is not architectural in the conventional sense, much less geometrical, but instead occurs through images that relate 'to an archetype lying dormant in the depths of the unconscious'.[11] Although the Bachelardian 'poetic image' is less optical and more prototypical than Benjamin's 'snapshot', it still evokes a spatial visualising that bears a personal, 'intimate' as Bachelard calls it, dimension.

In this context, and for both Benjamin and Bachelard, 'image' refers to an endowment of architectural space with a 'subjective', psychical quality, visuality therefore implies a creative engagement with the 'objective' world of architecture. Benjamin argues that we experience our environment going through a certain process of identification with it. In his essays 'On the mimetic faculty' and 'Doctrine of the similar', he describes that process as 'mimesis', using the term not in the Platonic sense of a compromised 'imitation' of an original, but rather in the psychoanalytic sense of a creative empathising with the object.[12] For Benjamin, the ability to identify with and assimilate to the environment refers to a constructive reinterpretation that goes beyond mere imitation and becomes a creative act in itself.[13] In that perspective, vision operates on a whole new level: Benjamin's phrase, 'For I was there ... when I gazed',[14] describing his experience of looking at postcards and feeling instantly transported into the places they depicted, describes a creative interchange between spatiality and visuality. Moreover, 'image' in its common usage as 'imitation', referring to an analogical representation, a re-presentation, an ultimate resurrection of an object, is subverted to be associated with imagination and a poeticising subjectivity.

> Just how guilty are we when the ceiling
> reveals no cracks that can be decoded? when washbowl
> maintains it has no more holy calling
> than physical ablution, and the towel
> dryly disclaims that fierce troll faces lurk
> in its explicit folds? or when the window,
> blind with steam, will not admit the dark
> which shrouds our prospects in ambiguous shadow?[15]

From a 'text' to be 'read' then, something to be gazed at from a certain viewpoint, architecture becomes something that interacts with the subject. Reading oneself into architecture and seeing oneself reflected in architecture renders architectural experience a discursive process with obvious implications for architectural representation. At this point, I think that Lacan's account of visuality becomes important. His theory of the 'gaze' or 'look', which presupposes that the object we are looking at looks back at us, implies also a certain mimetic attitude towards the environment.[16] But further, Lacan's idea of an 'I' that is 'photo-graphed'[17] to some extent by a world of inanimate objects, apart from reconstituting the subject as a being that exists 'in the spectacle of the world',[18] it marks a major shift in representation. As Lacan claims:

> When I am presented with a representation I assure myself that I know quite a lot about it, I assure myself as a consciousness that knows that it is only representation, and that there is, beyond the thing, the thing itself; behind the phenomenon, there is a noumenon. ... In my opinion, it is not in this dialectic between the surface and that which is beyond that things are suspended. For my part, I set out from the fact that there is something that establishes a fracture, a bi-partition, a splitting of the being to which the being accommodates itself, even in the natural world.'[19]

In these terms, there is no 'reality' to be represented, but rather an ongoing interaction between 'object' and 'subject', 'architecture' and 'user'. As vision becomes susceptible to subjectivity, seeing from a point of view that is always related to an object becomes inadequate; instead, representation should somehow provide us with a Lacanian 'look', which, as visual theorist Colin MacCabe argues, is not defined by a science of optics in which the eye features as a geometrical point, but by the fact that the object we are looking at offers a position from which we can be looked at – and this look is not punctual but shifts over the surface.[20]

Twenty years ago, the familiar tub
bred an ample patch of omens; but now
water faucets spawn no danger; each crab
and octopus – scrabbling just beyond the view,
waiting for some accidental break
in ritual, to strike – is definitely gone;
the authentic sea denies them and will pluck
fantastic flesh down to the honest bone.

We take the plunge; under water our limbs
waver, faintly green, shuddering away
from the genuine colour of skin; can our dreams
ever blur the intransigent lines which draw
the shape that shuts us in? absolute fact
intrudes even when the revolted eye
is closed; the tub exists behind our back:
its glittering surfaces are blank and true.[21]

Representation in that sense produces a different 'textuality', which not only allows meaning to be reconstructed over and over, but further reconstitutes the subject as a territory for transformation. A representation informed by the gaze of the Other is a critical representation; it subverts Cartesian space to open up the transcendental space of the relation to the Other.[22] The intrusion of the other that makes of the self a spectacle or object in relation to that other is accompanied by a radical decentring of the subject; and, although in Lacan that decentring takes the form of a threatening annihilation, in certain 'alternative' scopic regimes, as art historian Norman Bryson points out, is celebrated.[23] The subject's acknowledgement of itself in non-centred terms becomes a way of empathising with the world, and in Benjamin's terms, it is through empathy that we can, if not fully, understand the other.

What is important to note here, as far as it concerns architectural representation, is that, for Bachelard, empathy is further a matter of accepting spatiality. The relation of the self to the other, what Bachelard calls 'transsubjectivity', happens in that in-between space where boundaries get fuzzy, where, as he observes, 'inside and outside are not abandoned to their geometrical opposition'.[24] The fear of living without a 'geometrical homeland', in 'ambiguous space' of no clear distinction between inside and outside, refers to a certain misrecognition of the spatial contingency of life. Bachelard argues, however, that at the level of the poetic image this is avoided; through the image, there is a union 'of a pure but short-lived subjectivity and a reality which will not necessarily reach its final constitution',[25] that enables a kind of understanding of the self and other through each other.

In this particular tub, two knees jut up
like icebergs, while minute brown hairs rise
on arms and legs in a fringe of kelp; green soap
navigates the tidal slosh of seas
breaking on legendary beaches; in faith
we shall board our imagined ship and wildly sail
among sacred islands of the mad till death
shatters the fabulous stars and makes us real.[26]

It is becoming obvious so far that critical architectural representation, in terms of opening up architectural space to the subject's experience, interpretation and trans-formation, cannot escape to address issues of visuality and textuality as discussed above. For this, it will have to go beyond architecture's geometrical physicality, to recognise it as a 'hybrid' created out of material and psychic space, images and poetic narratives; and further, beyond simply re-creating, reflecting architecture, to creating that 'hybridity' and so critical environments. Drawing from a variety of sources, such as the visual arts, film practice or literary narratives, could be a way to do this. Apart from the obvious by now wish to draw links between visuality, space and narratives, my play on Roland Barthes' term 'image space text' in the title of this chapter intends to point out possible similarities between architectural design and film practice, in terms of combining together a variety of elements, which are perhaps worth exploring. A number of architectural theorists, such as Juhani Pallasmaa, Iain Borden and, more recently and more extensively, Jonathan Hill have pointed towards that direction. But also a number of practising architects have experimented with a variety of materials as part of their design process. Niall McLaughlin has worked with visual images, inspired by paintings or literature, as well as with narratives, either from the client's own brief or from the history of the site, to come up with an actual design proposal.

Such practices introduce new systems of visual and spatial representations, which somehow reflect 'a historical transition from the representational priority of "surface" to that of "interface" ',[27] rendering architecture from an 'object', a built 'thing', to 'a set of flows', 'a set of experiences and reproductions'.[28] To do so, they somehow bring into spatial representation 'the subject's psychical reality';[29] instead of the Latin *imago* of imitation, they draw more from the Freudian *imago* of 'unconscious representation' and imagination.[30] As this chapter has set out to demonstrate, critical representation cannot escape an engagement with subjectivity. In this way, the search for alternative visualities, spatialities, architectures, will not foreclose difference but, rather, keep it at play.

Notes

1   Plath, 1981, p. 275.
2   Foster, 1988, p. 10.
3   Burgin, 1996, pp. 148–149.

4   Foster, 1988, p. 9.

5   Plath, 1981, p. 24.

6   Leach, 2000, p. 28.

7   Ibid., p. 28.

8   Benjamin, 1992, pp. 230–231.

9   Benjamin, 1979, pp. 342–343.

10   Casey, 1998, p. 287.

11   Bachelard, 1994, p. xvi.

12   As discussed by Freud, the joke communicates through a certain empathising with the subject of the joke, which takes place in the imagination. For Freud, that kind of mimesis implies a creative engagement with the 'object' and could be of potential significance for aesthetics. See Freud, 1976.

13   Leach, 2000, pp. 30–31.

14   Benjamin, 1978, p. 328.

15   Plath, 1981, p. 24.

16   In 'The split between the eye and the gaze', Lacan refers extensively to Roger Caillois' account of 'mimicry' in nature. In Lacan, 1994, pp. 73–74.

17   Lacan, 1994, p. 106.

18   Ibid., p. 75.

19   Ibid., p. 106.

20   MacCabe, 1985, p. 67.

21   Plath, 1981, p. 25.

22   Lacan, 1994, p. 119.

23   Bryson, 1988, p. 104.

24   Bachelard, 1994, p. 230.

25   Ibid., p. xix.

26   Plath, 1981, p. 25.

27   Burgin, 1996, p. 157.

28   Borden, 2001, p. 6.

29   I further refer here to Victor Burgin's call for an introduction of 'psychical reality' into spatial representation in order to keep up with our apprehension of space in postmodernity; and his observation that 'attention to psychical reality calls for a *psychical realism* – impossible, but nevertheless ...' In Burgin, 1996, p. 56.

30   Laplanche and Pontalis, 1973, p. 211.

Bibliography

Gaston Bachelard, *The Poetics of Space*, Boston: Beacon Press, 1994.

Roland Barthes, *Image Music Text*, London: Fontana Press, 1977.

Walter Benjamin, *Reflections*, New York: Schoken Books, 1978.

Walter Benjamin, *One-way Street*, London: Verso, 1979.

Walter Benjamin, *Illuminations*, London: Fontana Press, 1992.

Iain Borden, *Skateboarding, Space and the City: Architecture and the Body*, Oxford and New York: Berg, 2001.

Norman Bryson, 'The Gaze in the Expanded Field', in Hal Foster (ed.), *Vision and Visuality*, Seattle: Bay Press, 1988.

Victor Burgin, *In/Different Spaces: Place and Memory in Visual Culture*, Berkeley, Los Angeles and London: University of California Press, 1996.

Edward S. Casey, *The Fate of Place: a Philosophical History*, Berkeley, Los Angeles and London: University of California Press, 1998.

Hal Foster, 'Preface', in Hal Foster (ed.), *Vision and Visuality*, Seattle: Bay Press, 1988.

Sigmund Freud, *Jokes and their Relation to the Unconscious*, London: Penguin, 1976.

Sigmund Freud, *The Standard Edition of the Complete Psychological Works of Sigmund Freud, vol. XXII (1932–1936)*, London: Vintage, 2001.

Sigmund Freud, *The Standard Edition of the Complete Psychological Works of Sigmund Freud, vol. XXIII (1937–1939)*, London: Vintage, 2001.

Jonathan Hill, *Actions of Architecture: Architects and Creative Users*, London and New York: Routledge, 2003.

Phillip Hill, *Lacan for Beginners*, London and New York: Writers and Readers Publishing, 1997.

Jacques Lacan, *Écrits: a Selection*, London: Routledge, 1989.

Jacques Lacan, *The Four Fundamental Concepts of Psychoanalysis*, London: Penguin Books, 1994.

Jean Laplanche and Jean-Bertrand Pontalis, *The Language of Psychoanalysis*, London: Karnac Books, 1973.

Neil Leach, 'Walter Benjamin, Mimesis and the Dreamworld of Photography', in Iain Borden and Jane Rendell (eds), *Inter/Sections: Architectural Histories and Critical Theories*, London and New York: Routledge, 2000.

Colin MacCabe, *Theoretical Essays: Film, Linguistics, Literature*, Manchester: Manchester University Press, 1985.

Niall McLaughlin, 'A Royal Gittern from the British Museum', presentation at the conference *Material Matters: Materiality in Contemporary Architectural Practice and Theory*, School of Architecture and the Visual Arts, University of East London, 2004.

Niall McLaughlin, *Niall McLaughlin Architects Profile*. Online, available at: www.niallmclaughlin.com/Profile.html (accessed 13 September 2006).

Harry Francis Mallgrave and Eleftherios Ikonomou, *Empathy, Form and Space: Problems in German Aesthetics, 1873–1893*, Santa Monica: The Getty Centre for the History of Art and the Humanities, 1994.

Maurice Merleau-Ponty, *The Visible and the Invisible*, Evanston: Northwestern University Press, 1968.

Juhani Pallasmaa, *The Eyes of the Skin: Architecture and the Senses*, London: Academy Editions, 1996.

Sylvia Plath, *Collected Poems*, London: Faber and Faber, 1981.

Acts of imagination and reflection in architectural design[1]

Peg Rawes

Introduction

Architectural designers are required to develop conceptual and critical skills about the urban, environmental, social and cultural design contexts that inform their design processes. In addition, these skills are informed by the individual's powers of judgement, which connect their ideas to broader design contexts. Architectural designers are therefore required to develop the ability to 'reflect' upon a range of cultural information, together with the processes, techniques and products that are involved in the discipline. Furthermore, the ability to actively embody these judgements in the design process directly informs his or her ability to generate an architecture, which 'reflects' the needs of the relevant social, environmental and cultural contexts, as well as the design context in which he or she works. We might therefore call this process 'reflective thinking'. Reflective thinking underpins the design processes of drawing, thinking and modelling the built environment, and the designer's personal experience of architectural and urban space.

This discussion examines the nature of these relationships with reference to Kant's theories of the imagination and the reflective subject in the *Critique of Judgment* (1790). In particular, I develop a discussion about reflective and imaginative thinking, which generate technical and aesthetic understandings of the material, cultural and theoretical relationships that constitute architectural design. I argue that Kant's 'reflective subject' enables these discussions about aesthetic and technical thinking in design, especially with respect to the role of geometry. Developing out of this argument, I consider how the processes of imagining and reflecting (i.e. reflective judgement) operate in the act of drawing, and in the experience of visiting a particular spatial art installation in a contemporary modern-art museum.

In the first section, I outline Kant's theory of reflection in order to highlight how it is valuable for a discipline that requires both geometric and spatial knowledge as part of its design processes, and to indicate how it informs the processes of drawing, experiencing and thinking about architectural design. I then develop the discussion to argue that Kant's theory is intrinsically concerned with the production of aesthetic experiences of space by examining the role of the imagination in relation to geometric powers of reflective thinking. The imagination is therefore significant because it enables the reflective designer to engage in aesthetic and technical modes of spatial thinking.[2]

Kant's theory is interesting for architects because it promotes the importance of an individual's ability to reflect as part of the production of aesthetic and technical judgements. In particular, his theory of the imagination reveals that geometric thinking and geometric relationships are inherently connected to the designer's reflective and aesthetic powers. In this respect, geometry in architectural design is integral to the aesthetic or reflective process because it is both a technical (e.g. a form of scientific or engineering knowledge) and an embodied (e.g. an imaginative) activity.[3] When understood as an example of both the technical and the aesthetic construction of space, reflective judgement therefore offers the designer an enriched understanding of geometric thinking.

Reflective thinking

In the first introduction to the *Critique of Judgment*, Kant highlights the difference between reflective thinking versus the individual's powers of reasoning and understanding. Reflective judgement is a special kind of thinking available to the individual because it is the ability to produce relationships between the individual, or a particular experience, and the world. Kant gives two descriptions of its powers: first, it is 'the ability to *reflect*, in terms of a certain principle, on a given presentation so as to [make] a concept possible', and second, it is 'the ability to *determine* an underlying concept by means of a given empirical presentation'.[4] Reflective judgement is therefore distinct from reasoning (the ability to determine the particular through the universal) and understanding (the ability to cognise the universal (i.e. rules)). Instead, the individual generates judgements about the world through his or her 'ability to *subsume the particular under the universal*'.[5] So, in the relationship between the individual and the particular experience, the reflective subject is able to generate a distinct set of judgements, which are more important than conceptual forms of knowledge or reasoning. Therefore, in a design context, this means the designer's powers of reflection may be more significant in the process of developing a specific and original judgement than his or her powers of conceptual understanding or reasoning.

Furthermore, Kant's examination of how the reflective subject engages with the world highlights the importance of the 'process' of constructing judgements because he draws attention to the relationship between reflective thinking and aesthetic judgements. Reflective judgement is not merely a cognitive form of thinking, but is a special kind of embodied thinking, which is also generated by the individual's powers of feeling or emotions. Reflective judgement therefore represents a special kind of aesthetic activity, in which the relationship between the individual and the world is developed out of his or her powers of thinking and feeling. As such, it represents a 'subjective relation' (rather than an objective, logical or mechanical relationship) in which aesthetic judgements are subjective, yet also technical (i.e. *techne*) powers derived from nature.[6] For Kant, then, the power to think reflectively is itself an aesthetic activity. In addition, he emphasises the importance of the 'technical' power of thinking in 'reflective judgment' which connects the subject and the world, rather than a harmony that is produced through a 'mechanical' or instrumental 'schema'.[7] Kant also stresses that a new kind of autonomy is established in the individual because it reflects the 'purposiveness' of nature; that is, a certain kind of agency is granted which is neither 'merely subjective, restricted to the sensibility of the individual, or exclusively cognitive'.[8] Thus, he defines this as 'a judgment' which he calls 'an AESTHETIC *judgment of reflection*'.[9]

Moreover, the relationship between the individual and the world is emphasised in the importance Kant gives to the act of making aesthetic judgements, so that procedures that might previously have been defined as determined concepts (e.g. the architectural diagram or plan) become understood as 'aesthetic acts'. As a result, scientific or technical procedures, such as geometry, become understood as 'technical' forms of aesthetic activity. Spatial and geometric judgements become defined in terms of their ability to express the powers of the sensing, reflective subject and his or her experiences in the world, not in terms of their status as concepts or abstract ideas. Central to reflective judgement's power, therefore, is its ability to generate relations in the form of an 'aesthetic of feeling'. This is especially evident in the capacities of the imagination to provide connections between a judgement or idea and the objects to which it relates, thereby enabling the exploration of an 'artistic and technical' (i.e. aesthetic) understanding of geometry.

Kant's definition of reflective thinking in relation to theoretical and practical forms of geometric figuration provides a link between the aesthetic act of drawing and the technical construction of a geometric figure; for example, in the shift from hypothesising a geometric figure out of an axiom to the act of drawing out a geometric figure. In the next section I explore this reflective thinking to suggest that geometry is not merely conceived as a scientific discipline, harbouring rational and idealised forms of knowledge, but is reconnected to its properties of aesthetic manufacture and construction.

Imagination and geometric thinking[10]

In this section I consider the way in which the activity of drawing plans, sections, lines, etc., are aesthetic activities that involve the imagination operating as a technique or tool within the event. I explore a common experience of drawing in architectural education in relation to Kant's analysis of the imagination's powers to suggest that the imagination is intrinsic to the technical and aesthetic processes of designing.

Imagine a student sitting at a desk, drawing the section for a housing project in Newcastle, on the north-east coast of Britain. In a purely mathematical account of this activity, the procedure of geometric drawing – of defining walls, boundary lines, floors, ceilings, windows, doors, cladding, external ground, foundations, load-bearing beams and so on – might focus on the attention to the correction and erasure of lines, the understanding and adjustment of angle, line or degree of curvature. The activity might be taking place using a computer, a CAD-cam package in which the plotting of lines and the direction of intention and decision is conducted through the manoeuvres of the mouse in the hand. However, in each case, a limited geometric account will omit the embodied activity of this person drawing from its description of the event.

Re-imagine the scene: she is sitting at her desk at 7.30am in the morning. It's cold and so she has dragged the duvet over from the bed to her chair and is wrapped up in it. For the first 15 minutes she looks over the work she left at 8.30pm last night, deciding which lines and spaces can stay, and which will have to be redrawn. There is a problem with the stairwell and access to the block of flats. According to this scale of 1:100 she now realises that, on a 1:1 scale, each stair would be 1.5 metres high. This will be the first area of the section that will have to be erased and redrawn. She goes down the hall to the kitchen to make the first of several very strong, hot, sweet coffees that she will drink over the next four hours. But it is also the day before her studio review in which she will be assessed by a group of tutors (some known, others not), and so the drawing will be, in part, a drawing of adrenaline, mixing desire, anticipation, worry and concentration in the process. Thus, her use of the instruments and tools of constructing spaces, which range from physical instruments – such as pens, pencils, rulers, erasers, compasses, set-squares, computer software, hardware, mouse and keyboard – to the powers of her imagination, will all be handled in the context of these feelings.

The drawing has become an enactment of geometric figures, planes and spaces that are imbued with the traces of emotional pressure, strain, relief, tension and change. A process that involves skills ranging from the ability to conceptualise, analyse, evaluate, draw, concentrate, apply dexterity, manipulate instruments, focus, apply editorial control, and the ability to keep out-of-mind the anticipation of the following day. Geometry has become an activity that is inherently constructed out of aesthetic experience, so that geometric figures become linked to the reflective powers of the individual subject. The event might be called an amalgam, a reflective 'subject–figure'[11] or an 'event–drawing' in which the relationship between the drawing and the individual represents a series of processes or reasoning in architectural design.

In the first introduction of the *Critique of Judgment* Kant examines the powers of the imagination in relation to geometric thinking. He argues that the individual's powers of reflection (i.e. reflective judgement) bring together the imagination and technical judgements in the act of drawing geometric figures. In a supplementary note to this passage, he also emphasises the aesthetic power of the imagination in the act, when he writes:

This pure and, precisely because of that purity, sublime, science of geometry seems to comprise some of its dignity if it confesses that on its elementary level it needs *instruments* to construct its concepts, even if only two: compass and ruler. These constructions alone are called geometric, while those of higher geometry are called mechanical, because to construct the concepts of higher geometry we need more complex machines. Yet even when we call compass [*Zirkel*] and ruler [*Lineal*] (*circinus et regular*) instruments, we mean not the actual instruments, which could never produce those figures [*circle* and (straight) *line*] with mathematical precision, but only the simplest ways [these figures can] be exhibited by our *a priori* imagination, [a power] that no instrument can equal.[12]

So the imagination transforms theoretical geometric ideas into 'practical and embodied actions in the individual'. For Kant, the imagination is a productive power through which ideas and feelings are generated. It is a constituent in 'reflective thinking' with the power to generate both aesthetic and technical judgements, including the production of practical geometric thinking. Therefore, if we reflect on the image of the student drawing, we are able to see how geometry is transformed from theoretical reason (idea) into a series of actions, instruments or enactments, which constitute the different forms of 'practical' or applied geometric methods. Importantly, it is the imagination's powers that provide the conduit for this passage, from the 'pure' geometric relations to the technical acts of artistic production, so that each is brought into harmony with the other, establishing heterogeneity in geometric thinking.

In contrast to scientific understandings of space and geometry, in which the 'technical' procedures are separated from the 'aesthetic' acts of producing geometric figures,[13] this discussion suggests that Kant's reflective subject maintains the connection between aesthetic and technical actions. As a result, a discussion about geometric 'techniques' can be rethought because they are aspects of the reflective subject, not external constructions of 'ideal' scientific truths. Space and geometry therefore become embodied in the actions of the designer as she draws. They are heterogeneous relations in the process of drawing, through which the student's aesthetic powers of reasoning, judging and imagining are transformed into mental, sensory and bodily actions. Kant's final *Critique* shows that idealised or homogeneous empirical forms of geometry are transformed into aesthetic acts in the reflective designer. Geometric procedures, instruments and figures constructed by the imagination do not represent objective forms of pre-given knowledge. Rather, they are technical and aesthetic actions that are produced by the designer's powers of imagination. In turn, geometric drawing and geometric thinking are embodied and reflexive processes because they express the designer's powers of construction.

Feeling magnitude

In this part of the discussion I consider how the individual's imagination operates in the experience of a contemporary spatial and aesthetic event. I explore the installation by the artist, Olafur Eliasson, in order to draw attention to the power of the imagination in the construction of the project's spatiality. The experience of visiting the art installation, *The Weather Project* (2003–4),[14] which Eliasson was commissioned to make for the Tate Modern in London, highlights the ways in which reflective judgement enables embodied spatial judgements to be made by the designer when he or she engages with modern architecture as part of the process of visiting a contemporary art museum.

The Weather Project consisted of a large representation of a yellow sun (made up of hundreds of sodium-yellow lightbulbs used for lighting streets), which was reflected from a suspended mirror onto the floor of the Turbine Hall in the museum. Smoke generators produced a fine mist that filled the hall to simulate a foggy, balmy day, and resulted in visitors sitting or lying on the floor, as if bathing in sunlight, or playing with their reflection generated by the mirror on the ceiling of the Hall.

This simulation of an environment in which visitors responded as if they were in an outdoor space (yet with the knowledge that it is artificially created inside a contemporary art museum) highlights how the experience of a modern art installation can involve the visitor in making reflective judgements. In particular, its illusory use of the sensory, meteorological qualities of light and water vapour enable a concatenation of geometric and spatial awareness to be generated through the combined sensory perception of the physical space of the installation and the geometric dimensions of the building in which it is housed. The visitor forms reflective and spatial judgements in a number of ways, partly because of the confluence between the large internal geometric scale of the reconditioned industrial building, and its contemporary context as a modern art museum, combined with the experience of inhabiting an installation that simulates the external, climatic environment of a late-modern industrialised city. Moreover, if we consider the experience in the context of how the imagination produces embodied geometric knowledge and spatial experience, geometry is generated by the visitor's judgements of the different scales that they 'feel' between their own body and the physical, geometric dimensions of the Turbine Hall. Thus, the visitor makes internally generated judgements about the magnitude of space, and geometry shifts from being an intellectual branch of mathematical reasoning into judgements that are formed by an individual's feelings.[15]

In addition, a contrasting set of judgements or feelings about magnitude are also evident that are derived from the simulation of being immersed in the limitless, external environment and horizon. The visitor's feeling of the potential limitlessness in the magnitude of the environment contradicts the real limits of the built architectural space of the museum and the material artifice of the installation, which generates a dynamic feeling of geometric magnitude. Therefore, geometric reasoning is also involved in the aesthetic experience, because it constructs the visitor's awareness of both the architectural proportions of the space and his or her experience of the art installation inside the museum. Consequently, geometric space is produced as a result of the individual's sensory awareness of the different scales of the physical space of the museum, the installation and his or her body. An embodied experience or cognition is generated in the museum visitor, underlining my discussion that reflective thinking is not 'just' produced through intellectual cognition or understanding. Rather, it is derived from an individual's feelings and aesthetic judgements. The experience also represents an aesthetic analogy of Kant's theory of the sublime, in particular in the individual's experience of the 'incomprehensible' dynamic between scale and quantity.

The imagination's ability to produce reflective judgements occurs partly in Kant's explanation of the sublime; for example, in his examination of how the imagination constitutes a link between the subject and the transcendental sublime where he highlights the boundaries or limits in this relationship, in particular. He explores two versions of this relationship; first, by explaining how the imagination subsumes formal, mathematical and external concepts into an internal state of 'agitation' and sensation in its attempts to cognise the magnitude of the sublime. Second, the mental agitation that results from the individual's attempts to understand the sublime, and the inevitable failure to do this, produces an 'intensive' kind of boundary between the reflective subject's feelings of pleasure and displeasure. Here, then, the imagination's activities represent the boundary between the desire to understand the unknowable, and the failure to do so, which generates the dialectical feelings of pleasure and excess versus displeasure and fear in the experience.

Thus, by emphasising the importance of 'activity' in the imagination's attempts to comprehend the division of the sublime into mathematical or 'sublime objects', the imagination's contribution is shown in the 'mental agitation' that it undertakes in the production of its judgements, aesthetic cognitions or desires.[16] The imagination is therefore significant for the individual because it enables space and geometry to become embodied, rather than merely being cognitive ideas. Geometric space is constructed, not through the production of geometric concepts, but in the 'movement between' feelings of pleasure and displeasure that are experienced by the individual. Kant's theory of the imagination is therefore central to his theory of reflective judgement. This aesthetic form of thinking enables the individual designer to make judgements about the world by means of his or her embodied powers or feelings. First, the individual's experiences of engaging with built architectural spaces are revealed to be intrinsically linked to the processes and powers of the imagination. In addition, the designer's powers of imagination represent a technique or tool in the process, therefore showing the imagination is both a technical judgement the designer uses in the process of drawing space, and an aesthetic power that links him or her to the built environment.

Conclusion

In conclusion, I am suggesting that the architectural design process involves the designer in making real material and physical links between abstract ideas and embodied experience, challenging the perception that the imagination, and the spaces, forms and ideas that it generates, are always inadequate, insubstantial or confused versions of pure theoretical ideas. The imagination is therefore a particularly important kind of embodied thinking and designing, through which the architect is able to construct images (drawings, models, renders, etc.) that have a material, aesthetic, cognitive and technical value.

The imagination and reflection are therefore intrinsic to architectural design, when re-evaluated as part of the critical tools that we use to draw, think, discuss and experience architecture as designers and users. Consequently, drawings, models and the subject's inhabitation of the built environment represent material constructions of an 'embodied' (not a disembodied) reason. The relationship between architectural design and the imagination is reconfigured so that its products become understood as material expressions of the process of reflective thinking in design. In addition, the activities of the imagination are an expression of the embodied subject's powers of production; it is a technical procedure that generates sensory relations between the individual and the world. The reflective self is 'both' the aesthetic experiences in the sensing designer, and the technical construction of geometric figures, challenging the suggestion that geometric figures are always products of deterministic scientific procedures. Rather, in the reflective designer, the aesthetic and technical expressions of geometry are brought together into a reflexive, thinking and perceiving agency.

Notes

1   This chapter is a version of a paper titled, 'Reflective Subjects in Kant and Architectural Design Education', in the *Journal of Aesthetic Education*, Spring 2007, Volume 41, no. 1, University of Illinois Press, 2007.

2   There are key differences between the powers of the imagination in Kant's first critical text, the *Critique of Pure Reason* (1781/1789), and in his final critical text, the *Critique of Judgment*. In the former, the imagination is seen as 'regulatory', i.e. it does not have the power to create legitimate, autonomous ideas. However, in the latter, it is considered to be 'productive' because it is able to produce legitimate content in thinking.

3   Geometry and mathematics are given different values in the *Critique of Pure Reason*. Here, Kant is concerned with determining the 'forms of knowledge', not the subject's powers of thinking or acting, so that mathematics and geometry are 'external forms' of knowledge, not internal or embodied modes of thinking in the subject. In addition, space and time are limited to 'sense-perceptions' for the individual not 'proper' forms of knowledge, like geometry and mathematics. Therefore, geometry is a pure but disembodied intuition, and space is a limited embodied form of sense-intuition.

4   Kant, 1790/1987, 211'/399.

5   Kant, 1790/1987, 202'/391.

6   Kant, 1790/1987, 214'/402.

7   Kant, 1790/1987, 212–3'/400–1.

8   Kant, 1790/1987, 218'/406. Kant's theory of 'art' is generated in this relationship between the subject and nature; for example, through the analogous powers of representation. Aesthetic judgement therefore registers the scope for agreement or

disagreement between the nature and the analogy, not on the basis of the conceptual value of the image. But he also writes that art can be generated in the agreement between the understanding and reason in the form of 'a unique concept', that is, 'the concept of nature as art' (Kant, 1790/1987, 203'–204'/392–3).

9   Kant, 1790/1987, 221'/409.

10   See the exhibition catalogue, *Spatial Imagination in Design*, Peg Rawes and Jane Rendell (eds), AHRC and EPSRC, and the Bartlett School of Architecture, UCL, 2005, for more examples of research into the cultural, historical, practical and theoretical role of imagination in architectural design that were developed by a group of architects, artists and writers during a year-long project, as part of the AHRC and EPSRC's joint-funded initiative, *Designing for the 21st Century*.

11   See Rawes, 2007 for further discussion of this term.

12   Kant, 1790/1987, 198'/388.

13   Perhaps most strongly demonstrated in the modern view that Euclid's *Elements* is an 'exclusively' scientific mathematical text. See, for example, Heath, 1956, v.

14   Tate Modern Unilever Series, 'Olafur Eliasson'.

15   Geometry can also be described as the science of magnitudes, in so far as it is the construction of geometric bodies through the division of a magnitude into parts. A link between geometry and feelings or perceptions of scale can therefore be suggested because both relate to the body.

16   Kant, 1790/1987, 259'/116.

Bibliography

Thomas Heath, *Euclid: the Thirteen Books of the Elements*, Volume 1, London: Dover Publications, 1956.

Immanuel Kant, *Critique of Judgment*. Translated by Werner S. Pluhar, Indianapolis: Hackett Publishing Company, 1987.

Peg Rawes, 'Reflective Subjects in Kant and Architectural Design Education', *Journal of Aesthetic Education*, University of Illinois Press, Spring, 2007.

Peg Rawes and Jane Rendell (eds), *Spatial Imagination in Design*, AHRC, EPSRC and the Bartlett School of Architecture, UCL, 2005.

Tate Modern Unilever Series, 'Olafur Eliasson'. Tate Modern. Online, available at: www.tate.org.uk/modern/exhibitions/eliasson (accessed 30 August 2005).

In the corner of perception

Spatial experience in distraction

Katja Grillner

> Our taverns and our metropolitan streets, our offices and furnished rooms, our railroad stations and our factories appeared to have us locked up hopelessly. Then came the film and burst this prison-world asunder by the dynamite of the tenth of a second, so that now, in the midst of its far-flung ruins and debris, we calmly and adventurously go traveling. With the close-up, space expands; with slow motion, movement is extended. The enlargement of a snapshot does not simply render more precise what in any case was visible, though unclear: it reveals entirely new structural formations of the subject.[1]

This remarkable vision of the powerful effects on human experience and perception of the invention of film is provided by Walter Benjamin in his classic essay from 1936, 'The Work of Art in the Age of Mechanical Reproduction'. In this essay, Benjamin argues for the potential of new media technology to liberate the subject by creating a new mode of perception, a new viewing position that combines distraction, absorption, criticality and distanciation.[2] Film and photography have provided access to a critical study of the world in which we are otherwise hopelessly immersed – now 'we calmly and adventurously go traveling'. Benjamin describes the filmic experience with its shock effects as mirroring the modern urban mode of existence, and argues that this makes it an appropriate training ground for coping with and, importantly, comprehending contemporary conditions of life.

Architecture plays an interesting role in Benjamin's argument. On the one hand, 'the taverns, our offices, our railroad stations' and so on have 'locked us up' in a 'prison-world' that only film could 'burst asunder'. On the other, architecture is brought to the fore as a privileged art form, the experience of which points humanity to a very particular and acutely relevant mode of appropriation, 'mastered' by habit and by impressions caught in 'an incidental fashion'. This observation, that architecture shies away from attentive contemplation, and demands to be perceived rather as a backdrop to life than as an object in life, points to an interesting dilemma facing the architectural critic: if the object under scrutiny, architecture, offers itself as a mere background event, appropriated primarily by habitual use and occasionally by attentive visual perception, how are we to capture it? How could such a delicate phenomenon be scrutinised if it cannot be held firmly before the eyes of the reader? It appears nearly impossible to represent and to critically engage with. Yet, as architectural critics, we are challenged and inspired to experiment with this condition. We construct, in different ways, temporary frames or lenses through which a critical point can be perceived. The phenomenon of architecture often, then, comes into focus, for a moment, then fades away again.

This chapter discusses these challenges for architectural research and criticism by examining more closely the particular notions of a distracted and de-focused architectural experience that Benjamin articulates, and by further presenting my own research into these notions in two recent writing and spatial installation projects, 'Writing architecture out of focus'[3] and *out of focus (in distraction)*.[4] These latter projects are propositional works.[5] They use literary, visual and spatial forms to indicate possible roles and modes of operation of a 'distracted critic' – a critic who picks up what is happening in the 'corner of perception' rather than what is evidently appearing on centre stage. The relationship in this chapter between my reading of Benjamin on the one hand, and my textual, visual and spatial installations on the other, is complementary but rather indirect and uncertain.[6]

Distracted experience, shock and the haptic

The notions of distraction and shock had an important critical and political function for Benjamin. Architectural appropriation is described as essentially tactile and governed by use. 'Architecture has always represented the prototype of a work of art the reception of which is consummated by a collectivity in a state of distraction,' he writes.[7] Its collective nature and the 'incidental fashion' in which it takes place promote architectural experience, for Benjamin, to a revolutionary force of 'canonical value'. While Benjamin's discussion of architecture in this essay is remarkably short, it continues to raise considerable critical interest within architecture theory. While his observations on the one hand might be used in isolation to underpin various haptic, synaesthetic and phenomenological studies of architectural experience, it is, on the other hand, important to fully recognise the political context in which (and purposes for which) Benjamin articulated these ideas.[8]

The distracting effects of media technology are celebrated in the essay, because they enable a radical break with traditional aesthetic values (the aura of the work of art, its cult-value).[9] Architecture plays a subordinated role in the argument and is addressed in order to point at an art form that has always complicated these traditional values, both depending on its inevitable connection to non-contemplative usage, and on the collective nature of its appropriation. Through the distracted everyday practices of architecture, cities and landscapes, humanity has been prepared for the new times (1930s Europe) and the necessary re-adjustment of its perceptual apparatus. Benjamin envisions that the shock, the fragmentation, the distractedness, that he spots in contemporary film, in combination with everyday practices, the goings-on of life, the habitual perception of architecture, will 'inoculate' humanity against the allure of fascism (presented as it is in an aesthetically comprehensible form). The modern subject, as seen by Benjamin, is devoid of fascism. S/he is a distracted critic.[10]

Distracted in use

> Buildings are appropriated in a twofold manner: by use and by perceptions – or rather by touch and sight. Such appropriation cannot be understood in terms of the attentive concentration of a tourist before a famous building. On the tactile side there is no counterpart to contemplation on the optical side. Tactile appropriation is accomplished not so much by attention as by habit. As regards architecture, habit determines to a large extent even optical reception.[11]

The chain of key-concepts in this central passage is 'use' and 'perception', transferred to 'touch' and 'sight', its qualities named as 'tactile' and 'optical', and their modes of 'appropriation' then referred to as 'attention' or 'habit'. Habit is given a more important role than attention in determining both optical and tactile reception in architecture. What we experience of an art form such as architecture while going about our daily lives is, in relation to the wholeness of its visual and material *gestalt*, rather fragments that reach us in a state of distraction (while doing something else). There is, in Benjamin's position, no alternative. To contemplate architecture visually, from a touristic viewpoint, is essentially meaningless. It says very little about the object of study.

Benjamin's pairing of touch and sight, tactile and optical, ties directly back to the distinction made by Aloïs Riegl in *Problems of Style* (1893) between the optical (delivering a survey) and the haptic (feeling its way along or around the world, experienced as surface rather than outline).[12] In the article 'Stereoscopy: modernism and the haptic', David Trotter discusses the experiential dimension of hapticity through the stereoscopic images of the late nineteenth century.[13] According to Trotter, Riegl chose to speak of the haptic rather than the tactile in order to avoid a literal understanding of that 'haptic regard' as one that 'touches'. Haptic comes from 'haptein' which means to fasten. While the optic gaze 'surveys' the world, the haptic look 'attaches' to it.[14] Benjamin lacks a corresponding word to 'contemplation' for 'tactile', or in Riegl's vocabulary, 'haptic', attention. According to Benjamin, this form of appropriation in architecture is never premeditated or intentional, it is rather a side-effect of use. It happens to the subject, whom it distracts. Distraction means, importantly, both to turn away from a certain activity or attentive focus, and to in its place focus on something else. To be distracted is to be 'called elsewhere'.

Imagining distraction

In the article 'Distraction and Digital Culture', William Bogard discusses the function of distraction in society as a mechanism that assumes different modes of operation in different cultures, and as a force that has both subversive and controlling effects on society as well as the individual.[15] He also makes the important observation that

> despite the fact that distraction is everywhere in experience, it is not at all difficult to imagine a world without distraction. Such an idea is in fact the norm if we consider it from the point of view of social control.[16]

The normative discourse of architecture, as reproduced in conventional reviews of new buildings and the accompanying architectural photographs, also manages very smoothly to avoid notions of a distracted use. This is not a surprise. For how could one, in rhetorically convincing ways, even begin to make those other perspectives appear and be understood without losing altogether the authority of the architect as a designer in control?[17]

The two projects presented here experiment in different media with the imagining of a world in distraction. The spatial installation, exhibited in the group show *Spatial Imagination* at domoBaal in London 2006, conveys a sensation of a de-focused, distracted, perception through a play with layers of mediation – still-images and sound distributed in space. Horizontal light boxes are distributed in the stairwell of the gallery space (see figures below). These boxes display three trip-tychs made up from photographs of TV-stills from DV-camera footage filmed in Haga Park, Stockholm. This eighteenth-century landscape garden is a public park (on royal grounds) bordering the inner-city and the northbound E4 highway. Three settings within this park are presented: the Temple of Echo, the ruins of the never-completed royal palace, and a hut in the woods (Eeyore's house). Listening closely, the sounds of these places (traffic, birds and rustling leaves) and fragments of their stories trickle out. The installation calls for the attention of visual, aural and corpo-real senses, while carefully steering away from any sense of a 'complete' or 'whole' experience.

This installation was developed out of a project initiated with an essay on Haga Park written in 2004 and presented at the *Critical Architecture* conference in London that year. The essay addresses particular places in the park. While being one of the most interesting examples of eighteenth-century landscape gardening in Sweden, the sites and experiences related were selected on the basis of rather vague (unimportant) personal memories from my own 'distracted' uses of this park as a child and teenager. Memories of past use were called forth by writing, in an attempt to 'defocus' the scholarly gaze of the grown-up critic, but also to invite the reader to imagine and simultaneously reflect on the park in terms of distraction. It challenges, in ways that I will get back to, the relative 'ease' with which we 'imagine a world without distraction', and that continue to reproduce that idealistic model.

Installation by Grillner in the *Spatial Imagination* group exhibition, Gallery domoBaal, London 2006. Three light/sound boxes are located on the walls of the gallery stairwell. They display three triptychs made up from photographs of TV-stills from DV-camera footage filmed in Haga Park, Stockholm. Listening closely, the sounds of these places (traffic, birds and rustling leaves) and fragments of their stories trickle out.

Plan of the domoBaal gallery for the *Spatial Imagination* group exhibition, London 2006. Grillner's installation *out of focus (in distraction)* is located in the stairwell. The three light/sound boxes are distributed along the walk up to or down from the main gallery space, here marked as a) Eeyore's House, b) The Ruin, c) The Temple of Echo. The stairwell and landing in addition displayed works by Stuart Munro, Peg Rawes, and Jane Rendell.

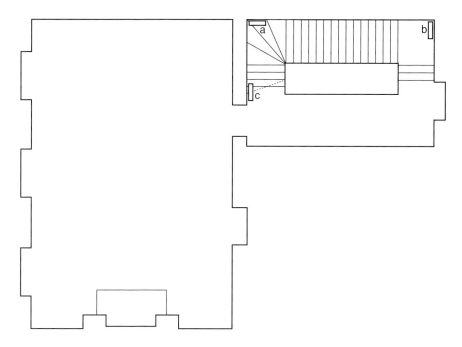

Magician and surgeon

> The surgeon represents the polar opposite of the magician. The magician heals a sick person by the laying on of hands; the surgeon cuts into the patient's body. The magician maintains the natural distance between the patient and himself; though he reduces it very slightly by the laying on of hands, he greatly increases it by virtue of his authority. The surgeon does exactly the reverse; he greatly diminishes the distance between himself and the patient by penetrating into the patient's body, and increases it but little by the caution with which his hand moves among the organs.[18]

If, in the experience of architecture, Benjamin saw the individual as somehow captured in habitual perception, where contemplation was meaningless, and tactile appropriation inaccessible to critical analysis, photography and film suddenly allowed the individual to access his/her own world of action as an engaged observer. Benjamin famously compares the magician to the surgeon to articulate how these new surgical tools, the camera, the film, the projector, penetrate more forcefully into the patient (the world) while simultaneously maintaining a critical distance:

> In short, in contrast to the magician – who is still hidden in the medical practitioner – the surgeon at the decisive moment abstains from facing the patient man to man; rather, it is through the operation that he penetrates into him.[19]

Through mediating technology, every observer (cinema-goer) could access the position of the camera operator (the surgeon) and, as Benjamin wrote, both extend 'our comprehension of the necessities which rule our lives' and manage 'to assure us of an immense and unexpected field of action'.

Trotter shows in his analysis of the stereoscopic image how the haptic look was invited by the use of low perspectives and protruding foregrounds, these typically having a significance that slightly disturbs the viewer. This corresponds to the shock-effect which Benjamin refers to in relation to Dadaist art as 'hitting the spectator like a bullet, happening to him, acquiring a tactile quality', effects that in film were created by close-ups, montage, rapid cuts, slow/rapid motion and so on. In contrast to the surgeon and camera operator (film director, editor, etc.), the cinema-goer cannot control his or her tools and the resulting structure of a mediated experience. Benjamin quotes the contemporary critic Georges Duhamel as having said 'I can no longer think what I want to think. My thoughts have been replaced by moving images'. This, means Benjamin, is something the modern subject just needs to accept. Filmic experience in fact trains the 'apperceptive apparatus' in a way that corresponds to modern urban experience and its demands on the subject.[20]

But how does this 'subject-in-shock' become a critic? Benjamin seems to imply that it is an automatic effect of the cinematic viewing position.[21] Essentially mediated through technology, this position combines, curiously, distraction, absorption, criticality and distanciation, notions that do not normally blend well. To be 'critical' means to be highly concentrated and focused. Not too 'absorbed' in the object of scrutiny, but rather able to put the object at a convenient, objective 'distance'. 'Distraction' has little room in this practice. Benjamin turns this logic around: distraction does not only hold a legitimate place within criticism, but is moreover necessary to address if we are to produce any spatial and architectural criticism of relevance to our contemporary conditions. The essay and installation that I present in this chapter came out of attempts to operate as a distracted critic. We will return to them and discuss in what way this critic appears to be distracted, in what way her resulting works might succeed in conveying a distracted mode of experience, and how critical positions are attained in these works.

A distracted critic in operation

Let us rehearse briefly the nature of the essay. It takes place in Haga Park, Stockholm, which is approached as an actual and a remembered place. The park is written as a site of everyday experience, not in the eighteenth century, not for Stockholmers today, but for the author (here 'the distracted critic'). What is the Haga Park that follows 'her' around? The remembered place that she stores in her mind, a place that expands, evolves, even disappears in part, as time and life goes on. In the attempt to write this place, my own remembered and current experiences were used as primary source material. To assist my observations I brought a DV-camera on my walks in the park, originally with the intention of using it as a mere registration device. Gradually I became quite interested in the crude footage. One of the sequences, filmed following the junio-high jogging-trail on a bike, made me seasick every time I watched it. I had to stop it. The quivering still on my TV had very particular qualities.

In what way does this critic seem distracted? The author of the essay relates to the reader an account of a Haga Park that obliges the reader to follow her train of thought, which moves between remembered and present time, as well as reflecting on the particular mode in which it is being told and why. It also addresses the notion of distracted experience and its critical and political function for Benjamin. So the text makes a double-layered performance. To some extent that essay has a similar scope to this chapter, but its mode of operation is essentially different. The particular effect of distractedness consists of the allowance made for the telling of parallel stories, and of making observations sometimes by association rather than by argument or narrative.[22] This leaves ample space for the reader to assume a critical position in relation to the landscape that is written for her imagination. Nevertheless, the narrating voice in the essay carefully guides the reader among these impressions and creates a critical space where some conclusions are drawn and arguments are put forward.

In what way might the resulting works convey a distracted mode of experience? By drawing on personal memories and experiences as a primary source, the author can only hope that the resulting account might bear a significant relation to potential readers who can recognise in it ways of experiencing and understanding particular places and landscapes. The choice of such an autobiographical method is based on a recognition of the importance of a cultural specificity in any discussion of spatial experience.[23] While these kinds of sources are, in some sense, always unique, the process of writing them – making a 'faithful' account – is of course wholly dependent on mediation. As soon as a memory is evoked and retold, it is severed from any original 'impression', which is also the only way that it may ever become useful. The distracted nature of the essay is further apparent in the way that it makes use of both a particular place, Haga Park, and a particular person's experiences, the author's, without having any ambition to give any complete or truly exhaustive account of either. It employs them merely to point at and give materiality to certain phenomena and experiences, which in turn demand the evocation of a slight interest in both the specific park and the author. The reading act might then, in itself, provoke a certain uneasiness, another level of distraction, that has to be carefully balanced (and might also stop some readers from ever reading through).

Establishing evidence

The scene of a crime, too, is deserted; it is photographed for the purpose of establishing evidence. With Atget, photographs become standard evidence for historical occurrences, and acquire a hidden political significance. They demand a specific kind of approach; free-floating contemplation is not appropriate to them. They stir the viewer; he feels challenged by them in a new way.[24]

In the installation, the images shown in light boxes relate to three places/settings/ scenes from the essay (echo temple, ruin, Eeyore's house) (see figures below). These triptychs are composed from DV-stills (the 'quivering still') photographed directly from their appearance on TV. These images had taken me by surprise while I was still writing the essay. I took one picture, then another.[25] I became fascinated by arresting these fleeting moments. To somehow pull the instances apart, and then, in composing the triptychs, to reassemble selected moments. There was also something curious in the rough, low-tech, mediating technology, the presence of the TV, the interference patterns, the strange colour patches.

Compared with the essay where I try very carefully and hard to actually remember, to capture, my 'actual' memories and experiences of this place, I here compose a scene, or sequence, that is distancing itself both from me, and possibly also from the viewer. When I appear as a person in some of these images, they might in a sense be looked upon as self-portraits, but that might also be beside the point. The surveillance camera associations that may be triggered by the coarse texture rather underlines a distance, very different from that between the reader and the narrator of the essay. The indication of a camera recording without a camera operator behind it twists the subjectivity around. The places now appear to look back at us, to survive us. To always be there as we pass by temporarily.

Eeyore's House.

The Ruin.

The Temple of Echo.

The sound leaking out of each light box is not to be conveniently audible from afar. Rather, it invites concentration, the impulse to put the ear rather close to the box. The sound consists of two basic tracks. First, the surround sound from the DV-recording of the particular place – lots of traffic, twittering birds, walking steps in leaves, joggers passing by, a quite particular echo-experiment in the echo-temple (see figure below). This first track gives a temporality and acoustic spatiality to the still-images in the light box. Second, my own reading of selected fragments of the written essay that positions a 'reading'/'accounting' subject in relation to the scene. This second track overlays the sound track of the surroundings.

The light (and sound) boxes are distributed on different walls and levels in the stairwell of the gallery space (see figure on page 275). The background sounds from the park from each box blends into one aural experience possibly transporting the listener momentarily to some other place. It is a recognisable outdoor sound. The place is not necessarily a park. But the attentive listener might imagine somewhere where there are enough trees and bushes to house crows, blackbirds and sparrows, and yet not arcadia, probably polluted due to the heavy traffic. When approaching each box the narrating voice will be heard: 'The temple of echo echoes ...', 'Spring 1980: I cannot recall how we get there. We run around the roofless rooms', 'I don't walk down. There is a path running north ...' To hear what she says, you must concentrate.

The installation creates a play with different modes of attention, evoking visual, aural and visceral senses, while carefully steering away from any notion of a 'complete' or 'whole' experience. While the reader of the essay is guided along the park and text by a narrator and author, who thereby rather carefully draws a critical

The triptychs on display are composed from DV-stills photographed directly from their appearance on the TV. The rough, low-tech, mediating technology, the presence of the TV, the interference patterns, the strange colour patches, the coarse texture, all trigger surveillance-camera associations, underlining a particular distance, a camera recording without a camera operator behind it, and twisting the subjectivity around.

space, this particular function is left out of the installation, or more precisely, it is not integrated, but appears in another space as a catalogue essay that one may read, or not. It leaves, then, to the 'visitor' an open critical space where the images could be from anywhere, and the voice and the woman portrayed could be anyone. The captions say: 'Temple of Echo', 'The Ruin' and 'Eeyore's House'. It could be fictional as well as real.

Out of control

To use Walter Benjamin's seventy-year-old essay in a contemporary context is not unproblematic. The age of mechanical reproduction looks very different today. It is not primarily mechanical at all. If the status of the 'original' in Benjamin's view had been radically devalued in the wake of reproductive technologies, that same notion has lost its significance today if we, for example, look at the implications of developments in the computer game or bio-genetic reproduction industries. Nevertheless, the remarkable popularity of Benjamin's essay among scholars in architecture, art and media theory does not appear to wane.[26] A significant reason for this might be that, however fast the world, and our conceptions of the world, appears to be changing, we cannot in fact escape the strong resilient discourse that holds on to the, as Benjamin writes, 'outmoded concepts such as creativity and genius, eternal value and mystery – concepts whose uncontrolled (and at present almost uncontrollable) application would lead to a processing of data in the Fascist sense'.[27] We seem to be helplessly stuck. Benjamin's enthusiasm for the film medium, when taken out of its 1936 context, needs to be qualified with references to the early films of the avant-garde tradition.[28] As with other artistic media, film may obviously be put to different uses, calling at times for critical shock and distraction, which is what Benjamin observes, but at other times for complete and essentially uncritical absorption.[29]

The highly condensed form of Benjamin's discussion of architecture means that several critical questions are left unattended to. Is architecture worthy of the canonical role given to it by Benjamin? Architectural aesthetics must surely be held to be as responsible as other art forms for its willingness to serve political leaders in providing a comprehensible view of the world as beautiful and whole. In fact, architectural discourse might even be considered as a particular stronghold for a resilient cult of values of authenticity, iconicity and artistic genius. Another interesting query concerns the possible relationship between technologies of 'mechanical reproduction' in architecture, and the particular value Benjamin ascribes to architecture as a training ground for the distracted critic. Issues of scale and programme in the architectural project have, throughout history, provoked the development of different forms of accessible representations (moulds, drawings, models, plates, mapping, surveying technologies and so on) that may be considered 'proto-mechanical' reproductive technologies. Questions of originality and authenticity in architecture have, in this respect, always been complex and they remain highly ambiguous still today. The Western, pre-modern and Renaissance understanding of architecture nevertheless clearly positioned God in the role of aesthetic authority and as an absolute anchor and divine original. Even if that particular anchor point has largely disappeared, the idea of (and desire for obtaining) that authorial position still haunts architectural discourse.[30]

The theoretical discourse in architecture (what Benjamin would translate through his Marxist filter to the 'superstructure') seems to be far behind the expected implications of current modes of architectural consumption and production. While the uses of architecture may have fostered a distracted critic long before mechanical reproduction speeded up this development in other art forms, the theoretical understanding of architecture continues to attach a definite cult-value to individual buildings, and has great difficulties incorporating the role of programme and use in the understanding of architecture as an art form.[31] Even in other fields it is evident today that Benjamin's vision of an efficient 'inoculation' of humanity against the fascist aesthetisation of politics is still unbearably far away. What does one conclude from that? Is the whole argument thereby invalidated? In terms of its historical analysis, it is a relevant question. But in the context of its time, the essay reads most of all as a forceful (and desperate) expression of a utopian hope, as well as warning against all accounts of wholeness, authenticity and uncompromising beauty. Read in that way, its basic premises may be taken as still valid, and of crucial importance in relation to the critical understanding of our contemporary spatial surroundings. What Benjamin identifies with the 'absent-minded examining public' is importantly a critic who is both out of control, but at the same time left with (and leaving to others) a space to manoeuvre – to experience *and* think. When Duhamel complained that in the movies 'his thoughts were replaced by moving images', one might wonder if he had ever thought about, or been troubled by, the kind of control a highly focused philosophical discourse really exerted on his thoughts?

Acknowledgements

The research for this chapter and the presented projects has been supported by funding from the Swedish Research Council through AKAD (www.akad.se), and by the Spatial Imagination in Design research cluster (www.spatialimagination.org). I wish to thank all participants of the cluster – in particular Penelope Haralambidou, Peg Rawes and Jane Rendell – for providing challenging and inspiring input to this research.

Notes

1   Benjamin, 1969, p. 236.
2   In the combination of these complex notions lie the contradictions and paradoxes which, I suspect, contribute strongly to the continued engagement by scholars and critics in this essay.
3   The essay, 'Writing architecture out of focus', was presented as a paper for the

AHRA conference *Critical Architecture* at the Bartlett School of Architecture, UCL, London, November 2004, and will be published in the forthcoming book from the event (*Critical Architecture*, ed. Mark Dorrian and others (London: Routledge, 2007)). It is a translated and revised version of my essay, 'Kritik och Förströelse (vi befinner oss I Hagaparken, Stockholm)', in *Varje dags arkitektur – Arkitekturmuseets Årsbok 2004*, ed. Christina Englund (Stockholm: Arkitekturmuseet, 2005) ('Critique and Distraction (we find ourselves in Haga Park, Stockholm)', in *The Architecture of Every Day* (Swedish Museum of Architecture, 2005)).

4   The installation *out of focus (in distraction)* was part of the group show *Spatial Imagination* that took place at the gallery domoBaal Contemporary Art in London, 9–20 January. The exhibition showed work from the research cluster *Spatial Imagination in Design*, funded by the EPSRC (Engineering and Physical Science Research Council) and the AHRB (Arts and Humanities Research Board) in the UK (www.spatialimagination.org). Production credits: Peter Tollmar for assistance with sound production, Göran Nilsson, model-maker at *Dekorteknik*, Stockholm, Sweden, for light/sound box production.

5   By 'propositional' I mean that they 'propose' particular modes of writing and representing spatial experience, instead of, or in addition to, what happens, for example, in this chapter, 'reflecting on' and 'discussing' those experiments.

6   A difficulty inherent in many critically oriented practice-led research projects in the arts and in architectural design is distinguishing between the different positions one might take as a scholar in relation to texts and works that are outside one's own practice, and as a writer, artist and designer in relation to one's own propositional projects. It is crucial, in my view, to avoid a setting up of simplistic binary relations between analyses that may be understood as more theoretically explicit, and others that are performed as material, sensual or poetic explorations; i.e. the former must not be understood to explicate, or legitimate, the latter. Rather, through different approaches, complementary perspectives are offered as layer after layer.

7   Benjamin, 1969, p. 239.

8   Here I am particularly concerned with how the interest for embodied experience in architecture, raised by Benjamin's remark, easily leads on to a phenomenological approach, whereby aspects of use and cultural specificity (highlighted by Benjamin through his reference to 'habit') might be pushed aside in favour of more generalised accounts. Iris Marion Young's critique of the undifferentiated phenomenological subject in the essay 'Throwing like a girl' is compelling. Regardless of why there exists such a motion-pattern as 'throwing like a girl', she argues that it does imply on a fundamental level a quite different mode of 'being-in-the-world' than the elegant projection performed by the one who throws a ball 'as one ought to' (Young, 2005, pp. 27–45. This essay was first published in *Human Studies*, 3 (1980)).

9   Benjamin, 1969, p. 218.

10 Benjamin, 1969, pp. 240–2.

11 Benjamin, 1969, p. 240.

12 Here as related by David Trotter in his article (2004, p. 39).

13 Trotter, 2004.

14 Trotter, 2004, p. 39.

15   To distract something is to elude its clutches; but also, as a consequence, to now clutch *it*, secretly and from behind. These qualities of clutching, elusion, of escape and capture, are what make distraction and its related strategies – simulation, disappearance, removal – games of *power*.

                                                                              (Bogard, 2000)

16 Bogard, 2000.

17 In his book *Actions of Architecture*, Jonathan Hill emphasises the building as a site of

action and discusses the implications of the unwillingness from the architects' side to acknowledge the users' roles as co-authors to the architectural work (Hill, 2003).

18 Benjamin, 1969, p. 233.

19 Benjamin, 1969, p. 233.

20 Benjamin, 1969, p. 238 and note no. 19.

21 The film makes the cult value recede into the background not only by putting the public in the position of the critic, but also by the fact that at the movies this position requires no attention. The public is an examiner, but an absent-minded one.

(Benjamin, 1969, pp. 240–1)

22 To write in such a way that brings to the surface several phenomena at once, and at the same time the presence of a distracted subject amid all this, the result may be a text that reflects the filmic effect Benjamin relates. This is not undone. Even Benjamin had several examples among his contemporaries. Virginia Woolf's stream-of-consciousness writing in novels such as *The Waves*, *Mrs Dalloway* and *Jacob's Room*, for example, appears to be aiming for a similar effect. At the same time, her essay-writing allows for considerably less distraction.

23 See comment in note 8 above. Other modes of working with such a specificity (experience grounded in a named, gendered etc., subject) may be achieved through discussing characters from film, literature and so on, or documentary characters, based on interviews, and relating the accounts of other individuals that we know or come to know.

24 Benjamin, 1969, p. 226.

25 In total, around 140 pictures were taken.

26 A Google search on 'Walter Benjamin' + architecture + 'work of art' gives, for example, 27,300 hits (accessed 1 November 2005).

27 Benjamin, 1969, p. 218.

28 Such as, for example, Dziga Vertov's *The Man with a Movie Camera* (1929), or Walter Ruttman's *Berlin. Symphonie einer Gross Stadt* (1927).

29 The mechanisms of absorption are, for example, explored in Mulvey (1975 and 1981) where she identifies and analyses the complicit role of narrative structure and close-ups in positioning the female subject as object of desire.

30 The history of and discourse on authorship in architecture is compelling and complex. In the research project *Architecture and its Mythologies* that I pursue in collaboration with Tim Anstey and Rolf Hughes, we are investigating these issues. We are currently producing a collection of essays entitled *Architecture and Authorship* to be published by Black Dog Publishing in spring 2007 (see www.auctor.se).

31 In the eighteenth century, architectural treatises begin to address notions of utility and programme in new ways. In an interview with Paul Rabinow from 1982, Michel Foucault argues that architecture did not become political until the eighteenth century. He qualifies this by saying that it is only then that its programme and organisation are considered from the point of view of political theories of government and social control. Interestingly enough, Foucault remarks that this change takes place primarily outside the discipline or discourse of architecture and is typically realised in building types such as the hospital and the prison. See 'Space, Knowledge and Power' (1998, pp. 430–9).

Katja Grillner

Bibliography

Walter Benjamin, 'The Work of Art in the Age of Mechanical Reproduction', in Hannah Arendt (ed.), *Illuminations*, New York: Schocken Book, 1969, pp. 217–51.

William Bogard, 'Distraction and Digital Culture', in Arthur and Marilouise Kroker (eds), *ctheory.net* (article: a088, published: 10 May 2000). Online, available from: www.ctheory.net/articles.aspx?id =131 (accessed 11 November 2005).

Michel Foucault, 'Space, Knowledge and Power', in Michael K. Hays (ed.), *Architecture Theory Since 1968*, Cambridge, MA: MIT Press, 1998, pp. 430–9.

Jonathan Hill, *Actions of Architecture: Architects and Creative Users*, London: Routledge, 2003.

Laura Mulvey, 'Visual Pleasure and Narrative Cinema', *Screen*, 16 (3, 1975).

Laura Mulvey, 'Afterthoughts', *Framework* (15–17, 1981).

David Trotter, 'Stereoscopy: Modernism and the Haptic', *Critical Quarterly*, 46 (4, 2004), 38–58.

Iris Marion Young, *On Female Body Experience*, New York: Oxford University Press, 2005.

Index

Illustrations are indicated by **bold** page numbers